Fans, Blockbusterisation, and the Transformation of Cinematic Desire

"This book is a truly impressive large-scale longitudinal study of the evolution of audience receptions of the *Hobbit* film trilogy. Based on rich data collected through a mixed method approach combining qualitative and quantitative methods, the book not only offers stimulating insight into the range of different viewpoints on this three-part 'blockbusterisation' of Tolkien's novel but also new and original methodological and theoretical approaches to audience studies. This is an important study which advances audience research significantly."
—Anne Jerslev, *Professor, Department of Media, Cognition & Communication University of Copenhagen*

"A smart book, adroitly deploying the best traditions of audience, fan and critical media scholarship to explain how the *Hobbit* film trilogy embodied politically significant shifts in global media culture. The authors blend a flair for cultural history with an enviable methodological skill, producing what will surely become a blueprint for many future projects on media industries and audiences, at every level of scholarship."
—Andy Ruddock, *Senior Lecturer, Communications & Media Studies, Monash University; author of Understanding Audiences: Theories and Methods (2001) Investigating Audiences (2007), Youth and Media (2013)*

Carolyn Michelle · Charles H. Davis
Ann L. Hardy · Craig Hight

Fans, Blockbusterisation, and the Transformation of Cinematic Desire

Global Receptions of the *Hobbit* Film Trilogy

Carolyn Michelle
Audience Research Unit
University of Waikato
Hamilton, New Zealand

Ann L. Hardy
Screen and Media Studies
University of Waikato
Hamilton, New Zealand

Charles H. Davis
RTA School of Media
Ryerson University
Toronto, ON, Canada

Craig Hight
School of Creative Arts
The University of Newcastle
Newcastle, NSW, Australia

ISBN 978-1-137-59615-4   ISBN 978-1-137-59616-1   (eBook)
DOI 10.1057/978-1-137-59616-1

Library of Congress Control Number: 2017949197

Cover design by Jenny Vong

Printed on acid-free paper

This Palgrave Macmillan imprint is published by Springer Nature
The registered company is Macmillan Publishers Ltd.
The registered company address is: The Campus, 4 Crinan Street, London, N1 9XW, United Kingdom

PREFACE

This book is the culmination of an ambitious project that sought to find out what kind of insights and potential applications could emerge within the field of audience studies by adopting an innovative longitudinal methodological approach to studying receptions of Peter Jackson's *Hobbit* trilogy (2012–14). Much of what we have attempted hasn't been done before on this scale, and the complexity of the project only really became apparent soon after we received the first rich accumulation of data in December 2012. Along the way, several new and unexpected issues emerged that warranted further investigation; we have done our best to give service to these. Writing this book has given us the opportunity to gather together our core findings and present these back to those who contributed to them, reflect on what these findings mean in the bigger picture and their possible implications for theoretical understandings of audience reception per se and Hollywood film franchises in particular, and to offer interested readers insight into the methodological design and conduct of a unique project that, we hope, may inspire similar studies in future.

The research that informs this book was the outcome of a collective effort over an extended period, and simply would not have been possible without the generous assistance and contributions of our respective institutions and the people associated with them. We have been extremely fortunate to receive modest funding at critical stages of the project from the Faculty of Arts and Social Sciences as well as the Research Trust at the University of Waikato, without which we could not have attempted a longitudinal project, let alone a multilingual study for one important stage of it. We particularly thank Emeritus Prof. Robert Hannah, former Dean of the Faculty of Arts and Social Sciences, for his active support of this project. Our sincere appreciation also goes to the many colleagues and graduate students who contributed in various ways to the success of this endeavour: Kim Schrøder, Christian Kobbernagel, David Mathieu, Cedric Courtois, Tonny Krijnen, Alejandro Fernández, José Javier Sánchez-Aranda, Stan Jones, Geoff Lealand, Darren Elliot, Nadia Gush, Debrin Foxcroft, Sheilah Jacay, Yana Wengel, Luis Cifuentes, Loic Dussart and Victoria Kirk. Many friends and family members have also provided invaluable support and encouragement throughout the course of our research and more recent book writing. Special thanks go to Jillian Smith, Rebecca Fraser and Roberto Saravia.

Last but not least, we extend our heartfelt gratitude to the several thousand survey respondents who gave so generously of their time to offer their comments and insights, often in considerable detail. Some of you have been part of this project from the outset, and many completed more than one survey at different stages. We have been truly humbled by your willingness to participate in our research and have found all of your responses extraordinarily useful in gaining a clearer insight into viewers' diverse reactions to the *Hobbit* film trilogy, both as a blockbuster event-film trilogy and a much-anticipated expansion of the fantastical world of Middle-earth. Each and every one of you has contributed to this book and the analysis it offers; for that, we are tremendously and enduringly grateful.

Hamilton, New Zealand   Carolyn Michelle
Toronto, Canada   Charles H. Davis
Hamilton, New Zealand   Ann L. Hardy
Newcastle, Australia   Craig Hight
February 2017

CONTENTS

ABBREVIATIONS

AUJ   An Unexpected Journey
BotFA   The Battle of the Five Armies
CGI   Computer-generated Imagery
DoS   The Desolation of Smaug
HFR   High Frame Rate
LotR   The Lord of the Rings
MEAA   Media Entertainment and Arts Alliance
RotK   The Return of the King

ACCENTS, SIGNS, SPECIAL CHARACTERS

Á   Álvarez
Ã   Mālama ãina
ä   Hirsjärvi, Häkkinen, Krämer, Välisalo
É   Éowyn, Rérolle
í   García
ö   Jöckel, Döbler, Pölönen, Göllner
ó   López-Sintas
ø   Schrøder
ü   Trültzsch-Wijnen, Wühr

LIST OF FIGURES

LIST OF TABLES

CHAPTER 1

Returning to Middle-Earth, in Blockbusterised Form

INTRODUCTION

This book traces the nature and evolution of audience receptions of Sir Peter Jackson's blockbuster adaptation of J.R.R. Tolkien's widely read and much-loved fantasy novel, *The Hobbit, or There and Back Again* (1937). Originally written for his children, *The Hobbit* has never been out of print, has been translated into over 40 different languages and has an enduring legacy within the fantasy canon. The *Hobbit* films (2012–14) were initially conceived in 2006 as a cinematic adaptation of that comparatively brief novel; given the remarkable popular, critical and financial success of Jackson's earlier *Lord of the Rings* (*LotR*) trilogy (Jackson 2001, 2002, 2003), anticipation was heightened among those who longed for a repeat of that extraordinary cultural phenomenon. Yet, as many readers will be keenly aware, the return to Middle-earth on screen was not without controversy, and the *Hobbit* films were ultimately less successful than their creators and many fans may have hoped—particularly when measured against Jackson's *LotR*, to which they effectively function as a prequel series.

Undoubtedly, the popular success of the *LotR* trilogy owed much to the enthusiastic and loyal following for Tolkien's novels that had been in existence since the 1960s, including an organised fan community initially based around various Tolkien societies and publications such as *Amon Hen* and *Tolkien Studies*, and later online newsgroups and forums such as alt.fan.tolkien and Theonering.net. This established enthusiasm for Tolkien's wider body of work meant there was a substantial pre-existing

© The Author(s) 2017
C. Michelle et al., *Fans, Blockbusterisation, and the Transformation of Cinematic Desire*, DOI 10.1057/978-1-137-59616-1_1

audience for Jackson's three-part cinematic adaptation of *LotR*. Most—although certainly not all—were well pleased with the result. Indeed, it would be difficult to overstate the significance of the *LotR* films and the aura of exceptionality which has grown around them. While not the first cinematic rendering of Tolkien's work—a Rankin/Bass animated television special of *The Hobbit* was released in 1977, followed by Ralph Bakshi's *The Lord of the Rings* animated feature film in 1978—Jackson's film trilogy has been by far the grandest and most widely viewed adaptation to date. A labour of love from a self-declared band of Tolkien fans, the *LotR* films helped revitalise the blockbuster franchise production model in the early 2000s, firmly established the credibility of fantasy as a genre, resuscitated New Zealand's flagging film industry, inspired a host of local film-related tourist ventures and in the process transformed Jackson into a national hero in his homeland.

Clearly, the *Hobbit* production had some extraordinarily large shoes to fill. Whether it succeeded in so doing, however, has been the subject of heated discussion and debate among fans and critics alike. In this book, we argue that the degree of ambivalence evident in *The Hobbit*'s public and private reception illustrates many of the unanticipated and largely unstudied consequences of what we term *blockbusterisation*; a film-industry phenomenon that, ironically, consolidated in the wake of the tremendous success of Jackson's *LotR* film trilogy.

BLOCKBUSTERISATION AND THE HOLLYWOOD FRANCHISE MODEL

We conceptualise blockbusterisation as the set of economic, industrial, creative and commercial strategies and related processes that work to transform a collective cultural property (in this case, a well-established property in the form of Tolkien's novel *The Hobbit*, but potentially any popular book, comic, video game or musical) into a blockbuster event-film. The term 'blockbuster event-film' denotes a genre of films that have extensive production budgets—today often exceeding $200 million (Owczarski 2015)—allowing for spectacular visual effects, high production value, well-known actors, broad-based appeal, extensive marketing and promotion campaigns and wide international release, all of which helps such films transcend the realms of cinema to become public *experiences* (Biltereyst and Meers 2006). Blockbuster event-films are produced by transnational entertainment conglomerates as part of a specific strategy to minimise commercial risks, maximise profits and counteract competition from other forms of screen media (Acland 2013; Cucco 2009; Epstein 2006; Langford 2005; Stringer 2003). As home entertainment systems become more visually and aurally impressive, attracting audiences into theatres becomes increasingly difficult. Hollywood blockbuster event-films thus seek to offer 'must-see' spectacular experiences that small screens cannot easily duplicate (Stringer 2003). Every major Hollywood studio today annually produces a handful of capital-intensive, technologically innovative, blockbuster 'tentpole' event-films intended for international consumption and designed to have very high earning potential, both at the international box office and through sales of ancillary merchandise such as DVDs and Blu-ray, books, video games and so on (Elberse 2013; Jöckel and Döbler 2006; Miller et al. 2005; Stringer 2003).

In order to cater to diverse global audiences, blockbuster event-films are specifically designed to offer a wide range of meanings, pleasures and forms of involvement through the use of multiple storylines, attractive ensemble casts, technologically enhanced visual and auditory effects and generic hybridity (King 2000; Kuipers and de Kloet 2009; Mikos et al. 2008; Wasko 2008). The blockbuster aesthetic emphasises spectacular and often violent action scenes over characterisation and dialogue, simple plots with clear visual differentiation between 'good guys' and 'bad guys' and the liberal use of storytelling conventions that can transcend national and cultural differences and thus be intelligible to non-English speaking audiences, which is important if the films are to maximise their global box-office takings (King 2003; Olson 1999; Schauer 2007). Increasingly, studios favour big action blockbusters aimed at international markets to offset lost profits from declining DVD sales and tumbling domestic (US) attendance, particularly in the wake of online streaming video services such as Netflix and Hulu. The huge profits often made by blockbuster event-films have become vital to the industry, helping to compensate for losses associated with the lower-performing, and more often original, films in a studio's portfolio (Elberse 2013).

As a set of imperatives and processes that work to transform an established collective cultural property into a blockbuster event-film, blockbusterisation is intimately connected to Hollywood's growing reliance on what is known as the *franchise* model. Particularly over the past decade or so, and again to minimise financial risks, major film studios have come to favour the creation of *serialised* blockbuster adaptations, prequels, sequels, reboots and spin-offs from already successful franchises

(Owczarski 2015). A related recent trend is to adapt popular novels into multi-part feature films, both to avoid having to condense material and to maximise a virtually guaranteed financial return from an established fan base as viewers are left hanging for part two—as occurred with *Harry Potter and the Deathly Hallows,* earning Warner Bros an extra billion dollars at the box office (Vaughan 2014). Through their extension and expansion of ready-made, proven successful storyworlds, blockbuster franchise adaptations, sequels, prequels and spin-offs benefit from a pre-assembled audience of knowledgeable readers and fans of an established 'brand', while also appealing to mainstream audiences (Owczarski 2015; Schauer 2007; Vaughan 2014). Consequently, films that are extensions of known cultural properties are often highly lucrative: 14 of the 20 top grossing films of 2016 were adaptations, prequels, sequels or spin-offs (Box Office Mojo 2017a). The pre-assembled audiences such films address can be carefully cultivated for forthcoming releases in the same series, and provide ready consumer markets for ancillaries such as books and video games as part of broader studio efforts to capitalise on multimedia product lines (Owczarski 2015; Schauer 2007).

These changes in the nature and focus of Hollywood film production since the late 1970s have met with criticism from various quarters on both aesthetic and creative grounds. The more trenchant of critics suggest Hollywood appears to have abandoned 'high-quality, artistic drama' focusing on narrative and character development 'in favour of large-scale, big-budget, action-based, computer-generated, cookie-cutter movies featuring robots, men in capes, and giant scary machines' (Brynes 2015)—all creatures of fantasy, as are hobbits and dragons. Such films are frequently panned by 'serious' critics for transgressing traditional aesthetic values associated with cinema as an art form, and for privileging style and visual spectacle over narrative complexity and in-depth characterisation (King 2003; Wyatt 2010)—two elements that, in the case of adaptations of literary works such as *The Hobbit,* might be presumed to have considerable importance for viewers familiar with the original work. As Schauer (2007, p. 191) notes, blockbusters are widely considered by film scholars and cultural critics to be 'faceless, escapist, mass produced popular entertainment' aimed at thrilling young people, and are often dismissed as existing 'primarily as advertisements for ancillary merchandise.' However, Lavik (2008), Schauer (2007), Thompson (1999) and others have defended this form of filmmaking, arguing that most franchise blockbusters retain a classical narrative structure, despite also offering impressive visual effects. Other scholars have understood the blockbuster franchise as a form of 'transmedia storytelling' that facilitates 'world building' (Jenkins 2006).

Our understanding of *The Hobbit* as a blockbuster franchise borrows from Derek Johnson (2013, p. 6), who theorises franchising as 'the ongoing industrial negotiation of tensions surrounding cultural production by social agents', including producers, creative workers and 'participatory consumers'—commonly known as fans. These networked organisations, groups and individuals must negotiate their interests in a shared cultural resource, within a set of social relations structured by unequal access to power and control over production processes. Johnson (2013, p. 7) argues that media franchises today are 'constituted by the shared exchange of content resources across multiple industrial sites and contexts of production operating in collaborative but contested ways through networked relation to one another.' He goes on to suggest that

> At each of these industrial sites, media institutions and producers laboring on their behalf have become stakeholders that, even when lacking ownership of a shared property, develop vested interests in its ongoing productive use. Conceived in this manner, the participatory consumers of contemporary social media too might be considered stakeholders, lacking economic claim, but developing a wide range of interests and sometimes even performing labor as part of the economic organization of franchised production.. .. [F]ranchising has situated multiple industrial stakeholders in economic but also creative production relations with one another. *The products and content offered by media franchising, therefore, might be considered as contested grounds of collaborative creativity where networked stakeholders have negotiated the ongoing generation, exchange, and use of shared cultural resources.* (Johnson 2013, p. 7; emphasis added)

In this book, we take the view that Tolkien's *The Hobbit* constitutes a shared cultural resource that became subject to an intensive process of blockbusterisation in the course of its cinematic adaptation, and that Jackson's blockbuster franchise adaptation can be understood as the product of a complex interaction between art and commerce that involved multiple industrial and creative stakeholders as well as fans. Furthermore, as we will show, the outcome of that interaction was deeply contested, and indeed rejected in full or in part, by a significant number of fans, who claimed a personal and psychological stake in the processes of translating book to screen. Peter Jackson's cinematic version of *The Hobbit*, we suggest, thus serves as a useful exemplar of contemporary processes of blockbusterisation and their potentially controversial and contested outcomes among fans of an established cultural property.

THE CREATION OF A NEW MIDDLE-EARTH BLOCKBUSTER FILM FRANCHISE

As readers will recognise, Jackson's *Hobbit* trilogy clearly satisfies the key criteria of a major Hollywood blockbuster event-film franchise. Much like the *LotR* production, *The Hobbit* was an extremely complex, expensive project that took several years to move from development into concurrent production and subsequent release. While the novel is a simple children's story of a homebody hobbit who discovers his courage and inherent wisdom in the course of an unexpected adventure, the process of translating book to screen presented significant challenges, in no small part because the *Hobbit* movies needed to align with the pre-established narrative and cinematic tone of Jackson's *LotR* films if they were to entice the many fans of these films back into cinemas. Just as Tolkien later amended parts of *The Hobbit* to create greater continuity with the themes and narrative threads of his successor series, the *Hobbit* films would become part of a wider story arc by foregrounding the momentous struggle between good and evil that transpires 60 years later, in Middle-earth terms. Successfully fulfilling these different requirements was never going to be easy.

Written by Guillermo del Toro, Peter Jackson, Fran Walsh and Philippa Boyens and initially to be directed by del Toro, the *Hobbit* production was confronted early on by a series of legal challenges from the Tolkien Estate and HarperCollins Publishers, delays arising from financial troubles at MGM and subsequent disruptions and controversies on set. Following del Toro's departure due to scheduling conflicts (Xoanon 2010), newly appointed director Jackson announced on 15 October 2010 that *The Hobbit*, by this time being co-produced by Warner Bros in conjunction with New Line Cinema, would proceed as a two-part 3D film. Then, on 30 July 2012, Jackson announced the production would be expanded into a trilogy by extrapolating from additional materials in Tolkien's unpublished revisions of *The Hobbit*, the appendices to *The Return of the King* and other notes (Riga et al. 2014) along with some entirely new scenes, in order to ease the transition into the darker, more adult themes of the *LotR*. As we discuss in Chap. 3, while this decision to transform *The Hobbit* into a three-part production was couched by Jackson and others as an opportunity to extend fans' enjoyment of the wider storyworld by telling more of the tale 'of Bilbo Baggins, the Dwarves of Erebor, the rise of the Necromancer, and the Battle of Dol Guldur' (Zakarin 2012), it likely also reflected the studios' awareness of the potential commercial value of enticing existing Tolkien readers and *LotR* fans back into cinemas for not two but *three* successive instalments, thereby maximising revenues with a film trilogy, three DVD/Blu-ray releases and sales of an array of licenced merchandise. Not without good reason, Warners, New Line and MGM were 'equally enthusiastic about bringing fans this expansive tale across three films' (Jackson, as cited in Zakarin 2012, n.p.).

The filmmakers also sought to widen *The Hobbit*'s appeal by offering a more complex and multilayered narrative than the original novel, adding a controversial non-canon love story while continuing to explore themes of friendship, loyalty, heroism, sacrifice and the perennial struggle between good and evil. To ensure continuity across the six-film franchise and recreate a similar visual and aural aesthetic for the prequels, several of the same creatives who worked on the art direction, illustration, cinematography, props, visual effects and score for the *LotR* films were recruited to work on the *Hobbit* production, including Alan Lee, John Howe, Richard Taylor of Weta Workshops and Howard Shore. The films also feature an attractive ensemble cast comprising several well-known actors in addition to five reprising their roles from the *LotR* trilogy. Alongside Martin Freeman as Bilbo Baggins, Richard Armitage as Thorin and Benedict Cumberbatch voicing Smaug the dragon, the production welcomed the return of Ian McKellen as Gandalf, Cate Blanchett as Galadriel, Andy Serkis as Gollum, Christopher Lee as Saruman and Orlando Bloom as Legolas. While Gandalf and Gollum do feature in Tolkien's original novel, Galadriel, Saruman and Legolas were written into the *Hobbit* trilogy to provide continuity with Jackson's earlier films.

The *Hobbit* trilogy's production budget was exceptionally large at around US$750 million (The Numbers 2017), meaning the trilogy cost nearly three times as much to make as *LotR* (Suzanne-Mayer 2016). Part of this inflated cost reflected a significant financial investment in advanced cinematic technologies following Jackson's bold decision to pioneer the use of high frame rate (HFR) 3D projection, which meant

The Hobbit would offer a truly unprecedented theatrical experience. By combining advanced computer graphics imagery (CGI) with stereoscopic 3D shot using 5 K resolution Red Epic cameras and double the usual frame rate to 48 frames per second, Jackson sought to transport viewers back into a Middle-earth more detailed, realistic and lifelike than ever before. On his Facebook page, he explained his decision to use 3D HFR as furthering his creative intent to provide a certain *kind* of viewing experience—one of immersive transportation: 'As a filmmaker, I try to make my movies immersive. I want to draw the audience out of their seats, and pull them into the adventure' (Jackson 2012). This unique combination of filming, digital and projection technologies, Jackson believed, would not only help recreate the characters, landscapes and heightened sense of wonder associated with Middle-earth, but also eradicate the cinematic 'fourth wall' to greatly enhance viewers' sense of physical presence within the fictional storyworld.

As a blockbuster event-film franchise, *The Hobbit* enjoyed a very wide international release, with the first film appearing on 4045 screens on its opening weekend in the USA, in addition to 2017 screens across the UK, Denmark, Italy, the Netherlands and the Philippines (IMDb, n.d.). Ticket sales likely benefited from *The Hobbit*'s status as a prequel series, meaning it stood to inherit a very large and enthusiastic audience of fans of the earlier *LotR* films, and was also likely to appeal to millions of readers of Tolkien's collective works. To facilitate the assembly of a large global audience, the release of each film was preceded by extensive marketing and promotion campaigns in major markets (Markowski 2012).

Many fans, as well as mainstream viewers, were thereby effectively primed to see these films: high levels of anticipation for *The Hobbit* were expressed on discussion boards such as Theonering.net, and for 18 months prior to its release, *The Hobbit: An Unexpected Journey (AUJ)* remained in IMDb MovieMeter's list of Top 100 movies as measured by users' search queries. By the time of its December 2012 release, *The Hobbit: AUJ* was the top-rated movie in the IMDb MovieMeter, the trailers had been viewed more than 10 million times, and 1310 other websites were hyperlinked to the official *Hobbit* website (Fiorelli 2012). Various signals thus suggested the prequel series was likely to benefit from what Mikos et al. (2008, p. 115) have termed an 'assured reception' among these positively predisposed fans of the wider Middle-earth franchise, who were already familiar with the story and its characters.

Whether the *Hobbit* trilogy would succeed in attracting and more importantly *keeping* this audience, however, was by no means guaranteed. Would it live up to the marketing hype and satisfy elevated fan expectations for a certain kind of experience, a certain kind of film series, particularly when assessed against the high standards of cinematic excellence and emotional resonance achieved in the *LotR* trilogy? *The Hobbit*'s potential audience was, after all, now more diverse than a decade earlier, when readers of the *LotR* novels first encountered Jackson's epic visual realisation of Tolkien's mythical world. It seemed likely that global receptions of *The Hobbit* would be variously shaped both by book readers' familiarity with the original novel and Tolkien's wider oeuvre, *and* by reactions to Jackson's *LotR* films among different segments of the global viewing audience—not all of whom had been satisfied by Jackson's rendering. Our book thus simultaneously addresses the complex relationship between the *Hobbit* film trilogy and what we have termed 'the transformation of cinematic desire.'

We are using 'desire' here in its generally understood sense as relating to what people *want*—what they hope or long for. As we show in Chap. 3, many respondents had formulated certain expectations and wishes for the *Hobbit* films in advance of their release, and were looking forward to seeing particular things realised on screen. Some hoped to see a certain *kind* of adaptation, others to relive a certain *kind* of phenomenon, or enjoy a certain kind of immersive experience. The nature of the focus of viewers' cinematic desires was often contingent on a complex set of prior affiliations, prefigurative activities and personal predilections, and clearly reflected different sets of interests. Audiences for *The Hobbit* did not all wish for the same things, and not all of their desires would be ultimately satisfied by Jackson's fully realised trilogy, leaving some in a quandary: should they modify or limit their expectations and desires to accommodate the likely difference between ideal and reality? As our research demonstrates, cinematic desires were formulated, modified and reasserted in an ongoing interrelationship between prefigurative hopes and expectations and the films *themselves* as they were progressively realised on screen. While some cinematic desires were initially relatively fixed, stable and clearly formulated, others were potentially fluid and mutable as some respondents attempted to reconcile the actual films produced by Jackson and his team with the idealised versions previously imagined and hoped for. The cinematic realisation of collective cultural properties, our research suggests, inevitably effects a *transformation* of cinematic desire among some, perhaps even many, viewers.

Complicating this process of negotiation between pre-existing affiliations, cinematic desires and the fully realised *Hobbit* films were a diverse array of factors relating to the nature of this production as a Hollywood blockbuster event-film franchise. As we shall illustrate, many of the more widely debated and indeed controversial aspects of the *Hobbit* trilogy's production, narrative and visual aesthetic reflect the influence of wider processes and imperatives of blockbusterisation. This phenomenon clearly has far-reaching implications for the production and reception of mainstream feature films in the contemporary era, as it effectively reshapes what kind of content is offered and in what forms, simultaneously reshaping audience tastes and expectations. As such, studying the *Hobbit* blockbuster franchise and its transnational reception provides a strategic vantage point from which to observe and better understand contemporary processes of transformation by, and resistance to, the capital-intensive commodification of culture.

A TROUBLED ADAPTATION?

To some readers, it may seem odd to be speaking of resistance to commodification, given the evident success of the *Hobbit* films among mainstream audiences and at the international box office. Yet a closer examination of *The Hobbit*'s performance both financially and critically reveals that it fell a long way short of matching the success of the *LotR* trilogy, which earned around $US2.912 billion in 2001–3 (Box Office Mojo 2017b),[1] not accounting for inflation and without the benefit of today's inflated ticket prices for 3D films. To match that extraordinary success, the *Hobbit* trilogy needed to make an amount in the range of $US*3.8 billion*. So, how did it do?

Overall, *The Hobbit* grossed just $US2.935 billion, suggesting its performance was considerably weaker than that of the *LotR* trilogy. According to Box Office Mojo (2017b), the most successful of the three *Hobbit* films was the first: *AUJ* earned US$1.021 billion in global box office receipts—somewhat less than the *LotR: The Return of the King*'s (*RotK*'s) $US1.119 billion (a figure unadjusted for ticket price inflation and achieved nearly a decade earlier!). Adjusted gross figures for domestic box-office takings make clearer the extent to which the first and most successful *Hobbit* film failed to match the top-performing film from the

LotR trilogy: *RotK* earned US $530,689,500 in today's figures; paling in comparison, *AUJ* earned just US$321,964,900. Clearly, the *Hobbit* films attracted lower attendance in cinemas from the outset: Vaughan (2014, p. 8) suggests that 'In the US, 32.3 million people saw *An Unexpected Journey* at the cinema, almost half as many as saw *The Return of the King*.'

Furthermore, while the *LotR* transcended its core fan base to enjoy mainstream appeal and progressively increased its box office takings over the course of the trilogy, earnings *declined* with each successive *Hobbit* instalment. *The Desolation of Smaug* (*DoS*) did not quite match the first *Hobbit* film's commercial success, grossing just US$958,366,855 globally. *The Battle of the Five Armies* (*BotFA*) was slightly weaker again, grossing just $US956,019,788. In most other cases such figures would be regarded as a commercial triumph. But this was *The Hobbit*, no less, and it is clear that rather than expanding its global audience over time on the back of the comparative success of the first film, *The Hobbit* progressively *shed* parts of its audience.

Declining box office receipts, we suggest, is one clear indicator of *The Hobbit*'s rather mixed reception among film critics, fans and the wider viewing public; another useful measure is aggregated audience ratings. Most readers will be aware that Jackson's first Middle-earth trilogy was almost universally acclaimed: average ratings for the *LotR* films were 94% on Rotten Tomatoes, 91.3 on Metacritic, and 'A' on CinemaScore, and all three instalments continue to feature among the top 20 of IMDb's 250 highest rated films (IMDb 2017). The *Hobbit* films, in comparison, feature nowhere on this list. Professional reviews of *AUJ* were lukewarm, with an overall 64% 'Fresh' rating on Rotten Tomatoes, alleviated somewhat by an audience score of 83%. On Metacritic, *AUJ* scored 58 out of 100 from reviewers, with a more positive user rating of 8.1 out of 10. Critics expressed mixed reactions to the film's use of HFR and its hyper-realistic aesthetic, with many also critiquing its extraordinary length, extraneous storylines and rather plodding pace. *DoS* fared somewhat better with critics, scoring 74% from Rotten Tomatoes reviewers and 86% from audiences, while Metacritic reviewers scored it at 66, with an average user rating of 7.8. The 'critics consensus' on Rotten Tomatoes suggested a still mixed, but more positive reception (Rotten Tomatoes, 2017). *BotFA*, in contrast, managed just 60% on the Tomatometer, with an audience rating of 75%, and 59 and 7.0 on Metacritic, making this the *least* favoured film overall. Critics suggested the final film concluded the trilogy 'in reasonably rousing fashion, but while the battle scenes are visually striking, the story is more than a little thin.... [It] lacks the human touch and weightiness that made the *Lord of the Rings* films such revered classics' (Ryan 2014, n.p.).

These and other perceived flaws perhaps help account for *The Hobbit*'s failure to match *LotR*'s stellar performance during award season. Whereas the first trilogy collectively won 17 Oscars from 30 nominations (in addition to more than 770 other awards and nominations), the *Hobbit* trilogy garnered just eight Academy Award nominations, winning a single Oscar in the less prestigious Scientific and Engineering category; the series received around 150 nominations and accolades in total.

Thus, while *The Hobbit* clearly delighted many viewers globally and did moderately well at the box office (although given its inflated production costs, it was clearly much less profitable than *LotR*), it was rather less successful than might have been expected in critical, popular and financial terms, for a complex set of reasons that this book seeks to illuminate. As we shall show, the *Hobbit* film production generated controversy even before the first film's release, and debate and discontent re-emerged and took on different inflections with each new instalment in the franchise. Whether related to the trilogy's conditions of production, its 'cavalier' handling of Tolkien's original novel, its hyperrealistic visual aesthetic or stereotypical formulae, most of the major sources of viewer antipathy, we suggest, fundamentally arose from *The Hobbit*'s subjection to the capital-intensive processes and imperatives of blockbusterisation.

In developing this argument, we draw from the results of an unprecedented longitudinal Q methodology study undertaken between 2012 and 2015, in which we charted the nature and evolution of transnational receptions of *The Hobbit* over its cinematic life course. Drawing on detailed qualitative and quantitative data provided by nearly 6500 respondents around the world, we demonstrate that the expansion of Tolkien's children's novel into a 'blockbuster' film franchise deeply divided audiences and alienated a significant number of otherwise positively predisposed viewers and fans. For certain audience segments, attributes intended to increase the trilogy's appeal to mainstream moviegoers—including the numerous action sequences, advanced computer-generated visual effects, a decidedly un-Tolkienish love triangle and the expansion of the story over three films— undermined deep engagement with the narrative storyworld. While this book primarily focuses on the nature and form of global audience receptions of Jackson's *Hobbit* films, it simultaneously offers insight into fans' resistance to the influence of corporate Hollywood on *The Hobbit's* production and content *as a block-buster franchise*; an influence which, for a significant and growing minority, undermined the quality and authenticity of this cinematic adaptation of Tolkien's original novel.

WHY STUDY AUDIENCES FOR THE *HOBBIT* BLOCKBUSTER FRANCHISE?

To date, much of the existing scholarship discussing blockbuster franchises examines this phenomenon from the perspectives of political economy, film production or textual aesthetics. With some notable exceptions, film scholarship is predominantly text-centred and often highly speculative about how audiences engage with and make sense of film productions. Where discussed at all, audiences frequently feature as 'ideal' or 'implied' viewers and are assumed to adopt the (singular) preferred spectator *position* encoded into films by their makers, as Barker and Mathijs (2008) have also noted. While exceptions to this trend began to emerge in the early 1980s following the ethnographic turn within media and cultural studies, much of the early research on film audiences was relatively small in scale, reflecting the predominant use of labour-intensive qualitative methods. There remains a lack of in-depth, large-scale research on audience responses to film in general and blockbuster film franchises in particular, and even fewer studies have explored the ways transnational texts are received and understood by differently located audiences (Hirsjarvi et al. 2016). In this book, we follow the lead of Barker and Mathijs (2008) in approaching the question of the blockbuster event-film franchise's status and value from the perspective of *audiences*. However, by drawing on a rather different methodology that recognises the complex and potentially highly variable processes of audience reception over the extended life cycle of a blockbuster franchise, we provide detailed insight into how different viewers, from a diverse range of backgrounds, variously engaged with and made sense of the *Hobbit* trilogy over time.

Understanding how audiences make sense of such productions is important for several reasons. Besides expanding our knowledge of media reception processes and related consumption practices, studying audience reactions to blockbuster franchises offers insight into the cultural as well as the personal significance of some of the most widely consumed, globally disseminated entertainment products of our time. Such research is also important from an industry perspective, given the degree to which reliance on the franchise model has become embedded within major Hollywood studios—a strategy which seems to rely on audiences' unwavering enthusiasm for more of the same. Some industry commentators have expressed concerns about the basis of that assumption, and warn of the dangers posed should audience tastes for blockbuster franchises change, or viewer fatigue set in. For instance, CLSA media analyst Vasily Karasyov warns that 'Hollywood is headed for a cliff', and suggests the 'continuously increasing reliance on non-original titles and sequels presents growing risk to film industry profitability' (Williams 2015, n.p.). Indeed, there are a few troubling signs for the industry following a series of expensive flops—most notably *Ben Hur* (2016), *The BFG* (2016), *Alice Through the Looking Glass* (2016) (Sakoui 2016) and the critically slated *Batman v. Superman: Dawn of Justice* (2016), which Warner Bros ambitiously conceived as the 'tentpole' film in a new DC Justice League film franchise that will extend to 10 films or more (Rose 2016). Studying audience reactions to *The Hobbit* as one example of the blockbuster franchise can potentially reveal much about how viewers are *already* responding to a production strategy that currently dominates contemporary filmmaking, influencing decisions about the kind of content that is seen as viable to invest in, as well as the particular form in which that content gets delivered.

In that sense, then, we regard the *Hobbit* films as exemplars of the blockbuster franchise adaptation *as a form*, and perceive parallels between their conceptualisation and realisation and that of other widely read serialised novels such as *Twilight*, *Harry Potter*, *The Hunger Games* and *Divergent*, and potentially also the wide assortment of interlocking superhero comic book adaptations that currently flood cinemas. While each of these examples is, in many important respects, unique—and the *Hobbit* trilogy even more so, given the long shadows cast by Tolkien's extraordinary legacy and Jackson's *LotR* films—we believe the patterns and trends we have identified in audience receptions of *The Hobbit* are not necessarily particular to this set of films alone. While different in content, they may be similar in *kind* to the reactions observed among viewers of the burgeoning array of serialised cinematic adaptations of other familiar cultural properties. Thus, our intent in studying global audiences for the *Hobbit* trilogy is not merely to document and reflect upon the specific content of audience reactions to these particular films: we also seek to contribute to theory-building in reception studies by offering critical insights into the nature and form of audience engagement and response itself, both in general and specifically related to this *kind* of entertainment product—the blockbuster franchise adaptation.

Chapter Overviews

The book addresses some of our major findings on a range of topics that we hope will be of interest to lay readers, including film and Tolkien fans, as well as academics. Part of our intention in writing this book was to give other scholars further insight into the research process we developed for this project, both in the interests of being transparent about our methodological assumptions and procedures, and because we hope our research will provide others with an alternative vision of *how* robust and reliable large-scale comparative research on transnational audiences for a serialised media form might be conducted.

Thus, we begin in Chap. 2 by outlining some of the key insights derived from previous studies of audiences for Jackson's earlier Middle-earth films that have informed our research, before highlighting the key questions that prompted our adoption of a longitudinal, cross-cultural approach in our own study of *Hobbit* audiences. Perhaps the key distinguishing feature of our project is its use and extension of Q methodology for large-scale, transnational online research; here, we introduce readers to this methodological approach and what it makes it possible to do, while also offering an overview of the particular understanding of the nature and form of audience reception that informs our conceptualisation and interpretation of key findings.

The following chapter fleshes out the first set of key findings, focusing on the various ways in which receptions of the *Hobbit* trilogy were 'prefigured' by the long shadows of both Tolkien's written works and Jackson's earlier *LotR* trilogy, and an array of marketing and promotions materials, news coverage, discussion and debate. Drawing on data from our online pre-viewing survey, we describe the main shared viewpoints expressed by our respondents before *The Hobbit: AUJ*'s release in cinemas and offer insight into the various prefigurative activities they were engaging in as they anticipated this film experience. Then, to further clarify the orientations and expectations of those who might later participate in our *AUJ* post-viewing surveys, we chart the specific constellations of meaning, value and affect that our respondents were ascribing to *The Hobbit* in advance of seeing it.

Chapter 4 focuses on a controversy that shaped public discussion and debate around the *Hobbit* production before the first film's release. The extended *Hobbit* union dispute, which threatened to derail the trilogy's New Zealand production and prompted widely criticised reforms to New Zealand labour law, reveals how processes and imperatives of blockbusterisation are currently reshaping transnational film production. Our respondents' reactions to this issue demonstrate how and why a transnational production such as *The Hobbit* can have varying degrees of salience for differently located audiences, while also demonstrating how cinematic desire for fetishised cultural commodities currently trumps consideration of the social conditions under which such commodities are produced.

In Chap. 5, we begin mapping the evolution of audience responses to the *Hobbit* film trilogy over time by describing and interpreting the major post-viewing perspectives that emerged in response to *AUJ*. We also present a unique comparative analysis of the responses of those who took part in *both* pre- *and* post-viewing *AUJ* surveys, illustrating the complex interaction between prefigurative expectations and audience receptions of the fully realised film. Chapter 6 sees our attention shift to the *Hobbit* sequels, *DoS* and *BotFA,* and identifies the major perspectives that emerged in the wake of each film. Here, we describe and illustrate shared viewpoints among different segments of the global audience for the *Hobbit* sequels, and show that their central preoccupations vary widely. While many respondents expressed deep satisfaction at a highly pleasurable, fully immersive return to Middle-earth, others were becoming increasingly troubled by a number of factors relating to the commercial and creative imperatives shaping *The Hobbit*'s production. These included questions of authorial intent and textual fidelity, the process of adaptation and the limits of creative licence, textual realism and *The Hobbit*'s unusual visual aesthetic, and the perceived intrusion of contemporary gender politics into the second and third *Hobbit* films.

In Chap. 7, we focus on audience reactions to the *Hobbit* trilogy's (then unique) visual aesthetic, produced through the combination of high frame rate stereoscopic 3D projection, extensive reliance on CGI and the use of green screens, and 5 K resolution cameras. While intended by director Peter Jackson to facilitate and intensify viewers' experience of pleasurable re-immersion in Middle-earth, the combination of these technologies appears to have produced contradictory effects and visual artefacts that some viewers considered jarring and displeasing. As we show, critical reactions to *The Hobbit*'s visual aesthetic had complex origins, being variously informed by individual commitments to a more traditional cinematic aesthetic, appreciation for *LotR*'s 'gritty' realism (achieved through greater use of practical effects), and an apparent clash between the technologies *themselves* which, we suggest, generated a hyperreality paradox that disrupted narrative immersion for a small but significant number of respondents.

From there, we offer deeper insight into the bases of the many variations in audience engagement and response our study has revealed. Chapter 8 addresses the diverse range of meanings ascribed to each of the films that constitute this blockbuster fantasy film franchise. Here, we illustrate and explain *The Hobbit*'s evolving significance for different kinds of fans, casual viewers and critics over the full course of the trilogy, and document, for the first time on a large scale, the progressive transformation of their engagement with and affection for a media product that had been long imagined and deeply desired by many. A dominant evolving sentiment for a significant minority was disappointment with a failed adaptation, and with the missed opportunity to replicate the heady success of the *LotR* film trilogy. Disappointment primarily centred on issues pertaining to the quality of the adaptation, and crystallised around a controversy surrounding the second and third *Hobbit* films: the introduction of a new female character, the Elf guard Tauriel, and a related love triangle. In discussing these and other issues that were especially salient among our respondents, this chapter adds depth and context to our understanding of the factors that led to continued engagement versus progressive disenchantment and disaffection among different groups of *Hobbit* viewers.

In Chap. 9, we explore the relationship between audience reception and important aspects of identity and social location, including gender, age, education and occupation, but also less frequently studied aspects such as political and religious affiliations, and of course fandom. Drawing on a comparison of responses to the post-viewing survey for *AUJ*, which was conducted in seven different languages, as well as our larger data corpus in which we received responses from over 85 countries around the world, this chapter documents a number of culturally and linguistically specific findings and offers an account of the possible basis for differences and similarities in *The Hobbit*'s transnational reception within different interpretive communities.

In Chap. 10 we conclude by highlighting what our project reveals about the issues that impacted upon the *Hobbit* creators' ability to attract and sustain an audience for a second Middle-earth themed fantasy trilogy. While our focus is on this particular film series, our findings speak to wider processes shaping the conceptualisation and realisation of blockbuster franchise adaptations more broadly, and thus have relevance to the growing number of similar films being generated by Hollywood studios today and into the immediate future. We also identify the key theoretical insights that can be gleaned from this research, and comment on the project's wider significance and contribution to audience and reception studies in particular. Finally, we revisit some of the major strengths and weaknesses of our research approach, acknowledging what our project has and has not been able to do, the methodological lessons we've learned, and offering suggestions as to how this approach might be adapted and extended in future research on audiences and media engagement.

In sum, then, this book addresses a wide range of themes relating to audience receptions of blockbuster franchise adaptations in general, and the *Hobbit* trilogy in particular. These include the public and private prefiguration of such films; fannish anticipation and the commercial elicitation of cinematic desire; the role of political affiliations and public controversies in shaping audience responses; the meaning(s) of blockbuster films for fans and others; expectations of genre and adaptation; modes of reception; identification; the role of social and cultural location in shaping audience response; gender representations in fantasy fiction; and responses to new cinematic technologies. We hope it offers much that is of relevance and interest to fans and critics of *The Hobbit* alike, while also providing a useful account for media and film scholars of a unique longitudinal project examining transnational audience receptions of a landmark blockbuster event-film franchise.

NOTES

1. These and all subsequent figures relating to the financial performance of *LotR* and *The Hobbit* were accessed from or calculated based on information provided by Box Office Mojo on 11 January 2017.

REFERENCES

Acland, C. R. (2013). Senses of success and the rise of the blockbuster. *Film History: An International Journal, 25*(1), 11–18. doi:10.2979/filmhistory.25.1-2.11.

Barker, M., & Mathijs, E. (Eds.). (2008). *Watching The Lord of the Rings: Tolkien's world audiences.* New York: Peter Lang.

Biltereyst, D., & Meers, P. (2006). Blockbusters and/as events: Distributing and launching *The Lord of the Rings.* In E. Mathijs (Ed.), *The Lord of the Rings: Popular culture in global context* (pp. 71–87). London: Wallflower.

Box Office Mojo. (2017a). 2016 domestic grosses. Box Office Mojo. Retrieved February 14, 2017 from http://www.boxofficemojo.com/yearly/chart/?yr=2016&p=.htm.

Box Office Mojo. (2017b). Franchises: Middle Earth. Box Office Mojo. Retrieved January 11, 2017, from http://www.boxofficemojo.com/franchises/chart/?id=middleearth.htm.

Brynes, P. (2015, 11 December). Why Hollywood movies have become so bad. *Sydney Morning Herald.* Retrieved October 8, 2016, from http://www.smh.com.au/entertainment/movies/why-hollywood-movies-are-so-bad-20151208-gli68i.html.

Cucco, M. (2009). The promise is great: The blockbuster and the Hollywood economy. *Media, Culture and Society, 31*(2), 215–230. doi:10.1177/0163443708100315.

Elberse, A. (2013). *Blockbusters: Hit-making, risk-taking, and the big business of entertainment.* New York: Henry Holt Macmillan.

Epstein, E. J. (2006). *The big picture: Money and power in Hollywood.* New York: Random House.

Fiorelli, G. (2012, 13 December). Prelaunch and the marketing of suspense: *The Hobbit* history case. *State of digital.* Retrieved 18, 2014, from http://www.stateofdigital.com/hobbit-history-case/.

Hirsjärvi, I., Kovala, U., & Ruotsalainen, M. (2016). Patterns of reception in Denmark, Finland, and Sweden: In search of interpretive communities. *Participations: Journal of Audience and Reception Studies,* 13(2), 263–288.

IMDb. (2017). Top rated movies. IMDb. Retrieved January 13, 2017, from http://www.imdb.com/chart/top.

IMDb. (n.d.). Box office/business for *The Hobbit: An Unexpected Journey.* IMDb. Retrieved February 14, 2017 from http://www.imdb.com/title/tt0903624/business?ref_=tt_dt_bus.

Jackson, P. (Director). (2001). *The Lord of the Rings: The Fellowship of the Ring* [Motion picture]. New Zealand and USA: New Line Cinema and Wingnut Films.

Jackson, P. (Director). (2002). *The Lord of the Rings: The Two Towers* [Motion picture]. New Zealand and USA: New Line Cinema and Wingnut Films.

Jackson, P. (Director). (2003). *The Lord of the Rings: The Return of the King* [Motion picture]. New Zealand and USA: New Line Cinema and Wingnut Films.

Jackson, P. (2012). Peter Jackson HFR Q & A. Retrieved May 14, 2014, from www.thehobbit.com/hfr3d/qa.html.

Jenkins, H. (2006). *Convergence culture*. New York: New York University.

Jöckel, S., & Döbler, T. (2006). The event movie: Marketing filmed entertainment for transnational media corporations. *The International Journal on Media Management, 8*(2), 84–91. doi:10.1207/s14241250ijmm0802_4.

Johnson, D. (2013). *Media franchising: Creative license and collaboration in the culture industries*. New York: New York University Press.

King, G. (2000). *Spectacular narratives: Hollywood in the age of the blockbuster*. London, GBR: IB Tauris.

King, G. (2003). Spectacle, narrative, and the spectacular Hollywood blockbuster. In J. Stringer (Ed.), *Movie blockbusters* (pp. 114–127). London and New York: Routledge.

Kuipers, G., & de Kloet, J. (2009). Banal cosmopolitanism and *The Lord of the Rings*: The limited role of national differences in global media consumption. *Poetics, 37*, 99–118. doi:10.1016/j.poetic.2009.01.002.

Langford, B. (2005). *Film genre: Hollywood and beyond*. Edinburgh: Edinburgh University Press.

Lavik, E. (2008). The battle for the blockbuster: Discourses of spectacle and excess. *New Review of Film and Television Studies, 6*(2), 169–187. doi:10.1080/17400300802098305.

Markowski, J. (2012). *The Hobbit* marketing: A not-so-unexpected journey in marketing diversity. *Branding Beat*. Retrieved March 20, 2016, from https://www.qualitylogoproducts.com/blog/the-hobbit-marketing-journey-in-marketing-diversity/.

Mikos L., Eichner, S., Prommer, E., & Wedel, M. (2008). Involvement in *The Lord of the Rings*: Audience strategies and orientations. In M. Barker & E. Mathijs (Eds.), *Watching The Lord of the Rings: Tolkien's world audiences* (Vol. 3, pp. 111–128). New York: Peter Lang.

Miller, T., Govil, N., McMurria, J., Maxwell, R., & Wang, T. (2005). *Global Hollywood 2*. London: BFI Publishing.

Olson, S. R. (1999). *Hollywood planet: Global media and the competitive advantage of narrative transparency*. London and New York: Routledge.

Owczarski, K. A. (2015). 'More than meets the eye': Transformers and the complexities of franchise film production in contemporary Hollywood. *Quarterly Review of Film and Video, 32*(8), 675–694. doi:10.1080/10509208.2015.10 78274.

Rankin, A., Jr. (1977). *The Hobbit*. [Animated TV film] USA and Japan: Rankin/Bass, Topcraft, ABC Video Enterprises.

Riga, F. P., Thum, M., & Kollmann, J. (2014). From children's book to epic prequel: Peter Jackson's transformation of Tolkien's *The Hobbit*. *Mythlore, 32*(2), 99–119.

Rose, S. (2016, August 3). From *Suicide Squad* to *Batman v Superman*, why are DC's films so bad? *The Guardian*. Retrieved February 14, 2017, from https://www.theguardian.com/film/shortcuts/2016/aug/03/from-suicide-squad-to-batman-v-superman-why-dc-films-so-bad-zack-snyder.

Rotten Tomatoes. (2017). *The Hobbit: The Desolation of Smaug*. Rotten Tomatoes. Retrieved January 2017, 13, from http://www.rottentomatoes.com/m/the_hobbit_the_desolation_of_smaug/.

Ryan, T. (2014). Critics consensus: *The Hobbit: The Battle of the Five Armies* is a solid sendoff. Rotten Tomatoes. Retrieved May 10, 2015, from http://editorial.rottentomatoes.com/article/critics-consensus-the-hobbit-the-battle-of-the-five-armies-is-a-solid-sendoff/.

Sakoui, A. (2016, 1 September). Hollywood's summertime bombs got a lot more disastrous this year. *Bloomberg Technology*. Retrieved February 14, 2017, from https://www.bloomberg.com/news/articles/2016-09-01/hollywood-s-summertime-bombs-got-a-lot-more-disastrous-this-year.

Schauer, B. (2007). Critics, clones and narrative in the franchise blockbuster. *New Review of Film and Television Studies, 5*(2), 191–210. doi:10.1080/17400300701432894.

Stringer, J. (2003). *Movie blockbusters*. London and New York: Routledge.

Suzanne-Mayer, D. (2016, 7 April). Why film franchises could change cinema forever. *Consequence of Sound*. Retrieved April 30, 2016, from http://consequenceofsound.net/2016/04/why-film-franchises-could-change-cinema-forever/.

The Numbers. (2017). Movie budget and financial performance records. *The Numbers*. Retrieved January 10, 2017, from http://www.the-numbers.com/movie/budgets/.

Thompson, K. (1999). *Storytelling in the new Hollywood: Understanding classical narrative technique*. Cambridge, MA: Harvard University Press.

Tolkien, J. R. R. (1937). *The hobbit, or there and back again*. London: George Allen and Unwin.

Vaughan, O. (2014, December 7). Return to Middle-earth—was it worth it? *The Hobbit: The Battle of the Five Armies* predicted to limp at box office. *The New Zealand Herald*. Retrieved December 14, 2015, from http://www.nzherald.co.nz/entertainment/news/article.cfm?c_id=1501119&objectid=11369366.

Wasko, J. (2008). *The Lord of the Rings*: Selling the franchise. In M. Barker & E. Mathijs (Eds.), *Watching The Lord of the Rings: Tolkien's world audiences* (pp. 21–36). New York: Peter Lang.

Williams, T. (2015, 25 September). Ridley Scott's latest 'Alien' announcement drives Hollywood's sequel problem. *Market Watch*. Retrieved February 14,

2017, from http://www.marketwatch.com/story/ridley-scotts-latest-alien-announcement-drives-hollywoods-sequel-problem-2015-09-25.

Wyatt, J. (2010). *High concept: Movies and marketing in Hollywood.* Austin: University of Texas Press.

Xoanon. (2010, 30 May). Guillermo Del Toro departs *The Hobbit.* The One Ring net. Retrieved August 12, 2012, from http://www.theonering.net/torwp/2010/05/30/36920-guillermo-del-toro-departs-the-hobbit/.

Zakarin, J. (2012, 30 July). Third *Hobbit* film confirmed. *The Hollywood Reporter.* Retrieved 14 February 2017, from http://www.hollywoodreporter.com/news/third-hobbit-film-confirmed-355817.

CHAPTER 2

Researching Audience Engagements with the *Hobbit* Trilogy: A Unique Methodological Approach

Introduction

In what follows, we firstly situate our project within the wider body of scholarship on audiences for adaptations of Tolkien's written works that has informed our core questions and research focus. Then, we explain our rationale for conducting a large-scale longitudinal investigation of transnational receptions of the *Hobbit* trilogy. These reasons reflect our interest in understanding whether and how a person's national or cultural identities, social location and affiliations might make a difference to their reception of these (and potentially other) films. Since we also wanted our project to contribute to theory-building about audience receptions in general and receptions of blockbuster film adaptation franchises in particular, our research and analysis have been informed by an established analytical framework, the Composite Multi-dimensional Model of Modes of Audience Reception (hereafter the Composite Model). For the benefit of readers, we outline the major distinctions charted in this model before detailing the specific methods employed to gather our research materials, which combined Q methodology with a conventional questionnaire. This approach, we believe, has allowed us to gain rich insight into the form and content of diverse global audience receptions of this Hollywood blockbuster fantasy film trilogy.

© The Author(s) 2017
C. Michelle et al., *Fans, Blockbusterisation, and the Transformation of Cinematic Desire*, DOI 10.1057/978-1-137-59616-1_2

AUDIENCES FOR *THE HOBBIT*: INSIGHTS FROM PREVIOUS RESEARCH

Our task in attempting to chart audience responses to *The Hobbit* was made more complex because of its status as simultaneously a literary adaptation, a prequel series to a much acclaimed earlier film franchise *and* a blockbuster event-film trilogy designed to appeal to global audiences. As noted in the previous chapter, *The Hobbit* clearly benefited from the existence of two 'pre-assembled' audiences in the form of dedicated Tolkien readers and fans of the *Lord of the Rings* (*LotR*) film trilogy eager to return to cinematic Middle-earth. We considered it likely that the pre-existing affinities of these two groups would colour their subsequent encounters with the *Hobbit* prequels. But, as we have previously noted (Davis et al. 2014), while we might imagine these two groups to be relatively distinct, there is considerable overlap between them and each is also internally diverse.

For instance, Brayton (2006) notes that even within the Tolkien fan community, there is a division between Tolkienists, whose primary allegiance is to the author and his wider corpus of literary works, and those who are more specifically fans of the *LotR* novels. Brayton also observes that there has been active online discussion of Jackson's adaptations of Tolkien's works since at least 1998, with Theonering.net being the key location for the articulation of fans' hopeful imaginings and anxious speculations before the release of the *LotR* films. Chin and Gray's (2001) in-depth analysis of these online fan discussions identified three distinct pre-viewing responses. First, a Tolkien purist position which regarded any potential deviations from the books as objectionable. This was countered by a second, more moderate Tolkien-oriented position, which sought to understand the need for modifications when translating books to screen while remaining apprehensive about the potential for unpalatable changes. The authors also observed a third position marked by wholesale enthusiasm for the long-awaited film version of a favourite book series, which many assumed was destined to enshrine its place in literary and cultural history. Thus, while many Tolkien readers expressed a strong sense of loyalty to and familiarity with the original works and their creator, not all were averse to changes being made in the process of cinematic adaptation (see also Thompson 2003).

Adding to this complexity, a new audience group has emerged in the wake of the commercial and popular success of the *LotR* film trilogy, one which Brayton (2006, p. 144) terms 'Ringers', or 'the fan of all things *Lord of the Rings*'. Yet within this new form of fandom there are different interests, loyalties, concerns and priorities, leading to internal debates and at time conflicts relating to the inclusion, exclusion or presentation of characters and scenes (Brayton 2006). As noted by Rae and Gray (2007), however, few reception studies have explored the significance of such distinctions and competing loyalties among audience groups, nor the ways differently interested and endowed viewers subsequently read and make sense of film adaptations (for further discussion see Davis et al. 2014).

One study that has attempted to address these issues explicitly is Martin Barker and Ernest Mathijs' (2008) Tolkien's World Audiences project, which traced transnational receptions of *The Return of the King*, the final episode in the *LotR* film trilogy. The various publications emerging from this extensive project offer detailed evidence of key lines of division among viewers across multiple dimensions, but their collective impact is hampered by the absence of a shared conceptual framework with which to make sense of connections across the different publications, which analyse different sets of data in disparate ways. For instance, four ideal 'types' of *LotR* film viewer were identified through cluster analysis of the Italian survey data, including 'the enthusiastic fan, the disappointed fan, the critic reader, and the mass spectator' (Barker et al. 2008, p. 229); while suggestive, these distinctions do not appear to have been taken up more widely in the World Audiences project. Kuipers and de Kloet (2009) also performed a cluster analysis of *LotR* audiences using three different variables and found just two groups. One contained highly involved and devoted fans, predominantly from Anglophone countries, who expressed greater appreciation for the film and the book on which it is based. The other contained less involved viewers from non-English-speaking countries, who offered a wider range of interpretations and themselves diverged more strongly from what these authors posit as Hollywood's assumed primary target market of young white males. While an interesting distinction, the lack of a shared conceptual framework makes it difficult to compare these findings with those presented by other scholars involved in the same project—including Jerslev's (2006) analysis of emotional engagement, de Kloet and Kuipers' (2007) and Barker's (2009) reflections on spiritual readings, Mikos et al.'s (2008) comparison of the reception strategies used by the 'literary' versus 'media' generations and Turnbull's (2008) discussion of disappointed book lovers. The eclectic foci and disparate analytical approaches also make it difficult to extract from this otherwise impressive body of scholarship a more unified and coherent understanding of audiences for blockbuster adaptations of literary texts. Nonetheless, each of the above works individually informs our analysis.

In preparing for our study, we thought it likely that responses to *The Hobbit* would be influenced by whether a viewer's primary loyalty was to Tolkien's written works or Jackson's *LotR* films, following Thompson's distinction between 'book-firsters' and 'film-firsters' (Thompson 2011, p. 43). We also imagined further distinctions according to which book(s) they were most loyal to—whether it was *The Hobbit*, *The Lord of the Rings* or Tolkien's wider corpus of works. While academic criticism has recently sought to expand the understanding of textual fidelity (in which original sources are given greater value and primacy than their screen adaptations [Stam 2000]), faithfulness clearly still matters for many viewers (Geraghty 2008), and thus remains an important concept in reception studies of literary adaptations such as *The Hobbit*. In addition to these pre-assembled audiences familiar with Tolkien's books and the Jackson-helmed films, we anticipated a wider viewership for this Hollywood blockbuster event-film, including film critics and scholars (who frequently denounce blockbusters as ostentatious and shallow); 'mainstream' casual viewers (who are often assumed to enjoy them as easily consumed but somewhat meaningless entertainment); fans of celebrities drawn to see their favourite stars perform on the big screen; fans of fantasy as a genre; and possibly more. In undertaking our research, we hoped to capture at least some of these distinctions among potential audiences for the *Hobbit* film trilogy and to trace their significance in shaping viewers' subsequent modes of engagement and response.

RESEARCHING *THE HOBBIT*'s GLOBAL RECEPTION

Informed by this scholarship on Middle-earth audiences along with the wider body of research on fans, film adaptation, audience reception and blockbuster film production, our project sought to chart major distinctions in viewers' perspectives on the *Hobbit* trilogy and explain how and why their perspectives may have evolved over time. The project's focus reflects the kinds of questions we were interested in exploring from the outset. In particular:

- How was this keenly anticipated blockbuster event-film trilogy understood, engaged with and made sense of by different viewers at key moments in its life course?
- To what extent did discussion, debate, marketing and promotion of *The Hobbit* before its cinematic release shape subsequent responses to it?
- How did individual and public reactions to the first *Hobbit* film shape engagements with its sequels?
- To what extent did global responses to the *Hobbit* trilogy transcend differences in terms of nationality, language and culture?
- Were there any significant differences in audience engagement and response based on gender, age, socioeconomic class, education, occupation, ethnicity, political views, religious beliefs, fan affiliations and so on?
- Which particular aspects of national, political, economic, social and cultural positioning were most influential in shaping audience responses to the *Hobbit* trilogy, and why?

Other questions emerged over the course of our research, as the films themselves and evolving audience reactions to them suggested new avenues for exploration. In particular, we wanted to know:

- Why were responses to this prequel trilogy so mixed and seemingly polarised, particularly compared to Jackson's *LotR* films?
- How did differently aligned viewers respond to the blockbusterisation of J. R. R. Tolkien's original novel as a familiar collective cultural property?
- What impact did this film trilogy's pioneering combination of CGI, high frame rate projection and stereoscopic 3D have on audience engagement and response?
- In what ways did New Zealand's central involvement in the transnational production of *The Hobbit* inform local and global perceptions of the films, their conditions of production and New Zealand as a sovereign nation?
- And, finally, in what ways did the meaning and significance of the *Hobbit* trilogy change over time?

Ultimately, we hoped that our research would offer in-depth understanding of how different audiences, each with prior experiences, desires and commitments, engaged with the *Hobbit* trilogy from the period immediately before the release of *An Unexpected Journey* (*AUJ*) to the post-release period following *The Battle of the Five Armies* (*BotFA*). In this respect, our research adopted a very different approach to previous research on audiences for the *LotR*. Most importantly, ours was a longitudinal as well as cross-cultural empirical investigation informed by an explicit theoretical understanding of audience reception, and utilised a unique mixed-methods research design that incorporated what is known as Q methodology. In what follows, we explain our research design and its rationale in greater detail, and outline the kinds of problems we hoped to overcome in developing our methodological approach.

A LONGITUDINAL INVESTIGATION INTO RECEPTIONS OF A BLOCKBUSTER FRANCHISE

The most obvious point of difference between our project and virtually all previous work in this area is our use of a longitudinal approach to data collection, which traced the evolution of audience responses to all three *Hobbit* films over the full course of the trilogy. Our research thus began in 2012, with our first online survey of potential viewers' opinions and forms of engagement being conducted in the three weeks before *AUJ*'s world premiere in Wellington, New Zealand, on 28 November 2012. This survey gathered 1000 usable responses from 59 different countries. This was followed by a survey of *AUJ*'s reception, conducted initially in English from February to June 2013, with translated versions going online in six other languages in April that year. From these multilingual surveys, a combined total of 2870 responses were collected from 85 countries. A third survey of *The Desolation of Smaug* (*DoS*) audiences took place from January to July 2014 and collected 1051 responses from 62 countries. The final survey of receptions of *BotFA* took place from January to May 2015 and collected 840 responses in total from 49 countries.

By surveying viewers at key moments in the *Hobbit* trilogy's cinematic release, we have been able to track the transformation of audience reactions to a wide range of textual features that reflect the economic, industrial, creative and commercial imperatives and processes governing the production of a contemporary blockbuster event-film franchise. This kind of longitudinal research on audiences is highly unusual. Most studies of film reception tend to focus in depth on responses to one particular film, even when it is part of a series. While so doing allows researchers to capture a 'snapshot' of receptions at a particular moment, it neglects to consider how those receptions might have evolved over time in response to repeated viewing or conversation with others, for instance. Such studies consequently tend to present reception as a fixed and static phenomenon. While our research is perhaps best thought of as a series of snapshots taken at different moments, it does allow us to hold steady and compare the responses of individuals and groups at key stages in the trilogy's life course. It means we can objectively contrast responses elicited before the first film's release, with those gathered following each instalment and after the final *Hobbit* movie appeared in cinemas two years later—a capacity that is exceedingly rare in the field of audience studies to date.

In effect, our longitudinal methodology has allowed us to capture evolving audience reactions to the currently dominant Hollywood production strategy of serialisation and the franchise model, in which filmmaking becomes deeply entwined with ongoing marketing and promotional efforts to ensure that a massive global audience is built and then sustained for various sequels or spin-offs. It has also afforded our project considerable flexibility. We were able to adjust and refine our research tools at each successive stage of the project and could add specifically targeted questions to the latter surveys to explore pertinent issues as they emerged, whether from our analysis of earlier survey data or wider public discussion around the films. For instance, it became clear from our first post-viewing survey that some respondents had been troubled by *AUJ*'s unusual visual aesthetic. In our subsequent surveys, we were able to add additional questions about *The Hobbit*'s pioneering use of high frame rate stereoscopic 3D. A graduate student was recruited to conduct a parallel project using an online questionnaire to gain greater insight into the views of 650 respondents from 49 different countries. This very useful information was supplemented by 39 Skype and email interviews with selected informants who represented the broad range of perspectives expressed in the questionnaire responses. Thus, our longitudinal approach allowed the project to expand and evolve to gain greater insight into the expressed interests and concerns of our respondents.

In all, then, we received 6450 responses from participants living in over 85 different countries. All were generous in contributing their thoughts and feelings about the *Hobbit* films, often in considerable depth. Several hundred respondents completed more than one survey, while 174 participated in all three post-viewing surveys. Of these, more than 50 completed all four core *Hobbit* surveys, offering an unprecedented opportunity to compare individual responses at key moments across the life course of a blockbuster film trilogy. The generous commitment of these respondents was extraordinary, and we are grateful to them, and indeed all our participants. Their willingness to share their views has allowed us to track the evolving opinions of different groups of viewers over time, pinpoint the attributes of the *Hobbit* films that caused enchantment, disinterest or disaffection, and interpret divergent responses to the film in terms of a more general model of audience reception, about which more shall be said below. To the best of our knowledge, the rich and extensive longitudinal data provided by our respondents is unprecedented in the field of audience studies.

A LARGE-SCALE INVESTIGATION

A second key difference from most existing studies of audience reception is the comparatively large scale of our *Hobbit* audience project. It is considerably larger than most other studies of film reception, but also smaller than two global projects led by Martin Barker and Ernest Mathijs, for quite deliberate reasons in both cases. In particular, the decision to recruit a large number of respondents relates to concerns regarding the generalisability of the findings obtained from most existing studies of audience reception, particularly within the ethnographic tradition of British cultural studies. To date, as Morley (2006) observes, there has been a wealth of qualitative research offering detailed insights into specific encounters between viewers and particular media texts, with small-scale ethnographic case studies being typical. As Barker (2006) suggests, the field has struggled to generate easily comparable observations that might support the formulation of stronger, testable generalisations, which is necessary to develop a clearer theoretical understanding of the nature of media reception per se. While having large numbers of respondents is not in itself sufficient to achieve greater generalisability and applicability of findings beyond the particular case in question, it does increase their reliability and validity, while guarding against potential idiosyncrasies in the interpretation of data derived from small and often unrepresentative samples.

Our decision to seek large numbers of respondents also stemmed from a belief that doing so would make it possible to explore a long-standing question concerning the degree to which individual receptions are shaped by wider social contexts of viewing. Since the early 1980s, researchers have sought to understand the influence of social positioning (in terms of gender, class, age, education, occupation and so forth) on people's receptions of media content. Seminal work includes David Morley's (1980) landmark study of the *Nationwide* audience, which identified distinct class-based differences in viewers' responses to a television news programme, Andrea Press's (1991) research exploring class and generational differences in women's receptions of American television drama and Tamar Liebes and Elihu Katz's (1990) detailed study of cross-national receptions of the US primetime television soap opera *Dallas*. Continuing in this tradition, we were interested in exploring possible relationships between receptions of *The Hobbit* and potentially important dimensions of social location—and not only the traditional ones of nationality, gender, age and class, but also education, professional experience in the media industries, political and religious beliefs, pre-existing fandoms and familiarity with key texts—such as the novel on which the *Hobbit* films were based, and Jackson's earlier *LotR* trilogy.

In the past, the possible relationship between individual receptions and aspects of social location has typically been examined using qualitative methods such as interviews and more especially focus groups. As a result, it has been difficult to generate reliable evidence of the relationships between reception and aspects of social location, for two reasons. First, the number of respondents involved in interview or focus group research is usually relatively small and unrepresentative of the wider viewing population, due to the resource-intensive and often exploratory nature of such research. Second, many researchers assume in advance that their respondents are members of particular interpretive communities with shared experiences, values and related reception strategies, and hence that it is reasonable to construct focus groups comprised either of naturally occurring groups, or of unconnected respondents who share the same nationality, ethnicity, class, gender, political interest and so on (see, for instance, Mikos et al. 2008). This common, inexpensive and convenient method imposes in advance certain assumptions about which particular aspect(s) of identity will be most significant in a given context. There is a danger that such thinking can become simplistic and reductionist, all too easily sliding into an implicit notion of social or cultural determinism.

To avoid making any such assumptions, we sought an approach that would allow us to explore possible links between social location, fan affiliations and audience receptions, in a way that did not assume prior knowledge of the relative importance of any particular aspect. We were also aware of the need to avoid reifying or naturalising either 'identity' or 'culture' as somehow singular, unified and uncontested. Identity, in the postmodern era, is increasingly regarded as somewhat unstable and intersectional, in the sense that we are never *just* women or men, English or French, fan or anti-fan, but are rather *multiply* positioned across various lines of difference that are themselves becoming increasingly complex. We may be women, men or possibly transgender, of a particular nationality that may differ to that of our birth, and may lay claim to multiple ethnic origins and fandoms, and so forth. Both 'class' and 'culture' have become more fractured, fluid and mobile phenomena in an age of globalisation and unprecedented rates of cross-border migration. The exponential growth and global spread of the Internet and social media has helped popularise identity politics 'old' and new, while playing a key role in forging transnational *communities of interest* based around shared cultural and political affiliations, media fandoms and so on. While these communities of interest remain tenuous and are often internally divided, they are nonetheless increasingly significant—and in the realms of global media fandoms, they may be more important than 'traditional' and supposedly stable markers of social identity such as gender, ethnicity or nationality.

We consequently sought an approach for our *Hobbit* Audience Project that would avoid making assumptions about the relative significance of any particular aspect of identity or national culture in shaping receptions, whilst also making it possible to explore the conditions under which a person's social or national identities, location and affiliations actually might make a difference, in what ways, and *why*. To avoid criticisms that our methodological choices shaped certain outcomes from the outset (and in particular, to avoid making presumptions about which aspects of identity would be most influential), we chose to explore such questions after the fact, working backwards from how our respondents actually made sense of the films to examine whether there were any patterns in the distribution of modes of response based on particular aspects of social location. To do this in a way that would provide statistically meaningful results, we aimed to recruit around 1000 respondents in each phase, achieving this for all but our final post-viewing survey.

CONTRIBUTING TO THEORY-BUILDING

While attracting large numbers of respondents was important, we realised it would not be sufficient, particularly given our wider aim of contributing to understandings of the nature of audience reception per se. To achieve this, our research needed to be clearly linked to an existing body of knowledge on how viewers engage with and make sense of screen media texts in general. This is the third key difference between our project and most other studies conducted to date. We have employed an explicitly elucidated model of reception to interpret our findings, known as the Composite Model (Michelle 2007). The distinct viewing modes charted in this model have been empirically observed and described within the larger body of audience reception research (using a variety of terminology), including seminal studies of television and (less frequently) film, such as those cited above.

Use of an explicit analytical framework was necessary because we wanted our project to go beyond merely describing similarities and differences in our participants' responses to these particular films. We wanted to contribute not only to our knowledge of how this particular group of viewers responded to *The Hobbit*, but to theory-building about audience reception in general, and of blockbuster film adaptation franchises in particular. To facilitate this, our results needed to be made sense of in relation to an existing model or theory of reception that other researchers could likewise draw on to interpret *their* findings, so that the two sets of findings might be compared in a valid and meaningful way (see Yin 2010, for a discussion of analytical generalisation).

As well as being grounded in an extensive body of scholarship on audience reception, the Composite Model has been applied in research on receptions of James Cameron's 2009 blockbuster film *Avatar* (Michelle et al. 2012), TV dramas including *Dexter* (Tager and Matthee 2014; Granelli and Zenor 2016), *The West Wing* (Zenor 2014), *Breaking Bad* (McKeown et al. 2015), and *The Sopranos* (Van Ommen et al. 2016), and reality TV shows *Rockstar: Supernova* (Michelle 2009) and *The Biggest Loser* (Holland et al. 2015). While these studies were conducted in a variety of locations—online/international, the USA, South Africa, the Netherlands and Australia—they draw on the same analytical framework, making it possible to observe parallels between their findings. Hence, there is a body of existing (and hopefully future) empirical research to which our results can be compared and insights generated across genres and cultural contexts. This facilitates theory-building and testing, because without a common set of analytical concepts or propositions it is difficult to compare findings relating to different texts, genres, cultural contexts of viewing and audiences—particularly if the methods used also differ. As Esser and Hanitzsch (2012a, p. 7) suggest, 'the objects of analysis need to be compared on the basis of a common theoretical framework and by drawing on equivalent conceptualizations and methods'. By using an explicitly articulated analytical framework to interpret data gathered via a standardised methodology, we hoped it would be possible to one day compare responses to *The Hobbit* with responses to other blockbuster fantasy adventure films, major literary adaptations and indeed films of entirely different genres, and to establish whether similar modes of response were evident, or not. This kind of approach, we believed, would ensure the project made a contribution to theory development and refinement, and to the progression of knowledge about audience reception per se.

To briefly outline our chosen theoretical framework, the Composite Model charts four broad modes of audience engagement and response: *transparent, referential, mediated* and *discursive* (Fig. 2.1). When watching a fictional narrative in a *transparent* mode, viewers temporarily suspend disbelief and critical distance to grant the fictional world the status of 'real life', entering fully into the story to derive the specific forms of pleasure and enjoyment intended by the text's makers (Michelle 2007). Media effects researchers have gone further in elucidating this mode of engagement in relation to entertainment media, citing as a key aspect the experience of being 'transported' into a fictional world by the narrative (following Green and Brock 2000; see also Green et al. 2004, 2012; Hall and Zwarun 2012; Tal-Or and Cohen 2015). Viewers in this mode experience deep engagement and full immersion in the text, feel 'swept away' by the story and often physically present in the storyworld, frequently report strong feelings of identification with the central character(s) or textual themes, lose awareness of the passing of time and may experience an intense emotional response (Michelle 2007). The transparent mode represents the preferred response to a fantasy adventure film such as *The Hobbit*, and is particularly relevant given Jackson's stated creative intent to transport viewers back to Middle-earth.

Conversely, in a *referential* mode, the text is primarily understood in relation to viewers' experiential knowledge(s) and perceptions of its relevance (or lack thereof) to the real world (Michelle 2007). In this mode,

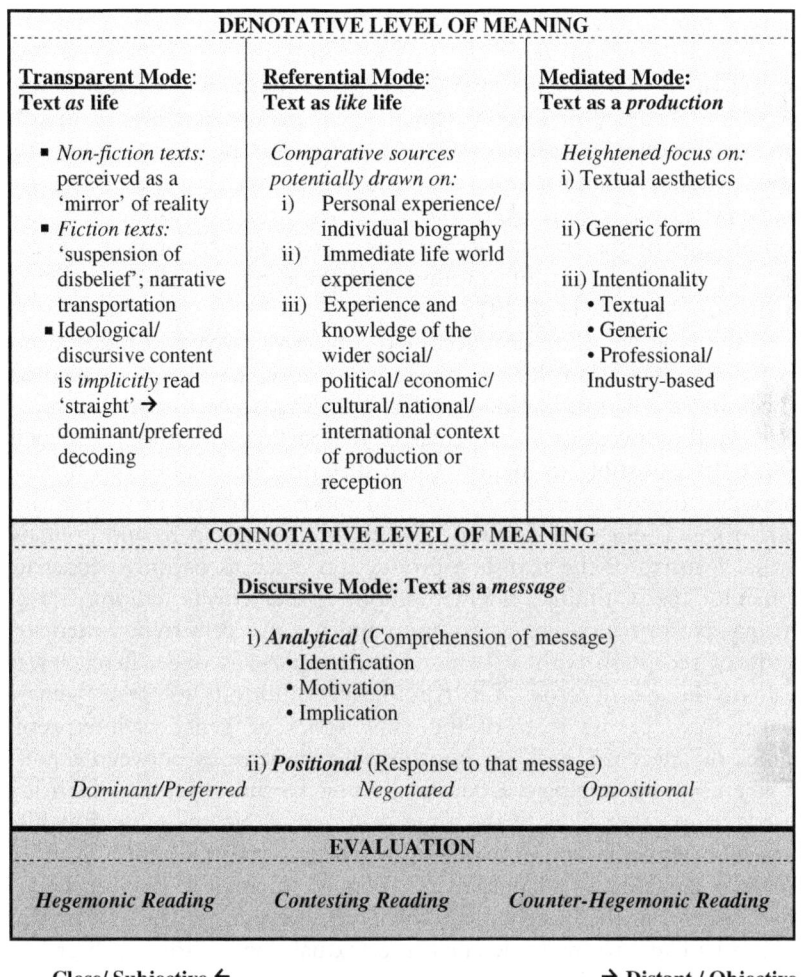

DENOTATIVE LEVEL OF MEANING

Transparent Mode: Text *as* life	**Referential Mode:** Text as *like* life	**Mediated Mode:** Text as a *production*
■ *Non-fiction texts:* perceived as a 'mirror' of reality ■ *Fiction texts:* 'suspension of disbelief'; narrative transportation ■ Ideological/ discursive content is *implicitly* read 'straight' → dominant/preferred decoding	*Comparative sources potentially drawn on:* i) Personal experience/ individual biography ii) Immediate life world experience iii) Experience and knowledge of the wider social/ political/ economic/ cultural/ national/ international context of production or reception	*Heightened focus on:* i) Textual aesthetics ii) Generic form iii) Intentionality • Textual • Generic • Professional/ Industry-based

CONNOTATIVE LEVEL OF MEANING

Discursive Mode: Text as a *message*

i) *Analytical* (Comprehension of message)
 • Identification
 • Motivation
 • Implication

ii) *Positional* (Response to that message)

Dominant/Preferred	*Negotiated*	*Oppositional*

EVALUATION

Hegemonic Reading	*Contesting Reading*	*Counter-Hegemonic Reading*

Close/ Subjective ← --- → **Distant / Objective**
(Relationship between text and viewer)

Fig. 2.1 The Composite Multi-dimensional Model of Modes of Audience Reception (Michelle 2007; revised)

viewers often make comparisons and analogies between the depicted reality and the world 'out there'. In so doing, they typically draw from aspects of their lives and experiences, observations and knowledges to assess the accuracy of textual depictions of people and events and the version of 'reality' presented. While it is certainly possible to adopt this mode when watching a fantasy adventure film such as *The Hobbit*, this kind of response is more likely to emerge when texts contain explicit allegorical content that makes overt references to objects or events within the 'real world'—as two of us found in our research on viewers' reactions to *Avatar* (Michelle et al. 2012).

In the typically more distanced and 'objective' *mediated* mode, viewers focus explicitly on the constructed nature of the text as an aesthetic object and media production that has been shaped by established media codes and conventions and created by particular authors (Michelle 2007). It is possible to identify three subcategories within this broader approach to sense-making. A mediated mode of reception with an *aesthetic* focus is one in which the viewer draws attention to and evaluates formal features of the text as a production, such as narrative construction, plot, pace, timing, cinematography, visual effects, editing, scriptwriting, performance, characterisation and so on. Conversely, a mediated mode of reception with a focus on *generic form* is one where viewers evaluate the text in terms of its typological conformity to certain generic conventions, or use texts of the same series or genre as interpretive frames of reference, drawing intertextual comparisons between them— as when viewers compare a film adaptation to the novel on which it is based, or to other films of the same genre or within the same franchise. This subcategory of response obviously has particular relevance given *The Hobbit*'s status as an adaptation of Tolkien's much-loved novel, by the same director as the hugely successful *LotR* film trilogy. The *Hobbit* films were thus likely to invite detailed intertextual comparisons with at least two pre-existing cultural properties—the original novel, and Jackson's *LotR* trilogy. The third type of mediated reception is one which draws on viewers' perceptions of the intentions and motivations of a text's producers in terms of meeting various textual, generic and professional or industry-based *imperatives*—such as the need to generate humour, interest or drama, to inform or entertain, or even to attract a lucrative viewing audience in order to generate profit for the television network or film studio—also highly relevant given *The Hobbit*'s status as a capital-intensive blockbuster adaptation franchise.

Finally, Michelle (2007) suggests that receptions framed in a *discursive* mode primarily and overtly address the text's propositional or 'message' content—in other words, its ideological connotations. Responses in this mode give particular credence to the text's perceived attempt to communicate a message about the wider social world and represent the viewer's reaction to that message. In assessing the connotative meaning of the text in relation to their unique stock of prior beliefs, assumptions and discursive allegiances, viewers may adopt one of the three positions theorised by Stuart Hall (1980)—preferred/dominant, negotiated or oppositional. While all texts and receptions clearly have a discursive element, some genres and texts are more clearly and immediately seeking to communicate an overt message, perhaps to persuade or inform. Thus, while it is certainly possible for viewers to adopt this mode when making sense of a fantasy adventure film such as *The Hobbit*, much depends on the emphasis given to deeper themes and messages throughout the production process.

While viewers potentially have access to all four modes and may shift or 'commute' (Schrøder 1986) between them at different moments, the four modes themselves remain distinct and potentially contradictory, since they utilise different sets of cultural and discursive competencies. Much of the variability of audience response, this model suggests, is due to the tendency for different segments of the audience to adopt (and in some cases commute between) distinct viewing modes which, working in tandem with the parameters imposed by textual encoding, shape the readings that are likely to be produced (Michelle 2007). Furthermore, certain kinds of text invite particular forms of interpretive engagement. Thus, while spectacular blockbuster event films may encourage a transparent mode of reading and use a range of techniques designed to facilitate narrative immersion, we assumed that a literary adaptation such as *The Hobbit* might also elicit a mediated mode of response focused on generic form and the quality of the adaptation, particularly among viewers who were deeply familiar with Tolkien's original novel.

A Cross-Cultural Exploration

A fourth key distinguishing feature of our research is that it is a study of transnational receptions of a globally disseminated transnational film production. Given that *The Hobbit* was specifically designed and intended for a global audience, we wanted to design a study that could transcend national and cultural borders in the process of data collection, without sacrificing the capacity to subsequently analyse the possible significance of national and cultural identity in shaping receptions of this blockbuster trilogy. By widely disseminating our survey online in several languages, we hoped to attract sufficient numbers of respondents from at least a handful of nations to be able to discern any culturally or nationally distinctive receptions of *The Hobbit*, whilst remaining open to the possibility that receptions might actually be more strongly shaped by deterritorialised communities of interest, including fan affiliations. Indeed, based on earlier research on global receptions of *LotR*, we thought it likely that certain receptions of this blockbuster film trilogy would be widely dispersed and perhaps universal, but designed the project in a way that made it possible to formally *test* this assumption, rather than taking for granted *The Hobbit*'s uniform appeal globally.

While this kind of large-scale comparative research has become somewhat more common in media and communication studies, only a few studies have focused on audience engagements with entertainment media: most notably, Liebes and Katz's (1990) landmark research on cross-national receptions of *Dallas*, Wasko et al.'s (2001) study of audiences for *Disney*, Mathijs and Jones' (2004) study of receptions of *Big Brother* and Barker and Mathijs' (2008) collaborative investigation of audiences for *LotR*. While resource-intensive and often difficult to accomplish, cross-national studies are important if researchers are to establish the wider applicability of their findings beyond specific geographical and cultural locations (Livingstone 2012), and essential to determine the 'generalizability of theories, assumptions, and propositions' (Blumler et al. 1992, p. 8; see also Esser and Hanitzsch 2012a; Stehling et al. 2016). Such an approach is especially important when studying globally disseminated media products viewed by audiences living in different countries, often in different languages: it would be impossible to make any general claims about *The Hobbit*'s reception without considering whether audiences in different countries had the same kinds of reactions to it. Indeed, Livingstone (2012, p. 417) suggests that 'it is no longer plausible to study one phenomenon in one country without asking, at a minimum, whether it is common across the globe or distinctive to that country or part of the world'. Other scholars have noted that comparative research aids in avoiding the 'parochialism and ethnocentrism' (Esser 2013, p. 113) that can ensue when broad generalisations are made based on findings derived from a single cultural or national context.

One significant benefit of comparative research lies in its potential contributions to analytical generalisation, theory development and contextualisation (Esser 2013, p. 113). As previously noted, the *Hobbit* Audience Project applies the Composite Model, which posits the existence of four *universal* modes of reception. To ascertain whether there are indeed underlying modes of reception that transcend differences of culture, gender, age and so on, our research needed to gather observations from a wide range of individuals in different countries and regions of the world. As Esser and Hanitzsch (2012b, p. 522) argue, 'Only comparative research allows us to test a theory across diverse settings and evaluate the scope and significance of certain phenomena'. A comparative approach was thus vital if this project was to fulfil our ambitions of contributing to theory-building in audience reception studies.

So, for each of the surveys we conducted, we endeavoured to attract a diverse sample of viewers from a wide range of geographical locations. This was particularly emphasised for the first reception survey, where invitations to participate were widely disseminated online in seven different languages (English, Spanish, German, French, Dutch, Danish and Flemish). We and our research collaborators and assistants targeted potential respondents via various fan forums such as Theonering.net as well as the Facebook pages of groups representing a diverse range of intertextual, professional and political affiliations in countries where these languages are predominantly spoken. In an effort to avoid this research being, in essence, only a study of fan receptions of *The Hobbit*, the invitation was posted on the pages of film societies and major film studios, fantasy fiction readers, political parties in several countries, film directors and cinematographers, the stars of the trilogy, online gamers and so on, as well as groups dedicated to Tolkien, the *Hobbit* novel and movies, and the *LotR* films and books in various languages. From there, a form of snowballing extended our reach as some individuals reposted the invitation on other sites, such as www.richardarmitagenet.com and a Russian Tolkien website. Press releases generated further coverage in some of New Zealand's national and regional newspapers and on two national radio stations, and the project received some media exposure in the USA and Canada. Finally, each member of the research team was asked to circulate the invitation through their professional, institutional and personal networks. The use of these recruitment strategies means that our respondents constitute a network-based convenience sample rather than a representative one, and this is important to bear in mind:

our findings are specific to our survey population, and do not necessarily reflect the distribution of viewpoints within the wider mainstream *Hobbit* audience.

Of course, there is more to doing cross-cultural research than recruiting multilingual respondents from a wide range of countries. Their responses have to be interpreted, and made sense of, often by researchers who do not share the same cultural or linguistic background. Much of the difficulty in conducting cross-cultural research lies in finding research tools that allow for meaningful and reliable comparisons to be made across national contexts and linguistic borders. As Schrøder (2011) notes, it is particularly difficult to make comparisons and formulate generalisations across different qualitative studies conducted in different contexts. This is one of the reasons why, for this study, we decided to adopt a hybrid or mixed-method approach that integrates qualitative and quantitative methods, using Q methodology in conjunction with conventional questionnaires administered online. This would ensure we could meaningfully compare our results, since all respondents were provided with the same 'tools' with which to express their unique viewpoint, and the analytical procedures used to analyse responses were the same in each case.

Grounded in Q Methodology: A Quali-Quantitative Hybrid

For those unfamiliar with this approach, Q is a true methodological hybrid, combining the mathematical rigour of quantitative methods with a strong interpretive component more commonly found in qualitative approaches to human research. It was invented by psychologist/physicist William Stephenson in the 1930s as a structured research tool specifically designed to analyse the nature and diversity of people's attitudes, beliefs, perspectives or subjective experiences relating to a given topic (Stephenson 1953), and is especially useful for revealing significant similarities and differences among respondents (Brown 1977). Q's quali-quantitative approach can potentially elicit insight into people's perspectives in the detailed and holistic way more typically associated with in-depth interviews and focus groups, whilst providing clear structure, capacity for replication, and robust measurement-based analysis (see Watts and Stenner 2012, for a detailed overview of the history and process of Q methodology; see Michelle and Davis 2014, for a discussion of Q's application within audience studies). We believe Q methodology offers a solution to a central methodological challenge facing audience researchers, as posed by Barker and Mathijs (2008, p. 9): how to preserve the rich complexity of respondents' qualitative data while still retaining the capacity 'to generalise from it (map the whole terrain of audience responses, distinguish different groups, demonstrate patterned connections, even show trends over time).'

In Q methodology research, participants are asked to rank-order a set of statements chosen to represent a wide range of ideas and opinions about the text or topic in question according to whether they agree, disagree or are neutral about the sentiment expressed. Through the ranking process, Q methodology allows each individual to 'map out' his or her viewpoint in a multidimensional sense, and to position themselves in relation to others on a range of relevant issues. What is more, it does so in a way that is almost entirely independent and *self-referential*, in that the process relies on respondents' self-directed actions and choices as they evaluate the statements according to their subjective values and preferences (Watts and Stenner 2012).

For the *Hobbit* Audience Project, the statements that respondents were asked to sort were derived from extensive 'cultural trawls' (Stenner and Marshall 1995, p. 626) of the wider discursive terrain or *concourse* around each film. This wide-ranging trawl aimed to identify the major issues, themes and concerns being expressed in public discussions of these films, and to capture a range of perspectives on them so that each individual respondent might, in turn, use these available resources to broadly convey his or her own viewpoint. Our four cultural trawls focused on print and online news coverage of the production, media and film commentary, early professional and amateur film reviews in the case of the post-viewing surveys, commentary on social media and in key fan websites such as Theonering.net, film blogs, discussion board comments, and comments on Peter Jackson's production videos and the *Hobbit* trailers on YouTube. The kinds of statements we considered for inclusion took the form of subjective opinions rather than facts. As such, all perspectives on the films were treated as potentially suitable to include, irrespective of origins. Our primary consideration in selecting a statement was whether it clearly reflected a particular shared *sentiment* or belief expressed in a succinct way, and we aimed to obtain a broad and inclusive impression of the range of things being said about different aspects of each film. By way of example, the cultural trawl conducted for our first reception survey sought to capture opinions relating to each of these categories:

> Story/narrative structure, director/directing, the decision to make three films, editing, aspects of film craft, issues relating to adaptation, the inclusion of additional materials, continuity with the *LotR* films, responses to stereoscopic 3D, CGI/visual effects, HFR 48fps, music/score/songs, narrative transportation, suspension of disbelief, excitement/enthusiasm, emotion/affects, characters/casting, character identification, meanings/ themes, real world/personal relevance, feelings of nostalgia, the social experience of viewing, opposition/dislike, disengagement, disappointment, other.

The selection of relevant statements continued until a degree of redundancy began to emerge among the themes expressed, although it quickly became apparent that certain issues were generating far more discussion and debate than others, which would need to be reflected in the final Q sample. Since sampling of the concourse and selection of the Q sample is one area where the researcher's subjective and cultural biases may influence findings in Q methodology research, we employed research assistants to undertake the cultural trawl and preliminary sampling of representative statements.

Since it is not practical to include large numbers of statements in online Q surveys (due to the risks of participant fatigue and the small size of many computer screens, which places constraints on the extent of the grid and the readability of Q items) it was then necessary to progressively whittle these statements down by eliminating repetition and redundancy in the categories and consolidating related ideas and themes. Ultimately, our surveys each contained 36–42 statements (see Appendices 3–6), which respondents read, sorted and placed into a ranked grid arrangement, as seen in Fig. 2.2.

Were completed, all the Q sorts were collectively analysed by person to identify statistically significant *factors*. A summary of the main audience segments identified in each survey can be found in Appendix A. These segments represent groups of individuals who ranked the statements in similar ways and can be said to share a similar perspective or viewpoint on the topic (Watts and Stenner 2012).

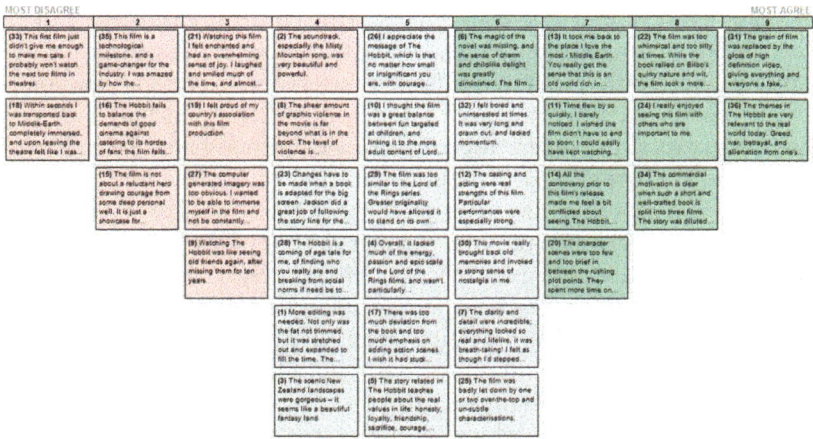

Fig. 2.2   A completed Q sort

To some readers, the categories produced via factor analysis may seem somewhat reductive. Critics sometimes claim that the desire of Q methodologists to assign respondents to categories obscures the complexity and inherent 'messiness' of individual perceptions. This accusation, we believe, arises from a misunderstanding of Q methodology's analytical processes, since the categories or shared viewpoints in fact emerge from the collective actions of individual respondents in independently sorting the Q statements provided to them according to their own preferences. Factor analysis is used to subsequently identify groups of respondents who sorted the statements in statistically similar ways, with very little, if any, mediation from the researcher. The viewpoints that emerged at each stage of our research can thus be said to have been naturally occurring but latent among respondents *themselves*, rather than being a product of us imposing a pre-existing schema on our data or attempting to force respondents into neat and tidy groups.

Furthermore, we take the view that analytic generalisation (and thus theory-building and testing) requires the creation of meaningful categories using a transparent, reliable and replicable process. While these categories cannot capture the full complexity of individual respondents' perspectives, nor their final views on the topic (both because the views expressed are in response to a specific *condition of instruction* and rely on the 'tools' provided, and because processes of reception may be ongoing with repeated re-engagement with both the main text and its intertexts), we nonetheless emphasise that they do reflect statistically significant and clearly meaningful distinctions in the expressed viewpoints of our respondents. As others have noted, Q makes it possible to identify and systematically compare the range of viewpoints shared by individuals within the population of respondents and to pinpoint their unique components, as well as any areas of consensus (Brown 1980; McKeown and Thomas 2013; Watts and Stenner 2012). This unique capacity proved to be extremely useful for our project, especially given the volume of responses with which we were working across four distinct stages. Making sense of all that very rich material would have been virtually impossible without some means of systematically and objectively categorising several thousand responses.

Our use of Q methodology is one of the most significant distinctions between our research and previous studies of film audiences. While quite often utilised in tourism and environmental studies, political science, policy studies, psychology, education, and nursing and health research, Q is less well known within media studies (see Michelle and Davis 2014). This lack of familiarity is something we hope our project will help change, as we believe the standardised methodological and analytical approach used in Q methodology provides a robust foundation for addressing some ongoing questions in the field, and also makes it possible to overcome some of the challenges of cross-national comparative research. This is because, as Schrøder (2011, p. 22) argues, Q data is both contextualised within the lifeworlds of respondents and 'can be translated into a standardized form, which makes it possible to perform common, standardized statistical procedures and to produce generalizations in the form of typologies that are transparent and immediately comparable.' What those typologies or viewpoints themselves mean and the underlying orientations they reflect, is, of course, subject to interpretation (see Watts and Stenner 2012). Our understanding of the factors that emerged was informed both by the extensive open-ended qualitative comments of our participants, and our chosen analytical framework—the Composite Model.

While there are considerable challenges in administering Q sorts online in a large-scale project such as this (a point to which we shall return in Chap. 10), doing so offers some significant advantages, including the ability to access geographically dispersed niche audiences for media texts, and the potential to explore cross-cultural and longitudinal differences in audience response in a highly structured, robust manner. As our project demonstrates, parallel multilingual Q samples can be constructed and administered relatively efficiently online. Adapting and expanding the capacity of Q methodology in this way, it has been possible to compare qualitative data across languages and national contexts, as we illustrate in Chap. 9.

Bolstered by a Conventional Questionnaire

To help us interpret the factors identified using Q methodology, we also asked our respondents to complete a conventional questionnaire, the first part of which asked several questions about levels of anticipation, enchantment and enjoyment, pre-existing fandoms and familiarity with Tolkien's novels and Jackson's *LotR* trilogy, and so forth. This section also included some open-ended questions seeking insight into the meanings our respondents' attributed to each film, what they would change, which character they identified with, their reactions to new cinematic technologies and so on. These comments are often fascinating and highly revealing, and by drawing on them in our discussion, we hope to convey a real sense of the individual personalities of the many and varied contributors to our research. In the final section, we asked questions about a wide range of socio-demographic group memberships as well as religious and political affiliations. We included several variables here, because we did not want to presume in advance which combinations would be most relevant in shaping audience interpretation and response, and also sought to explore a number of theoretically significant relationships in our analysis.

To give readers an indication of the kinds of questions asked and the wide range of data collected, we present our *AUJ* post-viewing questionnaire in Appendix B. As this shows, the surveys were relatively lengthy, which very likely contributed to a somewhat lower completion rate than might have been achieved had we chosen to use a simpler instrument. The use of a detailed questionnaire reflected a conscious decision on our part to privilege the quality and usefulness of the data collected over obtaining a potentially unmanageably large number of responses, given the limited resources at our disposal for the important analysis phase. The wisdom of this decision is, we believe, amply demonstrated by the wide range of significant insights our approach has garnered and by our capacity to explore various theoretical issues using our data sets, as shall be illustrated in the following chapters.

Our research thus adopts a mixed-method approach (Creswell 2015; Flick 2017); we have collected quantitative and qualitative data using two distinct methods, and analyse and integrate these different data sources to gain insight into the dominant trends among our respondents. While Q methodology is inherently hybrid in nature, combining it with a detailed questionnaire extends our study's capacity to employ what is called methodological triangulation, in which the use of two or more distinct methods means that results obtained using one technique can be corroborated and validated with reference to findings derived from the other(s) (Denzin 1970). To that end, the qualitative data from the open-ended questions was coded *independently* of the audience categories derived from Q sorting. That is, all data relating to each question in the questionnaire was coded without the coders having knowledge of how individual respondents had been grouped based on their Q sorts, or even how their responses to other questions had been categorised. This separation of the different analytical processes was necessary because inductive coding has a subjective component in terms of how coders classify open-ended comments; knowing in advance which viewpoint an individual was associated with could thus potentially influence the interpretation of their remarks. Avoiding this possibility of coder/confirmation bias means that each set of results can legitimately be used to validate the others through the convergence of findings, while also allowing us to extend our understanding of key issues well beyond what might have been possible using factor analysis alone. Our research thus surpasses the more basic use of triangulation, since we consciously used multiple methods 'as a source of *extra knowledge* about the issue in question and *not* just for confirming what is already known from the first approach (convergence of findings)' (Flick 2017, p. 53; original emphasis). By gathering both qualitative and quantitative data using two methods in the same survey, our project has benefited from a more sophisticated form of theoretical, methodological and data triangulation.

Combining Q methodology's unique capacity to reveal shared subjectivity in conjunction with a detailed questionnaire has allowed us to chart the evolution of *Hobbit* audience segments, pinpoint the attributes of the *Hobbit* films that caused enchantment, disinterest or disaffection, and interpret the widely divergent receptions of these films among fans, critics and casual viewers. It also allowed us to explore relationships between sharing a perspective on each film and sharing particular socio-demographic characteristics, intertextual affiliations and so on—and thus to offer insight into the respective roles of national cultural repertoires versus other possibly more relevant sources of difference in framing global audience receptions of this Hollywood blockbuster fantasy trilogy. For more detailed discussion of the specific procedures we followed in designing the project and analysing the extensive qualitative and qualitative data we have collected, we refer readers to the online methodological appendices for this book, available on the *Hobbit* Project website—http://tinyurl.com/kchjtbe.

CONCLUSION

The findings presented in the following chapters, we contend, make a significant contribution to our understanding of viewers' receptions of the cinematic adaptation of a much-loved cultural property—Tolkien's children's novel—and their reactions to its intensive blockbusterisation by Warner Bros and Jackson's production team. In what follows, we hope to illustrate the value of Q methodology and cross-cultural online research for audience studies of blockbuster film. While we don't claim to have been successful in all respects, we believe our approach offers a useful model of how reception research can successfully synthesise theory with empirical analysis in its effort to better understand diverse forms of audience engagement and response. Our findings add to understandings of audience reception more generally, and of audience reactions to issues that will be of interest to lay readers and scholars alike—including the relationship between pre-viewing anticipation and post-viewing receptions, the politics of transnational film production, processes of adaptation and the limits of creative licence, gender representations in fantasy film, the impact of new cinematic technologies, the relationship between reception and social location and more. We also maintain that while the methodological approach we have developed would benefit from further refinement, it provides a powerful tool for gaining rich qualitative insight while retaining the capacity for rigorous and productive quantitative analysis. Drawing on a large sample size and using a survey instrument that captures rich qualitative and quantitative data, we have been able to glean clearer insight into the meaning and significance of the *Hobbit* trilogy for differently positioned and interested viewers. We have been able to identify and describe distinct audience segments whose members share significant commonalities in their perspectives, preoccupations and (in some cases) socio-demographic characteristics. In the process, we have gained clearer insights into the respective roles of fandom, politics and idealised intertexts in shaping modes of engagement with a highly anticipated spectacular blockbuster event-film. We hope these insights might inform a more nuanced theoretical account of audience receptions of screen media, and of blockbuster film adaptations in particular.

REFERENCES

Barker, M. (2006). I have seen the future and it is not here yet ...; Or, on being ambitious for audience research. *The Communication Review, 9*(2), 123–141. doi:10.1080/10714420600663310.

Barker, M. (2009). Changing lives, challenging concepts: Some findings and lessons from the *Lord of the Rings* project. *International Journal of Cultural Studies, 12*(4), 375–393. doi:10.1177/1367877909104244.

Barker, M., & Mathijs, E. (Eds.). (2008). *Watching The Lord of the Rings: Tolkien's world audiences.* New York: Peter Lang.

Barker, M., Mathijs, E., & Trobia, A. (2008). Our methodological challenges and solutions. In M. Barker & E. Mathijs (Eds.), *Watching The Lord of the Rings: Tolkien's world audiences* (pp. 213–240). New York: Peter Lang.

Blumler, J. D., McLeod, J. M., & Rosengren, K. E. (1992). *Comparatively speaking: Communication and culture across space and time.* Newbury Park: Sage.

Brayton, J. (2006). Fic Frodo slash Frodo: Fandoms and *The Lord of the Rings.* In E. Mathijs & M. Pomerance (Eds.), *From hobbits to Hollywood: Essays on Peter Jackson's Lord of the Rings* (pp. 137–154). Amsterdam and New York: Rodopi.

Brown, S. R. (1977). Political literature and the response of the reader: Experimental studies of interpretation, imagery, and criticism. *American Political Science Review, 71*(02), 567–584.

Brown, S. R. (1980). *Political subjectivity: Applications of Q methodology in political science.* New Haven, CT: Yale University Press.

Chin, B., & Gray, J. (2001). 'One ring to rule them all': Previewers and pretexts of the *Lord of the Rings* films. *Intensities: The Journal of Cult Media, 2.*

Creswell, J. W. (2015). Revisiting mixed methods and advancing scientific practices. In S. Nagy Hesse-Biber & R. Burke Johnson (Eds.), *The Oxford handbook of multimethod and mixed methods research inquiry* (pp. 61–71). Oxford: Oxford University Press.

Davis, C. H., Michelle, C., Hardy, A. L., & Hight, C. (2014). Framing audience prefigurations of *The Hobbit: An Unexpected Journey.* The roles of fandom, politics and idealised intertexts. *Participations: Journal of Audience & Reception Studies, 11*(1), 50–87.

De Kloet, J., & Kuipers, G. (2007). Spirituality and fan culture around the *Lord of the Rings* film trilogy. *Fabula: Journal of Folktale Research, 48*(3/4), 300–319. doi:10.1515/FABL.2007.023.

Denzin, N. K. (1970). *The research act in sociology: A theoretical introduction to sociological methods.* London: Butterworths.

Esser, F. (2013). The emerging paradigm of comparative communication enquiry: Advancing cross-national research in times of globalization. *International Journal of Communication, 7,* 113–128.

Esser, F., & Hanitzsch, T. (2012a). On the why and how of comparative inquiry in communication studies. In F. Esser & T. Hanitzsch (Eds.), *The handbook of comparative communication research* (pp. 3–22). New York and London: Routledge.

Esser, F., & Hanitzsch, T. (2012b). Organising and managing comparative research projects across nations: Models and challenges of coordinated collaboration. In I. Volkmer (Ed.), *The handbook of global media research* (pp. 521–532). Malden: Wiley-Blackwell.

Flick, U. (2017). Mantras and myths: The disenchantment of mixed-methods research and revisiting triangulation as a perspective. *Qualitative Inquiry, 23*(1), 46–57. doi:10.1177/1077800416655827.

Geraghty, C. (2008). *Now a major motion picture: Film adaptations of literature and drama.* Lanham, MD: Rowman & Littlefield.

Granelli, S., & Zenor, J. (2016). Decoding 'the code': Reception theory and moral judgment of *Dexter. International Journal of Communication, 10,* 5056–5078.

Green, M. C., & Brock, T. C. (2000). The role of transportation in the persuasiveness of public narratives. *Journal of Personality and Social Psychology, 79*(5), 701–721. doi:10.1037//0022-3514.79.5.701.

Green, M. C., Brock, T. C., & Kaufman, G. F. (2004). Understanding media enjoyment: The role of transportation into narrative worlds. *Communication Theory, 14*(4), 311–327. doi:10.1111/j.1468-2885.2004.tb00317.x.

Green, M. C., Chatham, C., & Sestir, M. A. (2012). Emotion and transportation into fact and fiction. *Scientific Study of Literature, 2*(1), 37–59. doi:10.1075/ssol.2.1.03gre.

Hall, A., & Zwarun, L. (2012). Challenging entertainment: Enjoyment, transportation, and need for cognition in relation to fictional films viewed online. *Mass Communication and Society, 15*(3), 384–406. doi:10.1080/15205436.2011.583544.

Hall, S. (1980). Encoding/decoding. In S. Hall, D. Hobson, A. Lowe, & P. Willis (Eds.), *Culture, media, language: Working papers in cultural studies* (pp. 128–138). London: Hutchinson.

Holland, K., Warwick Blood, R., & Thomas, S. (2015). Viewing *The Biggest Loser*: Modes of reception and reflexivity among obese people. *Social Semiotics, 25*(1), 16–32.

Jerslev, A. (2006). Sacred viewing: Emotional responses to *The Lord of the Rings*. In E. Mathijs (Ed.), *The Lord of the Rings: Popular culture in global context* (pp. 206–221). London and New York: Wallflower Press.

Kuipers, G., & de Kloet, J. (2009). Banal cosmopolitanism and *The Lord of the Rings*: The limited role of national differences in global media consumption. *Poetics, 37,* 99–118. doi:10.1016/j.poetic.2009.01.002.

Liebes, T., & Katz, E. (1990). *The export of meaning: Cross-cultural readings of Dallas*. Oxford: Oxford University Press.

Livingstone, S. (2012). Challenges to comparative research in a globalizing media landscape. In F. Esser & T. Hanitzsch (Eds.), *The handbook of comparative communication research* (pp. 415–429). New York and London: Routledge.

Mathijs, E., & Jones, J. (2004). *Big Brother International: Formats, critics and publics*. London: Wallflower Press.

McKeown, B., & Thomas, D. (2013). *Q methodology*. Newbury Park: Sage.

McKeown, B., Thomas, D. B., Rhoads, J. C., & Sundblad, D. (2015). Falling hard for *Breaking Bad*: An investigation of audience response to a popular television series. *Participations: Journal of Audience and Reception Studies, 12*(2), 147–167.

Michelle, C. (2007). Modes of reception: A consolidated analytical framework. *The Communication Review, 10*(3), 181–222. doi:10.1080/10714420701528057.

Michelle, C. (2009). (Re) contextualising audience receptions of reality TV. *Participations: Journal of Audience & Reception Studies, 6*(1), 137–170.

Michelle, C., & Davis, C. H. (2014). Beyond the qualitative–quantitative divide: Reflections on the utility and challenges of Q methodology for media researchers. In F. Darling-Wolf (Ed.), *Blackwell companion to methods in media studies* (Vol. 7, pp. 1–23). *Research methods in media studies*. New York: Wiley.

Michelle, C., Davis, C. H., & Vladica, F. (2012). Understanding variation in audience engagement and response: An application of the composite model to receptions of *Avatar* (2009). *The Communication Review, 15*(2), 106–143. doi:10.1080/10714421.2012.674467.

Mikos, L., Eichner, S., Prommer, E., & Wedel, M. (2008). Involvement in *The Lord of the Rings*: Audience strategies and orientations. In M. Barker & E. Mathijs (Eds.), *Watching The Lord of the Rings: Tolkien's world audiences* (Vol. 3, pp. 111–128). New York: Peter Lang.

Morley, D. (1980). *The nationwide audience: Structure and decoding* (BFI Television Monograph No. 11). British Film Institute.

Morley, D. (2006). Unanswered questions in audience research. *The Communication Review, 9,* 101–121. doi:10.1080/10714420600663286.

Press, A. (1991). *Women watching television.* Pennsylvania: University of Pennsylvania Press.

Rae, N., & Gray, J. (2007). When Gen-X meet the X-men: Retextualizing comic book reception. In I. Gordon, M. Jancovich, & M. McAllister (Eds.), *Film and comic books* (pp. 86–100). Jackson: University Press of Mississippi.

Schrøder, K. C. (1986). The pleasure of *Dynasty*: The weekly reconstruction of self-confidence. In P. Drummond & R. Paterson (Eds.), *Television and its audience: International research perspectives* (pp. 61–82). London: British Film Institute.

Schrøder, K. C. (2011). Audiences are inherently cross-media: Audience studies and the cross-media challenge. *Communication Management Quarterly, 18*(6), 5–27.

Stam, R. (2000). Beyond fidelity: The dialogics of adaptation. In J. Naremore (Ed.), *Film adaptation* (pp. 54–76). London: Athlone Press.

Stehling, M., Finger, J., & Jorge, A. (2016). Comparative audience research: A review of cross-national and cross-media audience studies. *Participations: Journal of Audience and Reception Studies, 13*(1), 321–333.

Stenner, P., & Marshall, H. (1995). A Q methodological study of rebelliousness. *European Journal of Social Psychology, 25,* 621–636.

Stephenson, W. (1953). *The study of behavior: Q-technique and its methodology.* Chicago, IL: University of Chicago Press.

Tager, M., & Matthee, H. (2014). *Dexter*: Gratuitous violence or the vicarious experience of justice? Perceptions of selected South African viewers. *Communicatio: South African Journal for Communication Theory and Research, 40*(1), 20–33. doi:10.1080/02500167.2014.868366.

Tal-Or, N., & Cohen, J. (2015). Unpacking engagement: Convergence and divergence in transportation and identification. *Annals of the International Communication Association, 40*(1), 33–66. doi:10.1080/23808985.2015.11735255.

Thompson, K. (2003). Fantasy, franchises, and Frodo Baggins: *The Lord of the Rings* and modern Hollywood. *The Velvet Light Trap, 52*(1), 45–63. doi:10.1353/vlt.2003.0020.

Thompson, K. (2011). Gollum talks to himself: Problems and solutions in Peter Jackson's *The Lord of the Rings.* In J. Bogsrad & P. Kaveny (Eds.), *Picturing Tolkien: Essays on Peter Jackson's The Lord of the Rings film trilogy* (pp. 25–45). Jefferson, NC: McFarland & Co.

Turnbull, S. (2008). Beyond words? *The Return of the King* and the pleasures of the text. In M. Barker & E. Mathijs (Eds.), *Watching The Lord of the Rings: Tolkien's world audiences* (pp. 181–190). New York: Peter Lang.

Van Ommen, M., Daalmans, S., Weijers, A., de Leeuw, R. N., & Buijzen, M. (2016). Analyzing prisoners', law enforcement agents', and civilians' moral evaluations of *The Sopranos*. *Poetics, 58*, 52–65. doi:10.1016/j.poetic.2016.07.003.

Wasko, J., Phillips, M., & Meehan, E. R. (Eds.). (2001). *Dazzled by Disney? The global Disney audiences project*. London: Burns & Oates.

Watts, S., & Stenner, P. (2012). *Doing Q methodological research: Theory, method and interpretation*. London: Sage.

Yin, R. (2010). Analytic generalization. In A. J. Mills, G. Durepos, & E. Wiebe (Eds.), *Encyclopedia of case study research* (pp. 21–23). Thousand Oaks, CA: Sage.

Zenor, J. (2014). Reading the President: Audience reception of *The West Wing*. In J. Zenor (Ed.), *Parasocial politics: Audiences, pop culture, and politics* (pp. 9–18). Lanham, MD: Lexington Books.

CHAPTER 3

Adaptation, Anticipation and Cinematic Desire: Prefigurative Engagements with a Blockbuster Fantasy Franchise

INTRODUCTION

The term 'prefiguration' refers to the ideas and understandings that surround a cultural text—whether a book, television programme, film or video game—before it becomes available to consume. As Rae and Gray (2007) note, while audience reception is usually understood as a process that takes place when (and after) someone views a media text, discussion and imaginative activity often occur well before texts become publicly available. We wanted to investigate the period in which people were formulating and expressing ideas and opinions about the *Hobbit* trilogy before it had been released in cinemas. We thought *The Hobbit* might be a particularly interesting example to study in this regard, since it is one in a much longer series of 'Middle-earth' texts. Viewers for these films might range from those who, as children, read Tolkien's original novel back in the 1940s, to those who came to it after reading his more famous *The Lord of the Rings* series in the late 1950s and 1960s, to those who initially encountered Middle-earth via Peter Jackson's film adaptations of those works in the early 2000s. Alternatively, *The Hobbit: An Unexpected Journey* (*AUJ*) might itself be the first encounter someone had ever had with Tolkien's universe, even if they were otherwise highly knowledgeable about one of the film's actors or fantasy as a genre, for instance.

Rae and Gray (2007) note that few audience studies have explored the significance of these kinds of distinctions among prospective audience members and the different sets of knowledges, interpretive resources

53
C. Michelle et al., *Fans, Blockbusterisation, and the Transformation of Cinematic Desire*, DOI 10.1057/978-1-137-59616-1_3

and intertextual loyalties they might bring with them to their viewing encounters. Nor has this kind of analysis often been combined with an understanding of the various activities which encourage potential viewers to imagine, and form opinions about, a forthcoming film (although see Brayton 2006; Brooker 2012; Chin and Gray 2001). They might, for instance, imagine its aesthetic style or 'look', what events will happen in it, the appearance of particular locations, how the characters will interact with each other or what the soundtrack might be like. Envisaging and discussing these and other matters helps to generate what Jauss (1970) terms a *horizon of expectations*; 'the promise of pleasure, spectacle and imagination' that is yet to come (Biltereyst and Meers 2006, p. 72). Creating this horizon of expectations helps to give the film a public presence in advance of its cinematic release, and can in turn influence how others are able to imagine that 'which does not yet truly exist' (Chin and Gray 2001, p. 1). Some of the most obvious resources from which previewers might draw knowledge and inspiration are marketing and publicity campaigns, fan networks (which today operate predominantly online and can be influential sources of information, discussion and debate), and in the case of an adaptation such as *The Hobbit*, the original source text and the wider discourse around it.

Given the relative lack of empirical research in this area, we decided to study *potential* audiences for Jackson's forthcoming films as part of our longitudinal study of audience receptions of the complete film series. For our initial pre-viewing survey, we recruited 1000 English-speaking participants from 59 countries and set out to explore their different interests in the forthcoming *Hobbit* films as well as the forms and degrees of anticipation and expectation that were building in advance of *AUJ*'s release in cinemas. In so doing, we hoped to be able to later investigate connections between peoples' pre-viewing interests, hopes and expectations and their responses after seeing the *Hobbit* films in cinemas. Would viewers be disappointed by films that failed to live up to expectations, or thrilled by a trilogy that surpassed their hopes in ways never imagined? What modes of reception would differently oriented and interested viewers adopt once confronted with the films as fully realised by Jackson and his team?

As well as seeking insight into their pre-viewing perspectives, we asked participants whether, and what kinds of, prefigurative activities they had engaged in during the lead-up to *AUJ*'s cinematic release. To gain a clearer sense of our respondents' individual social positioning and interests, we posed various questions about their socio-demographic characteristics, political and religious affiliations, fandoms, knowledge of particular controversies around the films and so on. While an account of our prefiguration research process has been published in Davis et al. (2014), in what follows we offer new insights into the activities of *Hobbit* pre-viewers and the wide range of meanings they ascribed to this blockbuster event film trilogy before it fully 'existed' in the public sense of being available to consume.

We begin by discussing the extensive marketing campaign that preceded *AUJ*'s cinematic release, before addressing other potentially more important sources of knowledge and insight that would likely prefigure receptions of *The Hobbit* among those familiar with Tolkien's novel and his wider body of works. Then, we draw on data from our pre-viewing survey to chart the main perspectives expressed in the lead-up to *The Hobbit*'s cinematic release, and offer insight into the kinds of prefigurative activities prospective viewers were engaging in as they anticipated a long-awaited film experience. We also delve into the specific constellations of meaning, value and affect that our respondents were ascribing to *The Hobbit* in advance of seeing it, to clearly establish the orientations and expectations of those who might later participate in our post-viewing surveys.

Marketing *An Unexpected Journey*

The months and weeks before a film's first release is a prime period for encouraging and entrenching cinematic desire for the assumed future pleasures of the text. This is why the promotional divisions of corporations such as Warner Bros are willing to invest tens of millions of dollars on marketing new films: such promotional activities seek to build anticipation around a forthcoming film and encourage audiences into cinemas in the crucial first two or three weeks immediately post-release, during which most revenue is earned. In some cases, this lucrative period can be as brief as a week or two, especially if early professional reviews are unfavourable, or if audiences decide that a film's 'playability' is not as strong as promised and spread negative evaluations through word of mouth or via social media (Davis et al. 2016). While considerable revenues can be earned in later, subsidiary digital formats such as DVDs and Blu-ray, games, content on subscription services and associated merchandise (Wasko and Shanadi 2006), these secondary audiences for blockbuster products rely on the aura of having attracted large, satisfied, and hopefully proselytising audiences on first release (Davis et al. 2016).

In the case of the first *Hobbit* film, $81 million was spent on marketing, according to industry sources (Rosz 2012), in addition to the $250 million dedicated to production. Marketing began as far back as 2007 when it was announced that Jackson had signed a deal with New Line Cinema and MGM to executive produce a pair of movies based on *The Hobbit* (BBC News 2007). Every step, and setback, in the process of pre-production from that point on was extensively detailed on news and discussion websites, Facebook pages, YouTube posts, blogs and vlogs; formats that fostered low-key, intimate marketing bonds while providing facts alongside speculation (Davis et al. 2016). Many of these formats addressed the recipients as already 'fans'—of the *LotR* films, of Peter Jackson as a filmmaker or, perhaps, of anything associated with Tolkien's invented worlds. Most of these communication forums are traceable back to the production companies contracted to the studio, evidently so in cases like the official *Hobbit* website or Peter Jackson's production vlogs.

This promotional campaign intensified in the months leading up to the release of *AUJ* as it became more overtly marketed in public physical and digital spaces. Huge billboards were placed on tall buildings in city centres worldwide, while posters appeared at eye level along transport corridors (Markowski 2012). A teaser trailer had been released online in 2011 (Johnston et al. 2016), but now there were a variety of trailers featuring different character groups, landscapes and moods from the film, to appeal to diverse audience segments on television and online. (Interestingly, as Trultzsch-Wijnen and de Sousa (2016) note, the marketing and promotion of the *Hobbit* trilogy did not generally focus on the fact that it was an adaptation of a children's novel.) Stars from the film gave interviews on chat shows and took to Twitter to generate excitement about the forthcoming release. Inside Wellington's airport terminal, not far from Jackson's Miramar production facilities, large statues of Gollum and Gandalf's allies, the giant eagles, were installed, proclaiming the city as the 'centre' of Middle-earth. In the northern hemisphere, the restaurant chain Denny's put *Hobbit*-themed meals on its menu and Lego released a range of *Hobbit* building kits. There were competitions to win trips to the New Zealand premiere and tickets for early screenings available for advance purchase. These were only the most overt manifestations of the marketing campaign for the launch of the *Hobbit* trilogy; a final push to get uncommitted and new audience members into movie theatres through the widest possible interpellation of members of the public—especially, in this final stage, non-fan audiences.

Running in parallel to the vertically and horizontally integrated divisions of a global media conglomerate striving to produce receptive consumers through webs of television, newspaper, magazine and online coverage (Biltereyst and Meers 2006; Major 2008) were numerous other group and personal websites—at least 1310 directly concerned with *The Hobbit* (Fiorelli 2012)—where individuals also traded information, gossip, opinion and critique based on various forms of fandom, anti-fandom or even attitudes of studied indifference. Many of these people likely also engaged in discussions with friends and family about the upcoming films, thus using channels of opinion formation that are difficult for marketers to access. Online research does not give us access to those face-to-face communications either, but the generous descriptions many participants gave of their various prefigurative activities offer a fascinating insight into what those discussions might have involved. Certainly, one important area of interest was whether Peter Jackson would be as sensitive in adapting Tolkien's *Hobbit* as he had been with *The Lord of the Rings*.

THE CHALLENGES OF ADAPTING TOLKIEN

While our analysis of blockbusterisation emphasises the homogenising pressures by which a film idea is shaped in the hopes of becoming a successful 'blockbuster' and is, therefore, relevant to the several projects each year that aim to take more than a billion US dollars at the international box office, no other film property is in fact directly comparable to those adapted from Tolkien's written works. This is because of their history as the product of a scholar whose specific skills are reflected in his fictional creations, and the unprecedented popularity of those creations before their cinematic adaptation by Jackson and others. Shippey (2000), for instance, notes that more than 100 million copies of Tolkien's books had been sold by the year 2000, while another 25 million copies were sold from 2000 to 2003 (David Brawn, as cited in Rérolle 2012, n.p.). It is true that other film series may elicit comparable levels of passion from fans, particularly the *Star Wars* series

(Lucas 1977—), but the latter series originated in the cinematic realm and does not bear the burden of satisfying the imaginations of loyal book readers. For adaptations of recent 'blockbuster' novels such as *Harry Potter*, *Twilight* or *The Hunger Games*, the shorter time gap between publication and adaptation arguably also makes for a less entrenched set of reader expectations. Furthermore, these other cultural properties are not surrounded by the kind of institutional apparatus protecting, promoting and appraising Tolkien's writing—including the Tolkien Estate headed by J.R.R. Tolkien's son Christopher, the Tolkien and Mythopoeic Societies (the latter of which celebrates his work as part of the Oxford-based 'Inklings' group of fantasy authors), at least 60 book-length studies of Tolkien and his oeuvre (as listed on the website of the Tolkien Society) and several hundred academic journal articles. This apparatus, supported by serious readers of the books, plays an active role in guarding Tolkien's legacy and protecting his vision.

Born in South Africa to British parents in 1892, the concerns and atmosphere of John Ronald Reuel Tolkien's childhood and young adult life are branded into his imagined world, where they become touchstones for his fannish and scholarly gatekeepers, who avidly monitor the details of the books' screen translation. According to biographers Carpenter (1977), Shippey (2000) and Garth (2003), many of the things Tolkien found inspiring come from the few years he and his brother spent living in the village of Sarehole near Birmingham with their widowed mother. These included his love for the English countryside and the trees and creatures populating it, his commitment to the beliefs of Catholicism, his passion for fairy tales and myths (the translation and invention of fairy tales being a serious literary mode at the time) and his consequent interest in studying and inventing languages. His mother's early death when he was only 12 affected Tolkien deeply, and arguably influenced the infrequent but highly resonant characterisations of women in his novels (Croft and Donovan 2015). Another strand of Tolkien's thematics relates to his positive experiences of male 'fellowship' at preparatory school, Oxford University and during World War I, in which he served as a signals officer in the Somme region (Croft 2004; Garth 2003). Although he admired personal commitments to fight on patriotic and moral grounds, the battles and deaths Tolkien witnessed also connect with what he as a writer evidently loathed (Fowkes 2010), and represented in the characters of Saruman and Sauron: machines of war and the tyrants who controlled them, despoiling the environment and bringing death to others.

Criticised by some, not without reason, as ideologically conservative (Kellner 2006), masculinist (Drout 1996) and racist (Shieff 2006), Tolkien's books have nevertheless also resonated with progressive social discourses, particularly those related to environmentalism and anti-materialism, ever since the launch of their first paperback editions in the USA in 1965. That timing coincided with the rise of the counterculture movement and its critical reactions to the commodification and militarisation of culture (Barker 2006; Ciabatarri 2014). By providing resources for the imagining of alternative ways of living, Tolkien's books, especially *The Lord of the Rings*, became 'sacred' texts for a significant proportion of their readers (Davidsen 2013; De Kloet and Kuipers 2007; Hardy 2008; Jerslev 2006), several of whom have written about their formative and ongoing force in their lives (Barker 2006; Brayton 2006).

Indeed, we would suggest that Tolkien's books, *as well as* Jackson's *LotR* films, generate for many readers and viewers specific personal, collective and in some cases intergenerational constellations of meaning, value and emotional affect that are highly valued and intensely felt, prompting many serious fans of Tolkien's novels and Jackson's films to regularly re-immerse themselves in the written or visual representations of Middle-earth by habitually re-reading the books or re-watching the films. What those constellations of meaning, value and affect might be for particular readers and fans is worthy of further investigation, especially since Tolkien's *The Hobbit* and *The Lord of the Rings* have managed to provide affective attraction for many people in different societies for some sixty years now, through constantly changing contexts. Discussing fantasy texts in general, Fowkes (2010) argues that part of their appeal is their ability to provide a sense of 'home' within a risky world. Our data show a range of additional meanings and affective associations in the case of *The Hobbit*, including a nostalgic connection to intergenerational childhood experiences of reading Tolkien, echoing Fowkes' comments about 'home', but also ideas about returning to a familiar *place that feels like home*, with characters that feel like part of one's own family. While these meanings and associations varied considerably, what is clear is that a majority of our respondents came to *The Hobbit* expecting to *feel something* about something that mattered deeply to them—and not merely to be stunned and impressed by cinematic spectacle.

RESEARCHING PREFIGURATIVE AUDIENCES FOR *THE HOBBIT*

Our prefiguration survey was conducted in November 2012, almost nine years after *LotR: The Return of the King* (*RotK*) had premiered: a moment charged with both anticipation *and* ambivalence. Anticipation was grounded in a suite of factors: the ongoing, intense popularity of Tolkien's novels, the approbation that was given to Jackson's previous Middle-earth trilogy, and its outstanding financial and critical performance, all of which set a very high benchmark for the *Hobbit* films. These factors also produced a legacy of passionate fan communities among global audiences: some bonded with the original books, some with the films and many with both, which ought to have provided an 'assured reception' for any new adaptation of Tolkien's work (Mikos et al. 2008, p. 115). While the majority anticipated an immersive and satisfying experience, the announcement in July 2012 that *The Hobbit*, a children's book of modest length, would be turned into three long films was greeted with a certain ambivalence by some participants in online fora such as Theonering.net (Maegwn 2012). Commentators expressed anxiety as to whether the production team could produce a right-sized, Tolkien-respectful, emotionally satisfying version of *The Hobbit*.

We similarly wondered: could the phenomenal critical and popular success of the *LotR* be repeated? After all, much had changed in the interim period—not just in the nature of Hollywood filmmaking, but also in terms of the rise of social media and greater access to information and opinion about film productions and processes. In addition to the established *LotR* news, debate and archiving forums such as Theonering.net and Tolkien.movies.com, the *Hobbit* trilogy was preceded by the expanding influence of social media platforms such as Facebook, YouTube and Twitter. These newer networked platforms and sites make accessible widely dispersed communities of interest that otherwise only come into tangible existence during the time of a film's brief public release, or at fan conventions and gatherings such as ComicCon. Conveniently, they also make it relatively easy to reach large numbers of potential research participants, and so played a major role in our recruitment strategy.

Our survey of prefigurative audiences was conducted online in the three weeks before *AUJ*'s release. The 1000 respondents we successfully recruited sorted 38 Q statements from most strongly agree to most strongly disagree (see Appendix C), before completing a questionnaire

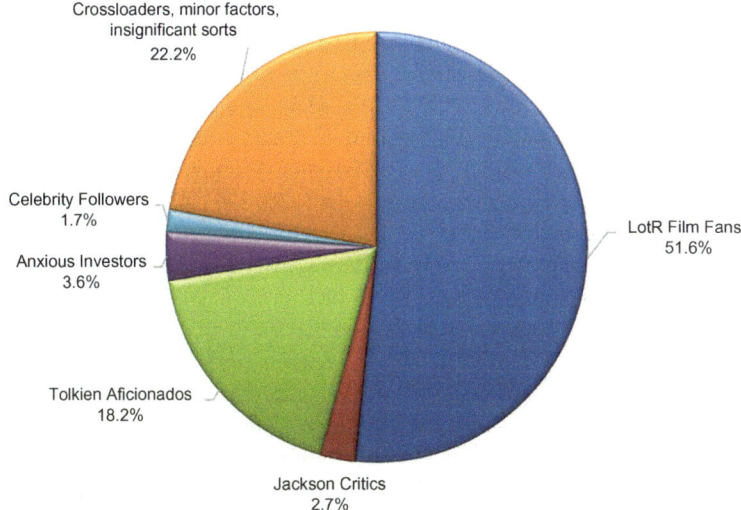

Crossloaders, minor factors,
insignificant sorts
22.2%

Celebrity Followers
1.7%

Anxious Investors
3.6%

Tolkien Aficionados
18.2%

Jackson Critics
2.7%

LotR Film Fans
51.6%

Fig. 3.1 Audience viewpoints, pre-viewing

combining a selection of forced-choice and open-ended questions. Their Q-sorts were then factor analysed by person to identify five major groups that accounted for 77.8% of participants (see Fig. 3.1). For convenience and to give readers an indication of their nature, we will refer to these groups as eager and enthusiastic *LotR Film Fans*, angry and disappointed *Jackson Critics*, *Tolkien Aficionados*, *Anxious Investors* and *Celebrity Followers*. In what follows, we summarise the perspectives of each group in turn, beginning with the largest and followed by a much smaller group of critics (since they expressed an inverted version of the *same* factor), before discussing the other groups in size order. For a more expansive description of the following categories and the method by which they were produced, see Davis et al. (2014).

LotR Film Fans

The 516 members of this largest group (51.6%) saw the creative leadership of Peter Jackson as the most important aspect of the forthcoming *Hobbit* films and adamantly believed he was the right person to produce an effective, satisfying adaptation-prequel. This group most strongly agreed with statements 10 and 27: 'Peter Jackson is a genius and I have complete faith that he knows what he is doing' (s10, +4),[1] and 'No one but Peter Jackson could tell this story and do it justice' (s27, +4). They also strongly agreed that Jackson was doing the best he could to bring the rich history of Middle-earth to life (s33, +3), and very strongly disagreed that Jackson and the film studio had stretched the novel out into three films to make more money (s24, −4). They also rejected statements criticising Jackson's directing skills (s26, −4) and use of new filming and screening technologies (s8, −3), and spurned the suggestion he was likely to diverge too far from Tolkien's story (s21, −3).

In other words, based on their love of the *LotR* trilogy as well as their appreciation of the *Hobbit* book, the members of this group constructed a powerful authorial figure in Peter Jackson and trusted that he and his design and production teams would again do a fine job of adapting Tolkien's source material. They expressed confidence that Jackson 'loves and respects' that material, and while they knew the book and the film could not be identical, believed that Jackson 'wants to bring it to life in the best possible way' (Finnish woman, 41). The were also adamant that his primary motivation in making a trilogy was creative, rather than financial:

> Peter Jackson has already given his reasons, and it is not because of money. He has a lot of that already. He just realised that there is more of the story to tell. Tolkien didn't write *The Hobbit* with *The Lord of The Rings* in mind, and so there were many things he explained that happened at the same time as *The Hobbit*, but [weren't] in the book. Peter Jackson is taking the opportunity to show a more complete picture. (Filipino woman, 18)

This comment expresses a common expectation among these respondents: that a longer version of *The Hobbit* would have space to include many of the characters and sub-stories that had been sketched out in the Appendices to *The Lord of The Rings* but did not feature in Jackson's previous films. There was, therefore, a long-standing desire among this group for an *extended* experience of their favourite fantasy world:

> I have wanted to see *The Hobbit*, the *LotR* trilogy and *The Silmarillion* filmed since I first read the books more than 35 years ago because the world created by Tolkien is so interesting, engrossing and fantastical. (British man, 49)

This desire expressed itself in strong agreement with statements 35 and 38 (both +3): 'this film can't get here soon enough, I've been waiting for this my whole life, and I can't wait to see this adventure on the big screen' and 'I am really looking forward to returning to the wonderful world of Middle-earth.'

Reflecting this trust, confidence and desire, 94% of this group considered it 'extremely' or 'very' important to see *AUJ*. On average, they had read Tolkien's *The Hobbit* eight times and seen the *LotR* trilogy an impressive 19 times. While 35.7% described themselves as fans of the *LotR* films, a larger proportion, just over 48%, actually said they were fans of the *Hobbit* novel or Tolkien's work, perhaps suggesting these individuals are what Brayton (2006) describes as 'Ringers'—fans of all things *Lord of the Rings*. The average age of this group was 34, and 61.8% of them were female.

Jackson Critics

This much smaller group of 27 respondents (2.7%) expressed the opposite position to that of *LotR Film Fans,* and thus most strongly disagreed that one could have 'complete faith' in Peter Jackson's ability to produce an excellent adaptation of *The Hobbit* (s10, −4). Indeed, they considered him an 'immature, sloppy, artistically tone-deaf director' (s26, +4) and vehemently refuted the suggestion that no one else could do justice to *The Hobbit* (s27, −4). This group most strongly agreed that *The Hobbit*'s three-part structure was determined by commercial considerations to maximise profit (s24, +4). They also strongly agreed the film had been over-hyped and were not impressed by what they had seen and heard so far (s7, +3), being particularly concerned about possible diversions from Tolkien's original work (s21, +3), and the likelihood that Jackson's focus on technology would undermine the films' cinematic quality (s8, +3):

> So far, all of Jackson's interpretations have been literal to the point of lacking any artistic vision. Seeing as how much thought was put into his books by Tolkien, adding random sequences to the story in the film can only do the whole thing harm. (German man, 38)

> . . . He's all about CGI, battles and technology and cares nothing at all about the story, character development or loyalty to the Professor's work. (American woman, 68)

With an average age of 45 years, these respondents were older than *LotR Film Fans*, with a slight gender skew towards males (53.8%), and more than half were New Zealanders. Indeed, we can perceive a further division between the New Zealander *Jackson Critics*, whose concerns typically lay with the political effects of Jackson's intervention in a local *Hobbit* labour crisis (discussed in more detail in Chap. 4), and the non-New Zealanders, who were more likely to be 'angry and disappointed' guardians of either Tolkien's work or the *LotR* trilogy, and thus more concerned with Jackson's aesthetic sensibilities. On average, this latter subgroup had read *The Hobbit* 14 times and had seen the earlier films 10 times, whereas the New Zealanders averaged just two readings of the book and two viewings of the *LotR* trilogy. For different reasons, both groups had come to share the same strongly negative feelings about Jackson's (aesthetic and/or political) contributions to the *Hobbit* project. Hence, only 11% of *Jackson Critics* felt that it was 'very' or 'extremely' important to see the films, and 30% were not planning to go at all.

Tolkien Aficionados

A sense of responsibility towards Tolkien's works was even more pervasive among this third group of 182 respondents (18.2%). Over 87% described themselves as Tolkien fans. Having read *The Hobbit* on average 10 times and having viewed the *LotR* films on average 13 times, *Tolkien Aficionados* were knowledgeable both about Tolkien's writings and Jackson's previous adaptations, which they clearly enjoyed—they did not share the former group's overwhelmingly negative view of Jackson's directing ability (s26, −3). *Tolkien Aficionados* tended to have encountered *The Hobbit* when they were much younger, and often expressed feelings of nostalgia related to reading the book as a child, or being read to (s1, +4). *The Hobbit* was thus a site of sociability for these respondents, which they hoped to reinforce by seeing the forthcoming film with family or friends (s20, +3). Because *The Hobbit* was a favourite book, they wanted the first film to be 'perfect' (s5, +4) and cared a great deal about seeing it (s2, −4). Like *LotR Film Fans*, this group very much looked forward to returning to the wonderful world of Middle-earth (s38, +3) and expressed a very high level of interest in seeing the film (s13, +3; s31, −4; s19, −3, s28, −3).

The emotional attachment that members of this group had to Tolkien's original novel led some to talk in terms of the 'spirit' of the book. Most understood that a film could not reproduce everything that was in a book, but they hoped, and expected, that the adaptation would retain *The Hobbit*'s undefinable 'essence':

> Even though choices will be made that I might disagree with. . . I hope that those decisions will be made in the spirit of the book. I hope that the changes will be done to propel the story forward, or to facilitate its transfer to the big screen, rather than made to attract audiences/money. *The Hobbit* was a big part of my childhood, so I hope they're able to recapture that. (Canadian woman, 23)

Tolkien Aficionados were the youngest group, averaging 30.4 years of age, and 55.9% of them were female. Jackson's *Hobbit* trilogy was clearly important to them as an adaptation of Tolkien's written works and a cinematic realisation of his vision; 89% considered it 'very' or 'extremely' important to see the first film.

Anxious Investors

Anxiety, in the form of concern that Peter Jackson make the most of the production possibilities of *The Hobbit*, but also fear that he might not excel at adapting the book to film, was a key feature of this small cluster of 36 respondents (3.6%). Nearly ninety percent of *Anxious Investors* were New Zealanders, who evaluated the forthcoming production from the perspective of what it might or might not do for their country and its economy. They were also likely aware that New Zealand taxpayers had already invested tens of millions of dollars worth of government subsidies into the film's production (Radio New Zealand 2012)—and would by the end have invested more than $191 million (Heather 2015). They strongly agreed with the proposition that the conversion of *The Hobbit* into a trilogy was commercially motivated (s24, +3), and expressed considerable concern about suggestions that Warner Bros was mistreating workers associated with the *Hobbit* production (s11, +3), but nonetheless still felt 'excited and proud' about their country's 'contribution to this major international film production' (s36, +3). They most strongly agreed that 'This film will really help to spur tourism in New Zealand, which is great for the economy' (s37, +4), and while they may have heard negative comments about the production, they preferred to reserve judgement until seeing the film (s25, +4). They also expressed confidence in Jackson's ability by strongly disagreeing that he is a sloppy director (s26, −4) while acknowledging that the project could have been directed by someone else (s27, −2).

The qualitative comments from the *Anxious Investors* were typically framed by the desire, or 'hope', that the film would be successful, but characterised by the balancing of probabilities:

> Hopefully, another great achievement for New Zealand on the world stage. I hope it succeeds hugely for that reason. Publicity, appreciation, all those things. Kiwis don't really realise how much *LotR* did for New Zealand in terms of tourism, so people saying that the amount of money spent is too much don't know what an effect *The Hobbit* will have. (New Zealand woman, 23)

The members of this group may have felt patriotic pride that *AUJ* was being made in their country, but it was less likely to have captured their imaginations as a prospective viewing experience. Their interest in this film related to its potential local impacts more than its status as an adaptation-prequel; while they expressed appreciation for the *LotR* trilogy (s31, −3), they didn't particularly enjoy discussing or speculating about the *Hobbit* production (s34, −3) and did not express high anticipation for the film per se (s6, −3; s35, −4). Only 14.7% of them said it was 'very' or 'extremely' important to see the film which, they were well aware, was primarily an industrial and commercial property, with the utilitarian tone of their comments reflecting that understanding. *Anxious Investors* had an average age of 36.8, and 61% of them were female.

Celebrity Followers

Our final segment consisted of a small but passionate group of 17 individuals (1.7%), all of them women and with an average age of 40, whose main interest in the *Hobbit* movies revolved around the opportunities they would provide to see particular actors in lead roles—76% of this group were attracted to the film by one of its stars. They most strongly agreed with statement 23(+4): 'I'm very happy that one of my favourite actors will appear in *The Hobbit*', and strongly agreed with statement 17(+3): 'What a great cast! Perfect choices in most cases!' Sixty-nine percent considered it 'very' or 'extremely' important to see the film, which they strongly believed was a 'must see' film and major cinematic event (s13, +4).

On average, members of this group had seen the *LotR* movies twice and were even less familiar with the novel of *The Hobbit*, having read it only once. It does not appear to have greatly impressed them, since they most strongly disagreed that *The Hobbit* was one of their favourite books (s5, −4). Nonetheless, they were still very interested in the film production (s7, −4), specifically because of the involvement of particular actors. While the participation of Martin Freeman, Sylvester McCoy and the voice of Benedict Cumberbatch were all attractions, it was the brooding presence of Richard Armitage as Dwarf prince Thorin Oakenshield which promised the greatest reward:

> The book itself means nothing to me as I've never read it and don't care to. The movie trilogy, however, is very important to me because it is a huge breakthrough role for my favorite actor, Richard Armitage. I have to see him in this important moment in his career, on the big screen, in such an important role. . . . I could say, also, that I'd have no interest in seeing the movie in the theatre if Armitage wasn't in it. (American woman, 35)

The identification of the *Celebrity Followers* group provides evidence that the casting of currently popular actors can be a significant (and successful) element in the efforts to make a blockbuster, in that audience members can be attracted to a movie by, and exhibit fannish behaviour around it in response to, aspects that are only tangentially related to the material or the production team (see also Brayton 2006; Chin and Gray 2001; Gray 2010). While the landscapes of Middle-earth were also attractions for this group (s12, +3) and they agreed the film would have benefits to New Zealand that justified government support (s37, +3), it is women's enthusiastic appreciation of individual male actors that gives this cluster its distinctiveness.

Prefigurative Activities

Although only three of these audience clusters had a majority of members who identified as Tolkien or *LotR* fans, in total these individuals made up more than 70% of respondents. It was those fannish clusters that reported the highest level of engagement with prefigurative activities. In our questionnaire, we asked respondents to indicate which prefigurative activities they had engaged in from a predetermined list (see Table 3.1). The most common activity was 'Viewing *Hobbit* film trailers', reported by 91.6% of *LotR Film Fans* and 89.6% of *Tolkien Aficionados*, but only 55.6% of *Anxious Investors*. The second most popular activity was 'Discussing the film with family or friends', very common among *LotR Film Fans* (88.5%), *Celebrity Followers* (88.2%), and *Tolkien Aficionados* (86.3%), but much less common among *Anxious Investors*, only 38.9% of whom were bothering to discuss the film with others. 'Watching *Hobbit* production videos' online was an activity favoured by *Celebrity Followers* (88.2%) and *LotR Film Fans* (85.4%); in stark contrast, just 37.0% of *Jackson Critics* and 27.8% of *Anxious Investors* sought knowledge from that source. It thus becomes apparent how different communities of interest can seek out, and accumulate, different types of information, building on existing dispositions and knowledges but also contributing to a critical mass of opinion and engagement in certain communicative channels but not others. For instance, whereas 60.7% of *LotR Film Fans* had '"Liked" the official *Hobbit* Facebook page', only 5.6% of *Anxious Investors* had done so and just 3.7% of *Jackson Critics*.

Also surprising to note is that while our sample clearly had a skew towards fans, their enthusiasm was predominantly directed towards arguably 'passive' consumption-based activities of viewing and reading as well as local communicative relationships, as opposed to more 'active' creative productivity and online interaction with other fans. For instance, in the 'Participated in online fan discussion' category, *Tolkien Aficionados* and *Celebrity Followers* were the most active, but at relatively modest levels (42.3 and 41.2%, respectively), followed by 37.2% of *LotR Film Fans*. 'Following news coverage of the film', 'Visiting the official *Hobbit* website' and 'Reading Jackson's production blogs' were the other principal prefigurative activities in which our respondents had engaged.

Seeking insight into other activities outside of those already identified, we asked respondents to tell us in their own words whether there were other things they had done in anticipation of seeing the first *Hobbit* film. More than half (54.6%) said they had. These prefigurative activities were categorised using a process of inductive coding (see Table 3.1). The two most significant reported activities were 'Consuming' and 'Re-engaging' with primary intertexts (the novel, or the *LotR* films, or both).

'Consuming' associated with the films was common, with 163 respondents (29.9%) telling us they had bought something recently, including 50 who had already purchased tickets or pre-booked them, and a further 59 who said they had purchased merchandise. For some, *Hobbit*-related consumption was a singular act, as these responses suggest: 'I bought an advance ticket for a midnight screening on the first day' (American man, 55); 'I have ordered the *Hobbit* stamps and

Table 3.1 Main prefigurative activities by viewpoint

	Audience segment				
Main activities (Yes/No)	LotR Film Fans (%)	Jackson Critics (%)	Tolkien Aficionados (%)	Anxious Investors (%)	Celebrity Followers (%)
Viewed the *Hobbit* film trailers	91.6	82.5	89.6	55.6	82.4
Discussed the film with family or friends	88.5	77.8	86.3	38.9	88.2
Followed news coverage of the film	85.8	77.8	76.9	55.6	76.5
Watched any of the *Hobbit* production videos online	85.4	37.0	77.5	27.8	88.2
Visited the official *Hobbit* website	75.3	22.2	60.4	2.8	58.8
Read Peter Jackson's production blogs	67.5	18.5	45.6	5.6	47.1
'Liked' the official *Hobbit* Facebook page	60.7	3.7	42.3	5.6	35.3
Participated in online fan forum discussions of the film	37.2	25.9	42.3	2.8	41.2

Q: Are there other things you have done in anticipation of seeing the film? Coded open-response question[a] (N = 546)	*Number of respondents (%)*
Consuming (merchandise, tickets, etc.)	163 (29.9)

(continued)

Table 3.1   (continued)

Q: Are there other things you have done in anticipation of seeing the film? Coded open-response question[a] (N = 546)	Number of respondents (%)
Re-engaging (reading the books, watching *LotR* films)	146 (26.7)
Planning (events, pilgrimages, viewings)	118 (21.6)
Impersonating (e.g. cosplay)	63 (11.5)
Creating (art, fanfiction, online content etc.)	51 (9.3)
Other	43 (7.9)
Researching (production news etc.)	41 (7.5)
Listening (score, podcasts etc.)	36 (6.6)
Watching (e.g. Air NZ *Hobbit* advertisement)	25 (4.6)
Multiple activities (more than three mentioned)	22 (4.0)
Encouraging engagement of others (family, friends, others)	21 (3.8)
Travelling (to film locations, premiere)	20 (3.7)
Participating (conventions, events etc.)	19 (3.5)
Discussing with others	18 (3.3)

[a]Up to three separate activities were coded for each respondent

maxicards from the New Zealand Post' (Hungarian male, 22). However, for others who were avid *LotR Film Fans*, consumption was a regular practice: 'Already purchased related movie books, calendars, NZ postage stamps, magazines!' (American woman, 63). Several *Celebrity Followers* primarily collected merchandise associated with particular actors starring in the films:

> I have purchased a copy of *Empire* magazine with Richard Armitage/ Thorin on the cover. I have purchased both of the Thorin action figures, and the New Zealand first day issue *Hobbit* stamps. I also check two forums every day to see if there is anything new about the film, which I have been doing since the cast first arrived in New Zealand almost two years ago. And I read the book for the first time after hearing that Richard Armitage was cast in the film. (American woman, 61)

The second major group included 146 respondents (26.7%), many of them *Tolkien Aficionados*, who said they had 're-engaged' with either Tolkien's book(s) or previous adaptations of them, or both. The adaptations were typically Jackson's *LotR* movies, but several respondents had also gone back to the Rankin/Bass (1977) animated feature. Some of these re-engagers were extraordinarily diligent in their preparation for viewing *AUJ*: their activities seemed more like serious work than an 'escape' to entertainment:

> Listened to a sneak peak of the score. Listened to *The Lord of the Rings* audiobooks as well the *Hobbit* audiobooks. Re-read *The Hobbit*. Watched the entire *LotR* trilogy extended editions. Surfing YouTube for all related *Hobbit* videos. (New Zealand, man, 30)

> I have been keeping a countdown of the total number of days left before the film's release, reading the book for the fifth time, watching the *LotR* movies, reading *The Lord of the Rings* books, reading information on Tolkien as an author and Peter Jackson as a director. . . . (American woman, 15)

A large number (118; 21.6%) were busy 'planning' special viewings, pilgrimages to film locations (such as Hobbiton) and to the Wellington premiere, and other *Hobbit*-themed events and activities. Several were travelling to New Zealand from as far afield as the USA, Canada, the Netherlands and Brazil.

In terms of creative activities, the most frequent was 'impersonation' (63; 11.5%), and more especially cosplay, with 50 respondents making or buying special clothing for film-related events or live action role-playing games. A more unexpected form of material enactment of fan identity was to eat the types of foods consumed by characters in the books and films. This ranged from savouring the spartan cuisine favoured by elves— 'I've found a lembas bread recipe which I am going to make for the premiere' (New Zealand woman, 15)—to Hobbit-inspired gourmandising:

> I cooked a *Hobbit* breakfast involving (with the exception of the scones and some of the beverages) all the various dishes that Bilbo served the Dwarves of the Unexpected Party (and two additional ones). (German woman, 27)

A further 51 respondents (9.3%) described engaging in other forms of 'creating'. They included half a dozen people who said they made artworks, a handful who wrote fan fiction and a similar number who engaged in academic writing about Tolkien's work or *LotR* fandom. Several people were webmasters, a handful had set up Facebook pages, a couple mentioned writing blogs and several were determined Tweeters or re-bloggers.

An unexpectedly distinctive feature of our data was the degree of *sociability*—both offline and online, but predominantly offline—that permeated the descriptions of prefigurative activities. A small number (21; 3.8%) stated that they had been actively encouraging family and friends to attend the films, to read the book, to appreciate production news, to dress up and attend parties, and to participate in reunions with the film as a pretext, as with one 23-year-old Belgian woman who said she had called 'my older brother and friends with whom I saw the *LotR* movies to see *The Hobbit* with them.' Several had been educating those they thought needed more preparation for the imminent film experience:

> Bought a tie-in picture book to prepare an octogenarian family member who will not have read the book. (British woman, 64)

> Making my nephews read *The Hobbit*. They are still too young to have read *LotR*. (British man, 36)

But in addition to these 'encouragers', many of those who were 'planning' activities were actively promoting sociability by organising *Hobbit*, and especially premier-related, events and group viewings, in some cases for very large numbers of others:

> Planning a mega party—a round green Bag End door for our front door, costumes, planning a menu for the party (400+ people), plus going to the movie as a group. (American woman, 54)

It is evident, then, that prefigurative activity is seen by many as an opportunity to help foster social relationships through both face-to-face and online contact, and that for some of those who were fans of the *LotR* films, certain social activities had become a custom or shared ritual. As an 'event' film, the forthcoming *AUJ* was motivating the creation of a myriad of smaller events which in themselves produced pleasurable emotions associated with real and anticipated social engagement and inclusion, quite some time before the film was available to be viewed. Being a prospective audience member, then, is a state that can include extensive *creative* and *material* (cooking, sewing, writing, making), *cognitive* (imagining, extrapolating, judging, justifying) and *communicative practices*, all in anticipation of engaging with the actual text.

PRE-VIEWING MEANINGS OF *THE HOBBIT*

Seeking further insight into the specific constellations of meaning, value and affect that were most significant for our respondents and to complement the insights derived from the Q sorts, we asked the following question: *What does The Hobbit mean to you, and why?* (Table 3.2). In hindsight, this question was insufficiently precise, since many interpreted it as referring to the novel rather than the forthcoming films—usefully revealing their basic orientation in the process. Others addressed the complex sets of meanings and feelings they associated with both the book and the films. Their answers were once again categorised using a process of inductive coding to identify common themes; many were complex answers for which multiple codes were necessary.

For some, answering this question entailed making a *generic* categorisation—in other words, they told us what kind of thing or experience they expected *The Hobbit* to be. Others told us about the *personal meanings* they associated with the books, the *LotR* movies or the *Hobbit* production. A third type of response was to tell us about the *intensity* of their feelings towards past or ongoing experiences provided for them by Tolkien and or Jackson, in other words, to tell us what *significance* the *Hobbit* trilogy's primary intertexts have had in their lives.

The results confirm that there were a smaller number of non-fans in our sample: 28 respondents (3.0%) were explicitly critical of the quality of the book, while a further 41 (4.3%) critiqued aspects of the film's production and marketing for various reasons, as with one 32-year-old New Zealand man who said *The Hobbit* meant 'Nationalistic hype, capitalist fantasies. Inanity on a worldwide scale.' At the other extreme were a more significant number of highly favourable meanings, with the largest category comprising 241 respondents (25.5%) who associated *The Hobbit* with reading the book as a thoroughly positive childhood experience strongly marked by close familial relationships:

> One of my favourite books since I was five, I've shared it with all my many siblings, and Bilbo is one of my heroes. I reread it all the time. It reminds me of when I was small ... and of my parents, because they read it with me .... (American woman, 21)

> *The Hobbit* means a shared history with my dad, who made sure I had copies of Tolkien at an absurdly young age .... (Canadian woman, 32)

Table 3.2   Meanings of *The Hobbit*, pre-viewing

Q: What does The Hobbit mean to you, and why? Coded open-response question[a] (N = 943)	
Primary-secondary codes	*Number of respondents (%)*
Book—life stage (childhood)	241 (25.5)
Book—favourite	175 (18.6)
Book—personal meaning	159 (16.9)
Book—significant	137 (14.5)
Book—positive	113 (12.0)
Book—important message	84 (8.9)
Book—genre	83 (8.8)
Book—Middle-earth	73 (7.7)
Book—social	68 (7.2)
Book—completion	63 (6.7)
Book—nostalgia	55 (5.8)
Book—life stage (other)	37 (3.9)
Book—critical	28 (3.0)
Book—escapism	26 (2.8)
Film—adaptation	195 (20.7)
Film—return to Middle-earth	118 (12.5)
Film—positive	112 (11.9)
Film—realisation	100 (10.6)
Film—significant	58 (6.2)
Film—cinematic experience	56 (5.9)
Film—completion	55 (5.8)
Film—social	49 (5.2)
Film—personal meaning	43 (4.6)
Film—critical	41 (4.3)
Film—actor	36 (3.8)
Film—life stage	31 (3.3)
Film—genre	29 (3.1)
Film—technology	17 (1.8)
Film—escapism	16 (1.7)
Film—important message	12 (1.3)
Imagination	21 (2.2)
Jackson	99 (10.5)
LotR books	52 (5.5)
LotR books—positive	45 (4.8)
LotR books—personal meaning	27 (2.9)
LotR books—significant	27 (2.9)
LotR films—positive	110 (11.7)
LotR films	50 (5.3)
LotR films—personal meaning	38 (4.0)
LotR films—significant	23 (2.4)
NZ—local product	56 (5.9)

(continued)

Table 3.2 (continued)

Q: What does The Hobbit mean to you, and why? Coded open-response question[a] (N = 943)	
Primary-secondary codes	Number of respondents (%)
NZ—landscape	29 (3.1)
NZ—economic benefits	13 (1.4)
Professional interest	47 (5.0)
Tolkien	195 (20.7)

[a]Up to three separate meanings were coded for each respondent

For 175 respondents (18.6%) the novel was a favourite book, while 84 (8.9%) said the book contained moral messages that they felt had significance, and possibly influence, in their lives:

> It's one of my favourite books, it's about greed as a destructive power and finding courage within ourselves that we didn't know existed. (Portuguese woman, 29)

> *The Hobbit* is a story of how people can have very different sides to them that sometimes the person doesn't even know. There's also the fundamental moral element in it: The treasure belongs to the Dwarves and Smaug stole it, and this is the story of how that was righted. (New Zealand male, 24)

Related to this pre-existing affection for the novel, considering *AUJ* a book-to-film adaptation was the most popular of our film-related codes; 195 people (20.7 %) ascribed it to that genre, very much hoping that the adaptation would be successful:

> *The Hobbit* is a story of transformation, encased in a fantasy adventure. It is a showcase for very important themes: providence, sacrifice, resourcefulness, reconciliation, greed, courage, faith and hope. It is a Faerie Tale fully realized ... seeing it in film, including in the newly developed immersive technology, will be another opportunity to wander in Tolkien's Perilous Realm .... (American man, 54)

As this quote suggests, many respondents associated the films primarily with J.R.R. Tolkien; so it is not surprising to note that a further 20.7% specifically associated *The Hobbit* with its original creator. Hence, the films were primarily meaningful for many as a visual 'realisation' of this author's influential works and the ideals conveyed by them (100; 10.6%).

'Returning to Middle-earth' was another important meaning for 118 respondents (12.5%), with comments such as this expressing the idea of returning to a place that felt familiar, almost like a second home:

> Middle-earth, to me, is like a home I miss, although I have never been there. There is something nostalgic, something warm, about seeing the lands and creatures of Middle-earth play out before me, and hearing Howard Shore's score draw me gently back into the land of magic. There is a spirit to the books and films that call you home to the Shire, or to Gondor, or to wherever your heart lies, and it just cannot be expressed with words. (American woman, 17)

For 47 respondents (5.0%), previous experience with Tolkien's imagined world, especially its realisation in the *LotR* trilogy, had been a factor in determining their career and 'professional interests':

> I am an enormous fan of all things Middle-earth. The *LotR* films (and after that the books etc.) have been such a huge, an important part of my life and have influenced my career decisions in massive ways. (American man, 28)

For a small subgroup of the 38 who discussed the personal meaning of the earlier films (4.0%), the influence of *LotR* extended not just to their daily lives but also their sense of self, as suggested by this 25-year-old Latvian man: '*LotR* changed my life. It inspired me at an all-time low. It gave me the courage to pursue what I wanted and to survive.'

Another sizeable group of 56 individuals (5.9%) were looking forward to the general 'cinematic experience', and to seeing a worthy successor to and continuation of Jackson's *LotR* film trilogy:

> I have always dreamed about watching something similar to *LotR* ever since [that] trilogy was completed .... It made me really happy that another such movie will be shown in the cinema and created by such a magnificent director, producer and scriptwriter like Peter Jackson. (Norwegian man, 21)

> It means watching and enjoying a really good movie, not regretting the price you pay for a ticket .... It's kind of a balsam for my eyes, regarding

all the beautiful places in the movie, for my ears, the music is great, again. (Slovenian woman, 25)

Viewing the Middle-earth saga on film would be a satisfying experience of 'completion' for 55 respondents (5.8%), as with one 23-year-old American woman who said 'It is completing the story of the *LotR* by telling its beginning.'

A large number of comments explicitly discussed the personal 'significance' of either the *Hobbit* book (137; 14.5%), the *LotR* films (23; 2.4%) or books (27; 2.9%), or/and the forthcoming *Hobbit* movies (58; 6.2%); that is, respondents told us what these Middle-earth texts meant to them *emotionally*. The majority were intensely hopeful about experiences they hoped to gain from the film:

> It means lots of warm, emotional, sad and happy feelings .... It means having a great time with my best friends sharing ideas, ideals, moments. (German woman, 26)

> This is getting to see my childhood, my adolescence, made into something I can watch again and again. This is art; this is poetry. This is dedication and craft. This is hobbits, dwarves, the original modern take on fairy tales and quests, of the unlooked for, average Joe hero. This is the book that has made all other fantasy in the modern age possible .... (American woman, 23)

Finally, there were smaller numbers for whom the primary meanings associated with *The Hobbit* related to aspects of the New Zealand production context, especially in terms of the trilogy being a local production (56; 5.9%), the possible economic benefits it might generate (13; 1.4%) and its showcasing of local landscapes (29; 3.1%). Others understood *The Hobbit* primarily in terms of Peter Jackson's key role as director (99; 10.5%) or as a vehicle for particular actors (36; 3.8%).

These comments from prefigurative audience members as to what *The Hobbit: AUJ*'s imminent arrival meant for them, couched in the confidence that more than half of our respondents had in Peter Jackson's ability to deliver another phenomenal Middle-earth trilogy, reveal the intensity of many *Hobbit* pre-viewers' cinematic desire for a similarly satisfying experience in its most pure and unsullied form. As we shall show, however, the nature and intensity of that desire were not static but rather evolved, in sometimes dramatic ways, over the course of the *Hobbit* trilogy's public presence in cinemas.

CONCLUSION

As this chapter has demonstrated, the five main pre-viewing audience segments each possessed different interests, orientations and associated constellations of meaning and emotion that shaped their hopes and expectations for *The Hobbit: AUJ*. For *LotR Film Fans, Tolkien Aficionados* and some *Jackson Critics* the knowledges, meanings and memories employed in discussing the forthcoming *Hobbit* trilogy were typically of long standing and were oriented towards Tolkien's and Jackson's various versions of Middle-earth. In contrast, *Celebrity Followers* and *Anxious Investors* tended to have more recent, specific and limited experience of the *Hobbit* text, instead drawing on knowledges, meanings and memories associated with other interests, such as being a fan of a particular star, or being familiar with localised debates around the costs and benefits of transnational film production. While *LotR Film Fans* were confident of re-experiencing the pleasures and satisfactions they had felt with Jackson's first trilogy, *Tolkien Aficionados* hoped to re-experience as much as was feasible of both the detail and spirit of Tolkien's Middle-earth. *Anxious Investors* looked forward to their concerns about potential economic and reputational benefits being eased by seeing the film succeed in various ways, while *Celebrity Followers* wanted a pleasurable vehicle for their attraction to certain actors. Possibly, *Jackson Critics* may have secretly hoped *AUJ* would prove less successful than the *LotR* trilogy, if only to validate their negative opinions about Jackson as director. And while among the latter group there was overt politically tinged criticism of the industrial contexts of the film's making and the detrimental effects of its blockbusterisation or 'up-sizing', such concerns were muted among other groups; if voiced, they were accorded less significance than other issues which apparently *mattered* more.

It is also evident that, among this international English-speaking sample of *Hobbit* pre-viewers, the already existing constellations of meaning were predominantly either personal or social, and related to a desire to rekindle feelings and emotions associated with reading the novel, or with first experiencing the phenomenal cultural event that was the *LotR* trilogy. While the originating pleasurable experiences might have been as long ago as childhood, they were often maintained and refreshed by repeated behaviours such as rereading the novel or regularly re-watching the *LotR* films, or by incorporating a Middle-earth-based world view and its associated values into personal decision-making, life choices and avocations. While some respondents related their individual and apparently solitary prefigurative interactions with *The Hobbit*'s primary intertexts, for the majority, prefigurative activities had a clear social dimension that involved discussing, or doing things with others, to the degree that this blockbuster production was *already* functioning as an important social resource for fans long before its widespread release in cinemas.

These findings thus affirm that reception is a fluid and dynamic process that may commence well in advance of actual moments of viewing. However, we caution against making too many assumptions about how these prefigurative perspectives and predilections might have subsequently shaped the viewing of differently interested and oriented members of *The Hobbit*'s global audience. While the insights we have gleaned from studying prefigurative meanings and activities are certainly fascinating, such knowledge does not diminish the importance of also engaging with actual encounters between viewers and films once fully realised and available to consume.

So, having identified the dominant pre-viewing perspectives and the optimism that characterised the majority of our respondents' anticipatory hopes, expectations and imaginings, we were eager to find out what happened when these pre-viewers later encountered the 'real thing'. How would their pre-existing intertextual affiliations, paratextual knowledges, fandoms and predilections shape their subsequent responses and evaluations of the first *Hobbit* film? Given that even the most well-informed pre-viewers could not possibly fully anticipate just what would become realised on screen and how they might feel about it, we wondered if the immense confidence of *LotR Film Fans* would be borne out once the final product was available to view. Similarly, we wondered where *Tolkien Aficionados* would draw the line between creative adaptation and desecration of a beloved childhood novel. We also had our own hopes as the *AUJ*'s cinematic release drew closer—specifically, that at least some of our respondents would have valued participating in our first survey enough to come back and complete another one once they had finally had the chance to see *AUJ* at the cinema, so that we could make direct comparisons between their pre- and post-viewing perspectives. The results of that second stage of our research are presented in Chap. 5. In the meantime, we delve deeper into the knowledge and evaluations of our respondents relating to particular controversies around the production of the *Hobbit* trilogy; controversies that provide additional insight into viewers' understandings of the processes and imperatives of blockbusterisation and their potential local and global effects.

80   C. MICHELLE ET AL.

Note

1. The rankings in parentheses should be interpreted as follows: (s10, +4) denotes that statement 10 was ranked +4 ('most strongly agree') on a scale from +4 to −4 in which 0 is the point of neutrality and −4 signifies 'most strongly disagree'. Hence, (s26, −3) would signify that respondents 'strongly disagree' with statement 26.

References

Barker, M. (2006). On being a 1960s Tolkien reader. In E. Mathijs & M. Pomerance (Eds.), *From Hobbits to Hollywood: Essays on Peter Jackson's Lord of the Rings* (pp. 81–100). Amsterdam and New York: Rodopi.
BBC News. (2007, December 18). Jackson to produce *Hobbit* movies. BBC News. Retrieved December 13, 2016, from http://news.bbc.co.uk/2/hi/entertainment/7150644.stm.
Biltereyst, D., & Meers, P. (2006). Blockbusters and/as events: Distributing and launching *The Lord of the Rings*. In E. Mathijs (Ed.), *The Lord of the Rings: Popular culture in global context* (pp. 71–87). London: Wallflower.
Brayton, J. (2006). Fic Frodo slash Frodo: Fandoms and *The Lord of the Rings*. In E. Mathijs & M. Pomerance (Eds.), *From Hobbits to Hollywood: Essays on Peter Jackson's Lord of the Rings* (pp. 137–154). Amsterdam and New York: Rodopi.
Brooker, W. (2012). *Hunting the Dark Knight: Twenty-first-century Batman*. London: I.B. Tauris.
Carpenter, H. (1977). *J.R.R. Tolkien: A biography*. London: George Allen & Unwin.
Chin, B., & Gray, J. (2001). 'One ring to rule them all': Previewers and pretexts of the *Lord of the Rings* films. *Intensities: The Journal of Cult Media, 2*.
Ciabattari, J. (2014, November 20). Hobbits and Hippies: Tolkien and the counterculture, BBC. Retrieved December 12, 2016, from http://www.bbc.com/culture/story/20141120-the-hobbits-and-the-hippies.
Croft, J. B. (2004). *War and the works of J.R.R. Tolkien*. Westwood, CT: Praeger Publishers.
Croft, J. B., & Donovan, L. A. (Eds.). (2015). *Perilous and fair: Women in the works and life of J. R. R. Tolkien*. Altadena: Mythopoeic Press.
Davidsen, M. A. (2013). Fiction-based religion: Conceptualizing a new category against history-based religion and fandom. *Religion & Culture: An Interdisciplinary Journal, 14*(4), 378–395. doi:10.1080/14755610.2013.838798.
Davis, C. H., Michelle, C., Hardy, A. L., & Hight, C. (2014). Framing audience prefigurations of *The Hobbit: An Unexpected Journey*: The roles of fandom, politics and idealised intertexts. *Participations: Journal of Audience & Reception Studies, 11*(1), 50–87.

Davis, C. H., Michelle, C., Hardy, A. & Hight, C. (2016). Making global audiences for a Hollywood 'blockbuster' feature film: Marketing, playability and *The Hobbit: An Unexpected Journey* (2012). *Journal of Fandom Studies, 4*(2), 105–125. doi:10.1386/jfs.4.1.105_1.

De Kloet, J., & Kuipers, G. (2007). Spirituality and fan culture around the *Lord of the Rings* film trilogy. *Fabula: Journal of Folktale Research, 48*(3/4), 300–319. doi:10.1515/FABL.2007.023.

Drout, D. C. (1996). The influence of J. R. R. Tolkien's masculinist medievalism. *Medieval Feminist Forum, 22*(1), 26–27.

Fiorelli, G. (2012, December 13). Prelaunch and the marketing of suspense: *The Hobbit* history case. *State of digital.* Retrieved February 18, 2014, from http://www.stateofdigital.com/hobbit-history-case/.

Fowkes, K. (2010). *The fantasy film.* London: Wiley Blackwell.

Garth, J. (2003). *Tolkien and the great war: The threshold of Middle-earth.* New York: Houghton Mifflin.

Gray, J. (2010). *Show sold separately: Promos, spoilers, and other media paratexts.* New York: New York University Press.

Hardy, A. (2008). There and back again: *The Lord of the Rings*, contemporary religiosity and cinema. In H. Margolis, S. Cubitt, B. King, & T. Jutel (Eds.), *Studying the event film: The Lord of the Rings* (pp. 205–213). Manchester and New York: Manchester University Press.

Heather, B. (2015, September 9). $191m in public grants paid to Hollywood for *Hobbit* trilogy. Stuff. Retrieved February 14, 2017, from http://www.stuff.co.nz/entertainment/71878242/191m-in-public-grants-paid-to-Hollywood-for-Hobbit-trilogy.

Jauss, H. R. (1970). Literary history as a challenge to literary theory. *New Literary History, 2*(1), 7–37.

Jerslev, A. (2006). Sacred viewing: Emotional responses to *The Lord of the Rings*. In E. Mathijs (Ed.), *The Lord of the Rings: Popular culture in global context* (pp. 206–221). London and New York: Wallflower Press.

Johnston, K. M., Vollans, E., & Greene, F. (2016). Watching the trailer: Researching the film trailer audience. *Participations: Journal of Audience and Reception Studies, 13*(2), 56–85.

Kellner, D. (2006). *The Lord of the Rings* as allegory: A multiperspectival reading. In E. Mathijs & M. Pomerance (Eds.), *From Hobbits to Hollywood: Essays on Peter Jackson's Lord of the Rings* (pp. 17–41). Amsterdam and New York: Rodopi.

Lucas, G. (Director). (1977, July 30). *Star wars* [Motion picture]. USA: Lucas Film.

Maegwyn. (2012, July 30). Peter Jackson confirms third *Hobbit* film. The One Ring. Retrieved October 20, 2012, from http://www.theonering.net/torwp/author/maegwen/.

Major, S. (2008). Cultivating a classic: Marketing strategies for the *Lord of the Rings* films. In H. Margolis, S. Cubitt, B. King, & T. Jutel (Eds.), *Studying the event film: The Lord of the Rings* (pp. 47–54). Manchester and New York: Manchester University Press.

Markowski, J. (2012). *The Hobbit* marketing: A not-so-unexpected journey in marketing diversity. *Branding Beat.* Retrieved March 20, 2016, from https://www.qualitylogoproducts.com/blog/the-hobbit-marketing-journey-in-marketing-diversity/.

Mikos, L., Eichner, S., Prommer, E., & Wedel, M. (2008). Involvement in *The Lord of the Rings*: Audience strategies and orientations. In M. Barker & E. Mathijs (Eds.), *Watching The Lord of the Rings: Tolkien's world audiences* (Vol. 3, pp. 111-128). New York: Peter Lang.

Radio New Zealand. (2012, October 8). *Hobbit* production company defends NZ film subsidies. Radio New Zealand. Retrieved February 14, 2017, from http://www.radionz.co.nz/news/national/117649/hobbit-production-company-defends-nz-film-subsidies.

Rankin, Jr., A. (1977). *The Hobbit* [Animated TV film]. USA and Japan: Rankin/Bass, Topcraft, ABC Video Enterprises.

Rae, N., & Gray, J. (2007). When Gen-X meet the X-men: Retextualizing comic book reception. In I. Gordon, M. Jancovich, & M. McAllister (Eds.), *Film and comic books* (pp. 86–100). Jackson: University Press of Mississippi.

Rérolle, R. (2012, July 9). Tolkien, l'anneau de la discorde. *Le Monde.* Retrieved November 12, 2016, from http://www.lemonde.fr/culture/article/2012/07/05/tolkien-l-anneau-de-la-discorde_1729858_3246.html.

Rosz, J. (2012, December 4). How much did the first *Hobbit* movie cost to make and market? *Media Market Journal.* Retrieved February 14, 2017, from http://www.mediamarketjournal.com/2012/12/how-much-did-the-hobbit-an-unexpected-journey-cost-to-make-and-market/.

Shieff, S. (2006). Well-laundered elves. In M. Kavka, J. Lawn, & M. Paul (Eds.), *Gothic New Zealand: The darker side of Kiwi culture* (pp. 111–119). Dunedin: Otago University Press.

Shippey, T. (2000). *J. R. R. Tolkien: Author of the century.* London: HarperCollins.

Trültzsch-Wijnen, S., & de Sousa, V. (2016). Watching *The Hobbit* in two European countries: The views of younger audiences and readers in Austria and Portugal. *Participations: Journal of Audience and Reception Studies, 13*(2), 469–495.

Wasko, J., & Shanadi, G. (2006). More than just rings: Merchandise for them all. In E. Mathijs (Ed.), *The Lord of the Rings: Popular culture in global context* (pp. 23–42). London and New York: Wallflower.

CHAPTER 4

Unexpected Controversies Cast a Shadow Over Middle-Earth

INTRODUCTION

If the emphasis in the previous chapter was on 'cinematic desire'—on what differently resourced and affiliated viewers were anticipating, imagining and hoping for in advance of seeing *An Unexpected Journey* (*AUJ*)—this chapter scopes similar territory but uses a different theoretical lens to understand it. Here, we are interested in our respondents' perceptions of the industrial processes of filmmaking, especially in the context of the intensification of size and spectacle we have referred to as blockbusterisation, which requires a commensurate increase in investment in production and marketing. Media corporations seek to help fund this expenditure by securing partnerships, subsidies and other cost efficiencies, and vigilantly guard their investments. In exploring this focus, we are contributing to a body of research which explores the complex interactions between contexts of cultural production, economic activities and audience responses to transnational cinema (Higbee and Lim 2010; Waetjen and Gibson 2007), with the intention of situating the meaning-making operations of potential and actual audience members within a structural-historical perspective that acknowledges the material conditions under which cultural texts are produced and consumed (Waetjen and Gibson 2007).

For many film viewers, information about the realities of production is usually filtered through processes of commodity sign production, circulation and desire. Our account of prefigurative activities in the previous

© The Author(s) 2017
C. Michelle et al., *Fans, Blockbusterisation, and the Transformation of Cinematic Desire*, DOI 10.1057/978-1-137-59616-1_4

chapter showed that reports on the successful aspects of the production process—in the form of blogs, vlogs and news items both on and offline—formed an important part of the marketing strategy used to build and maintain relationships with fans and other potential viewers. However, problems and controversies that occur during the pre-production and production phases are not usually actively publicised by a film's producers; rather, these become visible once reported by news media or perhaps related in online forums as rumour or 'insider information', the significance of which remains open to interpretation. Occasionally, these controversies themselves constitute moments that make evident the material *consequences* of the conflicts and concordances between global and national forces that are inherent within transnational filmmaking, rendering them subject to public discussion and debate.

This chapter relates to one such moment: an industrial dispute involving the Australasian actors' union that, in 2010, threatened to derail the New Zealand-based production of the *Hobbit* trilogy. In pursuing a solution to the dispute, Sir Peter Jackson, Warner Bros and the government of New Zealand inadvertently exposed the connections between flows of transnational capital and the political influence wielded by both globally connected media corporations and highly connected local citizens. In the aftermath, a series of documents relating to the case, released by the New Zealand Ombudsman in early 2013, revealed additional aspects of Peter Jackson's involvement as he had exerted direct influence on the government to ensure a favourable resolution for the project's sake. We propose that the interests of global capital prevailed in this instance both materially and discursively due to the production and naturalisation of a confluence of interests between Jackson's and Warner Bros' pursuit of their creative and commercial concerns, and the New Zealand government's furthering of its neo-liberal economic and labour policies.

As Chap. 3 illustrated, while different pre-viewers had various reasons for wanting to see *AUJ*, and a minority also had varying grounds to be guarded about the likely outcome, overall the prevailing mood at this time was optimistic. Here, however, we focus on moments of ambivalence to pursue two lines of enquiry. The first seeks to find out whether our respondents' awareness of the New Zealand *Hobbit* crisis would affect their feelings toward and desire to see the forthcoming trilogy. The *Hobbit* labour dispute and its controversial resolution had international implications and generated extensive media coverage locally and abroad; but was it known about, understood and evaluated in similar ways by international and local respondents? The second (related) line of questioning explores whether films aimed at a global audience do, in practice, evoke global readings and responses. Did *Hobbit* audiences around the world deploy globalised, deculturalised modes of response, as suggested by Kuipers and de Kloet (2009) in relation to the *Lord of the Rings* (*LotR*) films? Alternatively, were there discernible distinctions in audience receptions, perhaps reflecting the influence of more localised national, political and cultural affiliations?

CRITICAL TRANSNATIONALISM AND THE NEW ERA OF GLOBALISED FILM PRODUCTION

New Zealand is a small economy that has, for several decades, pursued a strategy of encouraging international capital investment in local industries. The growth of film production projects, which typically involve 'the global dispersion of production sites; the global dispersion of labouring agents . . . and cross-border partnerships, collaborations, and co-productions in terms of financial investment and creative talent' (Chung 2012, p. 28), has been seen as one field of opportunity which could capitalise on the country's human and natural resources. In particular, the government of New Zealand has promoted the country as a premium site for digital effects design, and has publicised both its spectacular scenery and its highly capable yet relatively inexpensive film workers in order to attract internationally funded location shoots and post-production projects (Jones 2008; Thompson 2007). Consequently, the New Zealand film industry has come to realise the instability involved with being only one of several comparable 'nodes' in a transnational film production network where control nonetheless remains in the hands of global media companies which frequently reappraise the relative risks and advantages of specific locations, as well as the competitiveness of suitable production facilities (Wasko and Erickson 2008).

While the sources and activities of personnel and facilities on such transnational collaborations are usually dispersed and heterogeneous, the nation state and the systems of regulation and governance that constitute its sovereign power nevertheless remain significant for both enabling and constraining the financial and legal manoeuvres that attract transnational projects to particular production sites and workforces (Jin 2011; Sassen 2006). As Gao (2009) has asserted, governments often use policies around film production to pursue specific economic, cultural and political objectives. Companies based elsewhere, in turn, rely on host nations to maintain local conditions favourable to capital accumulation (Wood 2002; as cited in Jin 2011). When those parallel agendas converge to produce a concordance of interests (Habermas 1991), a variety of concessions may be made (such as production subsidies and policy accommodations) which the less powerful party, usually the one seeking to attract the production work to its territory, may perceive as unavoidable and even highly desirable.

PETER JACKSON'S CHANGING STATUS AND INCREASING CHALLENGES

Within the transnational filmmaking environment particular individuals, often directors, come to represent what is, in fact, a complex apparatus of roles and sites of decision-making. As noted in the previous chapter, Peter Jackson filled this role for *The Hobbit* as he had done with *LotR*, and one line of clear differentiation among the pre-viewer perspectives we identified was the widely diverging opinions of Peter Jackson and his capabilities, related in no small part to the controversy addressed here.

The tremendous global success of the *LotR* film trilogy in the early 2000s had been particularly delightful—for Jackson and New Line Studios, for many Tolkien enthusiasts, and for the New Zealand filmmaking and tourist industries—because it had by no means been assured. Until that point, Jackson had been a successful regional director, beginning with low-budget splatter comedies and developing into a skilled director of genre films, including the ghost comedy *The Frighteners* (1996), in conjunction with USA-based DreamWorks Studios. However, the alchemy of a sufficiently faithful adaptation of Tolkien's *The Lord of the Rings* novels by Jackson and his writing team, the casting of a large ensemble of charismatic actors, the choice of spectacular natural locations and the creative labour of hundreds of technicians crafting real and digital effects changed all that, producing a series of films that earned more than US$3 billion at the box office and widespread professional recognition. By the time all the awards had been accumulated in 2004—the Oscars, BAFTAs and so on—Jackson had become one of an elite group of producer/director/writers who could be trusted to make a good return on the highest levels of media corporation ('Hollywood') investment, while also being able to command substantial production subsidies from his government.

Jackson and his partner Fran Walsh had wanted to make *The Hobbit* before making *LotR*, but ongoing difficulties over rights held by MGM had led them to film *LotR* first. Now, presumably, the success of that trilogy would make things easier. However, when such large sums of money are involved, cordiality in business relationships can sometimes be difficult to sustain. In March 2005 Jackson had filed a lawsuit in the USA against New Line for a larger share of the profits from merchandising associated with *LotR* (BBC News 2006). This action meant that, for a time, New Line were not prepared to work with Jackson again, before agreeing to take him on as *The Hobbit*'s producer (*not* director) in 2007 (BBC News 2007). The instability continued with, amongst other lawsuits, an eventually successful challenge from the Tolkien Estate for a profit share. That estate sued again, just before the launch of *AUJ*, demanding Warner Bros desist from producing *LotR*-themed slot machines (Belloni 2012). There was more change when Guillermo del Toro, the original director for *The Hobbit*, resigned from the role in May 2010, citing production delays and resulting conflicting commitments (Bierly 2010). It was not until July 2010 that Jackson announced that he would be directing the project after all, and not long after, that it would be filmed in 3D (Chitwood 2010). There was controversy, particularly among Tolkien loyalists, when he later announced, in July 2012, that the project would now be a trilogy (Maegwyn 2012). And, by the time we conducted our pre-viewing survey in late 2012, there was an additional controversy in the mix: allegations of animal abuse associated with the *Hobbit* production, a debate we do not have space to deal with here (see Artiquez 2013; Carlson 2012; Newkirk 2012). Fans from around the world who followed entertainment news (as did an overall 74.5% of the members of our pre-viewing groups) could not have failed to notice that the run-up to *The Hobbit*'s cinematic debut had been unusually turbulent.

Just as *LotR* had become a global phenomenon which needed to work for audiences in multiple locations despite being produced in New Zealand, Jackson, as a producer, director and partner in production and post-production businesses, now also operated from various positions within the networked apparatus of transnational filmmaking. Furthermore, as the following account of his handling of the *Hobbit* labour dispute demonstrates, it was sometimes not clear to onlookers when Jackson's decision-making was his own and when it was being influenced by the economics and protocols of the Hollywood studio system.

THE *HOBBIT* LABOUR DISPUTE SHAKES UP MIDDLE-EARTH

The New Zealand '*Hobbit* crisis' (Handel 2013) had three periods in the limelight. It first came to public attention in September 2010 when media reported that actors who belonged to the New Zealand union Actors' Equity, a subsidiary of the Australian-based Media Entertainment and Arts Alliance (MEAA), had given warning of their intention to withdraw their labour from the production until a satisfactory agreement on collective working terms and conditions had been negotiated (Kelly 2011). Due to MEAA's affiliation with the international Screen Actors' Guild, this proposed ban would also prevent international actors from working on the *Hobbit* set. Rather than negotiating with MEAA, however, Wingnut Films, Sir Peter Jackson's production company, began to claim that the production could be closed down or relocated offshore if the actors persisted in their demands (Cardy and Johnston 2010).

The conflicting claims around the dispute provided almost daily material for local news media during September–November 2010. It was also the subject of over 100 news items internationally (see for instance Handel 2010; Cieply and Rose 2010). Considering the importance of the production both to fans of Jackson and Tolkien worldwide and to New Zealand's filmmaking labour force, these threats aroused strong emotions on both sides. While New Zealand's umbrella union organisation, the Council of Trade Unions, stepped in to assist in settling the dispute, other craft workers fearful of losing job opportunities on the *Hobbit* production participated in a protest march in Wellington on 20 October 2010 (Smellie 2010) supporting Jackson's stance and demanding the right to work. The next day, MEAA/Actors' Equity announced the threat of industrial action had been withdrawn (Cheng 2010b).

Nevertheless, Jackson and associates persevered in asserting that the New Zealand production context was still too insecure for their comfort and that Warner Bros was still thinking about moving the production to another territory. A further public rally in support of the *Hobbit* production was held in Wellington on 25 October, addressed by the city's mayor. On 26 October, the president of New Line, Toby Emmerich, and the president of Warner Home Entertainment, Kevin Tsujihara, flew in from the USA and immediately had access to government officials, including the nation's leader, Prime Minister John Key. The next day Key held a press conference announcing that consequent to a commitment that the production would stay in New Zealand, and in return for material promoting the country as a tourist destination being included on DVD versions of the *Hobbit* films, Warner Bros would be the beneficiary of a further NZ$34 million in tax subsidies.

In itself, this set of negotiations was not exceptional. Other countries also make subsidies available to boost their attractiveness as production locations (Wasko and Erickson 2008). Such practices may signify submission to the business strategies of global companies such as Warner Bros Pictures, which characterises its commercial model on its website as one that 'mitigates risk while maximizing productivity and capital' (Warner Bros 2017). On the other hand, this kind of trade-off may also be read as part of a 'strategic' glocalised reaction to the assertive self-interest of transnational film productions, which demand a price from their hosts for enabling their participation in the global economy (Walker and Tipples 2011).

However, on 28 October there was an unexpected *policy* accommodation to Jackson's and Warner Bros' desire for a more 'secure' labour environment; one that would have a radical impact on New Zealand's employment law. Eschewing long-established customs of public consultation, the government forced through the Employment Relations (Film Production Work) Amendment Bill under the protocol of 'urgency'. This piece of legislation made it impossible for local screen-production workers any longer to hold the status of employees: they were redefined as workers on contract, thereby depriving them of the rights available to employees (Wilson 2011) and, as McAndrew and Risak (2012, p. 71) note, immunising 'the industry against both union-negotiated and legislated protections for workers, both for the *Hobbit* production and for the future'. This rushed amendment of labour law to prevent New Zealand film production workers (not only actors) from organising as a group in order to enjoy standard legal employment protections was a move without precedent within the international film industry (Handel 2013). It was, said Prime Minister John Key, designed to ensure 'that New Zealand law in this area is settled to give film producers like Warner Bros the confidence they need to produce their movies in this country' (Key 2010; see also Cheng 2010a). Coincidentally, the move was also consistent with previous efforts by the National Party-led government to limit the power of local trade unions, to liberalise employment law against the interests of workers, and to encourage global capital to invest in the country (Haworth 2011). We therefore suggest that the *Hobbit* employment law and tax changes constitute not merely a financial and legislative response to ameliorate Warner Bros' and Jackson's anxieties, but the material *outcome* of a concordance of interests between the goals of global capital, a select group of influential citizens, and the implicit anti-union agenda of a neo-liberal ruling party.

While public awareness of this issue had subsided once production of the *Hobbit* trilogy got underway, it came to prominence again in the last quarter of 2012: the period in which we were conducting our pre-figurative research. The majority of public sphere commentary was now critical of the roles played by Jackson, Warner Bros and the government in terminating the union threat to the production (see Chapman 2012; Wall 2012). There was a further intensification of coverage in January 2013 when the New Zealand Ombudsman made a ruling that previously inaccessible correspondence between various parties to the dispute and government ministers could now be made public (McGee 2013). These documents made it evident that Jackson and his partner Fran Walsh, as well as the Screen Production and Development Association (SPADA, which represents producers and directors), had easy access to government ministers at the time of the original dispute; moreover, the government had actively aided them by providing Jackson with legal advice that supported his decision not to negotiate with actors' union representatives. It was further observable that Jackson's statements to the media during the dispute were not always corroborated by information emanating from other parties. For instance, Jackson admitted in an 18 October email to an advisor in the Office of the Minister for Economic Development that Warner Bros' threats to relocate the production had not come about solely because of the union's demand for a collective agreement. Rather, they also stemmed from Warner's pursuit of a greater goal: to ensure that the legal status of the local workforce was determined in a way that suited them, thereby lessening Warner's financial exposure. The newly released materials also showed that MEAA had terminated its industrial action as early as 17 October, but had agreed to let Warner Bros announce that development. Warners' then held off making their announcement until *after* the 20 October protest march (Kelly 2011). The production workers taking part in that protest, therefore, did so under the misapprehension that they might still lose the opportunity to work on *The Hobbit*. This misapprehension, and the very fact the noisy and emotional march took place, also usefully stoked public and political anxieties about the possible loss of the *Hobbit* production.

The events of the '*Hobbit* crisis' have since become elements of an instructive case study of the risks of globalised business and labour cultures, written about by academics from several different disciplines (Conor 2015; Haworth 2011; Jess 2015; McAndrew and Risak 2012; Walker and Tipples 2013; Wynn 2015). One commentator has described the tactics used as representing a 'refeudalisation of the social sphere' (Wynn 2015, p. 3), while others have pointed to the undermining of New Zealanders' rights to self-governance (see Scherer 2010; Wilson 2011). It has been noted that the country was now 'the only nation with a non-unionized English-language film industry' (Handel 2013, p. 60), a precedent which has implications for other nation states thinking about ways to improve their competitive advantage. Nevertheless, the fact that a set of events is of historical significance does not necessarily mean that it will have the same salience for people who have a keen interest in enjoying a satisfying entertainment experience.

POLITICS, 'COMMON SENSE' AND DESIRE FOR A LONG-AWAITED CINEMATIC EXPERIENCE SHAPE AUDIENCE RESPONSES

An initial uncertainty about events and motivations in the labour dispute and confusion over the roles of key agents in it did shadow public discourse in the period before the release of the first *Hobbit* film. Nevertheless, the threat of disruption and the subsequent concessions made to ensure the smooth running of the *Hobbit* film production had been received and evaluated in various ways by differently-located audience members, who also possessed differing degrees of desire to experience this particular output of transnational filmmaking practices. Our data shows that whether respondents had access to, and were prepared to deploy, critical knowledge of the material environment in which the trilogy had been produced was dependent not only on geopolitical factors, but also on viewers' political leanings as well as their pre-existing attachment to a specific type of consumption experience. Generally, the tone of fan discussion of the labour issue during the period before production started had been one of anxiety that New Zealand might forfeit its status as the obvious physical location for the second Tolkien trilogy, and consequently that the *Hobbit* films might have lost an important aspect of their continuity with the *LotR* movies.

In the following section, we analyse participants' responses to a pair of questions in our pre-viewing survey asking 'Were you aware that New Zealand adapted its labour laws and gave Warner Bros a tax break to ensure this film production stayed in New Zealand?' and (if yes), 'To what extent does knowing about the labour laws/tax break impact on your feelings about the *Hobbit* film production?' (Table 4.1). Overall, 59.5% of our 1000 respondents said they had knowledge of the *Hobbit* employment law change and of the increased tax subsidy. The majority (89.5%) also completed the follow-up question, including many who had answered 'no' to the first question. We first discuss foregrounded themes amongst those who approved of the subsidy and law changes and, observing the dominant role of particular discursive framings, speculate on the power of commodity fetishism to shape cinematic desires. Next, we report on responses from people who expressed ambivalence or concern about the perceived 'downsides' of transnational film production, illustrating how these responses were framed by the intersecting dynamics of political and prefigurative orientations, differences in geographical and social proximity, and knowledge of subordinated discourses.

In our pre-viewing survey, most New Zealand and overseas respondents who provided qualitative comments either asserted that the *Hobbit* labour dispute had failed to impact on their feelings about the film (34.9%), or actually approved of the way the issue had been handled (27.9%), with most of the latter being identified as *LotR Film Fans*. One particular group of 62 'approvers' (6.9% of all who responded) emphasised the importance of the *Hobbit* films being shot in New Zealand to maintain visual continuity with the *LotR* trilogy, as suggested by this 25-year-old American man: 'New Zealand has already become uniquely associated with Middle-earth to many Tolkien fans and nonfans. It was an ideal setting for the *LotR* films and will, no doubt, be just as fitting for the *Hobbit* films. The films would probably not be the same filmed elsewhere' (*LotR Film Fan*).

A somewhat larger group cited the probable economic benefits that would result from the film's production staying in New Zealand (97; 10.8%). Participants from outside New Zealand were often somewhat vague in their assessment of these benefits; for example, 'New Zealand certainly takes Tolkien seriously! It's a money maker for the country so why wouldn't they invest in it?' (American woman, 18, *Tolkien*

Table 4.1   Categories of response to the handling of the New Zealand *Hobbit* labour crisis

Q: To what extent does knowing about the labour laws/tax break impact on your feelings about the Hobbit film production?
Coded open-response question (N = 895)

Primary categories of response	Major subcategories[a]	Number of respondents (%)
Ambivalent (*n* = 104; 11.6%)	Keeping it local vs implications	32 (3.6%)
	Questioned economic benefits to NZ	32 (3.6%)
	Critical of Warner Bros	29 (3.2%)
	Concerned about employment rights	21 (2.3%)
	Critical of NZ government	19 (2.1%)
	Pragmatic solution?	16 (1.8%)
	Concerned, but a separate issue	11 (1.2%)
Approved (*n* = 250; 27.9%)	Economic benefits to NZ	97 (10.8%)
	NZ location important	62 (6.9%)
	Local product	50 (5.6%)
	Industry support	31 (3.5%)
	Pragmatic solution	29 (3.2%)
	Unions the problem	23 (2.6%)
	Support NZ government	19 (2.1%)
	Support Peter Jackson	11 (1.2%)
Disapproved (*n* = 110; 12.3%)	Critical of NZ government	32 (3.6%)
	Critical of Warner Bros	31 (3.5%)
	Disapprove, but a separate issue	27 (3.0%)
	Concerned about employment rights	18 (2.0%)
	Critical of Peter Jackson	18 (2.0%)
	Critical of capitalism	12 (1.3%)
Neutral (*n* = 20; 2.2%) No impact (*n* = 312; 34.9%) Insufficient info/Other/ Unclear (*n* = 99; 11.1%)		

[a] Several smaller subcategories are omitted here; multiple codes were used in the case of complex responses

Aficionado). By contrast, New Zealand residents tended to be more aware of specific desirable outcomes: 'If it is for the betterment of New Zealand—tourism, promotion, bringing in investment dollars—and gives employment to many who would otherwise be unemployed, why not?' (New Zealand woman, 61, *Anxious Investor*).

For 31 respondents (3.5%), the labour law alterations and increase in tax subsidy were welcome evidence of the government's investment in its local film industry, as with this 44-year-old American woman who said 'I followed the news coverage, and I agreed with Peter Jackson and New Zealand. I think it is good to invest in local industry, especially art as industry. I wish my country did more of that' (*LotR Film Fan*).

Twenty-nine respondents (3.2%) viewed the increased tax subsidies as a pragmatic tactic that capitalised on the contemporary 'reality' of global capital flows, and several noted that other territories also paid subsidies to secure transnational film projects:

> I think it's a smart move of New Zealand. I wish our Dutch government gave film productions tax breaks; they're killing the film industry here. So yeah, clever move on New Zealand's part. (Dutch man, 24; *LotR Film Fan*)

> The UK has done vaguely similar things for productions such as *Harry Potter* (British man, 36; crossloader)[1]

These affirmative responses rarely brought up the regulatory or governmental outcomes of the controversy, nor showed awareness of the details of the labour law alterations, the unilateral nature of which was, as noted above, extraordinary. Those who did refer to the dispute often recycled formulations employed by the government to position the law changes as essential to keeping the *Hobbit* project in New Zealand, maintaining workforce participation in the domestic film industry, boosting economic activity and inspiring inbound tourism (Key 2010; NZPA 2010):

> The change to the labour laws was a clarification that made no difference really. The tax break was also necessary. Both resulted in hundreds of jobs and thousands of visitors. I have no hard feelings about the production at all. (New Zealand man, 43, *LotR Film Fan*)

I'm a lawyer who has studied New Zealand's labor laws. It was a specific exception that allowed them to continue using foreign actors . . . and it makes sense to me. It doesn't affect the vast majority of New Zealand workers, and it will bring hundreds of millions in revenue to New Zealand, so it was worth it. (American, 59, *Tolkien Aficionado*)

While disavowal of the more controversial aspects of the New Zealand government's handling of the issue is likely due to some respondents lacking a close connection to localised discursive framings of the events, it also indicates how, for many people worldwide, acceptance of the strategies that global conglomerates employ to maximise the value of their investments has come to be understood as common sense, as simply 'the way the film industry works' (New Zealand woman, 22, *LotR Film Fan*).

Other respondents were so hopeful that New Zealand would receive economic benefits from hosting the production of *The Hobbit* that they enthusiastically endorsed the steps taken to delegitimise the union protest. For 23 respondents (2.6%), most of whom were men and several of whom were New Zealanders, the unions were guilty of obstructing the *Hobbit* production. These respondents assumed the threat to relocate filming to another country was genuine, and expressed strong approval of the way the government had handled the problem:

The New Zealand labour law fiasco was the result of the idiocy of one group (NZ Equity) attempting to fight a corporate giant without realising that they never had a chance of victory and that they were also putting other people's livelihoods at risk without consultation. (New Zealand man, 33, *LotR Film Fan*)

It is clear, then, that although the New Zealand union movement had a different account of both events in the *Hobbit* actors' dispute and its own motivations in relation to them, it had been unsuccessful in asserting that account within the broader public domain, as Handel (2013) observes. Nor had many people picked up on the profound implications of the manner in which the dispute was settled. It was also apparent that many respondents, wherever they were located geographically, had a strong desire to see *AUJ*; one that frequently precluded or superseded any substantive or critical engagement with the material conditions under which the film had been produced. Cinematic desire, as we have already noted, was fermented by the production vlogs, official Facebook posts and other seemingly 'direct' insights into the *Hobbit* project, all carefully designed to promote a positive view of filming. As noted by Mathijs (2005, p. 456), 'Film companies have long capitalized on pre-production tales about the circumstances under which films were made, in order to invite a particular reception' and 'manage problematic discourses surrounding films'. For prefigurative audiences eager to see the first film, any strategy the production companies used to ensure viability was viewed as a valid means of materialising the story content:

> New Zealand seems to be willing to make certain that they are friendly to the film industry and as an American, I am all for free enterprise and commend them for being competitive … . Admittedly, I don't follow New Zealand labour laws or politics, but I have seen the production videos and did not see anything to concern myself with [and] have read no alarming accounts about the filming. (American woman, 41, *LotR Film Fan*)

As this comment reveals, official prefigurative materials clearly also provided resources with which to counter any allegations of disaffection on the *Hobbit* set.

It may also be the case that many fans of either or both Jackson's and Tolkien's world-making actively eschewed deeper consideration of the various controversies associated with the film's production in an effort to avoid the uncomfortable state of cognitive dissonance, which might undermine the anticipated pleasures of a longed-for entertainment experience. A sense of disengagement from issues associated with the labour dispute was palpable in the nearly 35% of respondents who told us that although they knew about the *Hobbit* labour controversy, that knowledge did not impact on their feelings about the forthcoming film. While the majority offered no further comment, those who did often distinguished between the film as an aesthetic object and the conditions under which it was produced, making comments such as 'It's all about the story for me, not what happened during the filming or any other controversies' (New Zealand woman, 16, *Tolkien Aficionado*); 'Don't care too much, just want to see the movie to be honest' (Indian woman living in New Zealand, 16, *LotR Film Fan*).

These and similar responses perhaps reflect the degree to which this film series, and the consumption experience it offered, had become fetishised cultural objects for many dedicated fans, inviting the classic Marxist analysis that commodity fetishism obscures awareness of exploitative capitalist labour processes. In these terms, both the original *LotR* trilogy and its soon-to-be-viewed *Hobbit* prequels could be regarded as highly desirable commodities ascribed with almost magical powers for facilitating immersive enchantment. As Mosco notes, 'the commodity not only congeals social relations and hides the struggle over value, but takes on a life and a power of its own, over that of both the producers and consumers' (2009, p. 131). Many of our research participants apparently hoped to consume *The Hobbit* as a 'pure' commodity, unstained by controversy over events that occurred out of sight during its production. Hence, they disengaged with, and in some cases actively disavowed, any criticisms that might diminish their future cinematic pleasures.

The Collision of Pleasure and Knowledge: Discursive Contestation and the *Hobbit* Labour Dispute

For others, awareness of this particular controversy was less readily set aside, with 104 (11.6% of) respondents expressing ambivalent views, being conflicted over competing interpretations of the actions of the parties involved: half of these respondents were resident in New Zealand. Their ambivalence particularly highlighted the disjunction between the claimed advantages of increasing the tax subsidies and changing the labour law, and the critiques advanced by unionists, academics and journalists. Thirty-two of these respondents (3.6% overall) were sceptical that the claimed economic benefits would result from hosting this transnational film production. A similar number, including several New Zealanders, were torn between their preference to see the production stay in the country and taking a cynical view of the actual intent and possible consequences of the government's fiscal and policy concessions (3.6%). The way in which a global conglomerate was perceived to have dominated a small country was also criticised by 29 respondents (3.2%), who disapproved of Warner Bros' actions. However, the removal of employee-status rights for workers on the *Hobbit* production was concerning mainly, but not exclusively, for local pre-viewers: only 21 respondents (2.3%) cited this as an important motivation for their ambivalence.

Of greater significance perhaps are the further 110 participants (12.3%) who expressed clear disagreement with the manner in which the

Hobbit dispute had been handled. New Zealanders comprised 62.9% of these respondents, with the strongest expressions of disapproval coming from local *Jackson Critics* and *Anxious Investors*, who often framed their comments by drawing on oppositional discourses circulating locally. The most frequent target of criticism was the government of New Zealand, with 32 respondents (3.6%) expressing disapproval of the concessions made: 'I don't like how the New Zealand government has held their ankles for Hollywood's best interests' (New Zealand woman, 34, *Anxious Investor*) and, 'It's no surprise that our current Government is willing to dismiss laws that New Zealanders value; I just hope the success of the film doesn't justify such acts' (New Zealand woman, 19, *Anxious Investor*).

Others judged that the incident had been caused by unsatisfactory processes associated with transnational capitalism, in that 31 (3.5%) directed their disapproval toward Warner Bros, as in these examples: 'It makes me annoyed that a company is, to my mind, abusing workers for extra profit. Warner Bros makes enough profit as it is' (New Zealand man, 19, *Anxious Investor*); 'It's scary how much power the studio has, and how easy it was for them to put successful pressure on our government. On the other hand, they've done the same with every other country, and are playing one off against the other' (New Zealand man, 69, *Tolkien Aficionado*).

The role that Peter Jackson had played in the affair interested many New Zealanders in particular, and featured prominently in comments made about specific Q items. Although just 18 respondents (2.0%) explicitly named Jackson in responses dealing with the employment law and tax subsidy issues, the tone of their remarks was often strongly critical: 'To me . . . it's par for the course for a Jackson production. He has no ethics or principles and this is just one more example of those character flaws' (American woman, 68, *Jackson Critic*); 'I'm disappointed in Jackson for not upholding high ethical standards' (American man, 43, *Tolkien Aficionado*). One local commentator picked up on the concordance of interests present in the conflict, asserting that:

> Peter Jackson colluded with the government and Warner etc. to disadvantage New Zealand actors. It doesn't fit with the feel good relationship that we had with him and the production team with *LotR* and the positive statements actors have made about New Zealand in the past. Our New

Zealand character was spoiled by these high finance deals. (New Zealand woman, 55, *Anxious Investor*)

The qualitative materials we gathered therefore demonstrate just how much some New Zealanders' evaluations of Jackson have altered since the release of the *LotR* trilogy more than a decade ago. At that time, Jackson was elevated to the status of creative, cultural and economic hero for several reasons: for not making the films outside New Zealand; for showcasing Kiwi technical innovation; for breathing new life into the local film industry; and for drawing attention to the country internationally (Haworth 2011; Jones 2008; Thompson 2007). Thornley (2006, p. 110) argues that Jackson's success with *LotR* symbolised an idealised 'Kiwi' ability to challenge and 'conquer Hollywood', as opposed to being seduced or suborned by the forces of globalisation (Jones 2008). Now, a dozen years later, with his personal wealth reported at NZ$560 million (Rogers and Steeman 2011) and having ascended the ranks of the New Zealand Honours system, *Sir* Peter Jackson had both been assimilated into the nation's business and cultural elites (Jackson and Court 2010), and evidently secured privileged access to government ministers (Haworth 2011; Walker and Tipples 2013). For some of our respondents, this change from outsider to member of the Establishment had, paradoxically, diminished Jackson's public reputation.

A further 18 respondents (2.0%) echoed concerns about employment rights while stating their disapproval of the rushed law changes, as in this instance: 'I strongly disagree that the rights of New Zealand workers should be compromised for the sake of producing a series of movies' (New Zealand man, 40, *LotR Film Fan*). However, amongst another group of 27 disapprovers (3.0%), the dynamic of commodity desire competing with political awareness was again evident. This 62-year-old American living in New Zealand neatly expressed the ensuing internal conflict:

It makes it impossible to get excited about seeing the films. I don't know if I can get past the ugliness and cynicism of the films' conception long enough to enjoy the finished product. Some of my responses probably seem contradictory because of this; I want to see the films, but can I get past the actions of the filmmakers enough to enjoy them? (*Jackson Critic*)

For others, however, any such conflict between politics and pleasure was consciously minimised: 'It does impact on my feelings, and I'm very sorry that a resolution could not be reached that was fairer to the New Zealand actors, but I am not going to think about that when I'm watching the film' (New Zealand woman, 57, *LotR Film Fan*); 'I don't necessarily agree with what was done, but it doesn't diminish my desire to see the film' (Singaporean man, 34, *Tolkien Aficionado*). So, even among some of those who were aware and disapproved of the actions undertaken to secure the production in New Zealand, commodity desire effectively prevailed over any residual political or ethical disquiet.

THE SIGNIFICANCE OF PROXIMITY IN THE RESPONSES OF PREFIGURATIVE AUDIENCES

Further analysis identified significant associations between pre-viewing perspectives, nationality, social location, and our participants' degree of awareness of and concern about the *Hobbit* labour dispute. As the above analysis suggests, geographical proximity clearly made a difference, since 78.6% of those resident in New Zealand knew about the controversy, compared with 52.1% of non-residents. *Anxious Investors* had the greatest level of awareness of the employment law and tax issues (91.4%), followed by *Jackson Critics* (80%), dropping to a low of 52% among *Tolkien Aficionados*. Within these groups proximity was clearly a factor, since it was New Zealand-based *Jackson Critics* who exhibited the strongest concern about Warner's actions in relation to the *Hobbit* labour issue, giving a related Q statement an average ranking of 7.9 out of 9 (with 9 signifying 'most strongly agree'). This group also more strongly disagreed with Q statements that expressed nationalistic pride in New Zealand's role in the production (2.3) or conveyed approval of the increase in government subsidy (3.9). By contrast, *Anxious Investors*, most of whom were locals, gave relatively high rankings to statements expressing concern about worker exploitation (6.5) and nationalistic pride (6.8), and expressed even higher levels of agreement with the government's move to subsidise the trilogy's production (7.6).

Geographical proximity to the context of production thus clearly sensitised respondents to factors affecting the material conditions under which the *Hobbit* films were produced. While some of the New Zealanders' responses were essentially similar to those of respondents from other territories, many were not. Both these differences and similarities indicate the complex discursive field within which contemporary audience members observed the contestation between a nation state, labour organisations, a major media conglomerate, and influential citizens with professional interests in a transnational film production as each struggled to define and assert interests which converged and diverged at different points.

The presence of competing understandings of a controversial issue within the local public domain also provided our local respondents with access to a range of discursive resources with which to formulate their own responses to the *Hobbit* labour dispute. These discursive frames largely echoed those being articulated within the broader public and policy domains, within which not all voices were equally powerful. Consequently, while the majority of the more critical assessments of Jackson's, Warner Bros' and the New Zealand government's actions came from people living in New Zealand, many others in the same location expressed *approval* of the methods used to resolve the *Hobbit* dispute and frequently draw on terminology very similar to that employed by local officials. Answers provided by locals also tended to have a stronger emotional tone than those from international participants, reflecting the greater prominence of this controversy within local media coverage as well as the more immediate salience of the issues to local respondents.

That said, our findings reveal that proximity is not merely geographical, but may also involve 'closeness' in terms of economic, political and other cultural affiliations. For example, certain occupational groupings exhibited stronger approval of the New Zealand government's actions, irrespective of location: 57.1% of government officials approved, along with 53.8 of tradespersons and small business operators. Noticeably lower rates of approval were evident among managers and executives (35.3%), as well as creative artists and media producers (34.1%). Those more likely to disapprove of the government's actions included higher-level professionals (21.1%), middle professionals and public servants (18.4%), and once again, creative artists or media producers (17.1%), suggesting polarisation among this special interest group. Approval, as well as disapproval, was positively related to income, with those on higher incomes expressing stronger feelings one way or the other.

Thus, it was not *exclusively* New Zealanders who expressed concern, positive or negative, about the employment dispute and the manner of its resolution. Rather, well-educated middle- and higher-level professionals were more likely to express strong views on this issue whatever their national location. This clustering around occupation, education and income suggests that while nationality remained a significant factor in shaping responses to a matter that was, on the face of it, locally specific, other interests and affiliations were also significant and sometimes more so. This is perhaps unsurprising: while the specifics may differ, the globalisation of blockbuster film production means that comparable controversies and discursive contestations are increasingly evident in multiple locations.

CONCLUSION

This chapter has shed light on the discursive resources that potential audience members drew on in evaluating the interplay of politics and power around a localised but globally significant production issue; one with clear salience for transnational film projects undertaken in other parts of the world. The lengths that both *The Hobbit's* producers and the New Zealand government were prepared to go to in order to 'secure' a favourable labour environment for the production has potentially significant implications for the employment conditions of film workers in other national contexts (Handel 2013; Wynn 2015). In terms of our findings, the various ways in which our participants engaged with, disengaged from or were ambivalent about these consequential legal and financial issues ultimately reveals the power of commodity desire to override concerns about the social and material conditions of transnational film production.

This case also illuminates the ability of experienced and influential global media companies such as Warner Bros to effectively leverage the anxieties experienced by many smaller nation states and their citizen workers, in a way that serves to further their commercial interests. Increasingly, nation states must compete in a globalised environment in which technical resources and expertise are widely dispersed. The availability of numerous production and post-production centres, which may have variable wage scales, different tax regulations and now also diverse employment environments, are factors influencing decisions about where films will be made. Indeed, these factors, which determine who can profit from a project and at what level, are probably now more influential than the availability of appropriate landscapes, since it is possible for these to be simulated digitally by skilled workers somewhere else—potentially a more cost-effective option. The resulting instability of transnational film production flows produces scenarios in which national players strive to position themselves as the most attractive sites for production within a constantly changing and rapidly expanding global marketplace.

Specifically, in the New Zealand case, the interests of global capital prevailed both materially and discursively through a process of strategic incorporation into the official discourse of the neo-liberal state, which implicitly reframed unprecedented labour reforms as the production of a *concordance of interests with* a global media conglomerate, rather than a *forced capitulation to* its troubling demands. This is similar to the processes that Saskia Sassen (2006) observes when she characterises globalisation as occurring through internal transformations of the state apparatus. The relevance of this insight is apparent in the comments of our respondents, many of whom employed similar discourses to those used by state agents to reframe financial as well as policy changes as the natural and *necessary* entry price for guaranteeing New Zealand's participation in the globalised film production economy. As our analysis illustrates, these localised discursive patterns were repeated internationally, demonstrating the extent to which similar accommodations have become familiar within free-market economies. They signalled many respondents' pragmatic acceptance of, and in some cases enthusiastic endorsement of, the 'common-sense realities' of global production systems, in which nations must strive to maximise their commercial advantages in the hopes of receiving significant reputational, and more especially economic, benefits. New Zealand has been relatively successful in this regard by building on its association with the *LotR* franchise to position itself as 'Middle-earth', and establishing a globally recognisable 'brand' (Thompson 2007). However, committing the local film industry to constantly competing in a global auction to secure the production of foreign-owned CGI-intensive blockbusters clearly has implications for the industry's longer-term sustainability (see Hunt 2013).

While the exchange value of Jackson's earlier *LotR* trilogy was inflated locally through its conflation with New Zealand's national identity and global ambitions (Thompson 2007), physical proximity to the *Hobbit* production, along with access to alternative discursive understandings via pre-existing political affiliations and varying degrees of knowledge of the movie industry, encouraged some of our respondents to query the actual costs and rewards of New Zealand's involvement. The presence of a local cluster of critical responses to actions and reactions in the *Hobbit* dispute suggests that pre-viewer opinions were not entirely shaped by the marketing and publicity endeavours of the Warner Bros production entity, but also took cognisance of public sphere and online debates around an issue geographically positioned in New Zealand, but having some degree of global relevance.

In designing this research we were curious as to whether we would identify globalised forms of engagement with *AUJ* in the lead-up to its international release. Blockbuster films are designed to be legible and enjoyable for people in many cultures—has geographical and cultural location therefore lost significance in relation to audience response? The answer, at least based on our findings, is both yes, and no. There was enough evidence of distinctively New Zealand-based characteristics and intensities of response to conclude that the increasing hegemony of transnational film productions does not prevent the emergence of glocalised forms of response grounded in geographic and experiential proximity. On the other hand, there was also clear evidence that dominant understandings were widely dispersed and highly influential, including in those settings where oppositional voices were vigorously articulated. Moreover, whatever the physical location of our participants, desire for another opportunity for immersion in the enchanted land of Middle-earth appeared to suppress most respondents' willingness to entertain any criticisms of the social and material conditions of the *Hobbit* production, lest such awareness detract from a longed-for consumption and cultural experience. In the following chapter, we trace the evolution of cinematic desire for the *Hobbit* trilogy from the pre- to post-viewing period. In so doing, we further demonstrate the potential for a fetishised cultural commodity to deliver such highly valued experiences that concerns about the social conditions of their production become effectively supplanted.

This chapter is derived, in part, from an article published in *Transnational Cinemas* on 31 August 2014, available online: http://www.tandfonline.com/doi/full/10.1080/20403526.2014.941185.

NOTE

1. The term 'crossloader' refers to respondents whose Q sorts were significantly associated with more than one of the distinct viewpoints identified through factor analysis.

REFERENCES

Artiquez, B. (2013). Animal holocaust in film: Researching the difference in animal welfare in film from 1903 to 2013 with regard to the work of the American Humane Association, established in 1943. *Dublin Business School*. Retrieved December 15, 2016, from http://esource.dbs.ie/handle/10788/1224.

BBC News. (2006, November 21). *Hobbit* goes ahead without Jackson. BBC News. Retrieved December 13, 2016. from http://news.bbc.co.uk/2/hi/entertainment/6167972.stm.

BBC News. (2007, December 18). Jackson to produce *Hobbit* movies. BBC News. Retrieved December 13, 2016, from http://news.bbc.co.uk/2/hi/entertainment/7150644.stm.

Belloni, M. (2012, November 19). Tolkien estate sues Warner Bros. over *Lord of the Rings* slot machines. *The Hollywood Reporter*. Retrieved December 12, 2016, from http://www.hollywoodreporter.com/thr-esq/tolkien-estate-sues-warner-bros-393212.

Bierly, M. (2010, May 30). Guillermo Del Toro drops out of directing *The Hobbit*. *Entertainment Weekly*. Retrieved February 14, 2017, from http://www.ew.com/article/2010/05/30/guillermo-del-toro-drops-hobbit.

Cardy, T., & Johnston, K. (2010, October 21). *Hobbit* looks headed overseas. *Dominion Post*. Retrieved February 14, 2017, from http://www.stuff.co.nz/business/4255670/Hobbit-looks-headed-overseas.

Carlson. E. (2012, November 12). Peter Jackson denies *Hobbit* animal claims. *Hollywood Reporter*. Retrieved December 15, 2016, from http://www.hollywoodreporter.com/heat-vision/peter-jackson-denies-hobbit-animal-392242.

Chapman, K. (2012, October 6). Some chance of too many takes. *Waikato Times*, p. A8.

Cheng, D. (2010a, October 27). *Hobbit* to stay in NZ. *NZ Herald*. Retrieved February 14, 2017, from http://www.nzherald.co.nz/business/news/article.cfm?c_id=3&objectid=10683486.

Cheng, D. (2010b, December 21). Sir Peter: Actors no threat to *Hobbit*. *NZ Herald*. Retrieved February 14, 2017, from http://www.nzherald.co.nz/nz/news/article.cfm?c_id=1&objectid=10695662.

Chitwood, A. (2010, November 28). Peter Jackson to shoot the *Hobbit* films in 3D with 30 new red epic cameras. *Collider*. Retrieved February 27, 2017, from http://collider.com/peter-jackson-the-hobbit-3d-red-epic-cameras/.

Chung, H. J. (2012). *Kung Fu Panda*: Animated bodies as layered sites of (trans)national identities. *The Velvet Light Trap, 69*, 27–37. doi:10.1353/vlt.2012.0011.

Cieply, M., & Rose, J. (2010, October 27). New Zealand bends and *Hobbit* stays. *The New York Times*. Retrieved February 14, 2017, from http://www.nytimes.com/2010/10/28/business/media/28hobbit.html.

Conor, B. (2015). The Hobbit law: Precarity and market citizenship in cultural production. *Asia Pacific Journal of Arts and Cultural Management, 12*(1), 25–36.

Gao, Z. (2009). Serving a stir-fry of market, culture and politics: On globalization and film policy in China. *Policy Studies, 30*(4), 423–438. doi:10.1080/01442870902899889.

Habermas, J. (1991). *The structural transformation of the public sphere: An inquiry into a category of bourgeois society*. Massachusetts: MIT Press.

Handel, J. (2010, October 24). Desperate to keep *Hobbit*, New Zealand officials meet with Warner Bros. Execs. *Hollywood Reporter*. Retrieved February 14, 2017, from http://www.hollywoodreporter.com/news/desperate-keep-hobbit-new-zealand-32291.

Handel, J. (2013). *The New Zealand Hobbit crisis: How Warner Bros. bent a government to its will and crushed an attempt to unionise The Hobbit*. Los Angeles: Hollywood Analytics.

Haworth, N. (2011). A political economy of 'The Hobbit' dispute. *New Zealand Journal of Employment Relations, 36*(3), 100–109.

Higbee, W., & Lim, S. H. (2010). Concepts of transnational cinema: Towards a critical transnationalism in film studies. *Transnational Cinema, 1*(1), 7–21. doi:10.1386/trac.1.1.7/1.

Hunt, T. (2013, October 26). Kiwi film industry 'on brink of a crisis'. *Business Day*. Retrieved February 14, 2017, from http://www.stuff.co.nz/business/industries/9329129/Kiwi-movie-industry-on-brink-of-a-crisis.

Jackson, P., & Court, D. (2010). *Review of the New Zealand Film Commission: A Report to the Hon Chris Finlayson, MP, Minister for Arts, Culture and Heritage*. Wellington, NZ. Retrieved December 15, 2016, from http://www.mch.govt.nz/files/100628NZReport.pdf.

Jess, C. (2015). 'The Hobbit dispute': Organizing through transnational alliances. *Global Labour Journal, 5*(2), 196–211. doi:10.15173/glj.v5i2.1158.

Jin, D. Y. (2011). A critical analysis of US cultural policy in the global film market: Nation-states and FTAs. *The International Communication Gazette, 73*(8), 651–669. doi:10.1177/1748048511420092.

Jones, D. (2008). 'Ring leader': Peter Jackson as 'creative industries' hero. In H. Margolis, S. Cubitt, B. King, & T. Jutel (Eds.), *Studying the event film: The Lord of the Rings* (pp. 93–99). Oxford: Manchester University Press.

Kelly, H. (2011, April 12). *The Hobbit* dispute. *Scoop*. Retrieved August 3, 2012, from http://www.scoop.co.nz/stories/HL1104/Soo081/helen-kelly-the-hobbit-dispute.htm.

Key, J. (2010, October 27). Hobbit movies to be made in New Zealand. *Beehive*. Retrieved February 14, 2017, from https://www.beehive.govt.nz/release/hobbit-movies-be-made-new-zealand.

NZPA. (2010, October 31). Key on *Hobbit* deal: 'It was commercial reality. We did the business.' *National Business Review*. Retrieved February 14, 2017, from https://www.nbr.co.nz/article/key-hobbit-deal-it-was-commercial-reality-we-did-business-132428.

Kuipers, G., & de Kloet, J. (2009). Banal cosmopolitanism and *The Lord of the Rings*: The limited role of national differences in global media consumption. *Poetics, 37*, 99–118. doi:10.1016/j.poetic.2009.01.002.

Maegwyn (2012, July 30). Peter Jackson confirms third *Hobbit* film. *Theonering.net*. Retrieved October 20, 2012, from http://www.theonering.net/torwp/author/maegwen/.

Mathijs, E. (2005). Bad reputations: The reception of 'trash' cinema. *Screen, 46*(4), 451–472. doi:10.1093/screen/46.4.451.

McAndrew, I., & Risak, M. E. (2012). Shakedown in the shaky isles: Union bashing in New Zealand. *Labor Studies Journal, 37*(1), 56–80. doi:10.1177/0160449X11429268.

McGee, D. (2013). *Ombudsman's opinion: Requests for information regarding the production of The Hobbit and film production generally*. Wellington, NZ: Office of the Ombudsman/Tari o te Kaitiaki Mana Tangata.

Mosco, V. (2009). *The political economy of communication* (2nd ed.). London: Sage.

Newkirk, I. (2012, December 13). The *Hobbit* movie is no fantasy for animals. *Independent*. Retrieved December 18, 2016, from http://www.independent.co.uk/voices/comment-the-hobbitmovie-is-no-fantasy-for-animals-8411487.html.

Rogers, C., & Steeman, M. (2011, July 28). NBR rich list shows Hart's wealth swelling. Stuff. Retrieved December 14, 2016, from http://www.stuff.co.nz/dominion-post/news/5355197/NBR-rich-list-shows-Harts-wealth-swelling.

Sassen, S. (2006). *Territory, authority, rights*. Princeton, NJ: Princeton University Press.

Scherer, K. (2010, December 3). The big picture. *New Zealand Herald*. Retrieved December 14, 2016, from http://www.nzherald.co.nz/business/news/article.cfm?c_id=3&objectid=10691502.

Smellie, P. (2010, October 20). Wellington film crews in large anti-union march. *Scoop*. Retrieved December 14, 2016, from http://www.scoop.co.nz/stories/BU1010/S00628/wellington-film-crews-in-large-anti-union-march.htm.

Thompson, K. (2007). *The Frodo franchise: How The Lord of the Rings became a Hollywood blockbuster and put New Zealand on the map*. North Shore, NZ: Penguin.

Thornley, D. (2006). 'Wellywood' and Peter Jackson: The local reception of *The Lord of the Rings* in Wellington, New Zealand. In E. Mathijs (Ed.), *The Lord of the Rings: Popular culture in global context* (pp. 101–108). London: Wallflower.

Waetjen, J., & Gibson, T. A. (2007). *Harry Potter* and the commodity fetish: Activating corporate readings in the journey from text to commercial intertext. *Communication and Critical/Cultural Studies, 4*(1), 3–26. doi:10.1080/14791420601151289.

Walker, B., & Tipples, R. (2011). Editorial: Introducing the forum. *New Zealand Journal of Employment Relations, 36*(3), 1–4.

Walker, B., & Tipples, R. (2013). The Hobbit affair: A new frontier for unions. *Adelaide Law Review, 34*(1), 65–80.

Wall, T. (2012, November 11). Hollywood's grip on govt. *Sunday Star-Times.* Retrieved February 14, 2017, from http://www.stuff.co.nz/entertainment/film/7933903/Hollywoods-grip-on-Government.

Warner Bros. (2017). Company overview. *Warner Bros.* Retrieved February 28, 2017, from https://www.warnerbros.com/studio/about/company-overview.

Wasco, J., & Erickson, M. (Eds.). (2008). *Cross-border cultural production: Economic runaway or globalization?* New York: Cambria Press.

Wilson, M. (2011). Constitutional implications of 'The Hobbit' legislation. *New Zealand Journal of Employment Relations, 36*(3), 91–99.

Wynn, M. (2015). Feudal societies and Hobbit law: The story of '*The Hobbit* amendment'. *Small Enterprise Research, 22*(2–3), 131–145. doi:10.1080/13215906.2015.1052343.

CHAPTER 5

The Saga Begins: Mapping Audience Reactions to *An Unexpected Journey*

INTRODUCTION

This chapter describes the main perspectives identified in our surveys of audiences for *An Unexpected Journey* (*AUJ*) conducted between February and June 2013. It also draws on our comparative longitudinal data to illustrate the kinds of transformations that occurred between the pre-viewing perspectives identified in Chap. 3 and those outlined here. In so doing, this chapter explores the question of whether, and to what extent, prefigurative structures of meaning and feeling came to provide important frameworks for interpretation in the post-viewing period. Would pre-existing affiliations, fandoms and commitments to certain kinds of anticipatory activities significantly pre-shadow the engagements of audiences with *The Hobbit* as a fully realised cinematic adaptation of Tolkien's beloved novel? Or would those anticipatory hopes, expectations and imaginings be revised or even displaced once viewers had the opportunity to appreciate the specific nature and content of Jackson's re-visioning of Middle-earth?

Released worldwide in December 2012, *AUJ* is undoubtedly the high point of audience satisfaction with the *Hobbit* trilogy. Our findings reveal that the majority were enchanted and delighted by the first *Hobbit* film, while others expressed more ambivalent and in some cases strongly negative responses. In these minority viewpoints, we see the emergence of what will become far more prominent and widely shared critiques following the release of the two *Hobbit* sequels. In total, 2870 respondents

© The Author(s) 2017   109
C. Michelle et al., *Fans, Blockbusterisation, and the Transformation of Cinematic Desire*, DOI 10.1057/978-1-137-59616-1_5

from over 80 countries completed a 36-item Q sort mapping their perspectives on *AUJ*, with these items being sourced from an intensive cultural trawl of media coverage and early professional and lay reviews of the film post-release. Most respondents also provided additional comments on the statements with which they most strongly agreed or disagreed. Their remarks variously reflect a range of understandings of Peter Jackson's role in translating the original book into a blockbuster franchise, a widespread attachment to and appreciation of his earlier *Lord of the Rings* (*LotR*) films, and an array of pre-existing knowledges, meanings and memories associated with Tolkien's *Hobbit* novel and wider written corpus. Our data clearly reflects the active participation of many respondents from within the established *LotR* and Tolkien fan cultures, and many were enthusiastic about sharing their views about the film, often in considerable detail.

As shown in Fig. 5.1, five major viewpoints were identified through factor analysis of all 2870 Q sorts, accounting for 89.7% of respondents. The most common perspective by a considerable margin was shared by *Enchanted Hobbit Fans*, while several alternative views express varying degrees of disappointment with certain aspects of the first *Hobbit* film. Some indication of the kinds of concerns articulated by these minor

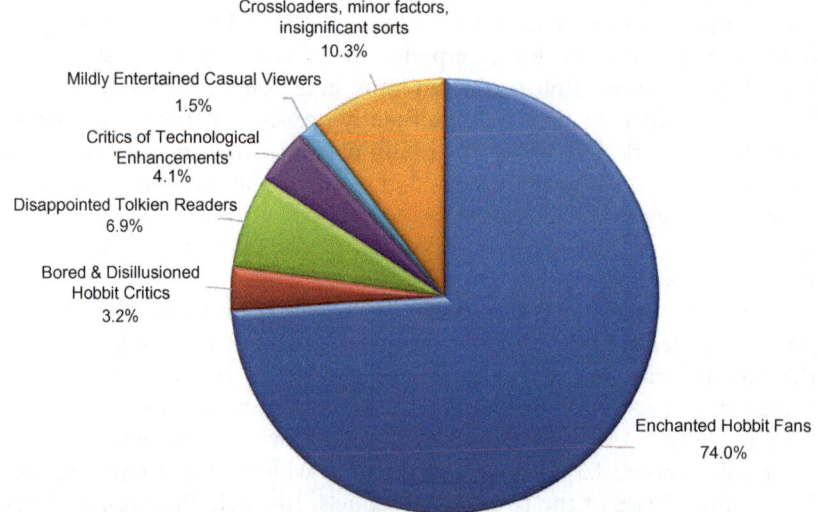

Fig. 5.1 Audience viewpoints, *An Unexpected Journey*

audience segments can be gleaned from the labels we have given them: *Bored and Disillusioned Hobbit Critics, Disappointed Tolkien Readers, Critics of Technological 'Enhancements',* and *Mildly Entertained Casual Viewers.* As our analysis reveals, while many viewers clearly appreciated the opportunity to re-immerse themselves in cinematic Middle-earth, various textual features led others to feel disengaged and even outraged by the level of artistic licence taken with Tolkien's work, and/or by Jackson's 'high-tech' approach to filming *The Hobbit.*

As expected given our earlier study of prefigurative structures of meaning, these concerns clearly related in important ways to respondents' competing intertextual and fan affiliations. However, they also reflected different understandings and expectations of genre (and more especially of *adaptation* as a cinematic form and process), varying aesthetic tastes, and competing understandings of the nature and intentions of contemporary blockbuster film production. As in Chap. 3, we discuss the perspective of the largest group of respondents first, followed by a much smaller group who expressed the *inverse* or opposite position (since in Q methodology terms, these two perspectives are positive and negative variants of the *same* factor). After that, we present each remaining group in descending size order.

Enchanted Hobbit Fans

The largest group by a considerable margin, *Enchanted Hobbit Fans* ($n = 2125$; 74.0% of all responses) collectively articulated a viewpoint that exhibits the characteristic features of the preferred *transparent* mode of reception (Michelle 2007). In the case of fiction texts, a transparent mode of reception is marked by the suspension of disbelief; narrative transportation and feeling present within the storyworld; identifying with fictional characters and events as though real; losing awareness of external reality; and intense emotional engagement and affect. This mode is evident in the viewpoint expressed by *Enchanted Hobbit Fans,* who experienced deep immersion in the fictional storyworld and barely noticed time passing (s11, +4), as suggested by this 72-year-old American woman: 'I could not believe the movie was over. I was so pulled into the story and the adventure—it was like stopping in the middle of your life and freezing.' The powerful emotional effect of the film was also evident as respondents reported feeling 'overwhelming joy' at times (s21, +3), as reflected in the comments of this 40-year-old South African respondent:

> I was immediately captivated. I wanted to jump into the screen and join in. I got misty-eyed, I was literally on the edge of my seat, I was clapping my hands in glee, I was mesmerised. After years and years of waiting, I was just so incredibly happy to have it all finally in front of me!

The film's hyperrealistic visual aesthetic was praised by these respondents as offering breathtaking clarity and detail (s7, +3), which appears to have enhanced strong feelings of immersion and presence in the world of Middle-earth (s18, +3; s13, +2), as these comments suggest:

> I found the clarity of 48fps 3D amazing, and actually felt like I was in Middle-earth locales like Bag End and Rivendell. I never felt that before in any other 3D movie. It brought me into the story immediately, and kept me there throughout the film. (American man, 56)

> The movie gave me such a feeling as if I am in Middle-earth and not in some cinema. I felt very attached to the film, and I was overwhelmed. The scenery and the landscapes and the characters represented Middle-earth very good, and they made me feel I'm with them on their adventure. (Slovenian woman, 15)

Unlike some other groups, these respondents were not averse to the many changes Jackson had made in adapting book to screen (s23, +2), believing that the differences in form made alterations necessary, and even desirable, since films and novels are subject to different creative forces and production imperatives, as Ilan and Kama (2016) note. This point was emphasised by a number of our *Enchanted Hobbit Fans*:

> A book is a medium to read. A movie is a medium to see and most importantly feel. If translated word by word the book will make a very dull and boring movie, therefore tweaks should be made in order to create a fluent visual and sonic by adding, retracting or altering some minor details for the movie's story to hold as one piece. (British woman, 18)

Possibly related to this acceptance of creative adaptations, *Enchanted Hobbit Fans* felt *AUJ* successfully recreated the fantasy world first depicted in the *LotR* films and allowed them to return to Middle-earth to 'see old friends' once again (s9, +2). They were also effusive in their praise of the cast (s12, +4), variously described as 'perfect', 'superb', and 'outstanding', and appreciated Howard Shore's beautiful score (s2, +2).

For these viewers, then, *The Hobbit* offered a deeply moving, fully immersive, visually spectacular experience that successfully transported them back to Middle-earth and evoked highly pleasurable feelings of nostalgia, all consistent with the preferred transparent mode of reception.

Our longitudinal approach allowed us to track the evolution of audience responses from the period leading up to *AUJ's* cinematic release through to the immediate post-viewing period, offering insight into whether prefigurative hopes, expectations and structures of meaning shaped interpretation and response in the post-viewing period (see Michelle et al. 2017, for an extended discussion). A sizeable cohort of respondents (277) completed both our prefiguration survey and the *AUJ* post-viewing survey; the transformation matrix in Table 5.1 shows the movement of these respondents between different categories of

Table 5.1 Transformation matrix showing movement from pre-viewing to post-viewing perspectives, *An Unexpected Journey*

N = 277	*Post-viewing perspectives, AUJ:*				
	Enchanted Hobbit Fans (n = 209)	*Disappointed Tolkien Readers (n = 13)*	*Critics of Technological 'Enhancements' (n = 12)*	*Bored and Disillusioned Hobbit Critics (n = 7)*	*Other[a] (n = 36)*
Pre-viewing perspectives:					
LotR Film Fans n = 160	143	3	4	0	10
Tolkien Aficionados n = 52	29	9	4	1	9
Celebrity Followers n = 5	2	0	0	1	2
Anxious Investors n = 4	0	0	0	1	3
Jackson Critics n = 3	0	0	0	2	1
Other[a] n = 53	35	1	4	2	11
%	75.5	4.7	4.3	2.5	13.0

[a]Crossloaders, minor factors, insignificant sorts

pre- versus post-viewing response. Among other things, it reveals how many of those who were previously categorised as *LotR Film Fans* subsequently evolved into *Enchanted Hobbit Fans,* while also illustrating how many instead shifted into one of the less appreciative groups identified in the *AUJ* post-viewing survey.

As this suggests, 89% of those who were pre-viewing *LotR Film Fans* went on to become *Enchanted Hobbit Fans* and were thus very satisfied with the outcome of a much anticipated cinematic event. While united by their appreciation of Jackson's earlier adaptations, this group was nonetheless internally diverse in terms of the meanings they ascribed to seeing the first *Hobbit* film: for some, *AUJ* presented an opportunity to return to Middle-earth; for others, it offered the chance to relive the amazing *LotR* phenomenon or to see Tolkien's literary milestone inspire the imaginations of another generation. While the things *most* looked forward to and the intertextual sources privileged varied, this group's post-viewing responses collectively described a very pleasurable experience of feeling fully engaged and immersed within *AUJ's* narrative story-world, as these comments suggest:

> **Pre-viewing:** I saw *The Fellowship of the Ring* in theatres when I was 11, and it completely changed my life ... Getting the chance to see a new trilogy based on books about my favourite universe, written by my favourite writer, directed by a director that I love ten years later is just too much. (Italian woman, 22, *LotR Film Fan*); **Post-viewing:** The *LotR* movies meant so much to me when they first come out, being transported to that world again was an incredible gift .../... It means coming back to a world populated with friends and values that are really important to me. (Same Italian woman, 22; *Enchanted Hobbit Fan*)

> **Pre-viewing:** *The Hobbit* was the first book I remember reading as a child, and it left a lasting impression on me. I'm excited to see the characters and places on the screen that I've only imagined for 30 years. (American man, 35, *LotR Film Fan*); **Post-viewing:** There was a great balance of whimsy and enchantment coupled with excitement and danger. I was emotionally invested in Bilbo, Thorin, Gandalf and Balin and their respective stories .../... *The Hobbit* was a wonderful vehicle to take me back to that place I love. (Same American man, 35, *Enchanted Hobbit Fan*)

Joining those *LotR Film Fans* who subsequently became *Enchanted Hobbit Fans* were 29 others (56%) who had previously been classified as *Tolkien Aficionados* (Table 5.1), a pre-viewing group that was somewhat more apprehensive about Jackson's second foray into cinematic Middle-earth (see Chap. 3). Among these 'converts' was a woman who initially expressed strong reservations about Jackson's ability to successfully adapt her beloved Tolkien's masterpiece, but found her concerns subsequently alleviated by an adaptation that greatly surpassed all prior expectations:

> **Pre-viewing:** [I]t's a big disappointment to me that Jackson is doing the movies instead of Del Toro.../... I did not like his *LotR* trilogy, and think that movies he did after *LotR* were progressively worse .../... I'm an avid fan of Tolkien's work; it played a huge part in my life. I was running a Tolkien fan community and invested a lot of expectations into PJ's *LotR*. It failed to meet my expectations, but I'm willing to give *[The] Hobbit* another chance. (Russian-American woman, 45; *Tolkien Aficionado*); **Post-viewing:** I didn't expect much, not being a fan of Peter Jackson's *LotR* trilogy, but I was blown away by *[The] Hobbit*. My expectations were greatly exceeded .../... I fell in love with all the characters .../... All characterizations were superb and true to Tolkien .../... I immediately bought the songs and couldn't stop listening to them for days .../... Magical .../... I watched the first movie six times, and I'm not done yet. Can't wait for the rest. (Same Russian-American woman, 45; *Enchanted Hobbit Fan*)

This respondent's earlier concerns about Jackson as a director thus created the particular 'structure of meaning' through which *The Hobbit* was subsequently evaluated, but far more *positively* so than anticipated. Importantly then, her prefigurative expectations were *disconfirmed* by her encounter with the fully realised text, which differed substantially from her imagined pre-text based on her dislike of Jackson's earlier films. Also significant here is the *degree* of this respondent's enthusiastic endorsement and affective response, expressed in references to the film's magical score and loveable characters and her desire to re-engage in highly pleasurable viewing—all consistent with her adoption of the preferred transparent mode of reception.

Many other *Tolkien Aficionados* also came to adopt the preferred viewing mode after seeing *AUJ*, despite initially expressing reservations. For one Ukrainian man, the novel's deep personal and emotional significance had underpinned a central pre-viewing concern about textual fidelity:

> **Pre-viewing:** This book really touched my heart once, it's like the first love memory .../... I want to feel the spirit of the book. **Post-viewing:** To me, it was like a window into my most favourite world .../... It was like meeting with very old and very good friends; I felt like I could touch

Tolkien's world for real. And this was amazing. (Ukrainian man, 38; *Tolkien Aficionado* turned *Enchanted Hobbit Fan*)

Expressed here is a sense of heightened realism flowing from the film's visual presentation, which appears to have partially displaced his pre-viewing structure of interpretation relating to textual fidelity. Similar responses were made by others among this subgroup who had been initially wary of the cinematic translation of Tolkien's *Hobbit*, but later clearly appreciated *AUJ*'s detailed realisation of the people and places of Middle-earth, despite some ongoing reservations about diversions from the original novel—as suggested by this 17-year-old Canadian woman:

> **Post-viewing:** While I didn't agree with some of the changes and additions ..., Middle-earth was still Middle-earth. Hobbiton still had its same charm, Rivendell its same mystery and wonder, the dwarf hall ... literally took my breath away with its majesty, and it was created just PERFECTLY. (*Tolkien Aficionado* turned *Enchanted Hobbit Fan*)

While most respondents thus adopted the preferred transparent mode of reception, several smaller groups expressed alternative viewpoints which appear to reflect the adoption of subcategories of the *mediated* mode. Respondents associated with these viewpoints commonly reported disruption of their immersion in the film's spectacular narrative, which different individuals attributed to how (and how well) the film was constructed, the agenda behind its production, its visual aesthetic, the manner in which Tolkien's work was adapted to become a global franchise, or some combination of these and other aspects relating to the film as a *media product*. As noted in Chap. 2, in a mediated mode of reception viewers may target various aspects of a text's production and execution for praise or criticism—with the three main subcategories of response emphasising textual aesthetics or production quality, generic form or type, or the 'intentions and motivations of cultural producers in terms of meeting various textual, generic, and professional or industry-based imperatives' (Michelle 2007, p. 204). While adopting a mediated mode of reception may yield certain cognitive satisfactions for fans and amateur film critics, it is not usually the textually preferred reading mode for a fantasy film such as *The Hobbit*. As we will see in subsequent chapters, the initial concerns about *AUJ* expressed by these small audience segments evolved into rather more forcefully expressed and also more widely shared critiques following the release of the second and third instalments of the *Hobbit* franchise.

Bored and Disillusioned Hobbit Critics

Taking the opposite viewpoint to that of *Enchanted Hobbit Fans* were a group of 91 dissenters to the pleasures of *AUJ* (3.2% of respondents). These *Bored and Disillusioned Hobbit Critics* considered the first *Hobbit* film to be uninspiring, overly drawn out, poorly edited and lacking in momentum (s1, +2; s32, +4, s11, –4), as reflected here:

> It seemed like the film was swallowed up by needless action scenes, with little time spent actually making me care about the characters. It was very long, very dull, and very poorly edited, and left me completely uninvolved emotionally. (Canadian man, 19)

> By the end of the film I was glad to leave the cinema, the film dragged on because we were shown battle after battle; by the final battle, any hope of tension or climax had been completely destroyed. The film was anticlimactic and underwhelming because of its repetition. (New Zealand man, 23)

These viewers evidently felt very disappointed and disengaged, and expressed no desire to see the *Hobbit* sequels (s 33, +4). Significantly, they attributed the film's many failings—including the decision to dilute the story by making three films—to the influence of industry-based commercial considerations (s34, +3), as suggested here:

> Making three movies out of such a short book, while reducing the pacing and stretching out the overall story—and even losing track of it during all the subplots—is more thinking about money than anything else. (American woman, 29)

> *The Hobbit* is simply following the template of the 'modern blockbuster' ... . The formula is this: (1) Remove any tension and drama from the plot. (2) Make each scene last about three times longer than it needs to. (3) Make the main characters invincible. (4) Add lots of CGI and keep adding more to the point of utter meaninglessness. (Irish man, 41)

Bored and Disillusioned Hobbit Critics also felt that, in seeking to maximise box-office takings, *AUJ* failed to 'balance the demands of good cinema against catering to its hordes of fans' (s16, +3). This viewpoint thus articulates a set of concerns relating to the blockbusterisation of *The Hobbit*; concerns that were also evident to some extent among *Jackson Critics* in our prefiguration survey.

Jackson's emphasis on showcasing new cinematic technologies and extensive use of CGI were also subject to critique as too obvious and as having disrupted the process of immersion (s27, +2), thereby detracting from the story and deeper meaning of *The Hobbit* (s15, +3): 'Peter Jackson clearly was more interested in making action scenes than realistic characters—character development is completely screwed up just to make way for him to show off his effects' (Australian man, 19); 'The obvious overuse of green screen gave it the feel of a children's TV drama. I'm amazed that such a big budget film could feel so "clunky" and I was completely distracted by the CG imagery' (British woman, 31). For these respondents, *AUJ* lacked the magic and charm of the original novel, and failed to convey its essence or spirit (s6, +2), while also failing to recreate the 'energy, passion and epic scale of the *LotR* films' (s4, +2).

In theoretical terms, such responses reflect the adoption of a deeply critical mediated mode of reception in which the industry-based commercial intentions and motivations of Jackson and his production team are subject to scathing critique for their negative impact on virtually every aspect of the production, an impact which has ultimately undermined the quality of this adaptation/prequel and fatally disrupted narrative engagement. The degree of this disengagement is clear from these respondents' rejection of all statements expressing pleasurable immersion, presence in the fictional storyworld and emotional affect (s:11, −4; s18 and s21, −3), as conveyed by this 22-year-old Belgian man: 'I was filled with disgust, annoyance and sadness when I saw—for three hours—what Jackson had done to one of the stories most dear to me, a story I literally grew up with.'

Among the cohort of 277 who completed both pre-viewing and *AUJ* post-viewing surveys, seven evolved into *Bored and Disillusioned Hobbit Critics* (see Table 5.1). Not surprisingly, two of these were formerly *Jackson Critics*, a group that had fully expected not to enjoy the first *Hobbit* film. As one such critic put it after seeing *AUJ*, '[E]ven I, whose opinion of PJ borders on contempt, was surprised that he managed to "exceed expectations" as to how low he could, and would, go to make a buck and play with his CGI' (American woman, 45). As noted by Gray (2010, p. 127), Jackson himself has become 'a brand and hence an inter- or paratextual framing device, a matrix of other (inter)texts.' While

Jackson's involvement in *The Hobbit* reassured many *LotR Film Fans* of its likely high quality, *Bored and Disillusioned Hobbit Critics* regarded director Peter Jackson's brand as tainted by disrespect for the integrity of Tolkien's works: 'PJ is not adapting, he is inventing' (Scottish man, 41); 'In his arrogance, the high school dropout believes he can pick Tolkien's bones and improve his tale' (American woman, 45).

Other respondents expressed a clear sense of frustration with what was regarded as a missed opportunity. For one former *Tolkien Aficionado* who earlier described the *Hobbit* novel as 'favourite comfort food reading', the first *Hobbit* film was uninspiring and over-long: 'The book is better, the pictures in my head better. Not worth the investment of time and money to go to a cinema' (Finnish man, 50). A former *Celebrity Follower* meanwhile lamented that she felt no emotional connection to *AUJ* due to the film's lack of narrative and character development:

> It failed to hold my attention and keep me engaged. ... All the running, battle, chasing scenes left little time for character and narrative development. ... I had a difficult time allowing myself to suspend my disbelief. (Canadian woman, 50)

One *Anxious Investor* had earlier hoped the film's success might bring 'a huge influx in tourism like the *LotR* trilogy did for us, added attraction to New Zealand as a film location and more work for Weta Digital' (New Zealand man, 23). Post-viewing, his concerns relating to the production of an 'American film made with a lot of our money and a tiny bit of our talent' were compounded by an *unexpectedly* disappointing textual feature—Weta Digital's visual effects, which were 'overdone and at times looked bad.' As these comments suggest, issues relating to textual aesthetics as well as textual fidelity disrupted pleasure and immersion among some viewers, including those we refer to as *Disappointed Tolkien Readers*.

Disappointed Tolkien Readers

The second largest audience segment ($n = 199$, 6.9% of all responses), *Disappointed Tolkien Readers* felt that the first film was a weak adaptation that failed to capture the spirit of Tolkien's literary classic due to the addition of too much poorly conceived extraneous material. Thus, their responses are strongly intertextual, with the film being judged, in relation to their familiarity with Tolkien's novel, as a flawed or even failed cinematic adaptation. These respondents shared the view that *AUJ's* many 'creative additions' and extended action scenes were unfaithful to Tolkien's 'charming' story (s17, +4; s6, +3), as the following comments illustrate:

> What I loved about the novel was that it was whimsical and funny yet full of hobbit heart ... . The *Hobbit* film felt forced and too contrived. It attempted to bring too much drama into the story and to present it as an epic, instead of a hobbit's tale of self-discovery. (Filipino woman, 39)

> The film tried to blend *The Hobbit* into the world of the *LotR* which had a much darker and more adult theme, whereas *The Hobbit* was originally a children's book and was more lighthearted in nature. (New Zealand man, 35)

> Very little of the original spirit of the novel was captured. The movie seemed more like a 'grown up' *Hobbit*, as if *The Hobbit* was supposed to have the same tone as the *LotR*. The movie is too bloated and too far from its roots in the novel. It's not really Bilbo's story anymore. (American woman, 23)

For these respondents, poorly rendered non-canon additions contributed to the film's unjustifiable length (s1, +3) and left little time or space for adequate character development (s20; +2). Like the previous group of *Hobbit Critics*, *Disappointed Tolkien Readers* held that the decision to make a trilogy was commercially motivated (s34, +4) and ultimately detrimental to the story, leading to the inclusion of storylines that detracted from Tolkien's primary message and themes (s36, +2):

> There's no question about the fact that Jackson milked this gentle little 320-page book into a three movie, battle-heavy, extravaganza solely to line his pockets. It's one of the most blatantly mercenary moves I've ever seen. (American woman, 69)

> We are only six chapters down in the original book, and we already have a three hours movie. Adding parts of the extended lore from Tolkien's texts wasn't always well done and only added to the overstretched feeling of the movie. Like butter scraped over too much bread. (French woman, 28)

In the view of these respondents, then, *AUJ* ultimately failed to strike the right balance between crowd-pleasing content aimed at maximising audiences and cinematic excellence (s16, +2). They felt neither transported nor enchanted (s11, −4; s18, −3), nor strongly emotionally affected by the film (s21, −3). However, they retained a more favorable view of the film's scenery (s3, +3) and musical score (s2, +2), and they still intended to see the sequels (s33, −2), while anticipating that these too would be disappointing in some respects: 'I'm sure the next two films will be disappointing in many ways that the first was, but there will still be redeeming elements' (American man, 48). Unlike *Hobbit Critics*, *Disappointed Tolkien Readers* were also somewhat more engaged by the film and did not share other groups' strongly negative views of high frame rate (HFR) 3D and computer-generated visual effects. Their primary concern relates to the quality of a film adaptation which diverged too far from the original novel in tone and emphasis for their taste, and it is with the novel that their primary allegiance clearly lies.

Drawing on our comparative data for this film (Table 5.1), we can see that only three former *LotR Film Fans* evolved into *Disappointed Tolkien Readers*. For these respondents *AUJ* failed both as an adaptation *and* prequel, with the novel and the *LotR* film trilogy providing dual intertextual reference points in judging *The Hobbit* to be ill-conceived and unfaithful to the original work(s):

> **Post-viewing:** Wherever violence was avoided in the book, it seemed to be relished in the movie. It was untrue to the spirit of the novel in that sense, and I felt it sold its soul to please the unthinking masses. ... *The Hobbit* fell short of the standard for storytelling set by *LotR*. ... He could have created a far richer and enveloping tale without trying to give every character a 'hero moment'. I feel Tolkien painted heroism differently than it came out in Jackson's roller coaster ride. (South African man, 36; *LotR Film Fan* turned *Disappointed Tolkien Reader*)

For a larger group of nine former *Tolkien Aficionados*, original concerns about Jackson's ability to faithfully translate the book to the screen were reinforced by *AUJ*'s numerous diversions from the original *Hobbit* story in tone and emphasis, as suggested here:

> **Pre-viewing:** I feel that Peter Jackson is unlikely to do the book full justice, and will try and make it more Lord-of-the-Ringsey to its cost, amping up special effects, battle scenes etc., .../... I think I will enjoy the *Hobbit* film a lot more if I think of it as a thing in itself instead of an adaptation. I expect it to be a poor adaptation. I hope it will be a wonderful

movie! (New Zealand man, 16; *Tolkien Aficionado*); **Post-viewing:** Bloodless video game battle scenes, lacking in both plausibility and any real sense that the major characters were under threat, were thrown in for no purpose. A bland cookie-cutter villain was added, presumably on the grounds that the book didn't have enough Orcs for our heroes to beat up. Tolkien's book was carefully and skilfully plotted. Peter Jackson's film is not. (Same New Zealand man, 16; *Disappointed Tolkien Reader*)

Evident in both sets of comments is the view that an adaptation/prequel should closely align with the original text from which it is derived and/ or with which it is continuous as part of a *series*, suggesting the adoption of a critical mediated mode of response focused on *generic form* (Michelle 2007). Hence, *AUJ* is judged lacking, not on its own terms, but in relation to the works that precede it (see also Rae and Gray 2007). For former *Tolkien Aficionados* who believed in the 'axiomatic superiority' of Tolkien's novel (Stam 2005, p. 4) and consequently adopted the post-viewing perspective of *Disappointed Tolkien Readers*, *AUJ*'s many deviations from the original work, although expected, were clearly a bridge too far.

It is important to note here that disapproval of the adaptation of Tolkien's literature into cinematic spectacles is not unique to audiences for the *Hobbit* franchise. Interrogations of textual fidelity were also clearly evident in some Tolkien fans' criticisms of Jackson's earlier *LotR* trilogy (Egan and Barker 2008; Rae and Gray 2007; Turnbull 2008). Fidelity is usually understood in terms of an adaptation's faithfulness to the original work, which is given primacy (Ilan and Kama 2016). Often, for 'serious' book fans, the more faithful the better. It is clear that for *Disappointed Tolkien Readers*, conveying the spirit or 'essence' of Tolkien's original novel (however conceived) was vital if Jackson's adaptation were to be considered a success.

However, we do need to stress here that post-viewing perspectives were not necessarily predetermined by respondents' prior allegiances to Tolkien's written corpus. As demonstrated above, other Tolkien-oriented respondents with very similar pre-viewing concerns about textual fidelity were quite effectively 'converted' to *Hobbit* fandom by *AUJ*. This variability in the reactions of Tolkien readers once again illustrates that individual receptions remain highly contingent, and cannot be 'read off' or assumed on the basis of viewers' prefigurative dispositions.

Critics of Technological 'Enhancements'

A fourth segment, which we have labelled *Critics of Technological 'Enhancements'* ($n = 119$, 4.1% of responses), also critiqued *AUJ*, but their primary concerns related to the quality of the film's CGI visual effects and the detrimental impact of HFR 3D projection on its visual aesthetic, which these respondents cited as barriers to immersion in the fictional storyworld. While they greatly appreciated the beautiful New Zealand scenery (s3, +3), the interaction between visual and projection technologies was not seamless for these respondents (s35, −4), instead producing displeasing perceptual artefacts, as noted by this 29-year-old American woman: 'While the high frame rate gave the film a very interesting look, it made it seem more fake, almost like a video game. It made the animated characters stand out more instead of blending in with the real actors.' This group most strongly agreed that the technological innovations gave the film a 'fake, artificial sheen', which 'spoiled the romantic illusion' by exposing the means through which cinematic magic had been constructed (31, +4):

> I could see how fake some props were and the colour was extremely saturated to the point of it looking ridiculously fake. (Singaporean woman, 24, residing in Australia)

> The illusion that is maintained by the limitations of film stock were not sufficiently compensated for by those who were doing the art direction and the graphics design, letting the film down quite badly. (New Zealand man, 50)

> Visually, the movements of the actors appeared insanely rushed and frantic, and it was actually very unnerving. I could not stop thinking about the effects and the high definition video the entire time, which completely pulled me out of the experience of getting lost in the film. (Filipino woman, 27, living in Canada)

Many in this grouping expressed frustration with Jackson's failure to effectively integrate special effects into a seamlessly plausible reality. These and other visually jarring elements disrupted narrative immersion (s27, +4; s7, −3), as noted here and above:

> I was expecting to see REAL PEOPLE in highly detailed and REALISTIC costume like in *LotR*. The computer imagery made the orcs and goblins look incredibly fake, unbelievable, and non-threatening. (American woman, 21)

The CGI in this film was very disappointing, especially the goblins and the goblin king, it definitely took away from the overall experience of the film. The CGI in the *LotR* films to me seems superior to *The Hobbit*'s CGI; even though there is a ten year difference and advances in technology it just looked clunky and far too fake, which made the believability of the film difficult and was distracting to the storyline, as I was constantly looking at how fake the monsters looked. (New Zealand woman, 21)

In theoretical terms, these respondents can be said to have adopted a variation of the mediated mode of reception focused on textual aesthetics. It is clear that rather than being deeply engaged in the fictional storyworld, they adopted a more distanced, objective perspective in which they critically evaluated the nature and (poor) quality of the film's aesthetic presentation and visual effects. Furthermore, for many of these respondents, the earlier *LotR* film trilogy clearly comprised the primary intertextual reference point, and the standard against which *AUJ* was judged as inferior. This is evident through references to experiencing nostalgia (s30, +3) while watching a film that allowed them to return to Middle-earth (s13, +2) and see old friends again (s9, +2):

When the *LotR* films came out, I was in my teens and was very obsessive about following them and obtaining all knowledge about them possible. Getting to anticipate something new that was related to Tolkien and Middle-earth was very evocative of that time in my life. (American man, 26)

The social experience of film viewing was also important for this group (s24, +2), and they greatly enjoyed both the casting/acting and soundtrack (s12, +3 s2, +2), possibly because these elements were closely related to the earlier trilogy, as this comment suggests: 'The soundtrack was on par with previous *LotR* films and kept the same essence and feel as the previous films' (Canadian man, 31).

Using our longitudinal data, we can trace the evolution of responses among the 12 *Critics of Technological 'Enhancements'* who also completed our pre-viewing survey, comprising equal numbers of *LotR Film Fans*, *Tolkien Aficionados* and crossloaders (see Table 5.1). These respondents shared a largely *unanticipated* negative reaction to the film's special effects and visual aesthetic, which prevented them immersing themselves fully in the fictional storyworld. Many were surprised by this, particularly those who we had previously identified as *LotR Film Fans*. As noted in Chap. 3, concerns about HFR 3D were not widely expressed among our respondents prior to *AUJ*'s cinematic release, and it seems many viewers simply assumed *The Hobbit* would live up to the elevated standards for visual effects set by the earlier trilogy, which was widely praised by fans and critics alike for its extraordinary attention to detail in realising the world of Middle-earth (Thompson 2007). But while *Enchanted Hobbit Fans* often appreciated the heightened sense of realism conveyed by HFR and CGI effects, *Critics of Technological 'Enhancements'* felt these same technologies 'spoiled the romantic illusion' by calling attention to the means through which cinematic magic had been constructed, as noted by this former *LotR Film Fan*:

> Cinema is about escapism, and for me, it only works if I am watching a grainy film and not some HD computer game. ... Azog looked like a computer figure. Some scenes reminded me of *300*. I prefer the graininess of film; otherwise, a movie loses its soul. (German woman, 24)

Furthermore, while *LotR*'s many accomplishments appeared to render even dedicated book readers more forgiving of diversions from Tolkien's original plot, in the case of *AUJ* it seems some former *Tolkien Aficionados* also could not look past the film's visual anomalies, again suggesting that unanticipated features of the fully realised text had the potential to supplant prefigurative preoccupations and frameworks of interpretation:

> [The] general decision to shoot in 3D, 48fps and, most importantly, to shoot on as little natural sets as possible has resulted in the very rough transitions between actors on set and [the] digital world around them. (Belarussian man, 26; *Tolkien Aficionado* turned *Critic of Technological 'Enhancements'*)

These very specific technological features of the fully realised text were so distracting that they made it impossible for these respondents to adopt or sustain the preferred transparent viewing mode of immersive enchantment; consequently, the text was experienced as less pleasurable. While efforts were subsequently made to address these and other criticisms of *The Hobbit*'s unusual visual aesthetic in the two sequels, our research suggests similar commentaries reappeared and broadened in audience responses to *The Desolation of Smaug* (*DoS*) and *The Battle of the Five Armies* (*BotFA*). Given the emphasis which the production team itself placed on the novelty of the technologies used in these films and the clear relevance of our findings for future film productions planning to combine HFR 3D with intensive CGI, we address the range of responses to *The Hobbit*'s particular combination of cinematic technologies in greater detail in Chap. 7.

Mildly Entertained Casual Viewers

Our final major audience segment, which we have labelled *Mildly Entertained Casual Viewers* ($n = 43$, 1.5% of responses), had rather ambivalent feelings about the first *Hobbit* film. They greatly enjoyed the 'breathtaking' New Zealand scenery (s3, +4), but did not feel overwhelmingly enchanted or transported by the film (s21, −2). They felt it lacked momentum, being overly long and in need of tighter editing (s1, +4; s32, +3, s11, −4):

> I was very conscious, while watching this movie, of its length. There were many scenes that did not advance or add anything to the story and could have been left out. (New Zealand woman, 49)

> There was no sense of urgency to the story. No rush to get to the mountain and no reason to root for the dwarves, so it was hard to get invested in the story. (British man, 38)

But while this group reported relative disengagement from the film's spectacular narrative, their dissatisfaction was not nearly as passionate as that of *Bored and Disillusioned Hobbit Critics* or *Disappointed Tolkien Readers*, nor focused on a sense of disappointment that the film did not measure up to treasured memories of the *LotR* trilogy. Like others, they attributed the film's generous extra padding to commercial motivations aimed at maximising profits (s34, +3), but they were rather more sympathetic to the need for some creative additions when translating books to screen (s23, +3): 'Splitting it into three movies is blatantly to make money. I don't know if it is a bad thing—fans get more movies, industry gets way more money' (New Zealand man, 22). They did not consider *AUJ* an unfaithful adaptation (s17, −2; s22, −3), perhaps in part because few were serious fans of the novel. They also praised the film's cast and performances (s12, +2), pioneering visual effects and projection technologies (s35, +2) and success as an adaptation/prequel (s10, +2), but found flaws with the filmmaking and also felt conflicted by controversies that emerged during the film's production (s14, +2) (see Chap. 4).

Mildly Entertained Casual Viewers can thus be seen to have adopted a mediated mode of reception focused on various issues relating to aesthetic quality; while some elements of filmcraft were found lacking, others were considered praiseworthy. That their response appears less strongly marked by pre-existing intertextual allegiances suggests these respondents are likely to be casual viewers and perhaps amateur (or professional) film critics, rather than dedicated fans of Tolkien or the *LotR* films. Unfortunately, very few of these respondents participated in our pre-viewing survey, so it was not possible to glean relevant insight into the evolution of this perspective drawing on our longitudinal data.

CONCLUSION

Our findings in this chapter support the general conclusion that the key factor shaping positive receptions of highly anticipated and extensively prefigured texts is the degree of alignment between viewers' predispositions and affiliations to particular intertexts, the nature of their imagined pre-texts and psychological investments in them, and the fully realised text itself. As the above discussion illustrates, prior hopes, expectations and structures of meaning evidently informed the foci of attention of many respondents but did not necessarily constrain the nature and tenor of audience engagements post-release. While the vast majority of existing *LotR* film fans had intensely hoped to re-experience immersive enchantment and were greatly satisfied by their subsequent viewing experience, a small number ultimately rejected the preferred reception mode, despite having had a similarly optimistic pre-viewing perspective marked, in many cases, by absolute *certainty* about Peter Jackson's ability to deliver. Others were less enthralled, if not actively repelled, by what they had seen and heard in *The Hobbit*'s prefigurative materials, leading them to lower or actively moderate their expectations—to anticipate some disappointing aspects. While some more cautious pre-viewers were ultimately recruited to the preferred reception mode, a significant number were not. Often, this was because *AUJ* failed to live up to their prior expectations of genre (for many *Tolkien Aficionados*, it was a poor adaptation), but for others, it related to the film's unanticipated and displeasing visual aesthetic. And while there were far more 'converts' among our sample, dissatisfied viewers may have been less inclined to complete the post-viewing survey: our subsequent studies suggest a significant group of disenfranchised 'former' *Hobbit*/Jackson fans has since emerged.

Despite living up to the hopes and expectations of many, *AUJ* retained the capacity to surprise, amaze, frustrate and disappoint in ways that exceeded viewers' prefigurative expectations and creative imaginings. Respondents cited specific features—such as added pieces of delightful dialogue, the enhanced realism or distracting effects of HFR 3D and the emotional impact of certain scenes—as unanticipated elements that significantly coloured their viewing experience. The potential of these textual elements to encourage or disrupt the preferred reception mode depended largely on how such elements were made sense of by viewers themselves. Because of the inherent complexity and specificity of both the text and its reception, the outcome of individual audience—text encounters remained variable and contingent upon a host of factors outside of the film's marketing, fan-based online discussions, and any number of related paratextual and intertextual materials.

Prefiguration might thus be said to play a complex and ambiguous role in shaping modes of reception. It clearly has the *potential* to define and delimit horizons of expectations to varying degrees and to cast particular shadows and spotlights which 'prefigure' the text's preferred reading for receptive audiences. Ultimately, however, the fully realised text can only ever be partially anticipated before release. Individual reactions thus remain indeterminate until viewing and may be subject to further revision and refinement with subsequent re-viewings, discussion and debate. Our research therefore serves as a timely reminder that the outcome of encounters between texts and audiences is not determined by public prefigurative discussions or marketing materials, and so cannot be predicted from careful studies of pre-viewer expectations and preoccupations with particular intertexts. It remains essential to engage empirically with actual—as opposed to implied or theoretical—audiences themselves, and to understand the specific nature of their complex and sometimes ambiguous interactions with even the most extensively prefigured texts, as our longitudinal study attempts to do.

Already striking in our analysis is the clear predominance of just two of the modes of reception described in Michelle's (2007) Composite Model (transparent and mediated), with neither the referential nor discursive modes being evident in the viewpoints described above. While as the following chapters demonstrate, this division persists throughout the course of our study, we should acknowledge that in addition to these five main viewpoints on *AUJ*, we also found two very minor perspectives that appeared to place greater emphasis on the messages and meanings of *The*

Hobbit and its real-world relevance, possibly reflecting the discursive and referential modes. However, due to their small size, bipolar nature and the difficulty of interpreting them given relatively few qualitative comments, we have omitted these viewpoints from our discussion in this chapter. Furthermore, it is clear that the fundamental division among respondents is between those who adopted the preferred viewing mode of immersive enchantment and those who did not, due to various aspects of *AUJ*'s status as *a constructed media product*—whether related to the intentions and imperatives behind its creation, its contested status as an adaptation/prequel, or its unusual visual aesthetic. This reasonably clear-cut division is interesting in itself and requires further explanation.

Speculatively, it might be that the wealth of prefigurative materials that preceded this blockbuster release helped to 'simplify' the type of audience this first *Hobbit* film attracted by providing clear cues for potential viewers (targeting existing fan cultures where appropriate) that there were familiar and expected cinematic pleasures being constructed—a return to Middle-earth, for instance, or more of Tolkien's work realised on screen—thus emphasizing certain structures of meaning over others, and perhaps also encouraging the adoption of particular modes of response. It might also be that blockbuster film adaptations/prequels as a cinematic form themselves tend to encourage the adoption of certain modes of reception among preassembled audiences who are deeply familiar with the source material, since such familiarity perhaps inevitably invites a series of intertextual comparisons and further speculation on why certain creative choices have been made. And of course, we acknowledge that our online survey most likely appealed to individuals with strong opinions about the film, as opposed to casual viewers for whom rather less was at stake. Our analysis likely overrepresents the views of self-selecting groups who were highly motivated to express their opinions on the kind of value and achievement *AUJ* might represent as an adaptation of Tolkien's novel, and as a continuation of a beloved film trilogy—again suggesting mediated modes of reception might figure more prominently among these kinds of viewers.

Our observations of disappointed *AUJ* audiences also confirm similar findings relating to cinematic adaptation. *Disappointed Tolkien Readers*, in particular, are a familiar group from *LotR* audience studies. Research conducted by Mikos et al. (2008) suggests that those who had read the *Lord of the Rings* books before viewing the final *LotR* film had distinctly different reception strategies to those who had not. While book readers often found the greatest pleasure in more faithful representations or those that were consistent with their imagined version of those texts, they nonetheless also derived enjoyment from exercising their expert knowledge and from engaging in a cognitive process of assessing the degree of textual fidelity. These findings are echoed by Jerslev (2006) and also Turnbull (2008), who highlights the disappointment of Australian book lovers.

In sum, *Critics of 'Technological 'Enhancements'*, *Bored and Disillusioned Hobbit Critics*, and *Mildly Entertained Casual Viewers* collectively represent a range of concerns which, in retrospect, anticipate the variety of critiques our respondents ultimately generated around the *Hobbit* sequels and the franchise as a whole. While pre-existing allegiance to Tolkien's written corpus clearly provided an important basis for rejections of this cinematic adaptation, it was certainly not the *only* such basis; *The Hobbit*'s visual aesthetic and its divergence from the look and feel of Jackson's *LotR* trilogy was also troublesome for some viewers, while concerns relating to the processes and imperatives of Hollywood blockbusterisation were evident in the views of others. As the trilogy unfolds, these increasingly critical perspectives come to represent the views of a larger proportion of our participant sample, as we shall illustrate in Chaps. 6, 7 and 8.

This chapter is derived, in part, from an article published in *International Journal of Cultural Studies* on 12 March 2015, available online: http://journals.sagepub.com/doi/pdf/10.1177/1367877915571407.

REFERENCES

Egan, K., & Barker, M. (2008). The books, the DVDs, the extras, and their lovers. In M. Barker & E. Mathijs (Eds.), *Watching The Lord of the Rings: Tolkien's world audiences* (pp. 83-102). New York: Peter Lang.

Gray, J. (2010). *Show sold separately: Promos, spoilers, and other media paratexts.* New York: New York University Press.

Ilan, J., & Kama, A. (2016). Where has all the magic gone? Audience interpretive strategies of *The Hobbit*'s film-novel rivalry. *Participations: Journal of Audience & Reception Studies, 13*(2), 289–307.

Jerslev, A. (2006). Sacred viewing: Emotional responses to *The Lord of the Rings*. In E. Mathijs (Ed.), *The Lord of the Rings: Popular culture in global context* (pp. 206–221). London and New York: Wallflower Press.

Michelle, C. (2007). Modes of reception: A consolidated analytical framework. *The Communication Review, 10*(3), 181–222. doi:10.1080/10714420701528057.

Michelle, C., Davis, C. H., Hardy, A. L., & Hight, C. (2017). Pleasure, disaffection, 'conversion' or rejection? The (limited) role of prefiguration in shaping audience engagement and response. *International Journal of Cultural Studies, 20*(1), 65–82. doi: 10.1177/1367877915571407.

Mikos L., Eichner, S., Prommer, E., & Wedel, M. (2008). Involvement in *The Lord of the Rings*: Audience strategies and orientations. In M. Barker & E. Mathijs (Eds.), *Watching The Lord of the Rings: Tolkien's world audiences* (Vol. 3, pp. 111-128). New York: Peter Lang.

Rae, N., & Gray, J. (2007). When Gen-X meet the X-men: Retextualizing comic book reception. In I. Gordon, M. Jancovich, & M. McAllister (Eds.), *Film and comic books* (pp. 86–100). Jackson: University Press of Mississippi.

Stam, R. (2005). Introduction: The theory and practice of adaptation. In R. Stam & A. Raengo (Eds.), *Literature and film: A guide to the theory and practice of film adaptation* (pp. 1–52). Oxford: Blackwell Press.

Thompson, K. (2007). *The Frodo franchise: How The Lord of the Rings became a Hollywood blockbuster and put New Zealand on the map*. North Shore, NZ: Penguin.

Turnbull, S. (2008). Beyond words? *The Return of the King* and the pleasures of the text. In M. Barker & E. Mathijs (Eds.), *Watching The Lord of the Rings: Tolkien's world audiences* (pp. 181–190). New York: Peter Lang.

CHAPTER 6

The Rise of the *Hobbit* Critic: From *The Desolation of Smaug* to *The Battle of the Five Armies*

INTRODUCTION

Our attention turns in this chapter to the diverse range of perspectives identified in the post-viewing surveys relating to *The Desolation of Smaug* (*DoS*) and *The Battle of the Five Armies* (*BotFA*). The former survey took place from January to July 2014, and collected 1051 responses from 62 countries, while the latter took place from January to May 2015, and amassed 840 responses in total from 49 countries. In what follows, we describe and interpret the shared viewpoints that were articulated by our respondents in the wake of each film, and use their comments to illustrate the core themes and concerns characterising each distinct perspective.

As this analysis suggests, whereas *An Unexpected Journey* (*AUJ*) received a very positive reception from the majority of respondents, the two *Hobbit* sequels were rather less well regarded. Furthermore, even those who quite enjoyed the second and third films appeared to adopt rather more defensive positions in response to increasingly trenchant critiques from others. The dominant trend, then, is the emergence of increasingly negative and indeed polarised perspectives on the cinematic value, quality and impact of Jackson's second and third *Hobbit* films. The critiques articulated by our respondents often also expressed a fundamental concern about the detrimental impact of key creative decisions; decisions that a growing number saw as reflecting, in turn, the commercial interests and imperatives associated with blockbuster

© The Author(s) 2017
C. Michelle et al., *Fans, Blockbusterisation, and the Transformation of Cinematic Desire*, DOI 10.1057/978-1-137-59616-1_6

film production. Whereas in Chap. 4 we explored the ways in which concerns about *The Hobbit*'s controversial social conditions of production were often suppressed or displaced by desire for a fetishised cultural commodity, our findings in this chapter suggest a gradual crystallisation and intensification of audience resistance to the processes and imperatives governing the cinematic adaptation, serialisation and blockbusterisation of Tolkien's original novel over time. This resistance, we suggest, is likely a by-product of the *thwarting* of that deeply felt desire, as viewers attempted to reconcile themselves to a series of films that, in many cases, failed to deliver the promised 'magic transport'. For a growing number, such failure clearly required explanation.

VIEWPOINTS RELATING TO *THE DESOLATION OF SMAUG* (N = 1051)

Concerns relating to the quality of the adaptation, artistic licence and textual aesthetics dominated the discursive terrain relating to *DoS* but became more immediately focused on two key issues: the addition of a new female character in the form of the elf guard Tauriel, and visual effects/textual realism. Our analysis identified five distinct viewpoints, representing three major and two minor audience segments: while varying greatly in size, each group is empirically observable and distinct from the others. Collectively, these five segments account for 91.8% of our survey respondents. For convenience and to signal each cluster's primary orientation toward the text, we shall refer to them as *Happy Hobbit Defenders, Disenchanted Hobbit Critics, Aggrieved Tolkien Aficionados, Hobbit Sceptics* and *Middle-earth Appreciators*. The relative proportion of each group is presented in Fig. 6.1. As in Chap.5, we discuss the perspective of the largest group of respondents first, followed by the much smaller group who expressed the *inverse* or opposite position, before presenting the views of each remaining group in descending size order.

Happy Hobbit Defenders

By far the largest group were 606 *Happy Hobbit Defenders* (57.7% of all respondents). Distinguishing this group was their sense of pleasurable re-immersion in the fantastical world of Middle-earth (s31, +4) where they relished the opportunity to reunite with their 'extended family' (s9, +2).

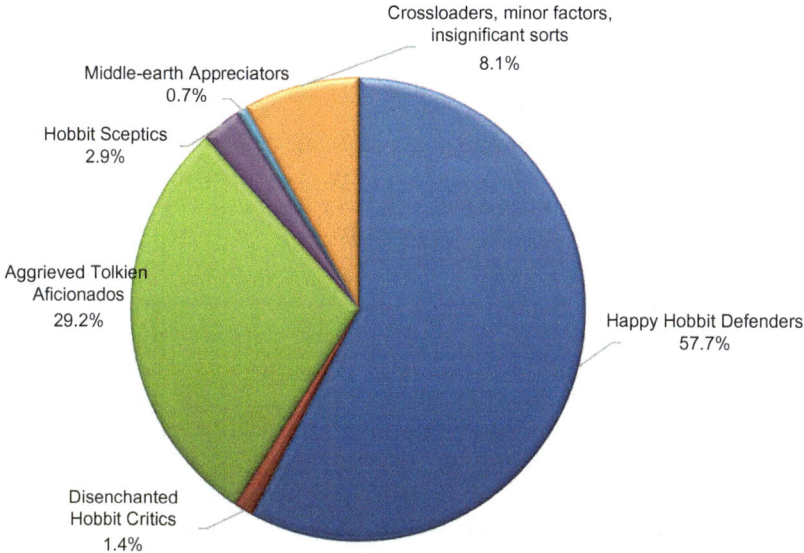

Fig. 6.1 Audience viewpoints, *The Desolation of Smaug*

They were fully transported, and reported feeling submerged and physically present within an exceptionally realistic narrative storyworld:

> All the set pieces were incredible, and they seemed so realistic. When I see the Woodland Realm and the inside of Erebor, I am blown away by its realism and how I never questioned the reality of it at all: I knew it was all green screen, but it sure didn't look like it! The amazing designs of all the settings were incredible, and it was wonderful to explore a new part of Middle-earth. (Chinese American woman, 17)

> For the 2.5 hrs that the film lasted, I felt as though I was in Middle-earth. I was completely immersed. (Manx man, 17)

> I just hadn't felt such a sensation since I was a child. The feeling of awe and wonder, like looking through a keyhole into a marvellous world. (Spanish man living in Greece, 28)

> I couldn't believe it when the credits rolled! This film pulls you in and moves you along at such a gallop that it is over before you know it. The detail—the peering under leaves to see the minute, then pulling back to reveal the majestic—it all worked for me. (Canadian woman, 68)

These respondents found the film to be exciting and fast paced, and they were mostly unaware of time passing (s18, +2). They were not especially concerned about the film's many deviations from Tolkien's novel; rather, they considered *DoS* an entertaining and highly creative adaptation that respected the source material, while updating the story to fit the expectations of modern audiences (s28, +2). They defended the film as a masterpiece in its own right (s35, +3), and welcomed this addition to the larger *Lord of the Rings* (*LotR*) franchise. They also regarded *DoS* as faithful to Tolkien's world (s10, +2), since it drew not only on the novel and Jackson's imagination, but also Tolkien's notes and the appendices to *The Lord of the Rings: The Return of the King* (*RotK*). For this group, creative changes and additions in the process of adaptation did not degrade Tolkien's classic Middle-earth tale (s17, +3) but rather were a welcomed recreation and extension of that world, and allowed for more depth and character development (s5, +2):

> It is a great story, and it is a classic. It is bound to be retold by different people in different mediums, and instead of nit-picking details, we should be happy that this story is reaching different people who never would have known about it if not for the movie. Why not think of it as a celebration of a well-loved story? (Filipino woman, 20)

> Exactly as Gandalf says in the first *Hobbit* [film]: 'Every good story deserves a few embellishments.' I enjoy Peter Jackson's storytelling and trust in his adaptions. This is also Hollywood; I'm sure in 20 years it will be remade again (as Hollywood loves to do). The world of Middle-earth deserves to be retold in many fashions. It's too fascinating to simply stay on the page. (American woman living in Germany, 29)

These respondents also generously praised the stunning New Zealand settings (s30, +4), the quality of the actors' performances (s13, +3), the CGI team's visual realisation of Smaug (s24, +4) and the exceptional craftwork involved in creating Laketown, Mirkwood Forest and Smaug's subterranean kingdom under the Lonely Mountain (s38, +3):

> Beautiful, stunning, artistic, lush, full of character and depth. Even thought Laketown was not my favourite of the three (the Elf-king's Halls were otherworldly, and Erebor was as majestic as imagined), it still suited the story. (Canadian woman, 26)

Importantly, while these respondents clearly adopted a transparent mode of reception, their post-viewing comments are somewhat more defensive than observed in our survey of *AUJ* viewers and draw more explicitly on discourses of film evaluation, presumably reflecting their recognition of the less than glowing evaluations of both *Hobbit* films offered by Tolkien adherents and other critics, for reasons our analysis helps elucidate.

Disenchanted Hobbit Critics

At the opposite extreme to these *Happy Hobbit Defenders* were a much smaller, but nonetheless distinctive and empirically observable, group of 15 *Disenchanted Hobbit Critics* (1.4%) for whom *DoS* did not evoke feelings of wonder and excitement, and who were neither deeply engaged nor positively emotionally invested (s15, +4). These critics considered *DoS* to be overly long and unnecessarily padded with new storylines and 'pointless invented characters' (s39, +3), as the following remarks suggest:

> Poor editing in cutting away from genuinely important character moments and scenes to spend time with substandard *World of Warcraft* invented characters badly shoehorned into the plot. (Scottish respondent, 42)

> It had the emotion of playing a video game. All the *LotR* movies had heart, and there was no reason why *The Hobbit* couldn't do the same. This is like a bad parody of the *LotR* films. (American man, 33)

Notably, these problems were attributed to commercial motivations and the filmmakers' desire to cater to the lowest common denominator by showcasing visual spectacle, crowd-pleasing additions and action scenes, all of which, these respondents believed, were ultimately detrimental to the film's storytelling, character development and emotional impact (s25, +3; s42, +4; s11, +4):

> The 'three films, all at Christmas' situation is certainly extremely exploitative and reeks of the corporate interference of Warner Bros. There is far too much CGI, often when not necessary. The films pander to simple whims, the desires for action and romance, rather than bothering to explore deeper themes in any detail. These films display and enhance only the superficialities of the narrative. (Australian man, 24)

Had I been able to actually see an artistic purpose behind the films, I would have been far more accepting (regardless of their relative closeness to Tolkien's story). What is most disappointing is the abominable story-telling, secondly the sacrifice of all attempts at ethical and/or philosophical depth on the altar of pampering to the least intelligent adolescent. (Danish man, 46)

Thus, we see explicit critique among this group of the film's commercial orientation as a blockbuster event-film aimed at general audiences. A dominant theme of this perspective is the view that *DoS* was just another formulaic blockbuster fantasy-adventure film, and failed to convey the powerful and meaningful messages of Tolkien's classic novel (s21, +3). These respondents were deeply angered by changes made to the story, its tone and themes (s1, +2), which diverged too far from Tolkien's original vision 'of truth, goodness, and beauty' (22, +2). In their view, the *Hobbit* films failed to convey the spirit or essence of Tolkien's work, which they felt was better reflected in *LotR* (s19, +2).

This concern was clearly related to a perception that *DoS* privileged visual spectacle over narrative and characterisation. This group observed that the film's combination of visual technologies (CGI, high frame rate [HFR] and 3D) generated distracting visual artefacts that undermined their ability to immerse themselves in the narrative storyworld (s37, +3; s26, +2), and particularly noted that characters seemed detached from their surroundings (s27, +2). In sum, these respondents appear to have adopted a critical mediated mode of response which ranges across all three subcategories—textual aesthetics, generic form and intentionality—suggesting a more generalised and wide-ranging critical reaction to the second *Hobbit* film amongst its most vitriolic detractors.

Aggrieved Tolkien Aficionados

Of more central concern for a much larger group of 307 *Aggrieved Tolkien Aficionados* (29.2%) was the perceived poor quality of *DoS* as an adaptation. Adopting a mediated mode of reception with a primary focus on generic form, these viewers were often scathingly critical of the film's creation of new characters and storylines (s33, +4) and its numerous diversions from Tolkien's original novel:

Peter Jackson took far too many liberties and creative license with the script and strayed too far from canon. ... Tauriel and her story arc go against canon and against everything Tolkien stands for. She felt like a fan fictional Mary Sue shoehorned into the script. (American woman, 44)

Jackson is just hungry for the crumbs of Tolkien's creation. Therefore he thinks that by inventing some bland and clichéd characters and storylines he has contributed to Tolkien's imaginarium. He has just descended into fanfiction. (Costa Rican man, 20)

As a result of these and other changes, this group believed Jackson's adaptation lacked the same spirit or essence of their beloved author's work (s8, +4), and had failed to convey its stirring vision and uplifting messages (s21, +3; s22, +3):

PJ's movies are entertainment. J. R. R. Tolkien's books are art. They serve a higher purpose of beauty and understanding. PJ's movies not only fail at this, but probably don't even attempt the task. (Italian man, 34)

I found that the over-importance put on the special effects, the battle scenes and the (canonically non-existing) love plots ended up creating a piece of entertainment rather than a successful homage to Tolkien's book. The desire to make a movie enjoyable to everybody took the focus away from the themes and spirit essential to the novel and to Middle-earth as a whole. (Canadian woman, 21)

Thus, for these viewers, the powerful story of a small, reluctant hero was lost (s14, +2) in the process of turning a gentle children's tale into a Hollywood blockbuster action adventure fantasy that would appeal to contemporary audiences. Like the previous group, *Aggrieved Tolkien Aficionados* attributed these unwelcome additions and changes to commercial motivations; they believed the film was 'catering to the lowest common denominator' and 'showcasing special effects at the expense of storytelling' (s42, +3; s11, +2):

It's all about marketing, about catering to the masses. Kili is the fan service for the tweenage fangirls, as is the romance subplot, Tauriel is eye candy for the guys, the action is ridiculously over-the-top and what gets lost? Exactly, the story telling! Jackson has, in essence, become the George Lucas of fantasy. (German woman, 29)

The story has been dumbed down much more than the first movie. Gone is the wordplay, gone is the brain over brawn, gone is the riddling, to be replaced by repetitive, boring battle scenes, some romance with an overly handsome dwarf for the girls—move over Legolas—and a movie that oozes Hollywood rather than Tolkien. (British woman living in New Zealand, 49)

The fundamental concern of this group, however, is the lack of respect shown toward Tolkien's written work and ethical vision in the process of adapting this novel for the big screen (s1, +3), which is now more explicitly attributed to the impact of commercial interests on the film's content and focus. Consequently, these respondents thought the film lacked the charm or appeal (s15, +2) of the book and author to which their loyalty primarily lies—their primary intertextual reference point is the written works of Tolkien. Hence, they did not feel especially invested in the film's outcome or the fate of its characters and experienced a lack of transportation and immersion in the storyworld (s23, −3). Nonetheless, many reacted more positively to the film's textual aesthetic, praising the beautiful New Zealand scenery (s30, +4) and admiring the creative realisation of Smaug (s24, +2) and key locations such as Mirkwood, Erebor and Laketown (s38, +2), while remaining less enamoured of other aspects of the film's visual realisation, such as the excessive use of CGI and the lack of textual realism.

Hobbit Sceptics

These latter issues dominated the responses of 30 *Hobbit Sceptics* (2.9%), for whom the key failing of *DoS* was its lack of narrative as well as visual realism and believability, which these respondents attributed to the overemphasis on visual effects that were of uneven quality. This group strongly believed that scenes often lacked tension and emotional impact, and attributed this to too much focus on action at the expense of adequate character development (s25, +4), as this 30-year-old Finnish woman explains:

The potential for great character interaction is there, but is only barely hinted at in the actual movie ... and all the one-word exchanges that are there are completely over-shadowed by the over-whelming pacing and the long 'trick-up-their-sleeve' battle-scenes ....

This group also believed that the protagonists' continued survival despite endless brushes with death lacked credibility (s34, +4):

> As far as these two *Hobbit* movies go, everyone other than those who are evil are completely invincible. In *LotR*, Boromir was killed in the first film, instating that these were just people (more or less). Now, not only do the dwarves always escape inevitable death, but the elves (specifically Legolas) have been made into superheroes, performing stunts that would have been laughed at in *LotR*. (Canadian man, 18)

> The violence and fighting were so much more gritty in *LotR*. When Frodo and Gollum fight, it hurts when they hit each other or bang their heads against stone. In this movie it's just lots and lots of chaotic and slightly ridiculous fighting, trying to cram all the dwarves into one shot. And it doesn't hurt. (Danish woman, 23)

Many of the concerns of *Hobbit Sceptics* appear to stem from a critical evaluation of the quality and execution of the CGI and other visual effects, and a perception that the interaction of these effects with the HFR 3D projection technologies was far from seamless. The film's artifice was insufficiently concealed for these viewers (s32, −3), and they could often tell what was real and what was fake on screen. At times, characters seemed like cardboard 'cut-outs' visually separated from backgrounds (s27, +2), and many scenes looked fake and video-game-like, rather than cinematic (s12, +3), particularly in comparison with the 'gritty realism' of the *LotR* trilogy:

> With the exception of Smaug, the CGI was terrible. I understand that using prosthetics like they did on Lurtz in *LotR* is a bit impractical, but my goodness did he look better than Azog. I recall the scene where they are riding towards the forest of Mirkwood, and it looked like a video game with bad graphics—you could just tell that the ponies were CGIed over the background. A scene like that would have NEVER been allowed to be shown in the *LotR*. Scenes like that instantly snapped me out of it and prevented me from 'submerging' into the story. (Canadian woman, 25)

The extensive fight and chase sequences and the barrel/river escape scene were identified as especially unconvincing. Conscious of the film's lack of visual realism in some places and the story's lack of plausibility in others, these respondents did not feel particularly immersed within the narrative storyworld (s15, +2); they also believed the movie dragged in places, being overly long.

However, they reacted more positively to other textual features and were not averse to changes being made in the process of the novel's adaptation for the big screen (s1, −2; 33, −4). They also strongly rejected the suggestion that the inclusion of additional material was purely commercially driven (s11, −4); so, unlike other groups, did not express explicit opposition to perceived blockbusterisation. Also unlike the previous group, these respondents showed moderate approval of the addition of Tauriel as a female elf guard (s6, +2), but were critical of the fact that she primarily featured in the context of an 'unnecessary' love triangle (s41, −3). They were impressed by the scenery (s30, +4) and the creative realisation of Smaug and key locations (s24, +3; s38, +3), the quality of most of the acting (s13, +2) and the soundtrack (s29, +3), but considered this lacked the 'heart-lifting epicness' of the *LotR* soundtracks. As this suggests, the *LotR* film trilogy was the primary intertextual reference point for these respondents. Overall, they believed that *DoS* failed to match the first trilogy's epic scale (s4, +2), realistic aesthetic and general level of excellence. In theoretical terms, we characterise this viewpoint as reflecting a mediated mode of response with a particular focus on textual aesthetics.

Middle-Earth Appreciators

Factor analysis allowed us to identify a second very small but nonetheless unique segment of seven *Middle-earth Appreciators* (0.7%) who praised the acting and craftsmanship of the film (s13, +3; s38, +2), as well as its beautiful scenery (s30, +4). This group were not averse to changes being made in the process of adaptation and believed the story of *The Hobbit* would inevitably be retold in different ways (s17, +2). They appreciated the film as Jackson's interpretative adaptation and accepted the need for some changes from the novel (s35, +3). But more especially, they relished the opportunity to be reunited with their extended Middle-earth family (s9, +4), and valued the film despite its various flaws, seeing it as fast-paced and exciting (s18, +3). While *somewhat* transported (s31, +2), they nonetheless considered *DoS* a lesser film in comparison to *LotR*, lacking the same epic scale and the extraordinary level of realism (s4, +3), yet they still valued it as part of the wider Middle-earth story. They were, however, particularly critical of the CGI (with the exception of Smaug [s24, +2]), and did not consider the film's visual effects to be seamless (s12, +4; 32, −4)—with the barrel scene being noted as especially weak (36, −4)—and considered the general look of the film to be un-cinematic and more like high-definition home video (s26, +2). Their primary point of reference, clearly, is the *LotR* film trilogy. While this cluster is more difficult to interpret due to its small size and thus the paucity of detailed qualitative comments, we suspect these respondents may have commuted between the transparent and mediated modes, particularly at moments that were visually jarring—textual aesthetics were clearly a concern for this group.

Viewpoints Relating to *The Battle of the Five Armies* (N = 840)

Similar patterns were apparent in our participants' responses to *BotFA*, with some further divisions emerging among more ambivalent viewers. Six distinct groups were identified: varying greatly in size, these groups together accounted for 87.0% of respondents. We have labelled these clusters *Fulfilled Hobbit Fans, Angry Hobbit Critics, Unhappy Tolkien Adherents, Ambivalent Middle-earth Enthusiasts, Appreciative Film Critics* and *Frustrated Middle-earth Fans*. That some of these descriptors are similar to those used in the previous section reflects a significant degree of continuity in the views expressed; however we have avoided using exactly the same nomenclature because these are (in most cases) different individuals responding to stimuli that are specifically related to the third *Hobbit* film. Figure 6.2 illustrates each group's relative proportion within our sample. While the largest and most enthusiastic group, *Fulfilled Hobbit Fans* (n = 405), again adopted the preferred transparent mode of reception, they comprised just 48.2% of our sample—a considerably smaller proportion than in the case of *AUJ*'s *Enchanted Hobbit Fans* (74.0%) and *DoS*'s *Happy Hobbit Defenders* (57.7%). Evidently, *BotFA* elicited even more mixed and often sharply critical responses than either of its predecessors, for various reasons that our analysis pinpoints.

Fulfilled Hobbit Fans

The proportionately smaller numbers associated with the most widely shared fan perspective were, nonetheless, effusive in their praise for the

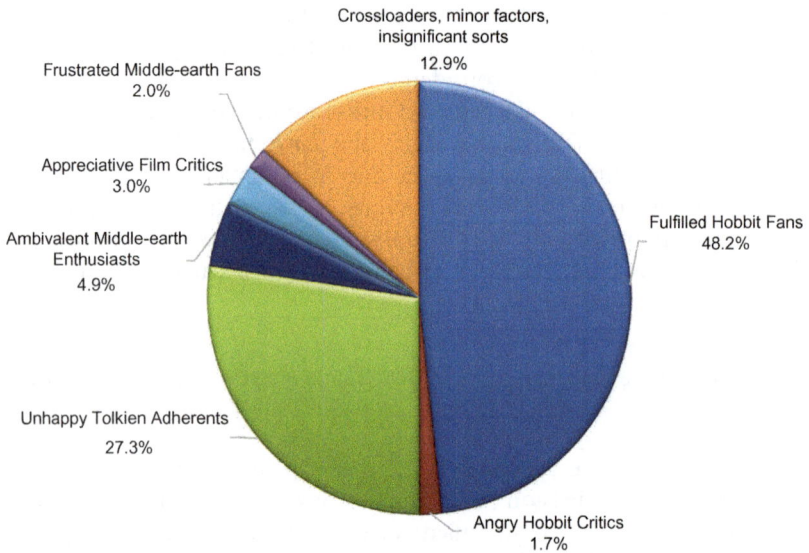

Fig. 6.2 Audience viewpoints, *The Battle of the Five Armies*

final film in the *Hobbit* trilogy. *Fulfilled Hobbit Fans* especially appreciated the consistently 'top notch' acting (s32, +4), which many described
as enhancing immersion and identification with characters: 'The actors
made me BELIEVE in dwarves and hobbits and orcs for the time I
sat in front of the screen. They came to life and were real. They exist'
(American woman, 53). Howard Shore's elegant and moving soundtrack
was also said to have evoked strong emotions and feelings of nostalgia
(s34, +3):

> Howard Shore's musical version of Middle-earth is just as important as the
> film and even more so in making the audience feel the emotions and land-
> scapes through his music. (Finnish woman, 44)

These viewers reported feeling deeply immersed and intensely engaged
in the narrative storyworld, and many said they lost awareness of the
external world and of time passing (s13, +3), suggesting that this group
primarily adopted the preferred transparent mode of reception:

When the movie finished I felt like it had just started some minutes ago. (Romanian man, 17)

As always in PJ's Middle-earth productions I feel like sitting IN that world and watching from a distance. Of course the popcorn is missing in that world—but to be honest, I forgot to eat it while watching the film. I totally ignored other people around sniffing, coughing, rustling. (German woman, 48)

Indeed, this group found the film to be an exciting and captivating combination of humour, romance, action and tragedy (s3, +2), and many enjoyed watching it with significant others (s38, +2). While most acknowledged a few flaws, they nonetheless regarded *BotFA* as a technically impressive and emotionally powerful visual spectacle (s17, +3), and praised Jackson and his team's skill in bringing the action to life in such dazzling detail (s23, +2):

I enjoyed the movie overall. It was entertaining and beautiful. I appreciate the obvious dedication, skill and love of all of those involved in the production. It showed in every frame. I was completely immersed in the world-building. The storytelling left a bit to be desired, however, particularly in developing character relationships and playing out key character moments on screen. Character seemed to have been sacrificed for spectacle too often but not quite enough to ruin the overall experience for me. (American, 51)

While enjoying *BotFA* from an aesthetic and sensorial perspective, these viewers also greatly appreciated the film's 'timeless' themes of 'honour, love and self-sacrifice' and its messages about finding and fighting for one's home, learning the value of the journey (s29, +4), and overcoming the corrupting influence of greed (s25, +2),[1] suggesting acceptance of textual messages—again consistent with the transparent mode of response:

This is the true spirit of the story. Not just the adventures of a funny hobbit, but a journey of discovery of values greater than what we find in our everyday lives. And about learning to give value to peace over war. Five Armies succeeds in delivering this message, thanks to Peter Jackson being able to find character driven moments amidst all the action. (Spanish man living in Germany, 29)

For these respondents, *BotFA* offered an emotionally satisfying and highly pleasurable conclusion to the *Hobbit* trilogy and a successful bridge to the *LotR* films; they gladly accepted it as part of the canon (s27, +3): 'I was very happy with the "dots" presented for connecting, leading the viewer right into *The Fellowship of the Ring*, the first instalment of the *LotR* trilogy. Well done' (American woman, 58). Seeing the film as an essential part of a much larger saga played out across both film trilogies, many expressed considerable sadness that their cinematic foray into Middle-earth was finally over (s30, +4):

> This is for two reasons: because of everything that happened in the movie with Thorin and Kili dying, and because I knew this is the end of the Middle-earth movie adventure, which I love. (Polish woman living in the UK, 30)

> This film was more than just a film, it was the end of an era that I have invested so much of my time and emotion into. So when it ended I couldn't help but feel emotional because I knew that I wouldn't go back to Middle-earth again. (American man, 20).

Angry Hobbit Critics

At the furthest extreme from this generally glowing reception were a much smaller group of 14 *Angry Hobbit Critics* (1.7%) for whom the film was deeply disappointing; several felt personally betrayed by Jackson. They most strongly agreed that the adaptation had 'destroyed a piece of my childhood soul' (s20, +4), and most wanted to walk out before the film ended (s16, +4):

> I really wanted to leave. I kept wishing we were at the last killing scene, and I didn't even want to go back to the Shire with Bilbo at the end of the movie. I really didn't want my feelings about the Shire tainted with any of the crap that Jackson had polluted the rest of the movie with. (New Zealand woman, 37)

Issues relating to the privileging of action and spectacle over narrative and characterisation were key sources of discontent. They believed the shift away from Bilbo as the central protagonist and the lack of character depth made it hard to feel empathy for major figures or care about their fate (s28, +4; s10, +2), and lamented the way in which excessively violent action and battle scenes supplanted quieter, character-driven moments (s, 14 +2):

> Thranduil's motivations are all over the place, his actions and speech constantly contradict each other, make little sense and so on. Thorin doesn't have real flaws, just some gold-induced psychosis. Bard is, of course, a perfect hero without flaws. (Danish man, 29)

> From Bilbo killing a Warg in single combat in the first film to this cinematic ruination Jackson has not just inserted one more crap-action star into the mix, he's sullied a true literary hero. (American man, 40)

These *Angry Hobbit Critics* also strongly agreed with s4 (+3): '*Five Armies* is a circus of freaks, marvels, and high-flying pageantry. Like any circus, we're there to gasp and to laugh, but not to feel.' In their view, *BotFA* was vastly inferior to the *LotR* trilogy, which had managed to retain Tolkien's intense spirituality (s12, +3; s37, +2). The film's many 'superfluous, self-indulgent' diversions from the concentrated brilliance and wonder of Tolkien's novel were regarded as deeply problematic (s22, +3): 'Too much action, too much focus on visual effects, where *LotR* was so much more focused on characters and story, and not just made-up plotlines like Tauriel/Kili, or taking Thorin's madness to such a boring and unbelievable level' (American, 21). Aspects of filmcraft such as direction, plot, the script, editing and CGI were also subject to critique (s18, +3; s35, +2). In sum, this perspective appears to reflect the adoption of a sharply critical mediated mode of reception with a focus on generic form that has extended into other aspects of media production such as textual aesthetics and intentionality, leaving these respondents extremely disillusioned by what they regarded as a tedious, bloated adaptation that disappointed in every respect. For these respondents, the *Hobbit* trilogy and this film, in particular, reflected the corruption of the wider Middle-earth franchise by Jackson's self-indulgence in tandem with commercial interests.

Unhappy Tolkien Adherents

A sizeable group of 229 *Unhappy Tolkien Adherents* (27.3%) similarly found the film very disappointing and disengaging, but focused their criticisms more centrally on aspects of adaptation; hence we see continuity with the *Aggrieved Tolkien Aficionados* discussed earlier, who similarly adopted a mediated mode of reception focused on generic form. For these respondents, *BotFA* was first and foremost a failed adaptation that deviated too far from Tolkien's original masterpiece (s22, +4). They were especially critical of its over-emphasis on 'non-stop bad action and battle scenes' instead of Tolkien's character-driven narrative (s14, +4):

> There is an extreme over-reliance on action to drive the story and what character-driven scenes there are seem to be exclusively non-canonical— such as the romance between a suspiciously human-looking and surprisingly beardless dwarf, and a feminist-appeasing, non-canon Elven Amazon. (British man living in Scotland, 19)

A lack of depth to the characters undermined identification and empathic response for these viewers (s28, +2), while unnecessary padding disrupted the story's momentum and detracted from its central narrative focus (s2, +3):

> Many of the scenes given to Legolas, Tauriel and Kili's relationship and Alfrid are either poorly-developed and often felt superfluous, shoddily edited, or characterized by bad dialogue. Since they are not central to the main themes of the story either, I think much of the time would be better spent concentrating on the main characters, their conflicts and dilemmas. (Norwegian man, 40)

Chief among the many unwelcome additions in *BotFA* were the (poorly rendered) comic-relief character of Alfrid (s26, +3) and the decidedly un-Tolkienesque love story between Kili and Tauriel (s31, +4), an issue to which we return in Chap. 8:

> I have been a life-long Tolkien fan. One of the reasons is that his books are about many forms of love; of kin, of home, of good over evil. To see relationships such as those between Thorin and his nephews, between Kili and his brother, between Bilbo and all the Dwarves sidelined for what I gather was a studio-requested, completely unnecessary and very badly written love triangle was bitterly, bitterly disappointing. (British/Australian woman living in the UK, 55)

Many considered this particular plotline especially cheesy and clichéd (s6, +3). Notably, they attributed the focus on action, romance and superfluous padding to the filmmakers' desire to appeal to as wide an audience as possible, in a cynical bid to maximise commercial box office takings (s8 +3; s33, +2):

> The problem I have with the additions made to the story is that none of them added anything to the story; they just inflated it into an action-heavy movie with barely any of the charm and core messages of the *Hobbit* tale. I feel that most of the additions to the film were simply made so that the filmmakers could make three movies, make as much money as possible by turning the story into a shallow action adventure, rather than try to enrich the plot. (New Zealand woman, 23)

We observed many comments of this nature in response to other Q statements, suggesting stronger objections to processes and practices associated with blockbusterisation had developed among Tolkien-orientated viewers by the trilogy's conclusion. While issues relating to textual infidelity and the negative impact of commercial interests on the adaptation of a Tolkien's important work were thus of central importance, these respondents were also somewhat critical of the film's CGI and seemingly 'weightless' gravity-defying action, which undermined the film's credibility as well their immersion in the narrative storyworld (s35, +2; s24 +2), something that was also noted by other groups.

But, as committed Tolkien enthusiasts grew more trenchant in their criticisms of the films over time—indeed, this viewpoint is marked by a rather more comprehensive sense of displeasure than observed among *Aggrieved Tolkien Aficionados* in our previous survey—others managed to find a few redeeming features in the final *Hobbit* instalment, suggesting further fracturing among fans of the wider franchise.

Ambivalent Middle-Earth Enthusiasts

Ambivalent Middle-earth Enthusiasts (n = 41; 4.9%) expressed strong reservations about many of the same elements, and were particularly concerned at the diversions away from Tolkien's strong spirituality in favour of unrelenting action, seeing *BotFA* as a lesser film to the *LotR* film trilogy (s37, +4; s12, +2):

By the end of the *LotR* even when I watch it today I am almost at the point of tears every time, it emotionally sucker-punches you. This was something I honestly didn't experience again with *The Hobbit*. Thorin, Fili and Kili's deaths should have had me in bits after spending nine hours with them on this journey, in comparison to Boromir's death after only three; it was absolutely more heartfelt, poignant and tonally very different. The same can be said for the action sequences; *The Hobbit* tended to, at times, lean towards the ridiculous and comedic. (British man, 24)

Everything about the *LotR* was superior, both in the book and in the movie .... Where the *LotR* saga omitted much from the book to fit into three movies, the *Hobbit* saga added much (too much) to fill up three movies .... It just doesn't have the same impact or nearly the depth of the *LotR* (the book or the movie), which I truly love. (American man, 54)

As in the case of *Unhappy Tolkien Adherents*, these viewers did not appreciate Tauriel's addition to the franchise (s7, −4) and strongly disliked her relationship with Kili (31, +4), seeing it as forced, superfluous, distracting and in some cases a violation of Tolkien's sacred canon, reflecting an in-depth knowledge of the wider series of books:

I think anyone who knows Tolkien lore knows just how deep the hatred runs between the elves and dwarves at this point in time in Middle-earth's history. I think the romance between Kili and Tauriel not only feels awkward, but it takes away from the importance of Legolas and Gimli's friendship in the *LotR* in bridging the divide between their two peoples. (Australian woman, 25)

I didn't like at all the subplot, not because it didn't happen in the book but for the lack of substance. I feel that it was forced into a romantic story because it had to have one, not because it was allowed for the natural development of the characters. (Uruguayan woman, 33)

This group also expressed concerns about the negative influence of commercial imperatives on the decision to make a trilogy and thus to pad the film out with invented scenes and storylines (s8, +3; s33, +3), weakening its quality and impact (s6, +3):

I came to the conclusion that a trilogy has been a mistake, even two parts are overmuch .... If it were a three-hour film, it would have been a small masterpiece, and the director didn't need to insert a pack of new characters. Tolkien's story is perfect, compact and linear. Jackson's [is] overstretched, overpopulated and often sagging. (Russian woman, 59)

Nonetheless, despite various criticisms of the quality of the adaptation and the film's failure to live up to the high quality seen in the *LotR*, this group recognised the film's overall achievements and appreciated the tremendous effort expended in bringing *The Hobbit* to cinemas (s19, +4):

> I have a lot of issues with how Jackson has adapted *The Hobbit*, especially his over-reliance on CGI and adding extra unnecessary characters and plots, but the films are still highly entertaining and full of heart. (American man, 20)

Hence, this group maintained that despite its many flaws, *BotFA* was still worth seeing, since it provided closure to the six-film Middle-earth series (s21, +3). They enjoyed the experience of watching the film with others (s38, +2) and much like *Fulfilled Hobbit Fans*, appreciated its messages and timeless themes (s29, +2). They also valued the clarity and sharpness of the imagery in fast-paced action scenes (s9, +2), achieved through the use of HFR. Unlike *Angry Hobbit Critics* and *Unhappy Tolkien Adherents*, they did not regard the film as an unremitting failure, but certainly expressed considerable ambivalence in their responses. In theoretical terms, this perspective appears to reflect the adoption of a variant of the mediated mode of reception focused on *BotFA*'s generic form as an adaptation/prequel, with *both* the novel and Jackson's earlier *LotR* films constituting significant intertextual reference points. While the group's predominant focus is on comparing *BotFA* with the superior works from which much of its value is derived, they also seek to acknowledge a few redeeming features as an entertaining media product that constitutes just one (somewhat disappointing) episode in an ultimately satisfying Middle-earth saga.

There are thus some important distinctions between this group and the more comprehensively disenchanted factions. Despite all three groups evidently adopting a mediated mode of reception, their responses emphasise different aspects of generic form, intentionality and textual aesthetics to which each group objects more or less strongly. Such subtle distinctions can be difficult to observe using traditional research approaches, as these typically aggregate respondents based on their reactions to discrete issues or questions which are then analysed in isolation from each other, when in fact respondents may have diverse opinions about *different* issues, agreeing on some but disagreeing—perhaps strongly—on others. Here, conversely, we can see the value of Q methodology in allowing for the empirical observation and characterisation of holistic perspectives where there may be certain areas of consensus—some common ground—but also specific areas of quite profound *disagreement* that, in other approaches, would be entirely obscured or downplayed, despite their evident importance to the individuals concerned. Furthermore, without the use of factor analysis and its capacity to objectively compare a very large number of Q sorts, systematically identifying among them distinct patterns of response, it would not be possible to characterise these highly significant commonalities in the shared subjectivities of the various audience groups: the number and complexity of the computations involved in delineating the shared perspectives that are latent within hundreds of individuals' rankings of 36–42 Q items is quite simply beyond the capacity of casual observation.

Appreciative Film Critics

This capacity of Q to recognise significant distinctions among viewpoints is also evident in the delineation of one further group of 25 *Appreciative Film Critics* (3.0%), who were not as highly engaged as *Fulfilled Hobbit Fans* but still considered *BotFA* a laudable effort (s19, +4) and worth seeing, if only to gain a sense of closure (s21, +4):

> I loved the *LotR* movies, and they remain a significant part of my life in that I re-watch them when I am feeling sad or am missing my siblings and friends, with whom *LotR* was part of our growing up together. *The Hobbit* was simply not as good as the *LotR*, but because it is part of Tolkien's world, it is an extension of my appreciation of the *LotR* films. In that respect, even though it did not measure up, it was still worth watching. (New Zealand woman, 19)

Unlike the previous groups, these respondents warmly welcomed Tauriel's addition to the Middle-earth franchise (s7, +4) and were less strongly averse to her romantic entanglement with Kili:

> I appreciate that Jackson recognized the lack of a strong female character for female viewers. I thought she was a fantastic balance: many people

disliked her relationship with Kili, but I thought it was nice. (American woman, 21)

I appreciated that Tauriel allowed us to get a glimpse of the stratification of Elven society (Silvan, Sindarin, and Noldorin) that isn't present in the original trilogy and wouldn't have been possible without the inclusion of her character. Also, ladies kicking ass. (Canadian woman, 25)

What is especially interesting in this group's responses is the focus on evaluating aspects of filmcraft. Whereas all previous groups tended to express a strongly subjective, emotionally charged response, this group instead articulates a more moderate evaluation of the film's quality across various dimensions. Hence, the acting was commended as excellent (s32, +3), they enjoyed the soundtrack (s34, +2), and they were impressed by the technical feat of mounting such an extensive battle scene (s11, +3). Also finding favour among these respondents were the film's visual effects (s5, +3); they enjoyed the clarity of the images, particularly in fast-paced action scenes (s9, +2). They also expressed approval of the film's messages and core themes of love, honour and self-sacrifice (s29, +2). Nonetheless, these respondents were clearly not particularly captivated nor engrossed by this film; they evidently did not feel transported into the narrative world, because the film lacked tension and emotional impact (s13, −3; s1, −3; s 36, −4):

One of my chief criticisms of the third film was how unemotionally involved I was with it. Perhaps it was because it was too choppy and felt rushed, or perhaps it was because the characters were re-established with their goals. I think the emotional beats are there, but it just didn't have a cohesive feel for me. (American man, 47)

Thus, this group appear to have primarily adopted a mediated mode of reception focused on aesthetic issues and on assessing the cinematic *quality* of the film. Their position is akin to that of the amateur film critic, offering reflections on *BotFA*'s various strengths and weaknesses. While some areas receive praise, others are found lacking—including the stretching of the story across three films (s33, +3) and the focus on action and battles in place of quieter, character-driven content (s14, +2).

Frustrated Middle-Earth Fans

Our final smaller grouping comprised 17 *Frustrated Middle-earth Fans* (2.0%), who were especially critical of the disruptive effects of the CGI and HFR 3D, and of scenes which lacked credibility in their defiance of fundamental laws of physics—most notably one in which Legolas is depicted leaping and scrambling his way up a hail of falling masonry during an extended battle sequence (s24, +4):

> I understand that Legolas is not human and that Middle-earth has magic deep within its roots, but the acrobatics in this movie were over the top. In the *LotR* trilogy Legolas had one or two acrobatic acts that I saw as natural due to my suspension of disbelief, but having full scenes dedicated to these physics-defying acrobatics made them very hard to ignore, and that took me out of the movie. (Dutch woman living in Norway, 23)

> It became more like a superhero movie and lost the serious weight that *LotR* had. PJ should have learned to press that 'stop-it's-too-much' button a long time ago. Some acrobatics, as in *LotR* is fine, but too much and you start to feel bored. (Swedish man, 20)

This group felt *BotFA* relied too heavily on CGI, the quality of which was variable (s35, +3), producing displeasing visual artefacts and undermining any sense that the antagonists posed a genuine threat. Their sense of immersion was continually disrupted by visually jarring elements which drew attention to the constructed artifice of the film. Many of these disruptive features were related to the use of high frame rate projection combined with CGI and 3D. Since these features undoubtedly shaped the responses of a significant minority of viewers for all three films, we shall explore *The Hobbit*'s use of new cinematic technologies in greater depth in Chap. 7.

Another key concern for *Frustrated Middle-earth Fans* was the film's lack of closure and its failure to tie up various loose ends (s39, +4). They were left wanting more, and in particular many had hoped to witness the funerals of Thorin and Kili:

> I didn't feel that the end was well tied up at all. Too many important conclusions were missing (the Arkenstone, who becomes king or whether Dain does, what happens with the gold). I think if I didn't have any knowledge of the book ending it would be even more of an issue, as it means the films are not internally consistent. (New Zealand woman, 22)

Troublesome too for these respondents were some of the non-canoni-cal additions and the film's generous 'extra padding'. They believed the film diverged too far from Tolkien's spiritual core, better expressed in Jackson's *LotR* films (s37, +2), but were generally pleasantly surprised by Tauriel's addition to an otherwise masculine domain (s7, +2). They were also critical of the script (s6, +2) and did not appreciate Alfrid's 'point-less' and 'cringe-worthy' comic-relief routine (26, +3). Unlike most other groups, *Frustrated Middle-earth Fans* felt sad when *BotFA* was over (s30, +4), but more because it signified the finale of a much-loved franchise rather than any deep affection for the film itself (s21, +3):

> I was left wanting more. I wanted to see certain scenes that I didn't get and most of all I wanted the movie not to end since that would mean the end of everything *LotR* [sad emoji]. (Belgian man, 23)

While they were not entirely transported and did not find the film utterly engrossing nor especially powerful emotionally, finding fault with many aspects, they nonetheless appreciated the achievements of Jackson and company in making it (s19, +3), and enjoyed the social aspect of watch-ing it with significant others (s38, +2). Like the previous group, such responses suggest the adoption of a mediated mode of reception focused on textual aesthetics as well as generic form, with particular emphasis on issues relating to the quality of the film's visual realism, narrative struc-ture, characterisation and related aspects of filmcraft, with the *LotR* film trilogy being the locus of intertextual comparisons.

CONCLUSION

What comes through very clearly in delineating these shared perspectives is the degree of similarity and overlap between them, along with some quite clear and highly significant lines of division. Whereas earlier studies have noted key distinctions between Tolkien readers, *LotR* film fans and fans of the extended Middle-earth franchise, our research suggests that these groups became internally fractured in response to elements that were quite specific to the content, narrative focus, visual aesthetic and perceived intent of Jackson's two *Hobbit* sequels *themselves*. That is to say, while our respondents possessed and expressed particular (and often multiple) intertextual allegiances—to the original novel, other works in Tolkien's wider oeuvre (including the appendices to *RotK*), the *LotR* films and books, and of course the first *Hobbit* film—these affinities were activated in relatively unpredictable ways in response to textual features that were largely unanticipated and to some extent unknowable prior to viewers' encounters with each of the three films in cinemas. Thus, how respondents reacted to particular story elements, changes from the novel and Jackson's creative additions varied considerably, in ways that our analysis has clearly illuminated.

For instance, while those following the *Hobbit* production knew that Evangeline Lilly would be playing the role of an invented female character, they were not privy to the particular narrative context in which Tauriel would be featured, although some had certainly expressed fears in our earlier surveys that she might be reduced to a token love interest. Nor were book readers able to anticipate that Tolkien's description of Legolas as 'light as a feather' might be rendered on screen as a capacity to entirely defy fundamental laws of physics—even feathers are subject to gravity, after all! While it might be presumed that 'serious' Tolkien readers would be more likely to object to the introduction of non-canonical elements, our data shows that many committed readers were nonetheless very satisfied by the three *Hobbit* movies, including several who said they had disliked the *LotR* films. Similarly, among the most *and* least enthusiastic of our respondents, we find fans of the wider Middle-earth franchise who claim to enjoy equally all things *LotR*. While there are certainly some significant patterns and trends in the form and content of audience engagement and response, the basis for divergent responses to the *Hobbit* films is rather more complex than a simple transposition of prefigurative desires and intertextual allegiances onto these fully realised films. The complicated relationship that exists between pre-existing fandoms, socio-demographic characteristics, discursive competencies and affiliations will be explored in greater depth in Chap. 9.

Before then, our attention turns in the following chapter to one unique feature of the *Hobbit* trilogy that evoked mixed reactions among many respondents—and that is the films' use of new and advanced cinematic technologies by combining extensive CGI and other digital visual effects with 5 K resolution, HFR 3D projection. Our focus on film technologies reflects the novelty of a mainstream feature film adopting a noticeably different visual aesthetic, not merely to conventional cinema, but also to the *LotR* trilogy to which it serves as a prequel series. Whereas the art design for the *LotR* was more strongly influenced by the sublime visual aesthetic of Alan Lee, who illustrated reprinted versions of

Tolkien's written works in the 1990s, the *Hobbit* films both continue and diverge from this tradition, with Lee's gorgeous panoramas being counterpoised by fast-paced, almost entirely 'weightless' aerial combat scenes that appear to emulate contemporary martial arts films such as *Crouching Tiger: Hidden Dragon* (2000), possibly in an attempt to appeal to *The Hobbit*'s international audience, given the growing importance of the Asian market. Other digitally rendered characters and scenes are reminiscent of those one might encounter in a very realistic high-resolution video game. This directorial decision to make a perceptible shift away from the practical effects for which the *LotR* was acclaimed toward more extensive reliance on digital visual effects, and a green screen used in combination with HFR 3D projection, brought with it unintended and unanticipated consequences that variously delighted and disturbed our respondents, for reasons we address in Chap. 7

NOTE

1. Among the 'timeless themes' noted by our respondents were courage, loyalty, friendship, the importance of home, the value of the journey, the dangers of greed and selfishness, personal growth through tackling new challenges, standing up for what you believe in and never giving up.

CHAPTER 7

Pioneering Cinematic Technologies and *The Hobbit*'s Hyperreality Paradox

INTRODUCTION

A distinctive aspect of the *Hobbit* trilogy, one intimately related to its blockbusterisation, was its deployment of a particular combination of cinematic technologies to create a unique digital aesthetic. Most recent Hollywood action/fantasy blockbusters rely heavily on what Allison (2011, p. 326) terms 'digital indexicality', meaning 'a blend of computer-generated images and material recorded from reality.' Live-action photography and prosthetics are now frequently used in combination with motion capture, digital stunt doubles, computer-generated characters, digital compositing and rotoscoping, and creature design. As Manovich (2001, p. 302) notes, contemporary digital cinema is now 'a particular case of animation that uses live-action footage as one of its many elements.' Ideally, the layering of what is real and what is artifice will be rendered seamless on screen, such that viewers cannot distinguish digitally created or enhanced characters, objects and settings from real-world ones. Peter Jackson's *Hobbit* trilogy aimed to radically extend the cinematic apparatus by combining advanced computer-generated imagery (CGI) with stereoscopic 3D and a high frame rate (HFR)—in this case, 48 frames per second, compared to the industry standard of 24 fps. Director Jackson promised audiences this new hyperreal digital aesthetic would effectively eradicate the cinematic 'fourth wall' and greatly enhance their sense of immersion in the fantastical world of *The Hobbit*. Jackson is among a small group of filmmakers pioneering

C. Michelle et al., *Fans, Blockbusterisation, and the Transformation of Cinematic Desire*, DOI 10.1057/978-1-137-59616-1_7

storytelling with this new extended apparatus[1]; an experimental collective of technologies that, when combined, present new technical challenges (Aylsworth 2012).

Importantly, given our overall thesis, the decision to invest in this extended cinematic apparatus and effectively pioneer the use of HFR 3D for global audiences was motivated by agendas and imperatives that are inherent to blockbusterisation. The contemporary revival of 3D was primarily driven by the demand to create and protect unique and compelling cinematic experiences in the face of intense competition for audiences from other media (Turnock 2013; see also Atkinson 2011). HFR, in turn, has been championed as a means to resolve perception problems with conventional 2D and its extension into 3D, since its use eliminates motion blurring and eases other troubling visual artefacts caused by dimness, ghosting and flickering (Häkkinen et al. 2008; Solimini 2013), thereby creating the perception of much smoother movement, as well as 'crisp, clear, realistic images' (Aylsworth 2012, p. 66). However, the level of production and distribution investment HFR 3D required virtually demanded that these innovative technologies be used with films that could attract large audiences. These pressures, in turn, reinforced the need to turn the *Hobbit* franchise into a cinematic 'event', to be promoted as the first realisation of a complete (digital) cinema (Elsaesser 2013). *An Unexpected Journey (AUJ)*, and to a lesser extent the rest of the trilogy, thus needed to promote and educate viewers about the benefits of this new aesthetic. These developments played across an inherent tension within CGI-driven digital cinema: the celebration of technical achievements (in paratextual material) is never intended to disrupt suspension of disbelief in the film's core narrative. As noted above, these are technologies designed to be seamlessly integrated with other visual effects; something that is essential for all digital cinema, but perhaps most fundamental to the creation of 'realistic' worlds within the fantasy genre.

Unfortunately for Jackson and his production team, our findings suggest that global audiences were divided on the value of these technological innovations, the particular combination of which seemed to generate paradoxical perceptual and experiential effects for different individuals. Whereas for most of our respondents, *The Hobbit*'s hyperrealistic digital aesthetic enhanced both spectacular *and* narrative immersion, a significant number experienced it as unconvincing and distracting, and as undermining suspension of disbelief—but for complex reasons. In what follows, we attempt to explain why the combination of extensive CGI with HFR 3D projection generated disenchantment among a significant segment of our respondents, and extend on our previously published work to consider the evolution of responses to new cinematic technologies across the life of the *Hobbit* trilogy (see Michelle et al. 2015). We suggest that their divergent reactions stemmed in part from an inherent hyperreality paradox that emerged from the combination of technologies that generate *contradictory* visual effects and artefacts.[2] Used together, CGI and HFR 3D produced noticeable and distracting effects for a significant segment of *The Hobbit*'s initial audience, leading them to report experiences that we categorise as indicative of a *mediated* mode of reception. Among the majority of others, those same effects either significantly enhanced perceptions of realism and textual presence, or else awareness of their distracting effects was actively suppressed in favour of close narrative engagement, thereby sustaining their adoption of the preferred *transparent* mode of response.

In a broader sense, the range of responses to the *Hobbit* trilogy's hyperreal digital aesthetic do more than provide convincing evidence of the ways in which cinematic engagement depends upon a variety of extra-textual factors; they simultaneously expose some of the inherent tensions within blockbusterisation itself and the challenges for media producers seeking to design innovative media content for globalised audiences. Responses to *The Hobbit*'s technological realisation were fundamentally shaped by different aesthetic tastes, competing cinematic values and pre-existing intertextual allegiances. Most notably, viewers' appreciation for the technical expertise and craftwork that contributed to the appearance and critical success of Jackson's earlier *Lord of the Rings* (*LotR*) trilogy undoubtedly complicated their reactions to *The Hobbit*'s digital aesthetic. These prior allegiances, in addition to other factors—such as the novelty effect, audience anticipation, gender, age and professional industry experience/media education—potentially shaped viewers' appreciation of technological enhancements, in turn variously reinforcing and undermining pleasurable spectatorship for different audience segments.

Technologically Mediated Immersion, or Distraction?

The broader context for Jackson's innovative deployment of multiple imaging technologies is a long history of critical commentary around the prioritising of visual spectacle in mainstream cinema, typically viewed as inherently antithetical to narrative (Wood 2002). Such criticism has been increasingly voiced in response to the growing reliance on spectacular digital visual effects since the early 1980s. Numerous critics have suggested that CGI has less value than film because it has no real referent; Neale (1983 p. 12), for example, dismisses effects celebrated as achievements in themselves as moments in which 'the narrative starts to freeze and spectacle takes over' (see also Pierson 2002; White 2013). Critical work in this area is only slowly moving beyond this assumption of a dichotomy between spectacle and narrative (see King 2000; Whissel 2014).

Not dissimilar debates have emerged about stereoscopic 3D film projection, which critics have described as 'gimmicky' nonsense and a distraction whose spectacular visual projections disrupt immersion and narrative engagement (Ebert 2010; Kermode 2009; see also Higgins 2012; Johnston 2012). Dissenters from these views have argued instead that 3D might work 'towards the common goal of immersion' (Brown 2012, p. 263) and thereby serve classical storytelling (Klinger 2013; see also Ross 2013). While these academic debates have been rendered somewhat mute recently with the consistent commercial success of CGI-heavy films as well as recent 3D productions—with 3D now in its 'third age' (Atkinson 2011) following short-lived appearances in the 1950s and 1980s (Kim 2013; Klinger 2013)—they clearly informed divergent responses amongst *Hobbit* fans and critics alike, as we shall show.

Even before *The Hobbit* appeared in theatres, quite similar themes and concerns became evident in critical evaluations of Jackson's use of HFR, which was showcased in the 10-minute *AUJ* preview screened at CinemaCon in April 2012. Whilst proponents touted HFR as radically redefining the future of cinema and uncritically reiterated a familiar discourse affirming the inherent desirability of greater realism (Turnock 2013), critics slated it as looking cold and 'tawdry, like a made-for-TV film' (Marks 2012, n.p.). While some felt HFR enhanced their sense of immersion, others felt the footage was so hyperrealistic it disrupted narrative engagement (Quesnel et al. 2013). Turnock (2013, p. 31) notes similar responses from those who deemed HFR's hyperrealistic filmmaking as 'uncinematic' and 'like a TV soap opera'. Having committed to this new apparatus, Jackson sought to address initial aesthetic critiques of *AUJ* by making image adjustments for *The Desolation of Smaug* (*DoS*) and *The Battle of the Five Armies* (*BotFA*), softening the image to 'make it look a bit more filmic. Not more like 35 mm film necessarily, but just to take the HD quality away from it' (Jackson, as cited in Child 2013, n.p.). By this stage, however, he also faced an overall narrowing of the trilogy's audience—for reasons that our research has sought to document.

ADDING TO EMPIRICAL RESEARCH: INSIGHTS FROM THE *HOBBIT* AUDIENCE PROJECT

While polarised assessments of the nature and possible effects of HFR 3D were clearly already circulating within the wider public domain before the first film's release, they were not a major feature of the previewing perspectives of our respondents, as noted in Chap. 3. Even those who did express some concerns tended to adopt a 'wait and see' attitude, while others remained confident of Jackson's and Weta Digital's ability to convincingly recreate Middle-earth on screen. We were thus very curious to find out how our respondents would eventually react to *The Hobbit's* pioneering digital aesthetic once *AUJ* hit cinemas.

The range and depth of our research on audience responses to *The Hobbit's* use of emergent cinematic technologies offers a useful counterpoint to the predominant approaches in research and scholarship on CGI/3D/HFR spectatorship, much of which either relies on theoretical conjectures, or abstracts technological mediations from the narrative and social contexts in which they are normally encountered. To date, there have been surprisingly few empirical studies of CGI's impact on viewers' perceptions of realism and related experiences of narrative transportation, immersion and emotional affect (Sobchack 2006). A significantly larger body of research has focused on audience reactions to 3D. Some of these studies measure viewers' experiences of physical *presence* in the virtual world, which refers to feeling part of a mediated environment (Häkkinen et al. 2008; Slater and Usoh 1993),[3] which may be further reinforced by the *genre* (Ji and Lee 2014; see also Baranowski et al. 2016; Michelle et al. 2012; Pölönen et al. 2012). Other research suggests viewers perceive 3D imagery as more 'natural', realistic and lifelike than 2D (Pölönen et al. 2009; Rooney et al. 2012; Seuntiens et al. 2005; Sobieraj and Krämer 2014).[4] There are also studies which have documented persistent physical discomfort for a minor segment of the 3D audience, including visual fatigue, motion sickness and headaches.[5]

While research on stereoscopic 3D projection is ongoing, the possibilities of combining HFR with 3D have only very recently become the subject of investigation. Jackson's commitment to using HFR was informed in part by small-scale laboratory experiments conducted by visual-effects specialist Douglas Trumbull in the 1970s and 1980s, which showed that the reduction of blurring made possible by HFR significantly enhanced viewers' sense of immersion and realism and substantially increased visual stimulation (Trumbull 2011). These effects appear to be broadly confirmed by other studies (Kim and Oh 2014; Kuroki 2012; Quesnel et al. 2013; Ruppel et al. 2015), particularly in relation to scenes involving rapid movement. To date, however, much of the existing research on audience responses to HFR 3D is very small scale and experimental. Our research is very likely the first large-scale 'real-world' study to explore audience reactions to these technological innovations in depth, and has captured rich qualitative data in the form of viewers' self-reported reactions and responses to the first mainstream HFR 3D film released, contextualised within wider social and discursive contexts of reception.

In what follows, we explore our respondents' diverse and indeed polarised responses to the particular combination of digital and projection technologies used in the *Hobbit* films. While it is difficult to separate out the specific effects and experiences of each of these technologies (given that they were encountered in combination and in a specific narrative context), it is nonetheless evident that the majority of respondents who expressed their views believed HFR enhanced their perception of textual realism and their feelings of physical presence within the 'world' of Middle-earth. Elaborate and richly detailed scenes and crisp action generated feelings of awe and excitement, while the greater intimacy and clarity conveyed by HFR intensified their emotional engagement and response to characters and scenes. For a smaller but still significant number of other respondents, however, the same technologies had the opposite effect and were too obvious and distracting as artificial constructs. In addition to introducing a number of visual artefacts that are essentially very similar to those observed by Quesnel et al. (2013), the combination of CGI, 3D and HFR intensified some viewers' awareness of the films' extensive reliance on technology to create the appearance of reality, one that was not perceived as natural or convincing. Perceptions of textual *realism* (and whether it remains seamless) thus lie at the heart of this paradoxical audience response to the *Hobbit* films.

Realism in this sense refers to a film's perceived authenticity and believability. In a transparent mode of reception, realism is assessed in terms that accept the basic textual premise that the depicted reality should be related to *as though* real. Viewers who adopt this mode suspend their disbelief and enter into the fictional storyworld on its own terms, accepting characters, actions, settings and events as true to life, realistic and believable given the internal parameters established by the fictional world, and in keeping with information and cues provided within the text itself (see Chap. 2). The images and scenes on screen must, therefore, be convincingly realistic, or sufficiently lifelike, or at the very least internally *consistent* with the on-screen storyworld, if they are to persuade the viewer to continue engaging in this way. As we will demonstrate, however, such judgements are largely subjective assessments formulated as the viewer encounters and evaluates the fully realised text in light of their own expectations, knowledges, aesthetic tastes, intertextual allegiances, affective predispositions and perceptual processing capabilities.

Visual Spectacle, Apparent Realism and the Transparent Mode of Reception: Appreciation for Technological Enhancements Among Viewers of *The Hobbit*

As noted in previous chapters, in each of our post-viewing surveys, the largest group of respondents adopted a transparent mode of reception and were extremely enthusiastic about the film and its technological realisation. *Enchanted Hobbit Fans (AUJ)*, *Happy Hobbit Defenders (DoS)* and *Fulfilled Hobbit Fans (BotFA)* all reported a high degree of narrative transportation and immersion, as well as powerful emotional responses to seeing Middle-earth realised on screen. For these viewers, the blending of artifice and reality was relatively seamless, allowing them to suspend disbelief and focus their attention entirely on the narrative, for the most part. Many among this group remarked that the greater clarity and detail provided by HFR 3D significantly enhanced their sense of wonder at the beauty, detail and believability of Jackson's rendering of Middle-earth. Many also reported intense sensations of physical presence in the fictional storyworld. They described feeling as though they had stepped through the screen into Middle-earth and could reach out and touch objects, and even participate in the action alongside characters, offering support to Casetti and Somaini's (2013, p. 421) contention that 'cinematic 3D … allows spectators to project themselves into the represented world, almost to the point of touching it.' For many of these respondents, the 'fourth wall' was effectively dissolved:

> The depth of the visual field into the vast backdrops of New Zealand was so breath-taking. I felt as though I was actually amongst the characters on screen participating in their journey. (American woman, 19; *Happy Hobbit Defender*)

> I saw *DoS* several times in HFR 3D, and I loved it. It looks so real and despite the big screen, action and effects somehow seemed more intimate. (Canadian woman, 60; *Happy Hobbit Defender*)

> Similar effect to the 3D, but a lot more immersive. Once the battle commences, you feel you are there; the movements are incredibly fluid and look more real. (Mexican man, 21; *Fulfilled Hobbit Fan*)

Confirming the hopes of Jackson and his production team, HFR was said to have greatly improved the quality and clarity of the imagery and the overall 3D viewing experience, with better colour and significantly less motion-blurring during panning, making fast action scenes smoother and easier to follow, and was also said to have enhanced respondents' feelings of immersion in the on-screen world. Several noted that HFR was more comfortable and enjoyable to watch than standard 3D, and resolved previously experienced problems such as eye strain and nausea.

However, even among those who were otherwise enchanted by *The Hobbit*, there were particular moments when narrative immersion was disrupted as the artifice of the films became more apparent, diverting their attention away from the story:

> The time when I watched *BotFA* in 3D was when I felt least emotionally connected to the story, to be honest. Because I spent too much time aweing over the spectacular camerawork and CGI effects, I found it harder to immerse myself in the story. (Vietnamese woman, 22; *Fulfilled Hobbit Fan*)

Several also noted that their feelings about HFR 3D changed as they became more familiar with this visual aesthetic, and in response to technical adjustments made by Jackson and his team for *DoS* and *BotFA*:

At first, the HFR makes you think you're actually in the studio looking at the cast and crew working, which I'm not a real fan of, because it's a 'fairytale' world and you don't want it to be too realistic, but that feeling quickly disappears and then it's better than normal 3D. (Dutch woman, 39; *Fulfilled Hobbit Fan*)

Once I adjusted to it, action scenes were clearer and easier to follow (e.g. less motion blur). At first, it had a somewhat fake look to it, until I became used to it. (New Zealand man, 30; *Appreciative Film Critic*)

I've grown to enjoy HFR; I didn't at first. I think PJ and WETA have been working on perfecting this format after *AUJ*. I think it's much clearer, better, now in *BotFA*. (American woman, 59; *Fulfilled Hobbit Fan*)

Tellingly, a number of these respondents said they had consciously chosen to pay selective attention to those features of the text which *facilitated* immersion, whilst downplaying distracting elements, as suggested by a 24-year old Australian woman who found the HFR 3D 'Distracting at first (the characters looked like cut-outs against a background), but once you stopped paying attention it was fine.' LeGrice (2002) suggests the spectator colludes with the text out of a desire for 'magic transport', and for this reason resists 'recognition of the artifice in favour of immersion in the illusion' (as cited in Hutcheon 2006, p. 143). Similarly, Pierson (2002, p. 103) notes that 'the audience knows very well that the impression of reality cinema is capable of producing is in fact fiction, but they choose to believe in these fictions all the same.' In effect, these respondents deliberately privileged engagement with narrative rather than visual spectacle, a capacity also noted by Thompson (1999, as cited in Ross 2013).

Many respondents were thus generally enthusiastic and optimistic about the new film technologies showcased in the *Hobbit* films, and relatively forgiving of occasionally disruptive visual effects and artefacts. While some acknowledged minor issues of quality and visual distortions, most *Hobbit* fans defended the films as praiseworthy for pioneering, if not yet perfectly executing, the use of cutting-edge film technologies. For a smaller group of others, however, these and other issues of quality and presentation undermined their ability to suspend disbelief and relax into pleasurable immersion.

ALIENATION AND DISAFFECTION: MEDIATED RESPONSES TO *THE HOBBIT'S* HYPERREAL DIGITAL AESTHETIC

Many of those who experienced the *Hobbit* films in a mediated mode were Tolkien readers whose attention was primarily focused on evaluating the quality of Jackson's adaptation of a much-loved novel, which many found lacking. However, in each survey, we identified other small but significant groups who articulated an alternative mediated response that was explicitly framed by a critical reaction to *The Hobbit's* visual aesthetic, which they experienced as disruptive and displeasing. These groups included 119 *Critics of Technological 'Enhancements'* (*AUJ*; 4.1%), 30 *Hobbit Sceptics* (*DoS*; 2.9%), and 17 *Frustrated Middle-earth Fans* (*BotFA*; 2.0%). Others also critiqued *The Hobbit's* over-reliance on CGI and noted distracting visual artefacts generated by the combination of CGI and HFR 3D, as part of more wide-ranging (and often scathing) critiques. These included 91 *Bored and Disillusioned Hobbit Critics* (*AUJ*; 3.2%), 15 *Disenchanted Hobbit Critics* (*DoS*; 1.4%) and 14 *Angry Hobbit Critics* (*BotFA*; 1.7%). For these respondents, the visual 'spell' of the *Hobbit* films was frequently fractured, and they could only perceive constructed artifice *as* artifice.

For many technology critics, the primary benchmark for assessing the success of *The Hobbit's* technological innovations was the earlier *LotR* trilogy, which enjoyed a reputation for high levels of craftwork in its production design, producing a 'gritty realism' which was often very favourably cited by our respondents. Many *LotR* fans remembered these films as having rendered an almost seamless realisation of Middle-earth (Cubitt 2008). Several nostalgically recalled the 'exemplary' quality of *LotR*'s prosthetics, modelling and 'bigatures' (small-scale replicas of structures), and its virtually imperceptible integration of CGI. Some intimated that *AUJ* and to a lesser extent *DoS and BotFA* looked 'artificial and cheap' in comparison, while others noted that *LotR*'s reliance on natural settings and carefully crafted props and prosthetics had been replaced by extensive use of 'bright and shiny' CGI in *The Hobbit*, resulting in many character scenes having to be filmed against a green screen:

> The problem with *The Hobbit* is that the effects take us further and further away from the gritty, realistic world that we grew to love in *LotR*. Eight weeks of location shooting for three 3 hour movies is a depressing statistic, especially when New Zealand itself was such a key character in the

original trilogy. The Extended Edition of *AUJ* shows us just how rushed post-production was after the decision to split into three films (with many effects-heavy sequences being added late, and the decision to make Azog fully CGI) and I think this was to blame for some of those effects seeming rushed and not up to Weta's usual high standard. I think in both movies, the replacement of miniatures with digital sets was a huge loss for realism, with neither new locations such as Laketown, or old locations such as Rivendell, feeling quite the way a Middle-earth location should. (British man, 23; *Hobbit Sceptic*)

Many other respondents stated that the CGI was too clearly apparent in places; lacking the 'random untidiness of natural objects' (Cubitt 2008, p. 187), scenes and characters appeared fake, undermining the credibility and believability of the visual rendering of Middle-earth. Scenes such as the barrel escape and characters such as the pale Orc, Azog, were frequently cited as exemplars of the films' failings in this regard:

> The CGI was not realistic looking; I wish it had been used more sparingly. I wanted to see a live action movie but I feel more like I saw an animated cartoon. Characters looked like 3D models from video games; it wrecked any sense of immersion. (American man, 21; *Angry Hobbit Critic*)

> If I want to experience a video game, I will play a video game. It jarred so much I've seldom felt its like, and it really, REALLY killed off so very, very much of the good feelings I sometimes built up during watching. No, if I disliked the shield- and Oliphaunt-surfing in the *LotR* trilogy, I positively loathed poor Legolas' video game sessions. After that, there was hardly any disbelief to suspend, so to speak. (Swedish woman, 30; *Frustrated Middle-earth Fan*)

As Purse (2007, p. 10) has argued, virtual bodies often appear unconvincing because they do not conform to the physical norms and laws that viewers associate with and recognise from actual human bodies, being subject to gravity and laws of physics governing mass, motion, impact and so on, and with particular muscular and skeletal movements (see also Lamarre 2006). By failing to observe physical laws governing movement associated with the real world, these scenes remained unconvincing. Ultimately for these respondents, *The Hobbit*'s extensive reliance on obvious CGI undercut the believability of the fictional storyworld and at times overwhelmed the narrative, disrupting or entirely precluding the pleasurable narrative immersion associated with a transparent mode of reception. Thus, they remained somewhat distanced, disengaged and more keenly aware of the films' flaws as constructed media products, reflecting their adoption of the mediated mode.

Other respondents focused more specifically on their experience of viewing in HFR 3D, and it is evident that HFR introduced additional tensions and perceptual artefacts. Many noted that the unprecedented clarity and visual detail revealed through HFR simultaneously drew attention to the artifice of *The Hobbit*'s sets and prosthetic effects:

> The HFR only served to highlight how artificial the filmmaking process was … It resembled a 'making of' rather than a film itself, with the peculiar result that it made everything—notably sets, lighting, costume, actors in the background you wouldn't ordinarily pay attention to—look somewhat cheap and ineffective. (British woman, 32; *Bored and Disillusioned Hobbit Critic*)

> The 'improved' high resolution or whatever he shot it in was hard on the eyes and didn't look like real life. It looked like a fakey movie set. (American woman, 44; *Disenchanted Hobbit Critic*)

A number of these respondents suggested the HFR made the films look and feel 'low-budget', 'clunky', and 'far too fake', thus supporting Turnock's (2013, p. 47) observation that HFR 'strips the footage of much of the sheen of its "cinematographic" effect, removing much of its expensive production value that has come to separate its look from that of television or video games.' Others noticed a visual artefact whereby scenes involving rapid motion seemed sped up, as though watching something on fast forward. Hence, the film appeared 'choppy' and 'disorienting': 'Visually, the movements of the actors appeared insanely rushed and frantic, and it was actually very unnerving' (Filipino woman, 27; *Critic of Technological 'Enhancements'*). For these respondents, a perceptible visual disjunction between real-life footage and digitally rendered characters, objects and settings further undermined believability, leading some to compare viewing *The Hobbit* to watching actors in a play, a 'making of' documentary, HD children's television programme or 'cheap Brazilian soap opera.'

Many of these more critical respondents had seen the films in multiple formats, and firmly believed these visual perceptual phenomena were specific to, or exacerbated by, the HFR 3D versions: 'Particularly in the high frame rate mode, I felt that characters (especially Azog) definitely suffered. I watched [*AUJ*] in a few different formats, and noticed it wasn't as bad in the regular frame rate' (American man, 37; *Critic of Technological 'Enhancements'*). The enhanced detail and clarity of HFR thus appears to have highlighted the presence of *overtly* artificial digital and prosthetic effects, rendering it impossible for these respondents to achieve or maintain suspension of disbelief, effectively precluding the desired (and preferred) transparent mode of reception and obstructing the process of narrative transportation.

DISCUSSIONS OF 3D, HFR AND CGI IN *DoS* WITH INTERVIEWEES

These polarised views over imaging technologies became immediately apparent in our first post-viewing survey, prompting members of our team to supervise a smaller, more focused project looking specifically at responses to the aesthetic of the second film in the trilogy, *DoS* (Elliott 2015). Combining an online survey with Skype interviews, this project allowed space for more detailed qualitative exchanges than our surveys could provide, and usefully supplemented the information gathered from additional questions on technologies that were added to the post-viewing questionnaires for *DoS* and *BotFA*.[6] These findings largely confirmed the patterns identified in our core project, while providing additional insight into specific positions on the use of HFR, 3D and CGI in the *Hobbit* trilogy. Perhaps the most useful reflections came from those interviewees who had watched both 2D and HFR 3D versions of *DoS* and who provided richly detailed explanation of their judgements on each, as in this example:

> It felt more like you were a part of the film with *DoS* rather than a spectator, which I felt like in *AUJ*. It's like I'm keeping up with everyone. As a spectator in anything, like a stage play, they would usually slow down their actions and exaggerate just so the audience can keep up. In HFR 3D it's like you're actually there moving naturally and organically as everybody else, so it's like you're a part of it ... the motion is realistic to me, because with HFR you're moving just as fast as they are. (Woman, 18–21)

Many respondents described themselves as experienced in watching 3D and argued that Jackson and his production team had learnt how to deploy these technologies within the film's narrative effectively. They appreciated the craft involved and the relative lack of emergent artefacts 'flying' into the audience (the use of negative parallax is often regarded by critics as an irritating distraction in 3D films). Interestingly, for most interviewees, the clear reference points for discussion were not just the earlier *LotR* trilogy but also James Cameron's *Avatar* (2009) as the contemporary exemplar for 3D, as well as a basis for critical comparison with its successful construction of a 'realistic' world within the fantasy genre.

Of the clear majority who provided positive reviews of *The Hobbit*'s HFR 3D aesthetic, many still reported initial unease and slight physical discomfort, or a period of adjustment to the nature of HFR images and the visual density they provided. And there were others who, while appreciative, noted that they were sometimes 'distracted' by the level of detail in parts of the screen not related to the main action; they were effectively lifted out of immersion in the narrative by the novelty of the (otherwise successful) aesthetic:

> The only thing I think that could hinder the films' narrative is that the HFR is so immersive, I found myself in awe at all the fine details in the set and environments. Maybe over time, our eyes will become used to such detailed environments. (Woman, 41–50)

Conversely, those expressing either critique of, or ambivalence toward, *The Hobbit*'s hyperreal aesthetic tended to focus on key moments such as the barrel scene in *DoS*, where Legolas appeared to them to be leaping about in completely unrealistic ways. Many also compared such sequences to Go-Pro video; needlessly frenetic, with too many point-of-view shots that did not work within the context of the rest of the film:

> In *LotR* they had really realistic combat where you feel like, 'Okay, this guy could die because he's not Superman', and they were like very mortal, it seemed ... The barrel scene ... when Legolas is like jumping around and stuff like that, I felt like that was really like 'okay, that CGI is so crap the whole Legolas is CGI right now.' (Man, 18–21)

For those expressing ambivalence toward the new hyperreal aesthetic, these contrasting points in *DoS* were evidence of inconsistency across the film in how successfully CGI, HFR and 3D were deployed in the service of successful storytelling. Those interviewees offering critical views pointed to some similar aspects which detracted from their enjoyment, typically while expressing variations of this comment: 'I really wish they would have stuck with the traditional viewing canvas [with] which people are used to seeing Middle-earth' (Man, 18–21). The failure to satisfy high expectations derived from the *LotR* trilogy was especially frustrating for these viewers:

> ... [I]t was overwhelming, because I've been waiting so long for these movies, seeing it for the first time was an overwhelming experience and then to see it look so bizarre and so different and weird, it really bothered me ... I hated it; I mean I really hated it. (Man, 26–30)

The most detailed negative assessments of *DoS* were often couched within a wider critique of the manner in which the adaptation of a classic book had strayed too far into the realm of cinematic spectacle. For some interviewees, there was just 'too much' of everything to enjoy the story the way it was designed to be experienced:

> I think you always say 'the book is so much better than the film', but I feel with *The Hobbit* it's too much jelly, too much tempo, too much action for this kind of story, for this kind of book ... It just made me feel like there was too much focus on the creatures, too much focus on the 3D, too much focus on the CGI, too much focus on the creature designs and the orcs, and too much beast. (Woman, 26–30)

Thus, while the underlying basis for objections to *The Hobbit*'s hyper-real digital aesthetic varied, it is clear that the visible presence of overtly artificial digital and prosthetic effects rendered it impossible for some respondents to achieve or maintain suspension of disbelief, effectively precluding the desired (and preferred) transparent mode of reception and obstructing the process of narrative transportation.

In our final survey relating to *BotFA* , we sought further information about the number of respondents for whom *The Hobbit*'s technologies were a visual distraction, and asked two open-ended questions that were then subjected to inductive coding (see Table 7.1). Of those who responded to a question asking *What impact, if any, did HFR have on your ability to immerse yourself in the story?*, 44.6% said HFR enhanced their viewing experience or was an otherwise positive experience, 18.3%

Table 7.1   Impact of high frame rate 3D and computer-generated imagery on enjoyment and narrative immersion, *The Battle of the Five Armies* post-viewing survey

Q: What impact, if any, did HFR have on your ability to immerse yourself in the story?	
Coded open-response question ($N = 278$)	Number of respondents (%)
A positive immersive or enhanced viewing experience	124 (44.6%)
A negative viewing experience	51 (18.3%)
Not important/no difference	47 (16.9%)
Mixed experience/response	43 (15.5%)
Other	13 (4.7%)

Q: Please share your views on the use and quality of the CGI and its impact on your immersion.	
Coded open-response question ($N = 741$)	Number of respondents (%)
Great/loved it	143 (19.3%)
Ambivalent response	122 (16.5%)
Preferred the practical effects of *LotR*	85 (11.5%)
Poor CGI undermined immersion/pleasure	79 (10.7%)
CGI was overused/would have preferred less	73 (9.9%)
Neutral/didn't notice/no impact	56 (7.9%)
CGI was poorly executed/poor filmcraft	43 (5.8%)
CGI enhanced immersion	29 (3.9%)
CGI was necessary/essential to the film	29 (3.9%)
Multiple categories/complex response	29 (3.9%)
Other/unclear	26 (3.5%)
CGI was unconvincing—like a videogame	19 (2.6%)
CGI detracted from the story/characters	8 (1.1%)

said it undermined immersion or was otherwise problematic, 15.5% expressed mixed views, and 16.9% said it made no difference to their viewing experience. A second question asked respondents to *Please share your views on the use and quality of the CGI and its impact on your immersion.* A more complex set of responses was identified, reflecting perhaps the greater familiarity with CGI among respondents and their ability to compare *BotFA*'s use of it with that seen in other key intertexts, most notably the *LotR* trilogy. The largest group (19.3%) expressed appreciation for the CGI in *BotFA*, with an additional 3.9% suggesting it enhanced immersion, and the same number again arguing CGI was essential or necessary to the film. More expressed negative views; 10.7% said it undermined immersion, 9.9% said it was overused and they would have preferred less CGI, 5.8% considered it poorly executed, 2.6% felt the CGI was unconvincing and video-game-like, and 11.5% preferred the practical effects of *LotR*; a further 16.5% offered ambivalent responses. Apparently, then, the quality of CGI was visually distracting for a significant number. While this may be due in part to poor technique or the rushed post-production period, our findings suggest it also clearly relates to the hyperreality paradox and the various perceptual artefacts that were generated by the trilogy's intensive use of CGI in combination with HFR 3D.

ACCOUNTING FOR DIVERGENT RESPONSES TO *THE HOBBIT'S* HYPERREALITY PARADOX

As we have shown, while the majority of respondents believed *The Hobbit*'s unique combination of technologies enhanced their pleasurable immersion in a hyperrealistic, life-like and utterly believable storyworld, others adopted a distanced—and in some cases antagonistic—variant of the mediated mode of response focused on evaluating the quality of *The Hobbit*'s aesthetic and technical execution, and its constructed artifice. It is also evident that some respondents alternated between these modes of response at different moments. The notion that viewers may shift or 'commute' between distinct modes of reception is explicit in the Composite Model that underpins our project (see Chap. 2) and has been acknowledged in previous theoretical work on special-effects spectatorship. For example, North (2005, p. 50) suggests that special effects 'derive maximum spectacular impact from their consumption as both convincing fictions and as artificial tableaux.' He also cites Buckland (1999), who describes endeavours to create digital effects that are so photorealistic and convincing that 'the spectator is not forced "out" of the text by special effects which betray their origins as mechanical craftwork' (North 2005, p. 51).[7] Concerning stereoscopic 3D, Ross (2012) suggests viewers are invited to move between subjective and objective modes of perception, and thus from a position of immersion *in* the text to a position of external reflection *on* the text—this being the fundamental distinction between transparent and mediated modes of response. Wood (2013) notes similarly ambiguous forms of engagement with IMAX.

Our research thus offers empirical support for recent theoretical claims, but also demonstrates that any assumption that these two modes of reception always pleasurably co-exist is problematic. Our findings suggest that when the mediated form takes a consistently negative aspect, transparent and mediated modes of reception potentially become incommensurate. That is to say, it is possible for viewers to find pleasure both in immersion (transparent mode) and evaluation (mediated mode) when evaluations of the text's construction are generally positive (or at least not derogatory) and where the assessment of textual quality supports and justifies close engagement: one can be both awed by the tremendous skill and technical prowess reflected in a film's special effects, and experience deep engagement with the storyworld, arguably at different moments. One can also acknowledge some aspects of weakness in the construction of a text but nonetheless accept it for what it is, and perhaps seek to redeem it out of loyalty to a particular director or franchise, for instance. Where such evaluations are markedly *negative* across a range of areas, however, the text may become irredeemably tainted. In such a case, the viewer may become so distracted by particular visual or textual elements that narrative immersion is no longer possible, nor desired.

Of course, some readers may object that not *all* viewers necessarily seek to experience such immersion in the first instance. No doubt this is true, at least of some. The film scholar, filmmaker or professional or armchair film critic may approach their viewing with a conscious intent to critically assess or perhaps learn from a filmmaker's demonstration of their film craft. Similarly, an avid reader of the novel on which a film is based may possess a more cerebral curiosity about how certain characters or scenes will be realised on screen, and experience pleasure in demonstrating their in-depth knowledge of the source text as they compare and evaluate the two forms. Such interests and foci may encourage the adoption of more distanced, evaluative, mediated modes of engagement from the outset. That said, our findings suggest that the vast *majority* of respondents did indeed hope to experience 'magic transport' back to a Middle-earth that, Jackson suggested, would be rendered in more compelling and immersive detail than ever before. (And, as previously noted, Jackson [2012] clearly articulated a specific authorial *intent* to facilitate narrative transportation: 'As a filmmaker, I try to make my movies immersive. I want to draw the audience out of their seats, and pull them into the adventure'.) Even in the case of avid readers, a commonly expressed hope was that the *Hobbit* films be 'as good as the book'—as compelling, as pleasurable and as effective in transporting them back into Tolkien's mythical universe. Unhappily, for a significant number, particular aspects of the films as fully realised clearly prevented or disrupted such immersion, effectively thwarting the fulfilment of these respondents' cinematic desire to return to Middle-earth.

Our research also illustrates how this process played out for individual viewers, and at different points in a film's viewing: a number of such moments or 'trigger' points were identified as especially disruptive and distancing, including the concluding sequence of *DoS* in which Smaug was smothered in gold (which one person said looked like 'nacho cheese'), the infamous barrel scene, and Legolas's gravity-defying antics, which in *BotFA* included him somehow scrambling up collapsing masonry as though entirely weightless—a number of respondents considered this scene particularly unbelievable, disrupting immersion.

Further analysis of our participants' socio-demographic data suggests that this kind of interpretive divergence may be related to levels of pre-release anticipation, media studies education/technical expertise, familiarity with digital effects and 3D, and prior intertextual affiliations—most notably, admiration for Tolkien's written texts and/or nostalgia for the look and feel of the earlier *LotR* trilogy (see Chap. 9 for a detailed analysis of these relationships). Häkkinen et al. (2008) suggest that viewing highly anticipated and emotionally significant content may lead a viewer to overlook or ignore stereoscopic distortions and visual artefacts that are distracting for others. This certainly seems true of many of our *Enchanted Hobbit Fans, Happy Hobbit Defenders* and *Fulfilled Hobbit Fans*, most of whom were existing *LotR* film fans who expressed a high degree of excitement and anticipation for the *Hobbit* films, and were thus primed and motivated to engage with the new trilogy on its *own* terms in order to enjoy the immersive pleasures promised by Jackson and in marketing materials. Just as LeGrice (2002, as cited in Hutcheon 2006) suggests, their strong desire for 'magic transport' and (re)immersion in Middle-earth perhaps led them to resist dwelling on the artificial means through which the cinematic illusion had been created.

For others, it was harder to overlook signs of artifice, for various reasons. Those *LotR* fans who expected or desired continuity with the authentic, grittily realistic look and feel of the earlier trilogy evidently found the hyperrealistic aesthetic of *The Hobbit* particularly jarring. Similarly, many Tolkien readers concerned that the films preserve the 'spirit of the book' suggested that the emphasis on CGI-enabled set pieces too often came at the expense of storytelling and character development. Both groups critiqued the CGI and HFR 3D, but for different reasons, including explicitly drawing upon previous experiences of (and preferences toward) CGI and 3D technologies.

CONCLUSION

We can tentatively offer some general conclusions regarding the ways that technologically enhanced cinema may reinforce pleasurable spectatorship, or undermine it. While we concur with Wood (2013) that the use of new formats may offer multiple points of engagement for viewers, perhaps leading them to commute, as Ross (2012, 2013) also implies, between being awed by and immersed within a spectacular narrative world (transparent mode) and reflecting on the skill behind its construction (mediated mode), we nonetheless suggest that the primary goal of those who produce fictional blockbuster entertainment—a goal explicitly articulated by Peter Jackson—is to encourage viewers to adopt a transparent mode of reception in which they experience suspension of disbelief, narrative transportation and pleasurable immersion. While some viewers may periodically commute to the more distanced and objective mediated mode and reflect on the quality of the text's production (in terms of visual effects, acting, the script, direction or soundtrack, for instance), consistently *negative* and even derogatory evaluations of textual quality undermine deep engagement with the narrative storyworld. Our research shows that cinematic spectacle was an important part of what audiences expected from *The Hobbit*, but primarily as a route to returning to their beloved Middle-earth and enjoying a new narrative in a familiar storyworld, rather than as an end in itself. Indeed, there is not *necessarily* a conflict between spectacle and narrative, as Wood (2002), Brown (2012) and Whissel (2014) suggest, but there most certainly *can* be when visual special effects are perceived as distracting, unconvincing or poor quality, as was true of a smaller but significant number of our respondents.

Our research also suggests that *The Hobbit*'s particular combination of stereoscopic 3D, HFR and CGI may have generated a hyperreality paradox in which there was a more apparent visual disjunction between real-life footage and CGI. This effect appears to have been compounded by additional visual artefacts which made real-life characters and scenes at times seem animated or artificial. As real-life footage was rendered significantly clearer and more like real life—indeed, hyperrealistic—with the use of HFR, it evidently outran the current capacity of CGI to replicate that reality in a believable way, and so undermined the films' perceived (seamlessly layered) realism. Hence, CGI looked more obviously fake; a problem likely exacerbated in 3D screenings due to additional visual artefacts produced by stereoscopic projection. The result disrupted narrative engagement for some otherwise primed and positively predisposed viewers of the *Hobbit* film franchise; responses which became more determinedly reinforced once *BotFA* hit cinemas. The example of the *Hobbit* trilogy, then, reveals many of the technical and perceptual challenges inherent to deploying innovative imaging technologies within globalised blockbuster franchise films.

This chapter is derived, in part, from an article published in *Convergence: The International Journal of Research into New Media Technologies* on 18 May 2015, available online: http://journals.sagepub.com/doi/pdf/10.1177/1354856515584880.

NOTES

1. At the time of writing, James Cameron is producing his *Avatar* sequels in 60 fps, while Ang Lee's *Billy Lynn's Long Halftime Walk* (2016) has been released in 120 fps format, to conflicting critical responses.

2. Buben partially accounts for this paradox by suggesting that 'the greater the memetic potential of the media image—that is the more faithfully the imaging process can reproduce the natural perception of the naked eye, the more apparent the artifice performed in front of the lens' (Buben 2007, p. 40).

3. Various studies have noted that the increased depth of 3D enhances viewers' sense of presence (Freeman and Avon 2000; Freeman et al. 2001).

4. Many of these and similar studies rely on small, laboratory-based research and offer contradictory findings (e.g. see Ji et al. 2013; Bombeke et al. 2013), while others have sought responses on 3D preference from audience immediately after reception (Cho et al. 2014; Rooney and Hennessy 2013). See also Wilcox et al. (2015) and Ruppel et al. (2015).

5. See Hakkinen et al. (2008); Pölönen et al. (2012); Solimini (2013); Tam et al. (2011); Urvoy et al. (2013); and Zeri and Livi (2015).

6. This project used a more conventional survey and interview methodology. There were 650 completed global responses to the survey, complemented by follow-up email and Skype interviews with 39 respondents who indicated they had seen both 2D and 3D versions of the film. This research was conducted by Darren Elliott, a postgraduate at the University of Waikato, and supervised by Craig Hight and Carolyn Michelle.

7. North further suggests that contemporary viewers have access to an 'exponentially expanding set of extra-diegetic, revelatory intertexts that enhance his/her ability to decode the spectacle' (p. 52) and to reflect upon the means by which cinematic texts are constructed, including, in the case of

The Hobbit, Peter Jackson's vlogs. Such material may encourage a mediated mode of response, in which viewers evaluate the execution of the text as an aesthetic object and media production (Michelle 2007).

References

Allison, T. (2011). More than a man in a monkey suit: Andy Serkis, motion capture, and digital realism. *Quarterly Review of Film and Video, 28*(4), 325–341.

Atkinson, S. (2011). Stereoscopic-3D storytelling: Rethinking the conventions, grammar and aesthetics of a new medium. *Journal of Media Practice, 12*(2), 139–156. doi:10.1386/jmpr.12.2.139_1.

Aylsworth, W. (2012). High frame rate distribution. *SMPTE Motion Imaging Journal, 121*(6), 66–68. doi:10.5594/j18215.

Baranowski, A. M., Keller, K., Neumann, J., & Hecht, H. (2016). Genre-dependent effects of 3D film on presence, motion sickness, and protagonist perception. *Displays, 44,* 53–59.

Bombeke, K., Van Looy, J., Szmalec, A., & Duyck, W. (2013). Leaving the third dimension: No measurable evidence for cognitive aftereffects of stereoscopic 3D movies. *Journal of the Society for Information Display, 21*(4), 159–166. doi:10.1002/jsid.164.

Brown, W. (2012). *Avatar:* Stereoscopic cinema, gaseous perception and darkness. *Animation, 7*(3), 259–271. doi:10.1177/1746847712456254.

Buben, J. (2007). The psychedelic sewing room. In R. Adelmann, A. Fahr, I. Katenhusen, N. Leonhardt, & D. Liebsch (Eds.), *Visual culture revisited: German and American perspectives on visual culture(s)* (pp. 40–66). Köln: Herbert von Halem Verlag.

Casetti, F., & Somaini, A. (2013). The conflict between high definition and low definition in contemporary cinema. *Convergence, 19*(4), 415–422. doi:10.1177/1354856513494174.

Child, B. (2013, December 13). Peter Jackson admits to 'softening' HD version of *The Desolation of Smaug. The Guardian.* Retrieved November 18, 2016, from www.theguardian.com/film/2013/dec/13/peter-jackson-48fps-tone-down-hobbit-desolation-smaug-hd.

Cho, E., Lee, K., Cho, S., & Choi, Y. (2014). Effects of stereoscopic movies: The position of stereoscopic objects (PSO) and the viewing condition. *Displays, 35*(2), 59–65. doi:10.1016/j.displa.2014.01.004.

Cubitt, S. (2008). Realising middle-earth: Production design and film technology. In H. Margolis, B. King, & T. Jutel (Eds.), *Studying the event film: The Lord of the Rings* (pp. 185–191). Manchester: Manchester University Press.

Ebert, R. (2010, May 9). Why I hate 3-D (and you should too). *Newsweek.* Retrieved May 10, 2014, from www.newsweek.org/2010/04/30/why-i-hate-3-d-and-you-should-too.html.

Elliott, D. J. (2015). *The Hobbit: The Desolation of Smaug*—A new era of realism? MA thesis, University of Waikato, Hamilton, New Zealand.

Elsaesser, T. (2013). The 'return' of 3-D: On some of the logics and genealogies of the image in the twenty-first century. *Critical Inquiry, 39*(2), 217–246.

Freeman, J., & Avons, S. E. (2000). Focus group exploration of presence through advanced broadcast services. In B. E. Rogowitz & T. N. Pappas (Eds.), *Proceedings of the SPIE: Human Vision and Electronic Imaging V* 3959, 530–539. doi:10.1117/12.387207.

Freeman, J., Lessiter, J., & Ijsselsteijn, W. (2001). Immersive television. *The Psychologist, 14,* 190–194.

Häkkinen, J., Kawai, T., Takatalo, J., Leisti, T., Radun, J., Hirsaho, A., Nyman, G. (2008). Measuring stereoscopic image quality experience with interpretation based quality methodology. In S. P. Farnard & F. Gaykema (Eds.), *Image Quality and System Performance V: Proceedings of SPIE-IS&T Electronic Imaging 68081B,* 1–12. doi:10.1117/12.760935.

Higgins, S. (2012). 3D in depth: *Coraline, Hugo,* and a sustainable aesthetic. *Film History: An International Journal, 24*(2), 196–209.

Hutcheon, L. (2006). *A theory of adaptation.* New York and London: Routledge.

Jackson, P. (2012). Peter Jackson HFR Q & A. Retrieved May 14, 2014, from www.thehobbit.com/hfr3d/qa.html.

Ji, Q., & Lee, Y. S. (2014). Genre matters: A comparative study on the entertainment effects of 3D in cinematic contexts. *3D Research, 5*(15). doi:10.1007/s13319-014-0015-6.

Ji, Q., Tanca, J., & Janicke, S. (2013). Does 3D increase the enjoyment experience? A comparative experiment on the psychological effects of 3D. *3D Research, 4*(2). doi:10.1007/3DRes.04(2013)2.

Johnston, K. M. (2012). A technician's dream? The critical reception of 3-D films in Britain. *Historical Journal of Film, Radio and Television, 32*(2), 245–265. doi:10.1080/01439685.2012.669887.

Kermode, M. (2009, December 23). Come in number 3D, your time is up. *Kermode uncut.* Retrieved May 16, 2014, from www.bbc.co.uk/blogs/markkermode/posts/come_in_number_3d_your_time_is.

Kim, J. (2013). Introduction: Three dimensionality as a heuristic device. *Convergence, 19*(4), 391–395. doi:10.1177/1354856513495325.

Kim, J., & Oh, S. (2014). Preference on high frame rate stereoscopic 3D in TV. *International Journal of Computer Science and Network Security, 14*(2), 37–40.

King, G. (2000). *Spectacular narratives: Hollywood in the age of the blockbuster.* London, GBR: IB Tauris.

Klinger, B. (2013). Three-dimensional cinema: The new normal. *Convergence: The International Journal of Research into New Media Technologies, 19*(4), 421–431. doi:10.1177/1354856513494177.

Kuroki, Y. (2012). Improvement of 3D visual image quality by using high frame rate. *Journal of the Society for Information Display, 20*(10), 566–574. doi:10.1002/jsid.107.

Lamarre, T. (2006). New media worlds. In S. Buchan (Ed.), *Animated Worlds* (pp. 131–150). Bloomington: Indiana University Press.

Manovich, L. (2001). *The language of new media.* Cambridge: The MIT Press.

Marks, P. (2012, May 2). Switch to high-frame-rate 3D movies may not be smooth. *New Scientist.* Retrieved May 10, 2014, from http://www.newscientist.com/issue/2863.

Michelle, C. (2007). Modes of reception: A consolidated analytical framework. *The Communication Review, 10*(3), 181–222. doi:10.1080/10714420701528057.

Michelle, C., Davis, C. H., Hight, C., & Hardy, A. L. (2015). The *Hobbit* hyperreality paradox: Polarization among audiences for a 3D high frame rate film. *Convergence: The International Journal of Research into New Media Technologies.* doi:10.1177/1354856515584880.

Michelle, C., Davis, C. H., & Vladica, F. (2012). Understanding variation in audience engagement and response: An application of the composite model to receptions of *Avatar* (2009). *The Communication Review, 15*(2), 106–143. doi:10.1080/10714421.2012.674467.

Neale, S. (1983). Masculinity as spectacle: Reflections on men and mainstream cinema. *Screen, 24*(6), 2–17.

North, D. (2005). Virtual actors, spectacle and special effects: Kung Fu meets 'all that CGI bullshit'. In S. Gillis (Ed.), *The Matrix trilogy: Cyberpunk reloaded* (pp. 48–61). London: Wallflower.

Pierson, M. (2002). *Special effects: Still in search of wonder.* New York: Columbia University Press.

Pölönen, M., Salmimaa, M., Aaltonen, V., Häkkinen, J., & Takatalo, J. (2009). Subjective measures of presence and discomfort in viewers of color-separation-based stereoscopic cinema. *Journal of the Society for Information Display, 17,* 459–466. doi:10.1889/JSID17.5.459.

Pölönen, M., Salmimaa, M., Takatalo, J., & Häkkinen, J. (2012). Subjective experiences of watching stereoscopic *Avatar* and *U2 3D* in a cinema. *Journal of Electronic Imaging, 21*(1). doi:10.1117/1.JEI.21.1.011006.

Purse, L. (2007). Digital heroes in contemporary Hollywood: Exertion, identification and the virtual action body. *Film Criticism, 32*(1), 5–25.

Quesnel, D., Lantin, M., Goldman, A., & Arden, S. (2013). *High frame rate (HFR) white paper.* Vancouver: S3D Centre, Emily Carr University of Art + Design. Retrieved May 14, 2014, from http://research.ecuad.ca/-/uploads/2014/02/VFR_WhiteSheet_v7_print.pdf.

Rooney, B., Benson, C., & Hennessy, E. (2012). The apparent reality of movies and emotional arousal: A study using physiological and self-report measures. *Poetics, 40*(5), 405–422. doi:10.1016/j.poetic.2012.07.004.

Rooney, B., & Hennessy, E. (2013). Actually in the cinema: A field study comparing real 3d and 2d movie patrons' attention, emotion, and film satisfaction. *Media Psychology, 16*(4), 441–460. doi:10.1080/15213269.2013.838905.

Ross, M. (2012). The 3-D aesthetic: *Avatar* and hyperhaptic visuality. *Screen, 53*(4), 381–397.

Ross, M. (2013). Stereoscopic visuality: Where is the screen, where is the film? *Convergence, 19*(4), 406–414. doi:10.1177/1354856513494178.

Ruppel, W., Alff, Y., & Göllner, T. (2015). Study on the acceptance of higher-frame-rate stereoscopic 3D in digital cinema. *SMPTE Motion Imaging Journal, 124*(1), 1–7. doi:10.5594/j18501.

Seuntiens, P. J., Heynderickx, I. E., Ijsselsteijn, W. A., van den Avoort, P. M. J., Berentsen, J., Dalm, I. J., Lambooij, M. T., & Oosting, W. (2005). Viewing experience and naturalness of 3D images. In B. Javidi, F. Okano, & J. Son (Eds.), *Proceedings of SPIE: Three-Dimensional TV, Video, and Display IV* 6016. doi:10.1117/12.627515.

Slater, M., & Usoh, M. (1993). Representations systems, perceptual position and presence in immersive virtual environments. *Presence, 2*(3), 221–233.

Sobchack, V. (2006). Final fantasies: Computer graphic animation and the (dis)illusion of life. In S. Buchan (Ed.), *Animated worlds* (pp. 179–180). Bloomington: Indiana University Press.

Sobieraj, S., & Krämer, N. C. (2014). Do 3D moviegoers enjoy screenings more than 2D moviegoers? On the impact of 3D fantasy movie perception on enjoyment. *Presence, 23*(4), 430–448. doi:10.1162/PRES_a_00210.

Solimini, A. (2013). Are there side effects to watching 3D movies? A prospective crossover observational study on visually induced motion sickness. *PLoS ONE, 8*(2), 1–8. doi:10.1371/journal.pone.0056160.

Tam, W. J., Speranza, F., Yano, S., Shimono, K., & Ono, H. (2011). Stereoscopic 3D-TV: Visual comfort. *IEEE Transactions on Broadcasting, 57*(2), 335–346. doi:10.1109/TBC.2011.2125070.

Trumbull, D. (2011). Douglas Trumbull sees a better filmgoing future. Retrieved May 18, 2014, from *Creative Cow Magazine*. http://library.creativecow.net/kaufman_debra/Douglas-Trumbull_Filmgoing-Future/1.

Turnock, J. (2013). Removing the pane of glass: *The Hobbit*, 3D high frame rate filmmaking, and the rhetoric of digital convergence. *Film Criticism, 37/38*(3/1), 30–59.

Urvoy, M., Barkowsky, M., & Le Callet, P. (2013). How visual fatigue and discomfort impact 3D-TV quality of experience: A comprehensive review of technological, psychophysical, and psychological factors. *Annals of Telecommunications—Annales des Télécommunications, 68*(11–12), 641–655. doi:10.1007/s12243-013-0394-3.

Whissel, K. (2014). *Spectacular digital effects: CGI and contemporary cinema.* Durham: Duke University Press.

White, A. (2013, June 1). Cinema is about humanity, not fireballs. *The New York Times*. Retrieved June 7, 2014, from http://www.nytimes.com/roomfordebate/2013/03/07/are-digital-effects-cgi-ruining-the-movies/cinema-is-about-humanity-not-fireballs.

Wilcox, L. M., Allison, R. S., Helliker, J., Dunk, B., & Anthony, R. C. (2015). Evidence that viewers prefer higher frame-rate film. *ACM Transactions on Applied Perception, 12*(4), 15. doi:10.1145/2810039.

Wood, A. (2002). Timespaces in spectacular cinema: Crossing the great divide of spectacle versus narrative. *Screen, 43*(4), 370–386. doi:10.1093/screen/43.4.370.

Wood, A. (2013). Intangible spaces: Three-dimensional technology in *Hugo* and IMAX in *The Dark Knight*. *Convergence: The International Journal of Research into New Media Technologies, 19*(4), 1–13. doi:10.1177/1354856513501414.

Zeri, F., & Livi, S. (2015). Visual discomfort while watching stereoscopic three-dimensional movies at the cinema. *Ophthalmic and Physiological Optics, 35*(3), 271–282. doi:10.1111/opo.12194.

CHAPTER 8

On the Transformation of Meaning and Cinematic Desire

INTRODUCTION

This chapter explores the diverse range of meanings ascribed to the *Hobbit* films among different audience segments, before drawing on our longitudinal comparative data to trace the major transformations that occurred over the life of the trilogy. Then, we use our extensive qualitative materials to pinpoint the key factors that led to continued pleasurable engagement among some, while provoking progressive disenchantment and ambivalence among others. As we show, many of the textual features that sparked criticism and prevented certain respondents from fully immersing themselves in the narrative storyworld reflect creative decisions that were partially shaped by underlying commercial considerations in terms of ensuring the trilogy's broad-based appeal, and thereby maximising box-office revenues. This appears true of what was, for many respondents, the *most* controversial creative decision—the introduction of a new female character and a related Elf–Dwarf 'love triangle' in the second and third *Hobbit* films. While some welcomed these additions to an otherwise heavily male-dominated franchise, Tauriel's storyline attracted protestation (and in some cases, outrage) from many others on a number of grounds. Indeed, central to the ambivalent reception of *The Hobbit* among certain audiences, we suggest, was its triggering of wider debates relating to contemporary gender politics. But before delving into these somewhat vexed issues, we take a step back to consider

© The Author(s) 2017
C. Michelle et al., *Fans, Blockbusterisation, and the Transformation of Cinematic Desire*, DOI 10.1057/978-1-137-59616-1_8

the diverse range of meanings that different audiences ascribed to each *Hobbit* movie and the wider franchise as the trilogy played out on screen.

A Contested Terrain: The Meaning of the *Hobbit* Trilogy for Fans and Critics

In each post-viewing survey we asked participants to respond, in their own words, to variations on the following question: *What does this film mean to you?* Here, we sought to provide an opportunity for respondents to do any number of things. For instance, they might convey something of the nature of their anticipation and cinematic desire for the film, or express their appreciation of it as a creative work, or comment on its significance in their own lives, or reflect on the messages communicated by it, or convey something of the heightened experience of watching it, or something else entirely—all of which would give us important information about their viewing modality. The question was open-ended because we wanted to avoid compiling a list of possible ways in which the film's meaning might be categorised a priori, in the belief that so doing would reflect our implicit assumptions about what film actually is, and how viewers should understand and relate to it. Comments were then categorised using an inductive coding strategy to identify the most common 'meanings' ascribed by respondents themselves, with 27 distinct categories emerging. As previously noted, to avoid coder bias, this process was undertaken without the coders having knowledge of individual affiliations to particular viewpoints. Independent coding of these open-ended questions thus constitutes a form of methodological triangulation which, in this case, largely confirms the validity of the analyses offered in previous chapters.

While continuity is clearly evident in the meanings ascribed to each *Hobbit* film, there are some important shifts in emphasis that confirm growing ambivalence among Tolkien followers as well as some fans of the *Lord of the Rings* (*LotR*) films. For reasons of space, we omit examples of individuals' comments from the preliminary discussion in order to highlight each group's specific constellation of meanings, as summarised in Table 8.1. We then delve more deeply into the specific issues that appear to have prompted a noticeable erosion of preferred receptions of the *Hobbit* trilogy over time.

Table 8.1   Most commonly expressed meanings of each film, by viewpoint

Q. What does AUJ mean to you? Coded open-response question Number of respondents (%)	Enchanted Hobbit Fans (n = 1392)^b	Bored and Disillusioned Hobbit Critics (n = 54)	Disappointed Tolkien Readers (n = 103)	Critics of Technological 'Enhancements' (n = 63)	Mildly Entertained Casual Viewers (n = 19)
Entertainment	44 (3.2%)^c				2 (10.5%)
A product/creative work/innovative film	70 (5.0%)	4 (7.4%)	4 (3.9%)		
Jackson and team's creative genius	125 (9.0%)		5 (4.9%)		
A story	43 (3.1%)		4 (3.9)		
Adaptation of a (favourite) book	312 (22.4%)	3 (5.6%)	17 (16.5%)	9 (14.3%)	4 (21.1%)
Tolkien's literary work/genius	48 (3.4%)			5 (7.9%)	
Return to Middle-earth	207 (14.9%)		4 (3.9%)	6 (9.5%)	
More of LotR—a prequel; continuity	74 (5.3%)		6 (5.8%)	12 (19.0%)	
First in a new trilogy	28 (2.0%)		4 (3.9%)		
An important influence/part of my life	55 (4.0%)	2 (3.7%)			

(continued)

Table 8.1 (continued)

Important messages/values	69 (5.0%)		4 (3.9%)	
Disappointment/failed adaptation	4 (0.3%)	34 (63.0%)	40 (38.8%)	8 (12.7%)
NZ connection—benefits, Kiwi pride	10 (0.7%)			2 (10.5%)
Other	30 (2.2%)	4 (7.4%)		3 (15.8%)
Nothing/not much/don't know	5 (0.4%)			2 (10.5%)

(continued)

Table 8.1 (continued)

Q. What does DoS mean to you?	Happy Hobbit Defenders (n = 542)	Disenchanted Hobbit Critics (n = 14)	Aggrieved Tolkien Aficiona-dos (n = 285)	Hobbit Sceptics (n = 28)	Middle-earth Appreciators (n = 7)
Entertainment	26 (4.8%)		16 (5.6%)	3 (10.7%)	
Adaptation of a (favourite) book	58 (10.7%)				
Return to Middle-earth	55 (10.1%)			3 (10.7%)	
Middle film in trilogy	78 (14.4%)		15 (5.3%)		
Important messages/values	42 (7.7%)				
Disappointment/failed adaptation	13 (2.4%)	10 (71.4%)	168 (58.9%)	10 (35.7%)	2 (28.6%)
Nothing/not much/don't know	5 (0.9%)		24 (8.4%)	3 (10.7%)	
A lesser film than the LotR	5 (0.9%)		12 (4.2%)	3 (10.7%)	

(continued)

Table 8.1 (continued)

Q. What does BotEA mean to you?	Fulfilled Hobbit Fans (n = 369)	Angry Hobbit Critics (n = 14)	Unhappy Tolkien Adherents (n = 214)	Ambivalent Middle-earth Enthusiasts (n = 37)	Appreciative Film Critics (n = 20)	Frustrated Middle-earth Fans (n = 16)
Farewell to Middle-earth	57 (15.4%)		8 (3.7%)	3 (8.1%)		3 (18.8)
End of an era	39 (10.6%)					2 (12.5%)
More of *LotR*—a prequel; continuity	28 (7.6%)					
Final film in trilogy	26 (7.0%)		6 (2.8%)	7 (18.9%)	2 (10.0%)	2 (12.5%)
Completion of the larger Middle-earth saga	36 (9.8%)		6 (2.8%)		5 (25.0%)	2 (12.5%)
An important influence/part of my life	22 (6.0%)			3 (8.1%)		
Important messages/values	22 (6.0%)					2 (12.5%)
Disappointment/failed adaptation	5 (1.4%)	12 (85.7%)	131 (61.2%)	5 (13.5%)	4 (20.0%)	2 (12.5%)
Nothing/not much/don't know	2 (0.5%)		20 (9.3%)	3 (8.1%)		
A lesser film than *LotR*	2 (0.5%)			3 (8.1%)		

[a]For comparative purposes, only the English-language responses to the *AUJ* survey are presented here

[b]All figures are based on the number of respondents in each group who responded to the question

[c]With the exception of the largest segment in each survey, only the five most frequently mentioned meanings for each group are included here and only when selected by two or more respondents associated with that viewpoint. In the case of *Enchanted Hobbit Fans, Happy Hobbit Defenders* and *Fulfilled Hobbit Fans,* comparative figures are provided in italics for additional meaning categories that were among the most frequently cited by other groups

An Unexpected Journey

What becomes immediately apparent in analysing the English-language survey responses to *An Unexpected Journey* (*AUJ*)[1] is the striking difference between the meanings assigned by the largest group of respondents and those reported by all other groups, a pattern that continues over the life of the trilogy. Among *Enchanted Hobbit Fans*, the most common meaning was that of 'an adaptation of a (favourite) book' (22.4%), followed by a welcome 'return to Middle-earth' (14.9%). Many expressed joy at returning to an imaginary literary and cinematic world that felt real and also felt like *home*, at visiting old friends if not family members, and immersing themselves in a wonderful place they have come to know and love, suggesting deep immersion in a familiar narrative storyworld. *Enchanted Hobbit Fans* also commonly perceived *AUJ* as an expression of 'Jackson and team's creative genius' (9.0%) that offered 'more of the *LotR*' in the form of an expansion of that series (5.3%), and as 'a product/creative work/innovative film' (5.0%). Together, these meanings suggest that *Enchanted Hobbit Fans* recognised Jackson's role in creating an excellent interpretative adaptation of Tolkien's novel.

In stark contrast, 'disappointment' was the most commonly cited meaning among *Bored and Disillusioned Hobbit Critics* (63.0%) and *Disappointed Tolkien Readers* (38.8%), and ranked third among *Critics of Technological 'Enhancements'* (12.7%). The underlying reasons for each group's discontent varied, and strongly resonate with those identified in our earlier description of these viewpoints in Chap. 5. *Bored and Disillusioned Hobbit Critics* typically regarded the film as a failed adaptation that also fell short of the high standards set by *LotR*, with several explicitly attributing this to commercial motivations trumping storytelling and fidelity to Tolkien's original vision—their comments relating to the film as 'a product/creative work/innovative film' (7.4%) were generally not complimentary. *Disappointed Tolkien Readers* placed greater emphasis on the film's lack of fidelity to the novel, evident also in their second most frequently cited meaning—'an adaptation of a (favourite) novel' (16.5%). A wide range of other meanings were also expressed within this group (see Table 8.1).

For *Critics of Technological 'Enhancements'*, conversely, 'disappointment' more often related to the film's failure to live up to the elevated standards set by the *LotR* films, both in terms of their technical excellence and extraordinary impact, culturally and personally. The primacy of this intertext is apparent in the most common meaning expressed by this group—'more of the *LotR*' (19.0%). However, others in this group understood *AUJ* as 'an adaptation of a (favourite) book' (14.3%) 'the product of Tolkien's literary genius' (7.9%), and a somewhat bittersweet 'return to Middle-earth' (9.5%). Meanwhile, some *Mildly Entertained Casual Viewers* noted *AUJ*'s status as 'an adaptation of a (favourite) book' (21.1%), while others highlighted aspects relating to the New Zealand production context in terms of 'economic benefits or "Kiwi pride"' (10.5%) or saw the film primarily as 'entertainment' (10.5%).

The Desolation of Smaug

While several categories persisted across the life of the trilogy, there were some revealing shifts in the meanings attributed to the second *Hobbit* film, the most significant of which relates to the trilogy's increasingly contested status as a cinematic adaptation. *The Desolation of Smaug* (*DoS*) was ascribed special significance by the largest and most satisfied group of *Happy Hobbit Defenders* as 'the middle film of the *Hobbit* franchise' (14.4%) and a highly successful sequel to *AUJ*. While some respondents emphasised the film's intertextual connections as 'an adaptation of a (favourite) novel' (10.7%), their closer mode of subjective engagement is evident in the third most common category—'return to Middle-earth' (10.1%). Tolkien's 'important messages and values' were emphasised (7.7%), and a few regarded *DoS* as excellent 'entertainment' (4.8%). While many among this group expressed mild dissatisfaction with particular creative choices, any unhappiness was vastly outweighed by their overall enthusiastic appreciation of the film.

Dominating the interpretive schema of all other groups, however, was a sense of deepened 'disappointment', this being the most commonly cited meaning for 71.4% of *Disenchanted Hobbit Critics* and 58.9% of *Aggrieved Tolkien Aficionados*. Prevailing themes in the views of *Disenchanted Hobbit Critics* were the negative impact of commercial values and the consequent degradation of Tolkien's work. Similar sentiments appear to have solidified among *Aggrieved Tolkien Aficionados*, many of whom expressed concerns about the underlying economic and industrial imperatives governing the trilogy's production, perhaps in an attempt to account for *why* the film fell short of the ideal adaptation of Tolkien's work they had imagined or hoped for. 'Disappointment' also dominated the meaning schema of 35.7% of *Hobbit Sceptics* and 28.6%

of *Middle-earth Appreciators*, but in these groups was noticeably more muted and often framed in relation to *The Hobbit*'s failure to match the high standards and quality of the *LotR* trilogy.

Also listed among the top five meanings for *Aggrieved Tolkien Aficionados* and *Hobbit Sceptics* was 'nothing/not much' (mentioned by 8.4% and 10.7% respectively). Significantly, 10.7% of *Sceptics* considered *DoS* 'a lesser film than the *LotR*'—again demonstrating the significance of this primary intertext. This sentiment was expressed by a smaller number of *Aggrieved Tolkien Aficionados* (4.2%). While some of the latter as well as *Hobbit Sceptics* considered *DoS* 'an entertaining film' (5.6% and 10.7% respectively), their comments suggest they wished for rather more than this. And, while the film offered some *Hobbit Sceptics* a pleasurable 'return to Middle-earth' (10.7%), the experience as a whole was evidently less satisfying than initially hoped.

The Battle of the Five Armies

A more noticeable shift occurs with the final film, as common themes emerge across all the groups emphasising sadness at the completion not merely of this trilogy, but of the wider Middle-earth franchise; for many, this sadness was tinged with disappointment at what might have been. For *Fulfilled Hobbit Fans*, though, *The Battle of the Five Armies* (*BotFA*) was celebrated as a fitting 'farewell to Middle-earth', its people and places (15.4%) and as marking 'the end of an era' that encompassed the wonderful *LotR* phenomenon (10.6%). They saw *BotFA* as very effectively 'completing the wider Middle-earth series' (9.8%) and understood this film both as 'a prequel' leading viewers into the events that transpire in the *LotR* films (7.6%) and as 'the final film in the *Hobbit* trilogy' (7.0%).

In contrast, for *Angry Hobbit Critics* the meaning almost unanimously ascribed to *BotFA* was once again 'disappointment' (85.7%). Criticisms ranged from the excessive violence to the corrupting influence of economic imperatives on the film's production. 'Disappointment' was also by far the most common meaning ascribed by *Unhappy Tolkien Adherents* (61.2%), who described the film as 'a failure', 'a wasted opportunity', 'an insult', 'a massacre', 'a travesty' and 'the butchery of Tolkien's fine works'. Disaffection, anger and frustration pervaded many of their comments; 9.3% stated the film meant 'nothing/not much' to them.

Among *Ambivalent Middle-earth Enthusiasts*, conversely, there was some sadness in recognising that *BotFA* was the 'final film in the *Hobbit* trilogy' (18.9%) and a final 'farewell to Middle-earth' (8.1%), but also a sense of 'disappointment' (13.5%) at what was, for many, 'a lesser film compared to the *LotR*' (8.1%). *Appreciative Film Critics* were somewhat more positively disposed toward the final film: 25% perceived *BotFA* as 'completing the wider Middle-earth series', while for 10% of this group its main significance lay in being 'the final film in the *Hobbit* trilogy'. However, a more significant proportion (20%) acknowledged their 'disappointment' relating to the failure of the film to live up to expectations. Finally, *Frustrated Middle-earth Fans* expressed appreciation for the films as a final 'farewell to Middle-earth' (18.8%), the 'end of an era' (12.5%), 'the final film in the *Hobbit* trilogy' (12.5%), and 'completing the wider Middle-earth series' (12.5%). Nonetheless, a number of *Frustrated Middle-earth Fans* also expressed a sense of 'disappointment' that the trilogy had come to an end in a way that was not entirely satisfying (12.5%).

Evident in the above discussion is the broad range of meanings ascribed to the three *Hobbit* films, with some important areas of continuity and a degree of overlap among certain audience groups, much as earlier chapters indicated. Also clear is that these meanings subtly shifted and evolved as the trilogy unfolded, progressively assuming a more negative aspect among all but the most transported *Hobbit* fans, as a larger proportion adopted variants of the mediated mode of reception. The comments of these dissenters reflect unhappiness, even dismay, that a desired viewing experience was effectively thwarted by the creative decisions of *The Hobbit*'s studio and production team, for reasons that will become more clearly apparent below.

Transformation of Desire and the Evolution of Viewpoints Over Time

Drawing on our longitudinal data set and extensive qualitative responses, we can trace these broader shifts in the views of our respondents over time and pinpoint the major sources of individual and collective discord that disrupted viewing pleasure at different moments of *The Hobbit*'s staggered release in cinemas. Such insights, we believe, would have been obscured had we only surveyed respondents at the trilogy's conclusion.

In the process, we illuminate the conditions under which an established franchise progressively disillusioned and even alienated a significant portion of its large and enthusiastic pre-existing fan base.

Figure 8.1 maps the major transitions in the distribution of viewpoints over the course of the *Hobbit* trilogy and reveals three important insights. First, the audience was *already* fragmented prior to the first film's release. Our pre-viewing survey documented high levels of excitement and anticipation among existing *LotR Film Fans*, as well as a degree of cautious optimism among *Tolkien Aficionados*, many of whom expressed concern about signalled and other potential diversions from the novel. Smaller numbers of *Jackson Critics* expressed strong opposition to the films' director, while others were primarily interested in certain cast members (*Celebrity Followers*), or concerned about the success of a product of the New Zealand film industry (*Anxious Investors*).

Second, the major audience groups remained relatively stable in their constitution throughout the life of the trilogy, with the largest group being loyal to Jackson and his Middle-earth trilogies, another sizeable group being oriented more toward Tolkien's written corpus, and several smaller groups expressing alternative or oppositional views focusing on particular issues such as visual aesthetics, textual realism and the negative impact of commercial imperatives. However, what does change is the relative size of these differently aligned segments. The largest and most positively predisposed group in the lead-up to *AUJ*'s release was *LotR Film Fans*. Post-release, this very enthusiastic group expanded from 51.6 to 74.0% of respondents, suggesting that *AUJ* won over a good number of previously apprehensive Tolkien-oriented viewers—evident also in the decline in the relative proportion of (pre-viewing) *Tolkien Aficionados* (18.2%) versus (post-viewing) *Disappointed Tolkien Readers* (6.9%). But while *AUJ* clearly delighted many among this group, a notable erosion of positive audience engagement was evident in the *DoS* post-viewing survey, with just 57.7% becoming *Happy Hobbit Defenders*. This decline accelerated in response to *BotFA* as the full extent of Jackson's amendments and additions became clearer. At the trilogy's conclusion, the most enthusiastic group (*Fulfilled Hobbit Fans*) had shrunk to just 48.2% of respondents overall, while the proportion of all other ambivalent or actively oppositional groups had increased, with the largest increase over the life of the trilogy as a whole being registered among disaffected Tolkienists.

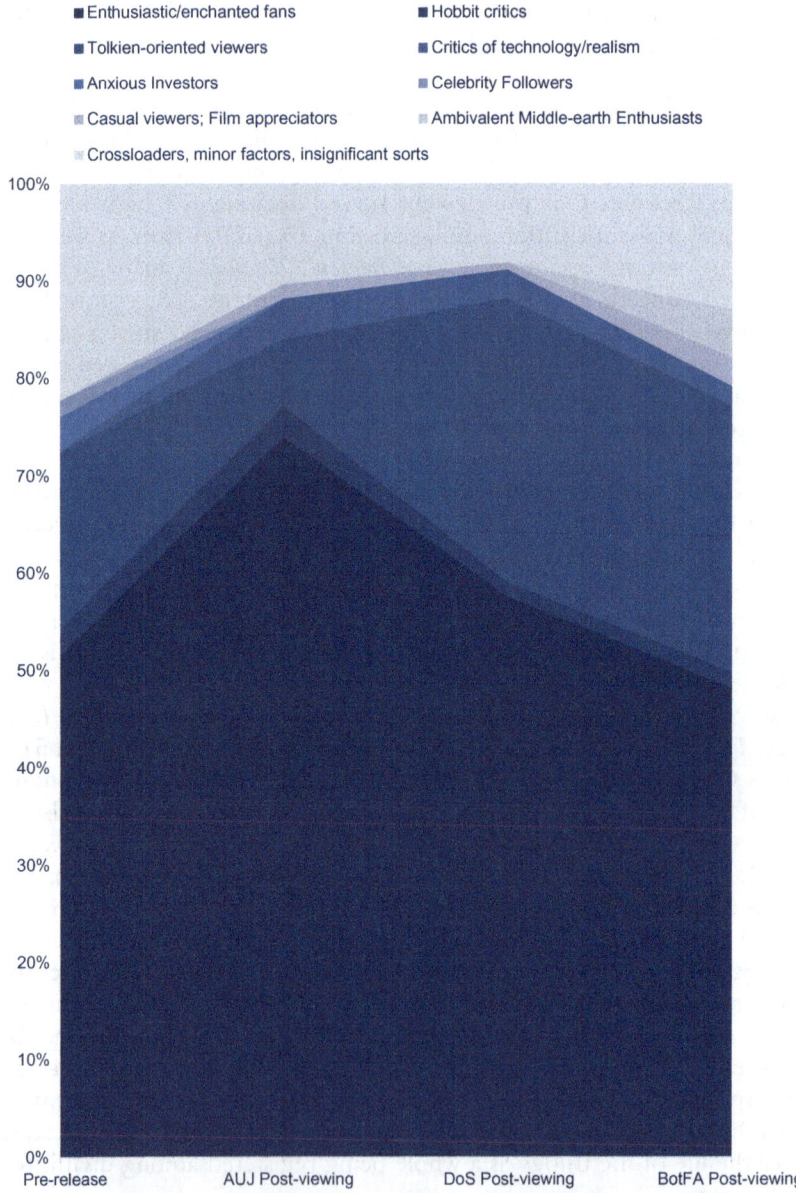

■ Enthusiastic/enchanted fans   ■ Hobbit critics

■ Tolkien-oriented viewers   ■ Critics of technology/realism

■ Anxious Investors   ■ Celebrity Followers

▨ Casual viewers; Film appreciators   ▨ Ambivalent Middle-earth Enthusiasts

▨ Crossloaders, minor factors, insignificant sorts

Fig. 8.1   Evolution of *Hobbit* audience segments, November 2012–May 2015

Table 8.2 Transformation matrix showing movement between viewpoints from *An Unexpected Journey* to *The Desolation of Smaug*

	Major viewpoints, DoS:				
N = 434	Happy Hobbit Defenders (n = 295)	Disenchanted Hobbit Critics (n = 4)	Aggrieved Tolkien Aficionados (n = 92)	Hobbit Scep-tics (n = 14)	Other (n = 29)
Major viewpoints, AUJ:					
Enchanted Hobbit Fans (n = 342)	275	0	49	7	11
Bored and Disillusioned Hobbit Critics (n = 9)	1	2	2	0	4
Disappointed Tolkien Readers (n = 32)	4	1	20	1	6
Critics of Technological 'Enhancements' (n = 14)	4	0	3	4	3
Other (n = 37)	11	1	18	2	5
%	68.0%	0.9%	21.2%	3.2%	6.7%

While mapping the viewpoints illustrates broader macro-level shifts in the collective views of our respondents over time, our longitudinal comparative data offers more nuanced insight into what such transformations mean at the micro or individual level. Two transformation matrices trace continuity and change among our unique cohort of 434 respondents who completed English language post-viewing surveys of *AUJ* and *DoS* (Table 8.2), 174 of whom also completed the final survey relating to *BotFA* (Table 8.3). They show, for instance, the number of *AUJ* viewers who were categorised as *Enchanted Hobbit Fans* (342), and of these, the number who became *Happy Hobbit Defenders* (275) as opposed to *Aggrieved Tolkien Aficionados* (49) after viewing *DoS*.

These figures suggest a considerable degree of continuity, in that the majority of those who greatly enjoyed the first *Hobbit* film also enjoyed the second, while most of those who were unhappy about the lack of textual fidelity in the first film 'evolved' into the *Unhappy Tolkien*

Table 8.3   Transformation matrix showing movement between viewpoints from *The Desolation of Smaug* to *The Battle of the Five Armies*

N = 174	Major viewpoints, BotFA:					
	Fulfilled Hobbit Fans (n = 93)	Angry Hobbit Critics (n = 1)	Unhappy Tolkien Adherents (n = 40)	Ambivalent Middle-earth Enthusiasts (n = 7)	Appreciative Film Critics (n = 7)	Other (n = 26)
Major viewpoints, DoS:						
Happy Hobbit Defenders (n = 121[a])	90	0	9	4	6	12
Aggrieved Tolkien Aficionados (n = 40)	2	1	25	2	1	9
Other (n = 13)	1	0	6	1	0	5
%	53.4%	0.6%	23.0%	4.0%	4.0%	14.9%

[a]The numbers in each *DoS* viewpoint differ from those shown in Table 8.2 because not all those respondents also completed the third post-viewing survey

Adherents identified in our final survey. However, we also see some surprising fluidity between the different categories, with the major trend reflecting defections away from the preferred viewing mode. Only four of the *Critics of Technological 'Enhancements'* from the *AUJ* survey become *DoS Hobbit Sceptics*, perhaps suggesting that those most put off by the first *Hobbit* film's unusual visual aesthetic may have subsequently chosen to view the sequel in 2D rather than HFR 3D. A more radical shift occurred in the case of one previously *Bored and Disillusioned Critic* turned *Happy Hobbit Defender*, who explained that better editing in *DoS* made viewing it a pleasure: 'The first of the *Hobbit* trilogy was edited horrendously; it had me bored instantly and was a challenge to sit through. However *DoS* was able to captivate me for the full 2.5 hours; it was edited well' (24-year-old New Zealand man).

While *DoS* did win over some 'converts', our evidence suggests an overall hardening of more critical viewpoints as earlier hopes for the franchise were progressively dashed, and more especially as ambivalent Tolkien readers become less forgiving of what some perceived as Jackson's 'self-indulgent' creative licence. Thus, the most significant shift occurred as previously *Enchanted Hobbit Fans* transformed into *Aggrieved Tolkien Aficionados* (49) and *Hobbit Sceptics* (7) after viewing *DoS*. One of these *Aggrieved Tolkien Aficionados*, a 24-year-old American woman, said 'I'm very emotionally invested in Middle-earth, and [after seeing *AUJ*] went into this film shaking from excitement. I left thinking of how Tolkien must be spinning in his grave. I've never been so disappointed'. Perhaps more revealing of the failure of *DoS* to effectively transport some *Enchanted Hobbit Fans* back to Middle-earth are comments from a 23-year-old Russian woman, who became a *Hobbit Sceptic* after seeing *DoS*:

> I expected to be taken to another world by this movie; I wanted magic and fireworks, but they never happened …/… After the first *Hobbit* movie I could barely think about anything else, for several months I had been re-reading Tolkien, watching other movies with the *Hobbit* actors, writing fan-fiction and drawing fan-art in order to make the magic of *AUJ* last. And I expected *DoS* to have the same effect on me, but somehow it didn't happen …. The magic didn't happen, and that was sad.

Expressed here is a much anticipated, intensely desired viewing experience of narrative immersion—that all-encompassing feeling of being 'taken to another world'. Sadly, for a significant minority, the fully realised film failed to deliver the same 'magic transport' as its prequel.

Table 8.3 shows that a second significant transformation occurred when a smaller proportion of *Happy Hobbit Defenders* 'defected' to become *Unhappy Tolkien Adherents* (9), *Ambivalent Middle-earth Enthusiasts* (4) or *Appreciative Film Critics* (6) in response to *BotFA*, for reasons alluded to by a 24-year-old American man and a 19-year-old New Zealand woman: 'This is the worst adaptation of Tolkien and will only be re-watched for completion rather than enjoyment, unfortunately' (*Unhappy Tolkien Adherent*); 'I was very disappointed that the spirit of the *Hobbit* book that I love and the *LotR* films that I love was not really conveyed though *BotFA*' (*Ambivalent Middle-earth Enthusiast*). The radical about-face experienced by some is evident in this comment:

> At first, I was really excited. I mean, it's *The Hobbit*! By Peter Jackson! I never imagined it would happen in my life! The first movie had me

content, and even more excited. The second movie left me confused, and scratching my head. What had Pete done?. . . The third movie left me analytical as hell . . . after I'd stopped sobbing my little *Hobbit* heart out. (Canadian woman, 15; *Happy Hobbit Defender* turned *Appreciative Film Critic*)

Delving Deeper into Evolving Audience Reactions

Hoping to complement these innovative analyses of audience transformations over time, we asked the following question in our final post-viewing survey: '*If you have watched all three Hobbit films, have your views and feelings about the trilogy changed since the first film's release? If yes, in what ways?*' Usefully, 89% of our respondents answered this question, and while we cannot convey all the nuances evident in their comments here, we can quantify some major trends in a way that illuminates the degree to which reactions evolved over time, and more importantly, *why*.

Altogether, 32.4% said their views did *not* change over the course of the trilogy. A significantly larger number (58.6%) suggested their views *had* indeed changed over time: among this group were 14.0% who (perhaps surprisingly) indicated their feelings had become more positive, and a further 35.6% who said their views had become more negative. The rest (8.5%) reported a vacillation in their views over time. Focusing on the latter two groups, various textual features caused a growing number of former fans to experience progressive disenchantment over the course of the *Hobbit* trilogy. For one 29-year-old Danish man, the declining quality of the script was a major factor: 'The script got worse and worse, dialogue deteriorated until it was cringe-worthy in every scene, the unsuitable comedy forced into every passage. It just got more and more terrible, and more lazy.' For others, the problems arose from the decision to stretch the story across three films rather than two, leading to additional 'padding' in the form of invented scenes and storylines, as noted by this 31-year-old Indian man living in the USA:

I was prepared for additional stories to be included into the *Hobbit* trilogy as long as they maintained the spirit of Tolkien. But it is now clear that the directors and screen writers didn't have a clear overview of the storylines they wanted to cover. Characterization of important characters (Gandalf, Radagast, Beorn) is diminished in favour of poorly written characters

(Alfrid) and stories (the love story). The *Hobbit* trilogy is a clear case of excess, making sitting through the 12 hour trilogy a chore.

Concerns relating to the fidelity of the adaptation and a sense of betrayal by the trilogy's creators were major themes among those whose appreciation declined with each subsequent film release, as expressed in the comments of these two women:

> The first films had its problems, yes. But I still liked it. I could overlook a lot, and I really thought it would get better. Back then, I trusted Jackson. Experience is a brutal teacher. And God's burning, did I learn. I am now firmly convinced that Jackson (and Boyens!) have no respect for Professor Tolkien whatsoever . . . . The trilogy is a travesty. The first half hour of *AUJ* is still perfect, but I can barely bring myself to watch the rest of the movie, *DoS* and *BotFA* have soured the experience too much. I also flat out refuse to ever see either *DoS* or *BotFA* as they are ever again. (German woman, 30)

> I was very excited for the release of *AUJ* because Peter Jackson had done such an excellent job of adapting the *LotR* trilogy. *AUJ* felt very authentic to Tolkien's book and made a good start on developing the characters and plot. It all went downhill with *DoS* as the lightheartedness of the story was abandoned for newly invented CGI battle sequences and poorly written additional story arcs. It no longer felt like it was in the spirit of Tolkien, nor a film worth my time. It required no emotional investment nor held any cerebral intrigue as the new changes made it as cliché and predictable as any other mainstream action film. *BotFA* carried on with this downhill trend, failing to conclude the main quest points that started *AUJ* for the sake of including more CGI action and pointless subplots. (New Zealand woman, 24)

Of the 8.5% whose views vacillated over the course of the trilogy, the most common shift was from negative to positive to negative:

> I was disappointed with the pacing and story changes of the first film. The second gave me hope because as a film I thought it was better although I still didn't love the story changes. The third proved to me that my concerns throughout were valid and I was left overall very disappointed. (American man, 30)

In other cases, the arc of change was inverted and it was the first and third films that were favoured, as suggested by this 30-year-old Chinese woman:

> I really love the first *Hobbit* film, it's full of songs and entertainment. When I watched *DoS* I was not quite used to the changing theme, but it is necessary to go darker and more connected to the *LotR* appendices because that war was what Sauron was plotting at that time. I love *BotFA* because it tells a great story of redemption, and this makes a connection between all three films.

Clearly then, the majority of respondents experienced considerable shifts in their affective orientation over the course of an evolving three-part *Hobbit* saga. Importantly, it would have been difficult to perceive, let alone accurately trace, the evolution of audience reactions to this blockbuster event film trilogy had we not adopted our unique longitudinal approach and quali-quantitative methodology. Surveying audiences before and after each instalment of the trilogy, in conjunction with a range of additional strategies, has allowed us to pinpoint, with a high degree of confidence, the primary sources of viewing pleasure as well as major discontents and their origins.

Thwarted Desire: Discontent and Its Origins

Implicit and sometimes explicitly articulated in our respondents' comments was a sense of the *Hobbit* films they really wanted to see—their ideal screen version of Tolkien's novel *The Hobbit*, as mentally visualised prior to seeing the actual films in cinemas (Barker 2006). While more committed book readers longed to see a faithful adaptation 'worthy' of the original novel and its author, others strongly hoped to enjoy an excellent successor to their beloved *LotR* films. For many of the latter, in particular, these pre-viewing cinematic desires were largely satisfied by a fully realised film trilogy that was everything they had dreamed of and more, or at least close enough to it. For others, any such gratification was thwarted by a series of films that differed significantly from what they had imagined: the processes and imperatives associated with the blockbusterisation of Tolkien's novel clearly produced a certain form of text that differed quite radically from the imaginative ideal in which many were psychologically and emotionally invested. As the trilogy

Table 8.4   Top 10 frequently mentioned desired changes to the *Hobbit* sequels

Q: If you could change one thing in [this film], what would it be?
Coded open-response question

The Desolation of Smaug (N = 999)	The Battle of the Five Armies (N = 813)
Fewer diversions from the book (16.5%)	Fewer diversions from the book (15.4%)
Change/omit the Tauriel love triangle (7.0%)	More/different character development (6.4%)
Omit or change the Tauriel/Kili romance (7.0%)	Omit Alfrid (5.5%)
Remove Tauriel (6.6%)	Show the funerals at the end (5.5%)
Change/omit the gold statue scene/final sequence (6.2%)	Omit or change the Tauriel/Kili romance (5.2%)
Less CGI/No HFR 3D (5.7%)	Not have certain characters die (4.3%)
Aspects of filmcraft/direction (4.7%)	Less CGI/No HFR 3D (4.4%)
Narrative structure/editing (4.7%)	Remove Tauriel (4.4%)
More of Middle-earth—places, people (4.3%)	Change the ending (4.3%)
More/different character development (4.2%)	Narrative focus/story elements (3.8%)

unfolded and the extent of divergence between ideal and reality become progressively revealed, all hope was lost for a significant number. For these viewers, the film adaptation of Tolkien's novel had become an irretrievably 'bad object' (Stam 2005, p. 15). Consequently, deep immersion was no longer possible, nor even necessarily desired.

One of the complementary strategies we used to try to gain a deeper understanding of the clear disaffection among a significant number involved asking respondents, in the final two post-viewing surveys, to tell us in their own words one thing they would change about the film in question. We asked this question in the assumption that it would help independently pinpoint which particular issues were most troubling and potentially disruptive of the preferred transparent viewing mode, since we knew the chosen Q items could not anticipate all the possible textual features that might have irked our respondents. As shown in Table 8.4, some closely related themes emerged relating to textual fidelity and the invention of objectionable characters and storylines, but among these were indeed several specific elements not featured in the statements chosen for the survey Q sets.

In both surveys, the largest category was 'fewer diversions from the book' (16.5% and 15.4%), reiterating the importance placed on textual fidelity by many respondents. A wide range of concerns were highlighted relating to the introduction of new material, such as the Azog chase scenes and Tauriel, and alterations to Tolkien's original story—including splitting up the company of dwarves following Kili's injury in Laketown, and insufficient or unfaithful characterisations of Beorn, the Elven King and Bard the Bowman. Underpinning these responses lay a shared frustration with the film's lack of conformity to the characters, scenes, moral themes and overall 'spirit' of Tolkien's novel. By far the most controversial of these 'divergent' textual elements was the introduction of Tauriel and the love triangle between her, Kili, and Legolas: these changes were so contentious that we had to develop five distinct categories in order to avoid conflating very meaningful distinctions. When re-aggregated, Tauriel-related changes were the most frequently cited by *DoS* respondents by a considerable margin, and a close second among *BotFA* respondents.

Among the remaining categories relating to *DoS*, noteworthy is one relating to the final sequence in which the dwarves confront Smaug and, after a prolonged chase inside Lonely Mountain, smother him in a river of molten gold, noted by 6.2%. One 24-year-old German woman said she wanted to 'Erase that whole Dwarves versus Smaug fight. It was extremely boring and just embarrassing and unnecessary', while an 18-year-old American woman went further, describing it as 'very unrealistic that the extremely clever Smaug wouldn't be able to fight off a couple of dwarves'. Furthermore, she argued,

> The idea that the dwarves could melt tons of gold in under five minutes and drench the dragon in it, all the while remaining completely unharmed, is utterly preposterous. That was the scene that really ruined the movie for me, even without the other changes.

Such concerns appeared to be related to the next most commonly cited issue highlighted by *DoS* respondents, whereby respondents wished there had been less *obvious* use of CGI or expressed criticism of the filmmaker's use of HFR 3D (5.7%).

In the case of *BotFA*, the second most frequently cited change concerned 'more or different character development' (6.4%), with some wishing to see more focus on characters and their relationships, rather than so much action. Several had hoped to see all of the dwarves featured more prominently, while others wished for greater focus on Bilbo as the central protagonist. Still others desired different characterisations of Tauriel, Galadriel, Thranduil and Legolas, in particular. In terms of other changes, 5.5% wished Alfrid had been omitted altogether. Others wanted the funerals of Thorin and Kili to be depicted (5.5%), while a smaller number wished they hadn't died at all (4.6%).

Of course, there are some important differences among the audience segments which are occluded in this analysis. For instance, the top five desired changes among *Fulfilled Hobbit Fans* in relation to *BotFA* were, in order, 'show the funerals at the end', 'fewer diversions from the book', 'not have certain characters die', 'change the ending', and 'omit Alfrid'. That three of these relate to the film's ending suggests sadness and a longing to see more of particular characters and events—to extend the viewing experience and provide a more satisfyingly comprehensive conclusion to the trilogy:

> Show the events following the Battle (the funeral of Thorin and his nephews, the placing of the Arkenstone and Orcrist on Thorin's tomb, the naming of Dain as the new King) as a way to bring a sense of closure to what feel like too many hanging plot points and to bring the story full circle back to the Erebor of the prologue. (American woman, 65)

Conversely, *Unhappy Tolkien Adherents* identified the following, most of which reflect their overriding concern with textual fidelity: 'fewer diversions from the book', 'remove Tauriel', 'more/different character development', 'omit/change the Tauriel/Kili romance', and a category that expressed universal discontent—'change everything', as articulated by a 21-year-old Finnish woman who said, 'I'd just scrap the whole movie and remake *The Hobbit* as two shorter ones (or even one), with less CGI, no extra romances and with minimal changes regarding the book.' A 27-year-old British woman echoed these sentiments, suggesting she would change 'pretty much everything':

> The characters needed proper development and resolution . . . . Tauriel needed to be revamped completely . . . . And Bilbo needed to be actually treated as the main character rather than an annoying hanger-on who the writers had to include but in whom they had no interest. Also, Alfrid needed to be eaten by Smaug.

Here, we can again perceive the usefulness of Q methodology for audience studies, as it has made it possible to distinguish between and reliably classify respondents who clearly have radically different cognitive and affective relationships to the *Hobbit* films.

MIDDLE-EARTH'S 'WOMAN PROBLEM' AND THE POLITICS OF GENDER REPRESENTATION

As noted, the second and third *Hobbit* instalments introduced viewers to a number of non-canon elements, the most controversial of which was the Woodland elf Tauriel, the 'Daughter of Mirkwood' and head of the Elven guard. A large number of respondents wished this character, the love story, or both, had been omitted entirely from the *Hobbit* films. Since this creative addition was clearly polarising, we devote the rest of this chapter to a discussion of audience reactions to Tauriel as a female action heroine and love interest for the handsome young dwarf Kili, and less overtly, Legolas.

To understand the divergent responses to Tauriel, it is useful to consider critical and fan scholarship on the role and representation of women in Tolkien's wider oeuvre, and in Jackson's cinematic adaptations (for further discussion, see Reid 2015). Some early commentators such as Stimpson (1969) argue that Tolkien expressed sexist and even misogynistic views of women in his personal life as well as his writings; few women feature in his works, and those that do are generally depicted in traditional, subordinated roles. Partridge (1983), for instance, contends that Éowyn's representation in *LotR* is modelled on courtly romance, and suggests that Tolkien proffers unrequited love as the source of her frustration at not going to war, rather than the constraints placed upon her as a woman (p. 192).

Others, however, dismiss such concerns as a form of presentism that overlooks the importance of Tolkien's broader themes. Hatcher (2007) notes that Tolkien lived and wrote at a time when sexist beliefs were normative and not subject to critique. She suggests that it is not appropriate for modern readers to draw on contemporary feminist ideals of gender equality when evaluating his works; rather, they should be judged on their own terms, and according to their internal merits. Furthermore, Hatcher suggests Tolkien *does* in fact offer powerful representations of women in the form of Galadriel, Éowyn and Arwen, while Croft and

Donovan (2015) argue that Tolkien's women are frequently essential to the plot (see also Crowe 1996; Yates 2000).

Scholarly discussions of Jackson's depictions of Tolkien's women address similar themes: Thum (2005) suggests that 'Women for Tolkien are positive figures whose influence extends far beyond their often brief appearances in the pages of his writings, and Jackson's film reflects that fact' (p. 254). Porter (2005) similarly observes that Jackson's *LotR* adaptations placed greater emphasis on and expanded women's roles into modern, independent and indeed heroic figures by drawing on additional materials produced by Tolkien in the Appendixes and his short story, *The Tale of Aragorn and Arwen*. However, while many viewers and critics have responded positively to the films' expansion of women's roles (Cubitt and King 2008), others note the relative marginalisation of Arwen and Éowyn within Jackson's wider narrative (Fredrick and McBride 2007).

While there has been much discussion of Tolkien's and Jackson's depictions of women in relation to *LotR*, it is significant to note that Tolkien's *Hobbit* provides no original materials with which to develop a more central female presence within the storyworld, in order to offer viewers a basis for 'feminine' identifications. The narrative follows the exploits of an exclusively masculine fraternity comprised of Bilbo, wizard Gandalf, and a company of 13 dwarves headed by the heir to the Dwarven throne, Thorin. Women, where mentioned at all in *The Hobbit*, feature as housewives or shrews, such as Rosie Cotton or Lobelia Sackville-Baggins. For writers Jackson, Philippa Boyens and Fran Walsh, *The Hobbit*'s overtly masculine orientation was clearly a problem that needed to be overcome. In response, they developed the character of Tauriel, to both 'expand the world of the elves of Mirkwood Forest—and to bring some more female energy to the otherwise male-dominated *Hobbit* narrative' (Rottenberg 2013, n.p.; see also McIntyre 2013).

Prior to the second film's release, Evangeline Lilly described Tauriel as a young and talented warrior, 'slightly reckless and totally ruthless' (as cited in Rottenberg 2013, n.p.). As a Silvan or Woodland Elf, Tauriel has less social status than High Elves such as Legolas and Galadriel, and hence Thranduil does not consider her a suitable match for his son, and warns her not to give Legolas 'false hope'. Thus, it is primarily the young dwarf Kili, Thorin's nephew, who becomes the object of her affections, in a decision that appears to have been informed both by creative considerations and by the studio's concern about increasing the film's appeal to female viewers by further developing their love story, as Lilly explains here: 'We came back for reshoots in 2012 … and they were like, "Uh, *the studio would really like to see….*" And I was like, "Here we go. Here we go". And sure enough I'm in another love triangle' (*Yahoo Movies* 2013, n.p.; emphasis added; see also Harp 2013; Sims 2013). Tauriel's inclusion in this fantasy action blockbuster thus reflects a common filmmaking strategy to appeal to female audiences, and simultaneously indulge heterosexual male viewers, by featuring an attractive action heroine who nevertheless primarily functions as romantic relief (Kartal 2014).

Our findings suggest significant polarisation in the responses to Tauriel as a non-canon female character in an otherwise exclusively masculine fantasy action narrative, and to her depiction as centrally involved in an invented romantic subplot. When asked to identify one change they would make if they could, 22.6% of *DoS* and 14.6% of *BotFA* respondents identified changes explicitly related to Tauriel and the love triangle. Of those respondents, 29.2% of *DoS* and 43.1% of *BotFA* respondents wished Tauriel had been removed from the plot entirely, while 30.5% and 36.2% would have omitted or changed the romantic storyline between Tauriel and Kili. A further 31.0% of *DoS* and 15.5% of *BotFA* respondents would have removed or altered the love triangle including Legolas.

Further insight into the basis of these objections can be gleaned from written responses to four Q statements specifically relating to Tauriel and the romantic storylines. Overall, 6.9% of *DoS* respondents most strongly agreed with this statement: 'Tauriel, even though an entirely new character, is frankly a welcome female face in a fictional universe that revolves around its men'; somewhat less than the 10.8% that most strongly disagreed. Rather more pronounced objections focused on the love story, as evident in response to the following: 'Jackson's risky move of inventing his own Tolkien character—the elf guard Tauriel—as a love interest for Legolas pays off. These two bring some badly needed heat to the woodlands', with 22.2% expressing very strong disagreement and just 1.2% most strongly agreeing. A similar pattern was identified in the responses to *BotFA*, where in response to the statement that 'Tauriel has been a fine addition to the series. I'm happy they added her', 22.3% most strongly disagreed, compared to 5.4% who most strongly agreed. There were also strong objections to the love story: in response to this statement, 'The love story between Kili and Tauriel detracts from the movie, rather than adding any value to it', only 4.6% most strongly disagreed, while a more significant number—19.5%—most strongly agreed.

The wide range of comments in response to these Q statements reflect a complex set of concerns. Some considered Tauriel's character to be poorly written, unnecessary, contrary to canon and a 'distraction' from the main story that 'destroyed' the plotlines of other main characters, most notably Kili. Many others expressed a striking degree of animosity and professed their hatred and loathing of Tauriel, whom they wished to be removed from *The Hobbit* altogether. Expressions of unveiled anger and intense disdain were not at all uncommon: Tauriel was variously described as 'horrible', 'a travesty', 'a fabricated Mary Sue elf', 'the Jar-Jar Binks of *The Hobbit*', 'one of the worst invented characters—EVER', 'a mistake' and a 'train wreck of a character'.

One set of objections to Tauriel both as a character and in terms of her romantic storyline stemmed from the numerous violations of Tolkien's sacred canon associated with her actions, attitudes and appearance. Several respondents argued at length that aspects of Tauriel's character and behaviour, and her relationship with a Dwarf, were completely out of step with the established 'laws' of Tolkien's universe. One 29-year-old American woman living in Poland remarked that

> Tauriel beggars belief. What is a mere 600 year old Silvan doing as captain of the guard? . . . . [S]he fails miserably in her duties. She has likely taken an oath to her king, yet she questions and defies him with impunity. In Tolkien's reality-minded world, this would be treachery and would merit execution. Thanks to Legolas's puppy love, it's brushed off like nothing.

Linked to this concern about the lack of textual fidelity, others took issue with the notion that a female character and love interest needed to be introduced to help 'correct' the conservative gender politics reflected in Tolkien's masculine fraternity between Bilbo, Gandalf and the dwarves, and thereby increase the trilogy's appeal to women. For many female respondents, the notion that *The Hobbit* needed a female character for them to 'identify' with was seen as tokenistic, insulting, patronising and as failing to acknowledge the possibility of cross-gender identifications, as theorised by Carol Clover (2004). This notion was expressed by a 54-year-old Italian woman, who suggested that 'Women don't need female heroes to identify in. I identify in a soul, in a complex character, its quest, its story, not its gender.'

Several respondents explicitly identified Tauriel as a classic example of the much-derided 'Mary Sue', a term referring to young and highly idealised female characters who are too good to be true, in the sense of being extraordinarily charming, intelligent, physically distinctive if not beautiful, and who possess extraordinary abilities and special gifts, engage in heroic feats and are loved and adored by, and often romantically entangled with, established male characters (Pflieger 1999):

> She's not only a female but the best fighter and a healer. She's got a dwarf and an elvish Prince fawning over her. She's got red hair, a rarity in the Tolkien realm, that's longer than even Lady Galadriel's or Arwen's. She has a dark and dismal past . . . and was taken in and favoured by the King. She's rebellious and yet was awarded the position of the Captain of the Guard . . . . And, she seems unusually complicated and conflicted for a Silvan elf. All of these combined = a Mary Sue. (American woman, 44)

As McCormack (2015) notes, the Mary Sue is often reviled within fandom as reflecting an obvious extension of the desires of the female author (usually of fan fiction), whose attempt to assert ownership over the text has 'overstepped reasonable or respectable bounds' (McCormack 2015, p. 322). Scodari (2012) observes that animosity also stems from a perception that the inclusion of a Mary Sue often outshines and diverts attention away from central male characters. Indeed, many of our respondents objected to Tauriel's insertion because her romantic entanglement with Kili altered his storyline, in the process perverting Tolkien's original denouement and intended message. Some criticised her addition as feminist or politically correct 'pandering', as suggested by this 48-year-old British woman: 'It is an insult to the audience that they cannot enjoy a film without a token female. Political correctness has no place in Tolkien's world.'

While many objected to Tauriel's mere presence in the films, the more significant bone of contention was her involvement in a non-canon love story with the young dwarf, Kili, and the implicit suggestion of a love triangle involving Legolas. Even on this issue we find a complex set of reactions that warrant careful unpacking. Of particular note are numerous comments reflecting deep disappointment at the missed opportunity to add a strong, well-rounded female character who could stand in her own right, rather than being reduced to the stereotypical role of a love interest:

If she is a strong warrior elf, then let her be one. The minute they had her mooning over the two male characters, it negated everything they said she was there for! Can't she be a strong fighter/person without also being looked upon as an object of romantic desire? (American woman, 51)

Such reactions echo those outlined by Porter (2005) in the fan and media reaction to the *LotR's* Éowyn. Many fans initially welcomed Éowyn's depiction as a more active and independent female figure, but became very critical of how her storyline unfolded. Whereas some *LotR* fans saw Éowyn as having 'sold out' by marrying Faramir, many of our respondents lamented Tauriel's reduction to a simpering, lovelorn shadow of her former warrior self.

While some merely sought changes to the way the *Hobbit* romance was presented, rather more wished it had been left out altogether, perceiving it as studio-contrived, unnecessary, stereotypical, unbelievable and entirely contrary to canon, as argued by a 20-year-old Welshman who said 'Her relationship with Kili is also very out of character for both him and any elf ever. We don't need them to "build a bridge between the two peoples." That's what Legolas and Gimli's love does!' Such views were echoed by several others:

It is so fabricated it reeks of studio interference, so forced it hurts, leads to the worst lines in the script, totally alters the way Kili dies making a beautiful moment of brotherly self-sacrifice for their Uncle a botched late addition to the script, and doesn't fit with Tauriel's character . . . . There is no "true love" felt for an enemy race dwarf after meeting him three times for a combined duration of five hours. I blame dumb executives at Warner Bros. for this and will never forgive them for the love triangle. (Canadian woman, 29)

Of course, there were those who nonetheless greatly enjoyed the addition of a strong female action heroine to the wider Middle-earth franchise, just as many women greatly appreciated the expansion of Éowyn and Arwen's roles in *LotR*. These respondents noted the importance of including powerful female characters as sources of identification and role models for younger viewers, and of contemporary films consciously addressing the underrepresentation of women and 'feminine' interests and attributes within entertainment media more broadly. As a 25-year-old American man observed, 'Not a single of Jackson's Middle-earth movies passes the Bechdel Test,[2] and Jackson should consider this an embarrassment ... . Adding a female character to *The Hobbit*'s line-up was a smart and, dare I say, socially conscientious move.' This sentiment was shared by a 30-year-old American woman, who felt 'Tauriel was a wonderful surprise to come out of Hollywood, which has a tendency to over-sexualize and under explore their female characters. The story would have lacked realism if it had kept to the book and included no women.' A smaller number enjoyed the romantic storyline and felt it added depth to the wider *Hobbit* narrative, while helping to account for certain aspects of the character relations depicted in the *LotR* films:

> Kili and Tauriel's doomed and delicate romance was a great way to take a step into the wider world of Middle-earth. To me they represented how individuals can overcome the long-held prejudices between peoples, and also it paved the way for Legolas to build his own friendship with Gimli in *LotR*. I am so glad that we got to see a female character in this movie trilogy, and I thought she contributed to the wider story and to Legolas' character development. (American woman, 56)

Significantly, Tauriel was the 'most like to be' preference of 11.5% of our respondents in our survey of *DoS*, the majority of whom were, unsurprisingly, women. This figure dropped to 9.1% in the *BotFA* survey, again suggesting growing disenchantment with her depiction, and specifically her reduction to the role of love interest, as the trilogy drew to its conclusion. This issue of character identification and its relationship to aspects of social location such as gender, age, nationality and modality of reception will be addressed in greater detail in the following chapter.

CONCLUSION

As demonstrated, the *Hobbit* trilogy was ascribed a diverse range of meanings by our respondents. Nonetheless, some very clear themes can be identified. For many, the trilogy offered heightened pleasures of re-immersion in and expansion of a fantastical world created in fiction and on film, allowing them to sustain a transparent mode of reception and return once again to their beloved Middle-earth. For others, the trilogy was clearly a source of disappointment and frustration on various counts, prompting the adoption of more distanced and critical mediated modes of response. Such responses, we suggest, stem from a fundamental mismatch between the ideal film versions of *The Hobbit* many respondents had mentally visualised and longed to see, and the films as actually realised by Jackson and his team. Whether they had hoped for an adaptation that would be faithful to the spirit of Tolkien's original novel, or a spectacular visual epic that matched the standard of cinematic excellence set by Jackson's *LotR* trilogy, it is clear that the processes and imperatives associated with blockbusterisation produced a certain form of text that differed quite radically from the imaginative ideal in which many were psychologically and emotionally invested. Confronted with films that failed to live up to their hopes and imaginings, a significant number of respondents found it impossible to sustain deep immersion in the *Hobbit* trilogy.

Still others were motivated to modify their hopes and dreams to better align with an initially unpalatable 'reality'. These respondents spoke of consciously minimising or 'transforming' their expectations prior to release, or over the course of the trilogy; of not allowing themselves to inflate their expectations, fearing disappointment—fears often based on rumour and speculation, and informed also by their encounters with the first and second *Hobbit* films. Post-viewing, some attempted to reconcile the films as fully realised by Jackson and company with the imagined versions they had originally desired or hoped to see—to make sense of why certain troubling changes had been made to the original story, to rationalise the choices of the films' creators, and to understand the wider production context that had led to their cinematic desires being ultimately thwarted. Several spoke of needing to watch the films several times before they started to appreciate them in their own right. Such practices of minimising or modifying expectations and post-viewing reconciliation have also been observed by Bacon-Smith and Yarbrough (1991) and Barker and Brooks (1998). While we do not have space to discuss these practices at length here, we conclude this chapter with two comments, one from a *Fulfilled Hobbit Fan* and the other from a *Disappointed Tolkien Reader*. These, we believe, capture the degree of conscious psychological effort that some dedicated fans of the franchise engaged in so as to recuperate *The Hobbit* for their fandom, or at least find it a tolerable addition to the wider canon:

> The first film left me feeling very disappointed and with a real sense of being conflicted about everything. I had gone into it with very high expectations from the epic majesty of the *LotR*, and loving the *Hobbit* story and

already happy with the casting of characters. But there were some very cheesy elements and bad CGI and poor changes to the storyline that took me by surprise . . . . It took me a long time to reconcile my feelings about the movie, because I wanted to love it so badly, but I had all of these negative impressions of it. Ultimately, I came to grips with this disappointment and learned to appreciate the good parts of the movies, which still had that flavour of the *LotR*'s majesty . . . . I decided to focus on the good parts of these movies rather than the things that bothered me. (Canadian woman, 26)

I had wanted *AUJ* to be a film version of a story that I have loved for years. I was upset that I didn't like it the first time I watched it. I watched it a few more times in an attempt to like it. I supposed I've gotten to the point that I was able to say that I liked it enough as a piece of entertainment. But as something that evokes the magic of the book, no. (Filipino woman, 39)

For these and other respondents, it was only through such active and deliberate processes of reducing and modifying expectations, post-viewing reconciliation and selective attention that the *Hobbit* trilogy become *worthy* of a revised and notably *diminished* form of cinematic desire.

Notes

1. For the purposes of comparison with the second and third surveys, only English-language responses are analysed here. The full multilingual data set is analysed in Chap. 9.
2. The Bechdel Test assesses the representation of women in film based on a simple rubric that a film should have at least two named female characters who talk to each other about something other than a man (see http://bechdeltest.com).

References

Bacon-Smith, C., & Yarbrough, T. (1991). Batman: The ethnography. In R. E. Pearson & W. Uricchio (Eds.), *The many lives of the Batman: Critical approaches to a superhero and his media* (pp. 90–116). New York: Routledge and London: BFI Publishing.

Barker, M. (2006). Envisaging 'visualisation': Some challenges from the international *Lord of the Rings* project. *Film-Philosophy, 10*(3), 1–25.

Barker, M., & Brooks, K. (1998). *Knowing audiences: Judge Dredd, its friends, fans and foes*. Luton: University of Luton Press.

Clover, C. J. (2004). *Men, women, and chainsaws: Gender in the modern horror film*. London: British Film Institute.

Croft, J. B., & Donovan, L. A. (Eds.). (2015). *Perilous and fair: Women in the works and life of J. R. R. Tolkien*. Altadena: Mythopoeic Press.

Crowe, E. L. (1996). Power in Arda: Sources, uses and misuses. *Mythlore, 21*(2), 272–277.

Cubitt, S., & King, B. (2008). Dossier: Adapting a script. In H. Margolis, S. Cubitt, B. King, & T. Jutel (Eds.), *Studying the event film: The Lord of the Rings* (pp. 195–204). Manchester: Manchester University Press.

Fredrick, C., & McBride, S. (2007). Battling the woman warrior: Females and combat in Tolkien and Lewis. *Mythlore, 25*(3/4), 29–42.

Harp, J. (2013, December 18). Evangeline Lilly on The Hobbit films: 'I didn't want a love triangle'. Digital Spy. Retrieved August 20, 2016, from http://www.digitalspy.com/movies/the-hobbit/news/a539345/evangeline-lilly-on-the-hobbit-films-i-didnt-want-a-love-triangle/.

Hatcher, M. (2007). Finding woman's role in *The Lord of the Rings*. *Mythlore, 25*(3/4), 43–54.

Kartal, E. (2014). It is a man's world: Romantic relief in the Hollywood blockbuster. *CINEJ. Cinema Journal, 3*(2), 165–174. doi:10.5195/cinej.2014.89.

McCormack, U. (2015). Finding ourselves in the (un)mapped lands: Women's reparative readings of *The Lord of the Rings*. In J. B. Croft & L. A. Donovan (Eds.), *Perilous and fair: Women in the works and life of J. R. R. Tolkien* (pp. 309–326). Altadena: Mythopoeic Press.

McIntyre, G. (2013, December 11). *The Hobbit: The Desolation of Smaug*. Philippa Boyens talks Tauriel. *Hero complex: Pop culture unmasked*. Retrieved August 20, 2016, from http://herocomplex.latimes.com/movies/the-hobbit-the-desolation-of-smaug-philippa-boyens-talks-tauriel/#/0.

Partridge, B. (1983). No sex please—we're hobbits: The construction of female sexuality in *The Lord of the Rings*. In R. Giddings (Ed.), *J. R. R. Tolkien: This far land* (pp. 179–197). London and Totowa: Vision; Barnes & Noble.

Pflieger, P. (1999, March 31). *'Too good to be true': 150 years of Mary Sue*. Paper presented at the American Culture Association conference, San Diego, CA.

Porter, L. R. (2005). *Unsung heroes of The Lord of the Rings: From the page to the screen*. Westport, CT: Praeger Publishers.

Reid, R. A. (2015). The history of scholarship on female characters in J. R. R. Tolkien's legendarium. In J. B. Croft & L. A. Donovan (Eds.), *Perilous and fair: Women in the works and life of J. R. R. Tolkien* (pp. 13–40). Altadena: Mythopoeic Press.

Rottenberg, J. (2013, June 5). 'The Hobbit': Evangeline Lilly as Tauriel. *Entertainment Weekly.* Retrieved May 10, 2014, from http://www.ew.com/article/2013/06/05/evangeline-lilly-hobbit-desolation-of-smaug?utm_source=feedburner&utm_medium=feed&utm_campaign=Feed%253A+entertainmentweekly%252Flatest+(Entertainment+Weekly%253A++Today%2527s+Latest)&utm_content=Google+Reader.

Scodari, C. (2012). 'Nyota Uhura is not a white girl': Gender, intersectionality, and *Star Trek* 2009's alternate romantic universes. *Feminist Media Studies, 12*(3), 335–351. doi:10.1080/14680777.2011.615605.

Sims, A. (2013, December 9). Evangeline Lilly on the importance of creating a female *Hobbit* hero, her one *Lost* condition. *Hypable.* Retrieved February 14, 2017, from http://www.hypable.com/hobbit-evangeline-lilly-tauriel-hero-new-character/.

Stam, R. (2005). Introduction: The theory and practice of adaptation. In R. Stam & A. Raengo (Eds.), *Literature and film: A guide to the theory and practice of film adaptation* (pp. 1–52). Oxford: Blackwell Press.

Stimpson, C. R. (1969). *J. R. R. Tolkien.* New York: Columbia University Press.

Thum, M. (2005). The 'sub-sub creation' of Galadriel, Arwen, and Éowyn: Women of power in Tolkien's and Jackson's *The Lord of the Rings.* In J. B. Croft (Ed.), *Tolkien on film: Essays on Peter Jackson's The Lord of the Rings* (pp. 231–256). Altadena: Mythopoeic Press.

Yahoo Movies. (2013, December 14). How 'Hobbit' filmmakers betrayed Evangeline Lilly. *Yahoo! News.* Retrieved from https://www.yahoo.com/news/blogs/movie-news/the-promise–hobbit–filmmakers-broke-to-evangeline-lilly-211339686.html?ref=gs. Accessed 11 January 2017.

Yates, J. (2000). Arwen the elf warrior? *Amon Hen, 165,* 11–15.

CHAPTER 9

Making Sense of Difference: How Social Location and Identity Shaped Engagements with the *Hobbit* Trilogy

INTRODUCTION

In this chapter, we revisit some of our guiding research questions to explore whether global responses to the *Hobbit* trilogy effectively transcended differences of nationality, language and culture. We also examine whether there were significant differences in our participants' engagements that might be linked to key socio-demographic variables and other relevant group memberships, including gender, age, socioeconomic class, education, occupation and fandoms—variables that we group together under the term 'social location'.

Our interest in these kinds of questions reflects a prevailing concern within the wider field in trying to understand the role that people's different social locations and identities play in shaping their receptions of screen media. Much of the early research in this area was informed by Morley and Brunsdon's landmark *Nationwide* study, which explored 'how the different subcultural structures and formations within the audience, and the sharing of different cultural codes and competencies amongst different groups and classes, structure the decoding of the message for different sections of the audience' (Morley 1980, p. 51). While receptions of television have received greater emphasis to date, a smaller body of research has explored the ways in which film responses may also be socially patterned. Collectively, these studies suggest that nationality, gender, age, socio-economic class, ethnicity, language and other affiliations potentially shape genre preferences, modes of engagement,

© The Author(s) 2017
C. Michelle et al., *Fans, Blockbusterisation, and the Transformation of Cinematic Desire*, DOI 10.1057/978-1-137-59616-1_9

emotional response, and feelings of affiliation and identification with characters.

The significance of these studies lies not merely in charting the relationships between audience receptions and important aspects of social location, but in exposing the complexity of those connections, since individuals are always located within multiple subcultural formations (Fiske 1989; Schrøder 1994). An individual respondent to our *Hobbit* surveys might, for instance, be a white British man who is also middle-aged, working class, politically left-wing, a Catholic and an avid Tolkien reader. Any of these aspects, or more likely a few in combination, may shape his response to these films. Social subjects may draw from various aspects of their identity along with other 'social alliances' when making sense of media texts (Dahlgren 1988; Jordin and Brunt 1988), depending on their immediate salience. Research on audiences inhabiting intersecting social categories (based on age and gender, for instance) confirms that social similarities and differences affect reception in complex ways (Alper et al. 2016; Leurs and Ponzanesi 2014; Press 1991b; Scodari 2012, 2014; Skeggs et al. 2008).

Adding a further layer of complexity, Hoffner and Cantor (1991, p. 76) suggest that 'the knowledge, predispositions, and cognitive abilities people bring to the viewing situation mediate the effects of specific depictions.' These may include familiarity with the 'types of people and situations depicted', familiarity with the characters in the context of the particular narrative/text (perhaps from having read the book on which a film is based), pre-existing stereotypes, developmental stage and an understanding of 'relevant social norms and conventions' (Hoffner and Cantor 1991, p. 76). Individual psychological factors also influence media selection, engagement and response (Chamorro-Premuzic et al. 2013), interacting with aspects of social location and identity to influence viewers' choices and receptions of media and shape their responses to particular characters—including whether they like them or want to *be* like them (Hoffner and Cantor 1991; see also Banerjee et al. 2008; Dill 2009; Giles 2003; Hall and Bracken 2011; Potter 2012). For example, personality traits—as measured by the 'Big Five' dimensions of personality—reliably predict individuals' preferences for music, books, and film and television genres (Potter 2012; Rentfrow et al. 2011). Indeed, in Rentfrow et al.'s (2011) study, sex and education level were found to have a strong relationship with entertainment media preferences while age and ethnicity were more moderately influential, but psychological dispositions also played a significant role that was independent of socio-demographic factors. Thus, extending the above hypothetical example, our white British working-class man may also be agreeable, conscientious, slightly introverted and a bit of a worrier, but ultimately open to new experiences—not unlike Bilbo, perhaps.

Drawing from the two (surprisingly disconnected) fields of audience studies and media psychology, our research is grounded in the understanding that different individuals could potentially construct substantially divergent interpretations of the *Hobbit* trilogy based on their particular constellation of socio-demographic memberships, cultural identities and locations, class positionings, political and moral beliefs, social and fan affiliations and individual psychological make-ups. Because of the complex intersections between these various subcultural formations, we have not made assumptions about which group membership(s) or affiliations will be most influential for particular respondents. Instead, we collected information about a wide range of characteristics that theoretically might be significant (based on the accumulation of previous research), and have tested these relationships among a diverse and naturally-occurring 'audience' for the *Hobbit* films, which we assembled by surveying a large number of viewers spread across various regions of the world.

In so doing, we have diverged from the more typical methodological approach used in media psychology research, in which a relatively homogeneous group of respondents (often undergraduate students) are studied in a laboratory or classroom setting. Our approach also differs from most reception studies within the ethnographic tradition, in which individual interviewees or participants in focus groups are selected on the basis of one or perhaps two aspects of their multifaceted identities. Whereas the latter approach assumes in advance that certain subcultural formations will be more salient than others (and thus potentially risks predetermining the outcome), our exploration of the relationship between reception and social location occurs 'after the fact', working backwards from our respondents' independently expressed reactions to the films to identify patterns in the distribution of their viewpoints based on country of residence, gender, age, socio-economic class, political belief, religion and fan affiliations.

At this point, we should acknowledge that, due to the inherent constraints in conducting online research and given the significant demands placed on our respondents through our use of Q methodology, we chose not to explore the role of psychological dispositions in any detail. However, our comparative neglect of this dimension should not be taken to suggest that we discount the possible importance of personality differences. In what follows, we highlight just some of our key findings and explore potentially meaningful differences within our longitudinal international data set, contextualising these in relation to the body of existing research. Then, we consider what our findings reveal about the relationship between modes of reception and subcultural formations, and highlight the contributions our project has made to the wider body of research addressing the factors shaping audience engagement and response.

We also acknowledge that our research findings may not be directly comparable with those derived from studies that used a different methodology to identify and interpret audience subjectivities and audience segments. Our use of Q methodology in tandem with a particular analytical framework—the Composite Model—constitutes a novel approach to cross-cultural audience research that differs in significant ways from most other studies in this field. The patterns we have identified should thus be interpreted with care, as should any apparent similarities to other studies. That said, we perceive some intriguing parallels between our findings and earlier research on *The Lord of the Rings* (*LotR*) viewers as well as the wider scholarship around cultural aspects of media reception and national repertoires of evaluation (Kersten 2014; Lamont 1992; Lamont and Thevenot 2000), and make note of these in the following discussion.

As we have maintained throughout this book, the intended effect of the *Hobbit* films on audiences (the film's 'preferred reading') was to induce narrative transportation and highly enjoyable immersion in the cinematic storyworld. In this *transparent* mode of reception (Michelle 2007), viewers suspended disbelief and entered the storyworld as though it were real, experiencing Middle-earth with a sense of enchantment and wonder. Viewers who experienced the films in the transparent mode were very enthusiastic about them, and in all our post-viewing surveys they constituted the largest audience segments, which we variously labelled *Enchanted Hobbit Fans* (from *An Unexpected Journey—AUJ*), *Happy Hobbit Defenders* (from *The Desolation of Smaug—DoS*) and *Fulfilled Hobbit Fans* (from *The Battle of the Five Armies—BotFA*). The pre-viewing audience contained a large segment of viewers who anticipated a highly enjoyable viewing experience; in theoretical terms, these respondents could be regarded as expressing a strong prefigurative desire to experience the forthcoming films in a transparent mode. We named this very eager and enthusiastic segment *LotR Film Fans*. In addition to the main audience segments which experienced or hoped to experience the films in a transparent mode, numerous viewers were disappointed by the *Hobbit* films, experiencing them in varieties of the mediated mode (see Appendix A for a summary of the main audience segments). As discussed in previous chapters, for many of these viewers the films' preferred reading was disrupted by factors which were increasingly attributed to processes and imperatives related to Hollywood blockbusterisation, and to excessive commercial influence on the *Hobbit* trilogy's content or conditions of production.

Our goal in the remainder of this chapter is to explore the social locations that are significantly associated with adoption of the *Hobbit* films' preferred reading. We report the results of tests of odds ratios,[1] which in this case express the likelihood of experiencing the *Hobbit* films in the transparent mode according to various aspects of social location. The use of odds ratios allows us to construct a portrait of the social dimensions of audiences who were most receptive to the *Hobbit* films. We also selectively discuss the social locations of dissenting audience segments. Although no conventions have been established (in audience or media studies, at least) for the measurement of social position, any definition would likely include age, gender, occupation, education, income and country of residence. These are the variables we have used; our core findings are summarised in Tables 9.1, 9.2 and 9.3. Other attributes of likely significance in measuring social location include race/ethnicity, sexual identity and family linkages—which we did not measure for reasons of economy.

THE ROLES OF CULTURAL LOCATION AND LANGUAGE IN SHAPING RESPONSES TO A GLOBAL BLOCKBUSTER EVENT FILM

Various scholars have studied the roles of cultural location, national identity and language in shaping encounters with media content, often as part of a broader response to the global dominance of US media and expressed concerns about American cultural imperialism.[2] In addition, an emerging body of research explores media use and engagement among diasporic audiences.[3] Collectively, these studies suggest that national culture does shape understandings of media content: cross-cultural reception involves an ongoing active process of selection, mediation and transformation as differently located audiences draw on their own

Table 9.1 Significant associations between viewpoints and social locations: *An Unexpected Journey*

	Overall Sample	Enchanted Hobbit Fans	Bored and Disillusioned Hobbit Critics	Disappointed Tolkien Readers	Critics of Technological 'Enhancements'	Mildly Entertained Casual Viewers
Number and % of all respondents	N = 2870	N = 2125 (74.0%)	N = 91 (3.2%)	N = 199 (6.9%)	N = 119 (4.1%)	N = 43 (1.5%)
Average age	30.9	34.0	31.2	32.0	26.0	27.9
Age range (with significant correlations shown)	10–14 (1.0%) 15–18 (11.9%) 19–23 (25.8%) 24–29 (18.2%) 30–39 (18.6%) 40–49 (13.1%) 50–59 (8.3%) 60 + (3.2%)	10–14* (1.2%) 15–18** (13.0%) 24–29## (16.6%) 50–59* (8.9%)	15–18## (0%) 50–59*(15.4%)	30–39* (24.2%)	24–29** (30.3%) 40–49# (6.9%) 50–59# (2.5%)	
Female	1590 (55.4%)	1250** (58.8%)	37## (40.7%)	96# (48.2%)	51## (42.9%)	24 (55.8%)
Principal countries of residence (with significant correlations shown)	US (827, 29.2%) Germany (226, 8.0%) Spain (224, 7.9%) UK (175, 6.2%) France (174, 6.2%) NZ (148, 5.2%) Belgium (140, 5.0%) Canada (132, 4.7%) Australia (121, 4.3%) Denmark (118, 4.2%) Mexico (43, 1.5%)	1250** (58.8%) US** (31.5%) Germany (7.7%) Spain## (7.3%) France (6.4%) UK (6.3%) Canada (5.0%) Australia (4.5%) NZ ## (4.4%) Belgium## (4.1%) Denmark## (2.7%)	37## (40.7%) NZ** (15.4%) UK (9.9%) US## (9.9%) Belgium* (8.8%) Germany* (8.8%) Spain (7.7%) Denmark (6.6%)	96# (48.2%) US (28.6%) Germany* (12.2%) Spain (9.2%) Denmark* (7.7%) UK (7.1%) France (5.1%) Netherlands** (3.6%)	51## (42.9%) US (26.7%) Denmark** (11.2%) France (8.6%) Germany (6.0%) NZ (6.0%) Spain (6.0%) Australia (5.2%) Belgium (5.2%) Canada (5.2%) UK (5.2%)	24 (55.8%) Belgium** (16.3%) NZ* (14.0%) Denmark* (11.6%) Spain (11.6%) US# (9.5%) Germany (9.3%) Australia (7.0%) Canada (7.0%) UK (7.0%)

(continued)

Table 9.1 (continued)

	Overall Sample	Enchanted Hobbit Fans	Bored and Disillusioned Hobbit Critics	Disappointed Tolkien Readers	Critics of Technological 'Enhancements'	Mildly Entertained Casual Viewers
Resident of English-speaking country (Anglosphere)	1446 (51.2%)	1110** (53.0%)	42 (46.2%)	90 (45.9%)	57 (49.1%)	20 (46.5%)
Graduate degree	557 (20.5%)	386## (19.6%)	33** (36.7%)	55** (27.9%)	20 (16.9%)	8 (19.0%)
High income	426 (15.2%)	301 (14.5%)	14 (15.6%)	37 (18.9%)	18 (15.5%)	10 (23.8%)
Advanced media education or production experience	458 (16.2%)	291## (13.9%)	33** (37.5%)	31 (15.6%)	35** (29.4%)	12* (30.0%)
Any religious affiliation	1501 (56.0%)	1156** (58.0%)	35# (44.3%)	103 (54.8%)	45 (47.8%)	17 (42.5%)
Christian	1149 (42.9%)	891** (44.7%)	24# (30.4%)	78 (41.5%)	43 (38.1%)	14 (35.0%)
Political orientation:[a]						
Left	1106 (39.0%)	793# (37.7%)	35 (39.3%)	88 (44.2%)	53 (44.9%)	15 (35.7%)
Centre	376 (13.2%)	260# (12.2%)	11 (12.4%)	29 (14.6%)	17 (14.4%)	6 (14.3%)
Right	489 (17.2%)	367 (17.4%)	14 (15.7%)	36 (18.1%)	20 (16.9%)	11 (26.2%)
Neutral/None	581 (20.5%)	466** (22.1%)	12 (13.5%)	33 (16.6%)	20 (16.9%)	6 (14.3%)
Number of times members have read The Hobbit (mean)	6.0	5.9	7.8	8.2*	5.5	2.7#
Motivated to see The Hobbit by the LotR films[b]	802 (28.0%)	600 (28.3%)	22 (24.2%)	33## (16.2%)	46** (38.7%)	19* (44.2%)

Note Pearson correlations: * / # = positive/negative significance at 0.05 level; ** / ## = positive/negative significance at 0.01 level

[a]These categories were created by combining a wider list categories as follows: Left—progressive/liberal/social democrat, communist/socialist, anarchist; Centre—centrist, libertarian; Right—conservative/republican, nationalist, monarchist, faith-based; Neutral/none—neutral, none

Table 9.2 Significant associations between viewpoints and social locations: *The Desolation of Smaug*

	Overall Sample	Happy Hobbit Defenders	Disenchanted Hobbit Critics	Aggrieved Tolkien Aficionados	Hobbit Sceptics	Middle-earth Appreciators
Number and % of all respondents	N = 1051	N = 606 (57.7%)	N = 15 (1.4%)	N = 307 (29.2%)	N = 30 (2.9%)	N = 7 (0.7%)
Average age	33.1	35.1	33.6	30.8	27.8	35.6
Age range (with significant correlations shown)	10–14 (0.5%) 15–18 (10.0%) 19–23 (20.8%) 24–29 (22.2%) 30–39 (15.5%) 40–49 (14.6%) 50–59 (11.5%) 60 + (5.0%)	24–29## (17.7%) 40–49* (17.0%) 50–59* (14.9%) 60 + * (6.4%)	40–49* (38.5%)	24–29* (26.4%) 50–59# (8.2%)		
Female	631 (61.0%)	392** (65.3%)	5# (35.7%)	163## (54.3%)	20 (66.7%)	6 (85.7%)
Principal countries of residence (with significant correlations shown)	US (469, 45.3%) UK (97, 9.4%) Canada (71, 6.9%) Australia (58, 5.6%) NZ (45, 4.3%) Germany (35, 3.4%) Finland (31, 3.0%) Netherlands (20, 1.9%) France (18, 1.7%) Philippines (16, 1.5%)	US (45.3%) UK (9.3%) Canada (7.2%) Australia (5.7%) NZ (5.0%) Germany (3.3%) France (2.3%) Finland# (2.0%) Philippines# (2.0%) Russia* (1.8%)	US (28.6%) Australia** (14.3%) + individuals from eight other countries	US (48.7%) UK (9.3%) Canada (7.0%) Australia (6.3%) Germany (3.7%) Netherlands (2.7%) Finland (2.3%) NZ (2.3%)	USA (33.3%) Finland** (13.3%) Canada (10.0%) UK (10.0%)	UK (28.6%) US (28.6%) + individuals from three other countries
English spoken at home	750 (72.9%)	443 (74.2%)	7 (58.3%)	220 (73.6%)	19 (63.3%)	5 (71.4%)

(continued)

Table 9.2 (continued)

	Overall Sample	Happy Hobbit Defenders	Disenchanted Hobbit Critics	Aggrieved Tolkien Aficionados	Hobbit Sceptics	Middle-earth Appreciators
Resident of English-speaking country (Anglosphere)	757 (73.2%)	448 (74.7%)	10 (71.4%)	220 (73.6%)	19 (63.3%)	5 (71.4%)
Graduate degree	266 (25.6%)	140# (23.3%)	7 (46.7%)	86 (28.2%)	12* (41.4%)	1 (14.3%)
High-school education or less	187 (17.8%)	109 (18.0%)	1 (6.7%)	53 (17.3%)	4 (13.3%)	3 (42.9%)
High income	138 (13.2%)	79 (13.2%)	2 (14.3%)	39 (12.8%)	4 (13.3%)	1 (14.3%)
Advanced media education	114 (13.9%)	74 (12.4%)	4 (26.4%)	38 (12.5%)	11** (36.7%)	2 (28.6%)
Media production experience	118 (11.6%)	61 (10.4%)	6** (40.0%)	28 (9.3%)	5 (17.2%)	1 (14.3%)
Any religious affiliation	548 (59.4%)	329 (62.0%)	7 (53.8%)	162 (59.8%)	11 (44.0%)	4 (57.1%)
Christian	409 (42.6%)	248 (44.9%)	4 (30.8%)	123 (43.8%)	8 (28.6%)	2 (28.6%)
Political affiliation (with significant correlations shown)	Progressive: 192 (20.9%) Liberal: 120 (13.1%) Centrist: 43 (4.7%) Conservative/Republican: 117 (12.7%) None, neutral, apolitical: 146 (15.9%)			Progressive: 42 ## (15.4%)		
Number of times members have read The Hobbit (mean)	7.5	6.9##	11.3**	8.7**	4.1#	6.0
Principal motivation to see DoS: Fan of LotR films	170 (16.2%)	122** (20.1%)	2 (13.3%)	27## (8.8%)	8 (26.7%)	2 (28.6%)
Hobbit/Tolkien book fan	641 (61.5%)	315## (52.4%)	7 (46.7%)	245** (80.1%)	14 (50.0%)	3 (42.9%)

Note Pearson correlations: * / # = positive/negative significance at 0.05 level; ** / ## = positive/negative significance at 0.01 level

cultural tastes, values, practices and experiences to make local sense of foreign media content (Morley 1992).

Moreover, the degree of cultural distance between the context of production and that of reception significantly shapes audience engagements, in line with Straubhaar's (2003) theory of cultural proximity. While closer proximity to the production context and the cultural 'reality' depicted on screen may generate feelings of familiarity, recognition and affinity, cultural distance and a lack of understanding of culturally specific references may create gaps in meaning. In response, some viewers may attempt to 'fill the gaps' by drawing on information and experiences from their own cultural location, history and practices.[4] However, such cultural 'translation' work can often be mentally taxing, and hence audiences often express a preference for media content produced in contexts that are relatively similar to their own in terms of expressed cultural values, tastes and customs. Media audiences also prefer content in their native language (Hasebrink 2012). Not surprisingly, then, Fu's (2012) analysis of global box-office receipts shows that 'countries tend to cluster, more or less, within cultural, linguistic, historical, or geographic boundaries' (p. 14). This author notes that Anglosphere countries that are linguistically as well as culturally proximate to the USA tend to like or dislike the same kinds of Hollywood films and have similar preferences for genres, narrative plots and aesthetic forms. East Asian Confucian countries prefer action, adventure, fantasy and thrillers over comedy, romance and drama, while tastes in France and Germany tend to be more similar to the USA, but with a higher interest in action-oriented genres. Similar clusters in terms of genre preferences were found for Eastern and Central European countries (Fu 2012).

Preference for culturally familiar and thus more readily interpreted content is reflected in a 'cultural discount' at the level of box-office sales in countries that differ significantly from the country in which a film was made (see Fu 2012; Hoskins and Mirus 1988; Lee 2006, 2008; Moon et al. 2015; Volz et al. 2010). However, global flows of entertainment content seem to be decreasingly affected by a steep 'cultural discount'. While the USA remains the dominant global supplier of high-end entertainment film (and television) products, screen media content in several regions of the world is becoming increasingly similar irrespective of where it is produced, suggesting a growing convergence between local and American genre tastes and preferences (Fu 2012). Furthermore, as previously noted, in the case of Hollywood blockbuster event-films seeking a global audience, deliberate efforts are often made to achieve a high degree of 'narrative transparency' (Olson 1999) in order to minimise culturally specific references and maximise cultural translatability (see also Miller et al. 2005; Sigismondi 2011; Tan 2011). While certain aspects of Olson's theory of narrative transparency are controversial, some genres—such as fantasy, science fiction and action-adventure—appear to have more universal cross-cultural appeal than others, possibly due to their focus on visual effects and action rather than complex narrative and dialogue, which may ease the cognitive load for those viewing dubbed or subtitled versions of a film (Bielby and Harrington 2008; see also King 2003; Wyatt 2010). These insights are significant for our research, as they suggest a blockbuster film trilogy such as *The Hobbit* likely has a high degree of cross-cultural portability 'built in', as it were—helping to extend the appeal of these films beyond contexts that are culturally similar or in which English is widely spoken or understood.

Seeking to gain some insight into how cultural location might shape global receptions of the *Hobbit* trilogy, we turned to the findings of the Tolkien's World Audiences study. Barker (2008) reports that American respondents had the highest overall score for a question about the importance of seeing *LotR: The Return of the King* (*RotK*), while UK respondents ranked second behind Chile in their appreciation of the film—ahead of US respondents, who ranked 13th on this measure (Kuipers and de Kloet 2008). Barker (2008) furthermore observes that viewers in Australia, Germany, Greece, Spain, the UK and the USA exhibited similar responses in the sense of a notable distinction between what he terms 'engaged' versus 'vernacular' modes of response. These are countries, Barker notes, where Tolkien has 'had a longstanding presence' (p. 178). Yet different forms of response were observed in France and Germany, despite Tolkien's similarly lengthy presence in both countries. Seeking to explain these anomalies, Barker suggests wider philosophical criteria were drawn on to assess the film in France, while German receptions appeared to be shaped by locally relevant concerns about war.

In their research on the effects of national location on reception, Kuipers and de Kloet (2008) compared 24 countries in terms of their appreciation of *RotK* and found significant although small differences. Appreciation was consistently high, and higher still in Commonwealth countries, while generally lower in countries relatively distant from British culture. In subsequent work, Kuipers and de Kloet (2009) posit

Table 9.3 Significant associations between viewpoints and social locations: *The Battle of the Five Armies*

	Overall Sample	Fulfilled Hobbit Fans	Angry Hobbit Critics	Unhappy Tolkien Adherents	Ambivalent Middle-earth Enthusiasts	Appreciative Film Critics	Frustrated Middle-earth Fans
Number and % of all respondents	N = 840	N = 405 (48.2%)	N = 14 (1.7%)	N = 229 (27.3%)	N = 41 (4.9%)	N = 25 (3.0%)	N = 17 (2.0%)
Average age	34.9	36.9**	33.2	31.3##	34.2**	39.5**	26.8##
Age range (with significant correlations shown)	10–14 (1.0%) 15–18 (6.4%) 19–23 (18.5%) 24–29 (20.2%) 30–39 (18.3%) 40–49 (16.8%) 50–59 (11.9%) 60 + (7.0%)	10–14 (1.0%) 15–18 (7.2%) 19–23 (16.4%) 24–29## (15.4%) 30–39 (17.6%) 40–49 (18.1%) 50–59* (14.1%) 60 + (10.2%)	10–14 (0%) 15–18 (7.7%) 19–23 (15.4%) 24–29## (15.4%) 30–39 (23.1%) 40–49 (15.4%) 50–59 (15.4%) 60 + (0%)	10–14 (0%) 15–18 (5.9%) 19–23 (22.5%) 24–29**(30.2%) 30–39 (18.9%) 40–49 (12.2%) 50–59 (7.7%) 60 + (2.7%)	10–14 (5.0%) 15–18 (5.0%) 19–23 (15.0%) 24–29## (25.0%) 30–39 (15.0%) 40–49 (17.5%) 50–59 (12.5%) 60 + (5.0%)	10–14 (0%) 15–18 (4.0%) 19–23 (16.0%) 24–29## (8.0%) 30–39 (20.0%) 40–49 (24.0%) 50–59 (24.0%) 60 + (4.0%)	10–14 (0%) 15–18 (5.9%) 19–23** (47.1%) 24–29 (17.6%) 30–39 (23.5%) 40–49 (0%) 50–59 (0%) 60 + (5.9%)
Female	504 (62.8%)	270** (70.3%)	5 (38.5%)	123# (56.2%)	23 (57.5%)	14 (60.9%)	11 (64.7%)

(continued)

Table 9.3 (continued)

	Overall Sample	Fulfilled Hobbit Fans	Angry Hobbit Critics	Unhappy Tolkien Adherents	Ambivalent Middle-earth Enthusiasts	Appreciative Film Critics	Frustrated Middle-earth Fans
Principal countries of residence (with significant correlations shown)	US (364, 43.9%) Canada (75, 9.0%) UK (56, 6.8%) NZ (48, 5.8%) Australia (41, 4.9%) Germany (34, 4.1%) Finland (15, 1.8%) France (15, 1.8%) Spain (13, 1.6%) Sweden (12, 1.4%) Russia (11, 1.3%)	US (46.3%) Canada (8.0%) UK (7.5%) Australia (4.7%) Germany (4.5%) NZ# (3.7%) Finland (1.7%) France (1.7%)	US (42.9%) NZ* (21.4%) + individuals from five other countries	US (42.4%) Canada (10.7%) UK (6.3%) Australia (5.4%) NZ (4.5%) Germany (4.0%) Finland (2.2%) Netherlands (2.2%)	US (39.0%) NZ* (14.6%) Australia (7.3%) Germany (7.3%) UK (7.3%)	US (41.7%) Canada (16.7%) NZ* (16.7%) + individuals from six other countries	US (29.4%) Australia (11.8%) Mexico (11.8%) Sweden (11.8%) + individuals from six other countries
English spoken at home	608 (73.3%)	290 (72.1%)	11 (78.6%)	164 (73.5%)	29 (70.7%)	22* (91.7%)	11 (64.7%)
Graduate degree	206 (24.8%)	86# (21.4%)	5 (35.7%)	50 (22.0%)	17* (41.5%)	11* (45.8%)	3 (17.6%)
High income	14 (1.9%)	4 (1.2%)	0	6 (3.1%)	2 (5.0%)	0	1 (7.7%)

(continued)

Table 9.3 (continued)

	Overall Sample	Fulfilled Hobbit Fans	Angry Hobbit Critics	Unhappy Tolkien Adherents	Ambivalent Middle-earth Enthusiasts	Appreciative Film Critics	Frustrated Middle-earth Fans
Advanced media education	145 (17.6%)	57# (14.5%)	4 (28.6%)	48 (21.2%)	5 (12.2%)	6 (25.0%)	5 (29.4%)
Media production experience	110 (13.3%)	45 (11.3%)	4 (28.6%)	29 (12.9%)	6 (15.0%)	7* (29.2%)	4 (23.5%)
Any religious affiliation	418 (53.9%)	219* (58.6%)	7 (53.8%)	104 (49.1%)	25 (64.1%)	10 (41.7%)	6 (35.3%)
Christian	327 (42.7%)	175* (46.8%)	5 (38.5%)	85 (40.1%)	17 (43.6%)	4# (16.6%)	3# (17.6%)
Political affiliation (with significant correlations shown)	Progressive: 230 (33.5%) None, neutral, apolitical: 123 (17.9%) Conservative/ Republican: 72 (10.5%) Green: 71 (10.3%) Socially liberal, fiscally conservative: 63 (9.2%) Centrist: 51 (7.4%)	Conservative**: 43 (12.7%)	Libertarian/ anarchist right*: 1 (7.7%) Communist/ socialist*: 2 (15.4%)			Progressive: *: 16 (69.6%)	Progressive *: 9 (60.0%)

(continued)

Table 9.3 (continued)

	Overall Sample	Fulfilled Hobbit Fans	Angry Hobbit Critics	Unhappy Tolkien Adherents	Ambivalent Middle-earth Enthusiasts	Appreciative Film Critics	Frustrated Middle-earth Fans
Number of times members have read The Hobbit (mean)	7.5	6.9	7.9	8.9*	6.1	4.5	9.4
Number of times members have seen the LotR trilogy	15.8	16.9*	8.9	15.9	12.8	12.6	16.9

Note: Pearson correlations: */# = positive/negative significance at 0.05 level; **/## = positive/negative significance at 0.01 level

that national 'repertoires of evaluation' may be giving way to global or transnational repertoires 'which are more readily available to viewers closer to the cultural and geographic centre' (p. 99). Using cluster analysis, they identified two major groups of *RotK* viewers within the World Audiences data. The first contained viewers from English-speaking countries and also Greece, France, Italy, Spain and most of Latin America who preferred more central characters and expressed greater appreciation for both the film and the novel, as well as stronger allegiance to the 'preferred' genre ascription of 'epic'. These viewers were regarded as generally closer to the centre of global media culture in terms of geography, gender and age, and included a larger proportion of young males. The second group contained less-involved viewers, mainly from non-English-speaking countries, who offered a wider range of genre ascriptions and preferred more fantastic characters that were less central to the plot. This latter group included more women than the first group, as well as more of the older and very young respondents.

Such findings suggest that cultural location is not the only factor shaping film receptions: language, gender and age also play important roles. Kuipers and de Kloet's (2009) research is of particular relevance to our own, since the distinction they observed between viewers who were highly engaged versus those who were more distanced and disengaged echoes our analysis of *Hobbit* audience segments, in which we identified a core distinction between those adopting the transparent (preferred) mode of reception and others adopting more distanced (and often critical) mediated modes. However, our data clearly show a rather different pattern in terms of the socio-demographic composition of the most enthusiastic audiences for these films.

Given this previous research on *LotR*, we assumed that greater familiarity with the cultural context and language in which Tolkien wrote *The Hobbit*, and within which the earlier *LotR* films were made, might influence the nature of audience engagement and response among different national groups. We therefore tested several possible cultural predictors of the prevalence of the transparent mode of reception and considered whether residency in the UK, US, New Zealand, Europe or the English-speaking world might significantly affect audience responses.

With the exception of New Zealand and the USA, we found no significant relationships between residency in any of the above-mentioned countries or regions and adoption of the preferred reading. Despite the incorporation of imagery evocative of rural England and medieval

Europe, none of the *Hobbit* films resonated significantly more strongly with UK audiences—arguably the group most culturally proximate to *The Hobbit*. Furthermore, European viewers, viewers in the Anglosphere (outside the USA) and viewers in all other countries with more than a few participants in our survey were not significantly more likely to adopt the preferred reading.

On the other hand, residents of the USA were more likely (odds ratio = 1.54) than non-US residents to experience the first *Hobbit* film, *AUJ*, in the transparent mode. US residents also reported relatively higher levels of anticipation, higher expectations and higher levels of their fulfilment, and greater levels of enchantment. These findings possibly reflect greater exposure to *The Hobbit*'s marketing and promotional hype (see Chap. 3), along with the closer cultural proximity of US viewers to filmmaking as a business, given the historically dominant role of Hollywood. Support for this interpretation can be drawn from Kersten (2014), who analysed national cultural repertoires of evaluation among film critics from four countries and found American film critics to be the most pragmatic, de-emphasising 'formal and intellectual aspects of film' (p. 723) in favour of practical issues such as decisions about casting and locations, realism and believability, and whether they felt moved, transported and excited as viewers—a key facilitator of this being actors and the quality of acting. This leads us to suspect that US respondents may have adopted a more 'pragmatic' response to *The Hobbit*'s various production issues—and their significant underrepresentation among both pre-viewing *Jackson Critics* and *Bored and Disillusioned Hobbit Critics* (post-viewing) lends weight to this interpretation. Notably, 38.5% of those in our prefiguration survey who identified 'actors' or 'the acting' as the thing they most looked forward to about *AUJ* were US residents—a significant degree of overrepresentation. This finding, along with the higher levels of enchantment expressed by US respondents in the *AUJ* post-viewing survey, is consistent with Kersten's (2014) observations about the prominence given to actors in US cultural repertoires and US viewers' greater emphasis on emotional and experiential dimensions of film viewing.

Striking evidence of the potential for cultural location to influence audience receptions can be seen in the responses of our New Zealand participants, which were very different from those of residents of other countries. This was evidently due to their closer proximity to key issues that beset the film's production and greater familiarity with debates about the roles of Peter Jackson and Warner Bros in the New Zealand *Hobbit* labour dispute and its troubling resolution, as outlined in Chap. 4 (see also Davis et al. 2014; Michelle et al. 2015). From the outset, New Zealand residents were more conflicted about the *Hobbit* trilogy, being more likely (odds ratio = 3.69) than non-New Zealand respondents to be angry and disappointed *Jackson Critics* (51.9% of all respondents in this segment) and much more likely (odds ratio = 30.28) than non-New Zealand respondents to be *Anxious Investors* (88.9%). They also expressed lower levels of anticipation and ascribed less importance to seeing the first *Hobbit* film. A significant degree of national antipathy was also evident in the *AUJ* reception survey, where New Zealand respondents reported lower levels of anticipation as well as enchantment, and were less likely (odds ratio = 0.56) than other respondents to be *Enchanted Hobbit Fans* while being more likely (odds ratio = 3.50) to be *Bored and Disillusioned Hobbit Critics*. New Zealanders also ascribed less importance to seeing *DoS* than other groups, and were significantly less enchanted and transported by *BotFA*, being less likely to be *Fulfilled Hobbit Fans* than other respondents (odds ratio = 0.47), and more inclined to be *Angry Hobbit Critics* (odds ratio = 4.67).

Although national residence predicts receptions in the preferred reading mode in only a few cases, it predicts adoption of various mediated modes of response in a larger number of cases, which we shall briefly review. Among *AUJ* audiences, *Disappointed Tolkien Readers* were more likely to be found among residents of Germany (odds ratio = 1.68), Finland (odds ratio = 3.90), the Netherlands (odds ratio = 3.25) and Denmark (odds ratio = 2.03). Residents of Denmark were more likely than other viewers to be *Critics of Technological 'Enhancements'* (odds ratio = 3.09). *Mildly Entertained Casual Viewers* were more likely to be found among resident of Denmark (odds ratio = 3.16), New Zealand (odds ratio = 2.99) and Belgium (odds ratio = 3.94). Although these groups were relatively small in number, they suggest that in some cases national characteristics may foster a tendency to adopt non-preferred reading modes.

These differences raise an obvious question: how significant was language in shaping receptions of *The Hobbit*? Of the seven different languages used in our multilingual *AUJ* post-viewing survey, responses to the English-language version were the most positive, with higher levels of anticipation as well as higher expectations, greater enchantment, greater liking of the technological enhancements and the largest proportion of *Enchanted Hobbit Fans*. Respondents in the English- and French-language surveys were more likely to adopt the preferred reading than other respondents. Participants in the German-, Flemish-, Dutch-, Spanish- and Danish-language surveys were significantly less likely to adopt the film's preferred reading. Notably, however, nearly 49% of respondents in the English-language *AUJ* survey resided outside the Anglosphere. Although these respondents expressed a lower-than-expected degree of anticipation to view *AUJ*, they did not disproportionately affiliate with any of the five audience segments. This suggests that anticipation may be more closely linked to cultural proximity to the centres of production (and presumably also marketing and promotion), while shared language may be more important in shaping *reception*. Indeed, English comprehension appears to have been more influential in shaping transnational receptions of this blockbuster film trilogy than the degree of distance from the centre(s) of cultural production.

The fact that there were no significant differences in the distribution of non-Anglosphere English speakers across the viewpoints suggests a degree of homogenisation of responses to this blockbuster film. Our findings also appear to indicate that preferred modes of reception are more easily secured when consuming a text that uses one's first language, rather than a version that has been dubbed or subtitled—the latter was the case for nearly 90% of the respondents completing the non-English-language surveys. That English-language competency (or lack thereof) played a role in shaping responses to the *Hobbit* trilogy is evident in our finding that those who did not speak English at home had more trouble making sense of some parts of *DoS*, a difficulty that may have been exacerbated by this film's more significant diversions from the novel than *AUJ*. Also, audiences viewing subtitled versions of *AUJ* were less likely to experience the film in the preferred mode, as *Enchanted Hobbit Fans*, than viewers of non-subtitled versions (odds ratio = 0.69). Interestingly, however, this picture is complicated by the fact that those who spoke languages other than English at home reported higher levels of enjoyment of *BotFA* than English speakers, perhaps suggesting the final *Hobbit* film more successfully transcended linguistic and cultural boundaries (or alternatively, that larger numbers of native English speakers disliked elements of *BotFA*'s narrative or visual realisation). Fu (2012) and others suggest narrative transcendence is more easily achieved by special-effects-intensive action-fantasy blockbusters than films of other genres, presumably due to their greater emphasis on action over narrative. Clearly, *BofFA* is not short on action, with its extensive and visually impressive final battle scene being evocative of *RotK*. The narrative, such as it is, is also relatively straightforward and conventional, including a clichéd love scene and dialogue, and (for those familiar with the book) a somewhat predictable denouement. All of these elements may have made this final film more easily digested by non-English speaking audiences.

While these findings are certainly intriguing and might usefully inform future research, we caution against ascribing too much significance to them given considerable variability in the size of our national samples and that fact that they are neither representative of national audiences nor matched to other national samples to ensure comparability (in terms of having similar gender, age and class distributions, for instance). Nonetheless, we present them here, as our primary purpose in undertaking this analysis was to explore new ways of investigating the nature of transnational film reception while illustrating the value of Q methodology for cross-national audience research, even as we recognise the need for much more work in this area. It is also important to acknowledge that each of these national groups is itself fractured along other lines of difference that may be rather more salient than either language or cultural location for individual respondents, as the following discussion reveals.

The Role of Gender in Shaping Interpretation and Identification

Various studies have explored patterns of media use and engagement linked to gender. One consistent finding relates to gender differences in genre preferences: while men generally express a stronger preference for action-adventure, horror and war movies, women tend to prefer romances and melodramas.[5] Women also report greater enjoyment of sad films featuring relational and emotional themes such as relationship break-ups or the death of loved ones, while men prefer movies that feature competition and adventure (Oliver et al. 2000). Further, Oliver et al. (1998) found the men report greater enjoyment of violent depictions and less enjoyment of tragic sequences than women, while women report greater empathic responsiveness in both situations.

Such findings suggest that *The Hobbit*, as an action-adventure fantasy film with an abundance of fast-paced and often violent imagery, might have greater appeal to male viewers. This seems even more likely given the common perception that blockbuster films that heavily rely on high-tech special effects and multiple action sequences primarily appeal to adolescent boys and 'male geeks' (Klinger 2008, p. 69). However, in their research on global receptions of *LotR*, Kuipers and de Kloet (2008) found that on average, women actually liked *RotK* slightly more than men, possibly reflecting the fact that the *LotR* trilogy was not merely an action-adventure fantasy but rather, a highly complex narrative featuring tragic, romantic and relational themes alongside extensive CGI-enhanced battle scenes. These things are also true of *The Hobbit,* and thus it seems likely that a similarly gendered pattern of response might be evident in our survey data.

This was indeed the case. In all three *Hobbit* post-viewing surveys, women expressed much more favourable responses than men. In our *AUJ* survey, women reported significantly higher levels of anticipation, fulfilment of expectations, enchantment and (surprisingly) even greater liking of the film's technological enhancements. They were more likely than men to adopt the preferred reading, as *Enchanted Hobbit Fans* (odds ratio = 1.70), and were underrepresented among the various disaffected audience segments. This general pattern persisted, with women ascribing greater importance to viewing *DoS*, expressing higher levels of anticipation of *BotFA* and reporting greater enjoyment, enchantment and transportation in response to both films; they were also more likely than men to be *Happy Hobbit Defenders* (odds ratio = 1.53). A pronounced gender difference is also evident in our final survey, in which women were more likely than men to be *Fulfilled Hobbit Fans* (odds ratio = 1.86). This shows an apparent tendency for male respondents to adopt overtly critical perspectives on the *Hobbit* trilogy, while female respondents were more likely to assume the preferred transparent mode of response for all three films.

While there has been scant research specifically exploring whether modes of reception might be gendered, Livingstone's (1994) study of men's and women's responses to television talk shows implicitly suggests this might be so. She found that women more commonly engaged with the participatory discussions presented in shows such as *Donahue* and *Oprah Winfrey,* and were especially appreciative of 'the opportunity to hear the voices and experiences of ordinary people talking about issues relevant to their everyday lives' (Livingstone 1994, p. 445), suggesting a tendency to adopt transparent and referential modes of reception in relation to the talk-show genre. Male participants, on the other hand, were more interested in the views of the 'expert' guests and in how the programme was made, and expressed concern about the motivations and intentions of the host and producers in making it—suggesting the adoption of mediated modes of engagement (Michelle 2007). More recent studies applying the Composite Model also point to possible gender differences in modes of reception. In an online survey of audiences for James Cameron's Avatar (2009), women were more inclined to adopt a discursive mode of response (Michelle et al. 2012), while in McKeown et al.'s (2015) study of *Breaking Bad*, men were overrepresented among two distinct viewpoints, one which the authors categorised as reflecting the transparent mode, and the other which appeared to commute between transparent and mediated modes (see also Zenor 2014).

While no firm conclusions can be drawn based on these studies, they suggest that any gendered tendency to adopt particular modes of response is likely shaped by genre *in tandem with* the narrative, commercial/ authorial intent and perceived ideological message content of the text in question. It is also important to note that, if they do exist, gendered patterns of engagement and response should not be assumed to express essential or innate differences between the two sexes. Rather, they more likely reflect broader (and very much generalised) distinctions in men's and women's attitudes and dispositions that are themselves the products of gender socialisation and enculturation into gendered subcultures, rather than being entirely 'natural'.

Identification with characters also displayed highly gendered patterns, which for reasons of space we address only very briefly here in relation to our final post-viewing survey in which a clear candidate for 'feminine' identifications was offered in the form of Tauriel. We asked respondents to indicate which characters in *BotFA* they would like to be. Wishing to be Bilbo, Thorin, Gandalf, Galadriel or Thranduil had no significant relation to the adoption of the preferred reading. However, viewers who wanted to be Tauriel were more likely than all other viewers to adopt the preferred reading of *BotFA*, as *Fulfilled Hobbit Fans* (odds ratio = 2.38), and women were much more likely than men to wish to be Tauriel (odds ratio = 20.77). The undoubtedly complex relationship between character identifications and modes of reception is one we shall explore in greater detail elsewhere.

WHAT DIFFERENCE DOES AGE MAKE IN SHAPING RECEPTIONS OF *THE HOBBIT?*

Various studies suggest age can also be a factor in shaping interpretation and response (Barwise and Ehrenberg 1988; Lacalle 2015; Press 1991b; Riggs 1996; Willis 1995). As noted above, it is often assumed that CGI-intensive spectacles appeal primarily to younger male viewers, while the greater appeal of 3D among younger viewers and children has also been documented (Banks et al. 2012; Pölönen and Aaltonen 2012). In the Tolkien's World Audiences Study, Kuipers and de Kloet (2008) found lower appreciation among the very oldest group of viewers of *RotK* (those aged 70 +), while de Kloet and Kuipers (2007) and Barker (2009) note that older respondents were more likely to choose the genre descriptor of 'spiritual journey' when asked to categorise this film. Their research also suggests differences in character identifications, with older viewers pre-ferring Gandalf and Sam, while younger viewers preferred Merry, Pippin, Arwen, Eowyn and Legolas. Further distinctions based on the intersection of age and gender were also identified, with Aragorn, Gimli and Gollum being preferred by younger males in particular (Mikos et al. 2008).

Regarding our findings, a slightly different pattern emerged in each survey, but there were some consistent trends. The most striking over-all trend is the trilogy's relative failure to appeal to young adults, nota-bly those in the 24–29 age range. That is, in general, younger and older persons expressed significantly stronger engagement with the films than did individuals in the 24–29 age bracket. Initial anticipation for the *Hobbit* trilogy was highest among the youngest respondents, who also expressed the highest levels of enjoyment of *AUJ*. But later instalments of the trilogy appealed more strongly to older viewers. Viewers in the 24–29 demographic were less likely to be *Enchanted Hobbit Fans* than other age groups (odds ratio = 0.67). They were also less likely to be *Happy Hobbit Defenders* (odds ratio = 0.54) and *Fulfilled Hobbit Fans* (odds ratio = 0.55). Counterintuitively, viewers over 50 were more likely than younger viewers to adopt the preferred reading of *DoS* and *BotFA* as *Happy Hobbit Defenders* and *Fulfilled Hobbit Fans.*

Our observations thus appear to challenge conventional wisdom about audience tastes for CGI-intensive action blockbuster films, assumed to appeal to younger (and predominantly) male viewers pri-marily. In the case of the *Hobbit* trilogy, enjoyment and enchantment were related to age in ways that differed depending on the particular film in question, with each appealing more to those at either end of the age scale. Respondents in the middle (between 24 and 39 years) were consistently less enthusiastic than other age groups, with lower levels of anticipation and enjoyment and a greater tendency to adopt mediated modes of response for all three instalments.

Conceivably, these very unusual patterns may reflect something about the *Hobbit* movies themselves as simultaneously a three-part adaptation of a children's book published in the 1930s (thus appealing to an older audience than might usually watch CGI-intensive action-fantasy films) *and* a technologically intensive blockbuster spectacle designed to attract a broad and diverse audience, but with a large volume of ancillary merchandising specifically aimed at young adults and children. Both much younger and older viewers may be less familiar with CGI and 3D than other age groups, and thus perhaps more easily impressed by them due to the effects of novelty and habituation, following the reasoning of Häkkinen et al. (2008) and Ji and Lee (2014). Younger viewers may also have been less intimately familiar with the novel, and thus less concerned about deviations from it, or may have felt more enchanted by the first *Hobbit* film's light-hearted tone with its songs and slapstick humour. Older viewers, conversely, may have appreciated the darker and rather more dramatic presentation of the second and more especially the final instalment, with its emphasis on extended large-scale battle scenes reminiscent of the *LotR* films, while also presenting some deeper and more serious themes.

Indeed, older viewers clearly had a greater appreciation for *The Hobbit*'s deeper messages and thematic content. We found highly significant age differences relating to agreement with statement 5 in the *AUJ* reception survey: 'The story related in *The Hobbit* teaches people about the real values in life: honesty, loyalty, friendship, sacrifice, courage, faith and hope. Such stories are very uplifting, and can help us become better people.' This message resonated more strongly with those over the age of 50 than it did younger viewers ($p = 0.001$), a pattern confirmed in the *BotFA* survey in relation to statement 29: 'This film is about finding home, fighting for it, and learning the value of the journey. It reflects timeless themes of honour, love and self-sacrifice' ($p = 0.002$ for persons 50–59 and $p = 0.001$ for persons 60 and over). While these findings may reflect less interest in philosophical introspection among younger people more generally, an alternative explanation might be that older respondents were more familiar with the novel, having had more opportunity to reread it over time, and thus to study and appreciate its deeper meanings. To test this, we compared the rankings of those who had read the novel more than 10 times with those who had read it less than 10, and found no significant differences in the importance ascribed to *The Hobbit*'s message. This suggests the different emphasis placed on messages and themes is indeed more likely age-related.

The Role of Socio-Economic Class in Shaping Interpretation and Response

While nationality, language, gender and age clearly have potential to shape audience receptions, a number of researchers have followed Morley's suggestion that socio-economic class is perhaps the most significant factor in the production of distinct 'clusterings' in audience reception.[6] Some of these scholars also highlight an apparent association between socio-economic class and modes of reception. For instance, in studying women's receptions of the American police drama *Cagney & Lacey*, Andrea Press (1991a) found that middle-class women were consistently more detached and critical, and commonly shifted away from discussing the text's content to focus instead on its formal and aesthetic limitations and on technical features such as production imperatives, textual realism, the acting and whether they felt moved by it—all indicative of a mediated mode of response in terms of the Composite Model. Working-class women, conversely, responded more directly to the narrative content and were much less inclined to comment on the programme's formal or generic qualities. They also resisted the idea that the programme was biased, instead highlighting its educational potential. These women clearly enjoyed the programme more than their middle-class counterparts and responded to it more positively—suggesting a transparent mode of response was primarily adopted by these viewers.

Similar findings relating to a different generic and cultural context emerged in Skeggs et al.'s (2008) analysis of British women's responses to reality television. They found that middle-class respondents 'produced scholarly and critically distanced views' (p. 9) of a culturally derided genre, describing it as exploitative and manipulative of reality, and in the process demonstrating their awareness of it as a constructed media product—again consistent with a mediated mode of reception. Their working-class respondents, however, approached reality TV as entertainment—a source of pleasure—and evidently felt little need to justify

Table 9.4 Effects of social location on membership in audience segments associated with the preferred reading—all surveys

	Pre-viewing survey	AUJ post-viewing survey	DoS post-viewing survey	BotFA post-viewing survey
Age 18 and under	NS	1.57	NS	NS
Age 24–29	NS	0.691	NS	0.428
Age 40–49	NS	NS	1.949	NS
Age 50–59	NS	NS	3.068	NS
Age 60+	2.37	NS	3.159	3.21
Graduate degree	NS	0.619	NS	NS
Bachelor's degree	NS	NS	1.459	NS
Professional occupation	0.612	NS	NS	NS
Higher professional occupation	0.381	NS	0.58	NS
Manager or executive	NS	NS	NS	0.293
Student	NS	0.689	NS	NS
Times read *The Hobbit* book	0.986	NS	NS	0.971
Times viewed the *LotR* film trilogy	0.969	NS	NS	NS
Times read the *LotR* books	NS	NS	0.974	NS
Worked in or studied media production	NS	0.67	NS	NS
Hobbit/Tolkien fan	NS	NS	0.503	NS
Times viewed *DoS*	NS	NS	1.555	1.088
Times viewed *BotFA*	N/A	N/A	N/A	1.628
NZ resident	NS	0.48	NS	NS
Belgium resident	NS	0.501	NS	NS
Germany resident	NS	0.649	NS	NS
Denmark resident	NS	0.374	NS	NS
Australia resident	NS	NS	0.043	NS
Politically neutral	NS	1.376	NS	NS
Gender (reference category: female)	NS	1.517	NS	1.785
Percent of cases classified correctly:				
Null model	51.8%	74.3%	56.5%	54.0%
Model with all independent variables	66.2%	75.2%	72.6%	72.2%

Note Shown are odds ratios for variables that are significant at 95% or better

their enjoyment. They reacted to participants in the shows as though they were real people and made moral judgements about them and their behaviour, offering primarily affective reactions in line with a transparent mode of response. More recent research applying the Composite Model further demonstrates the potential for modes of reception to be shaped by professional experiences and membership of related moral subcultures (van Ommen et al. 2016).

In attempting to explore the possible relationship between socio-economic class and receptions of the *Hobbit* trilogy, we were cognisant of the complexity of social class as a category and the challenges of operationalising it for research. As Press and Rosenman (2016) note, social class is comprised of an array of factors relating to educational attainment, occupational category or position and its associated social status, and also financial resources in terms of access to wealth and income. Each of these may be understood and measured quite differently in different contexts, making it difficult to determine suitably universal categories that would make sense to respondents regardless of the country in which they lived. Even collecting comparable data about income levels across countries is notoriously difficult given the use of different currencies and exchange rates; more difficult still is the task of interpreting, as a cultural outsider, what those income levels might mean locally in terms of class positioning. Seeking a workable solution, we assumed most respondents would have an approximate idea of the local average income, and thus of where they sat in the income scale compared to their fellow citizens. We therefore asked respondents to tell us whether they considered themselves to be lower income/ unpaid, lower-middle income, middle income, higher-middle income or high income, *relative to the average income in their country of residence*. This allowed us to create a five-point scale to measure income. We classified the various levels of education and kinds of occupations into a six-point scale and a seven-point scale, respectively. We then summed the occupation, education and income scales into a social class scale. With these scales, we sought to measure possible effects of income, education, occupation and social class on adoption of the preferred reading of the three *Hobbit* films.

Results show significant trends that are consistent with what we might expect to see based on previous research in this area, and these trends were persistent across the life of this longitudinal project. Most notably, across all four surveys, those with advanced degrees expressed less enthusiasm and were ultimately less enchanted by the films, tending to adopt mediated modes of reception rather than the preferred transparent mode characterised by pleasurable enchantment.

Delving deeper, responses to *AUJ* clearly differed based on education, with those with master's or doctoral degrees reporting lower levels of anticipation, lower expectations and less fulfilment of them, and less enchantment than others. An increase in level of education lowered the odds of being an *Enchanted Hobbit Fan* (odds ratio = 0.87). This general trend was evident to some extent also in the responses to *DoS*, where those with advanced degrees again ascribed less importance to seeing the film, had lower expectations, and reported less enchantment and enjoyment than other respondents. However, the level of education per se was not significantly related to the adoption of the preferred reading. Likewise, in the case of *BotFA*, those with higher degrees were once again less enchanted and also less transported, but the level of education did not predict adoption of the preferred reading.

Regarding occupation, significant patterns first emerged in the prefiguration survey, showing an inverse relationship between the level of occupation and odds of being a *LotR Film Fan*. An increase in the level of occupation decreased the odds of being a *LotR Film Fan* (odds ratio = 0.86). A similar inverse relationship between the level of occupation and engagement emerged among *AUJ* audiences; the odds of being an *Enchanted Hobbit Fan* decreased with each increment in the occupation scale (odds ratio = 0.91). Although we did not observe significant systematic inverse relationships between occupation and adoption of the preferred reading among *DoS* and *BotFA* audiences, we found that some of the higher occupations (such as executive manager and higher-level professional) were much less likely to adopt the preferred reading than other categories of occupation.

Not surprisingly, given these trends, we also found some suggestive patterns relating to income, with high-income respondents reporting less enthusiasm for the film before and after viewing, and viewers at lower income levels being more enthusiastic. In the prefiguration survey, an increase in the level of income decreased the odds of being a *LotR Film Fan* (odds ratio = 0.87). But income (as measured by our scale) did not predict adoption of the preferred reading for any of the three films.

Combining income, education and occupation into an index of social class, we observed a significant negative effect of class on the disposition to enjoy the film among the pre-viewing audience, with the odds of being a *LotR Film Fan* inversely related to higher social class (odds ratio = 0.89). A similar inverse relationship between higher social class and likelihood of adopting the preferred reading was found among *AUJ* audiences, but not among *DoS* or *BotFA* audiences. In sum, then, our findings suggest the *Hobbit* films were somewhat more favourably received by those with lower levels of education and working in occupations traditionally associated with the lower-middle and middle class, while appealing less strongly to the most highly educated respondents and those with high-income, upper-middle-class occupations. The results also suggest that education, income and occupation do not smoothly operate in combination to affect receptions of cultural texts.

Alongside these findings relating to aspects of socio-economic class are significant findings relating to viewers' existing *discursive knowledges and competencies*, some of which are clearly related to particular forms of education, training and occupational membership. Specifically, experience working in the film or television industries or advanced media production education was a significant predictor of lower appreciation of *AUJ*'s technological enhancements, and also lower levels of enchantment. Those with media industry experience or with advanced knowledge of media production were less likely than respondents without such experience or knowledge to be *Enchanted Hobbit Fans* (odds ratio = 0.55), and they were overrepresented among those expressing mediated viewpoints in the *AUJ* survey. In several cases, these 'dissenters' offered extensive and clearly well-informed critiques of the film's HFR 3D projection and the quality and execution of the CGI and other special effects. This suggests that technical expertise and perhaps also a stronger allegiance to a more traditional 'cinematic' aesthetic shaped responses to *The Hobbit*'s uncommon combination of technologies.

While distracting visual elements appear to have been less problematic in *DoS*, those who had experience of working in the industry were nonetheless highly overrepresented among *Disenchanted Hobbit Critics*, being more likely than persons without industry experience to adopt this viewpoint (odds ratio = 5.32), while those with advanced media production education were more likely than those without such education to experience the film as *Hobbit Sceptics* (odds ratio = 4.06). In response to *BotFA*, those with advanced media production education reported lower levels of anticipation, enjoyment, enchantment and transportation, and were less likely than those without such education to be *Fulfilled Hobbit Fans* (odds ratio = 0.65) while being more likely to adopt the viewpoint of *Unhappy Tolkien Adherents* (odds ratio = 1.45). Those who had industry experience, on the other hand, were more likely to be *Appreciative Film Critics* (odds ratio = 2.79), perhaps suggesting a more distanced, objective evaluation of the final film as a creative work by those familiar with the practical challenges of filmmaking.

While we have identified some highly suggestive patterns regarding education, occupation and income, we caution against essentialising such associations. In particular, the seemingly more critical mediated modes of response evident among wealthier, more highly educated and higher-level-professional respondents should not be assumed to be a *natural* or inevitable feature of socio-economic class membership. Rather, following Pierre Bourdieu's (1984) dissection of judgements of taste, this mode of interpreting entertainment media draws on (and requires access to) various forms of cultural capital that are more often acquired by members of higher socio-economic classes, in the sense that they are more likely to be exposed to certain kinds of formal education and training for extended periods and consequently more likely to enter higher-level professional occupations. Class membership also implies, as part of enculturation, acquisition of certain cultural tastes that in turn reflect particular aesthetic, social, moral and political *values*. These shared tastes and values inform the ways in which more highly educated members of the middle and upper classes tend to engage with media texts in general as objects for critical evaluation, reflection and appreciation, rather than vehicles for pleasurable immersion and escapist entertainment, which has traditionally been derided as part of 'low' or popular culture. This tendency is also linked to the transmission of class-based understandings of the symbolic value of particular forms of culture and a shared disdain for cultural expressions that are 'tainted' by commercial (as opposed to artistic and creative) values. Historical debates over the status of film as art as opposed to commercial entertainment are thus, in an important sense, an expression of a wider class-based struggle to define the symbolic value of film as a cultural form.

THE ROLE OF FANDOMS IN SHAPING ANTICIPATION, ENGAGEMENT AND RESPONSE

Finally, we turn to one of the more significant distinguishing features among those studied—pre-existing fandoms. Earlier research has addressed the role that prior intertextual and paratextual affiliations played in shaping audience engagements with the *LotR* film trilogy (see Chin and Gray 2001; Klinger 2008; Mikos et al. 2008; Turnbull 2008). Mikos et al. (2008), for instance, found that non-readers (whom they define as the 'Media Generation') responded more positively to *RotK*'s love story elements than Tolkien readers (the 'Literary Generation'). While non-readers were more focused on genre elements (fantasy, romance, action) and the film's impressive visual effects, readers drew on their often extensive knowledge of Tolkien's novels to offer 'expert' evaluations of the accuracy and fidelity of Jackson's adaptation—a tendency we also found among avid Tolkien readers.

While we caution against assuming prior affiliations are definitive in shaping the nature of individual engagements and response, it is clear that some of the subjective perspectives we identified were shared by those respondents who possessed a deeper than average familiarity with the novel, while other viewpoints were shared by those who expressed greater affinity for the *LotR* films (as measured by the number of repeat viewings). In our pre-viewing survey, higher frequency of viewing the *LotR* films was positively correlated with attributing greater importance to seeing the first *Hobbit* film. Heavy *LotR* film viewers were (not surprisingly) slightly more likely to adopt the viewpoint of *LotR Film Fans* (odds ratio = 1.03). Conversely, the frequency of having read *The Hobbit* was inversely related to the level of anticipation, slightly decreasing the odds of expressing the *LotR Film Fan* viewpoint (odds ratio = 0.98); heavy book readers were in turn overrepresented among *Tolkien Aficionados*, as one might expect.

This trend continued in relation to *AUJ*, where those primarily motivated to watch because they were fans of the *LotR* films expressed higher anticipation for the first *Hobbit* instalment. These respondents were also overrepresented among *Critics of Technological 'Enhancements'*, a group that felt *AUJ* failed to live up to the benchmark of cinematic excellence established by Jackson's earlier trilogy. Those motivated by being a fan of the novel or Tolkien expressed lower anticipation and expectations and were overrepresented among *Disappointed Tolkien Readers*. In response to *DoS*, the frequency of viewing *AUJ* was significantly correlated with reported greater importance of seeing the sequel, along with higher expectations, enchantment, enjoyment and transportation, greater odds of being *Happy Hobbit Defenders* (odds ratio = 1.60), and underrepresentation among *Disenchanted Hobbit Critics* and *Aggrieved Tolkien Aficionados*. Conversely, greater frequency of having read *The Hobbit* was significantly correlated with lower expectations, lower enjoyment, over-representation among *Disenchanted Hobbit Critics* and slight underrepresentation among *Happy Hobbit Defenders* (odds ratio = 0.99). Much the same patterns continued in response to *BotFA*: those with higher rates of watching *LotR* expressed greater anticipation, higher expectations and were more transported, being overrepresented among *Fulfilled Hobbit Fans*, while more committed book readers conveyed lower anticipation, were less transported and were, not surprisingly, overrepresented among *Unhappy Tolkien Adherents.*

CONCLUSION

This chapter has identified numerous significant relationships between multiple aspects of social location and modes of reception of the *Hobbit* films. We note that very few *Hobbit* audience segments are dominated by just one or two attributes of social location: the two clearest examples are the prefiguration survey's *Celebrity Followers*, all of whom were women, and *Anxious Investors*, 88.9% of whom were residents of New Zealand.

The other audience viewpoints are characterised by rather more complex combinations of social attributes. Our results show that while gender, age, education, country of residence, income, occupation and socio-economic class did indeed contribute to shaping engagement with and responses to the *Hobbit* trilogy, these aspects of social location did not *determine* the variations in the nature and forms of reception we have charted. This is because such affiliations, while significant, generally have very small effects and also interact with each other and with other sites of difference that can be equally, and in some cases *more*, influential. Indeed, even in combination, the attributes we investigated have very modest predictive power. Table 9.4 shows the results of binomial logistic regression with independent variables that are significant predictors of affiliation with the preferred readings of each of the three *Hobbit* films, and of the pre-viewing audience segment most expectant of experiencing narrative transportation. It shows the 'social locations' of those who were disappointed by the films on various grounds: young adults in the 24–29 age range; highly educated individuals; students; individuals in professional and managerial positions; residents of New Zealand, Belgium, Denmark, Germany and Australia; viewers with work experience in the screen industry or with advanced education in media production; those with greater exposure to the Tolkien books and Tolkien fandom, and so on. It also shows the disproportionate engagement of women, viewers below the age of 19 and over the age of 40, individuals professing political neutrality, those with greater frequency of viewing and those with undergraduate education.

Interestingly, the models are perhaps better at identifying social locations associated with *dis*enchantment rather than enchantment. Our results suggest that social location has very complex effects on film reception, especially when the various attributes and aspects of social positioning and identity are in interaction with each other; that other factors are at work, which may be unidentified contextual factors or perhaps even factors related to individual psychological dispositions and preferences; and that creative products may have powers to enchant or dismay that are not directly affected by immediately identifiable social factors. Clearly, there is a need for more research exploring how these kinds of factors may also shape modes of reception, most likely in tandem with the key socio-demographic variables and other affiliations explicitly addressed in this project.

NOTES

1. The tests use binary logistic regression to test for the ability to predict membership in the audience segment reporting reception in the transparent mode. The confidence level is 95% or better. The statistic reported is the *odds ratio*. Unlike percentages, which measure the extent of something in a population, odds compare the occurrence of something to its absence. Odds ratios greater than one indicate that an increase in odds of membership in the predictor category is associated with an increase in odds of membership in the predicted category. Odds ratios of less than one indicate the inverse relationship. Strictly speaking, an odds ratio of 1.5 means that the odds of A having a particular characteristic are 50% greater than the odds of B having that characteristic. For the sake of simplicity in our discussion, we use the term 'likelihood' to interpret the meaning of odds ratios.
2. See Ang (1985), Artz and Kamalipour (2003), Bil[tereyst (1991, 1995), Boyd-Barrett (2015), Elasmar and Bennett (2003), Gillespie (1995), Hamelink (1983), Katz and Liebes (1985, 1990), Liebes and Katz (1990), Miller et al. (2005), Thussu (1998), Weaver et al. (1993) and Wilson (2001).

3. See Athique (2011, 2016), Chan (2005), Dekie et al. (2015), Harindranath (2005), Smets (2012, 2014), Smets et al. (2016) and Zalipour et al. (2014).
4. See Bore (2011), Desilla (2014), Gould et al. (2010), Gray (2007), Gudehus et al. (2010), Haag (2014), Haluza-Delay et al. (2013), Mankekar (1999) and Zalipour et al. (2014).
5. See Banerjee et al. (2008); Brown et al. (1990), Gray (1999), Hoffner and Cantor (1991), La Pastina (2004), Livingstone (1994), Morley (1986), Oliver et al. (1998, 2000), Ratnasingam and Ellis (2011), Rentfrow et al. (2011), Richards and Sheridan (1987) and Wühr and Schwarz (2016).
6. See Allen and Mendick (2012), Gray (1992), Jensen (1995), Kim (2004), Lopez-Sintas and Garcia-Alvarez (2006), Press (1989, 1991b), Press and Rosenman (2016), Seiter (1999), Seiter et al. (1989), and Skeggs et al. (2008).

References

Allen, K., & Mendick, H. (2012). Keeping it real? Social class, young people and 'authenticity' in reality TV. *Sociology, 47*(3), 460–476. doi:10.1177/0038038512448563.

Alper, M., Katz, V. S., & Clark, L. (2016). Researching children, intersectionality, and diversity in the digital age. *Journal of Children and Media, 10*(1), 107–114. doi:10.1080/17482798.2015.1121886.

Ang, I. (1985). *Watching Dallas: Soap opera and the melodramatic imagination.* London: Methuen.

Artz, L., & Kamalipour, Y. R. (Eds.). (2003). *Globalization of corporate media hegemony.* Albany: SUNY Press.

Athique, A. (2011). Diasporic audiences and non-resident media: The case of Indian films. *Participations: Journal of Audience & Reception Studies, 8*(2), 1–23.

Athique, A. (2016). *Transnational audiences: Media reception on a global scale.* Cambridge: Polity.

Banerjee, S. C., Greene, K., Krcmar, M., Bagdasarov, Z., & Ruginyte, D. (2008). The role of gender and sensation seeking in film choice: Exploring mood and arousal. *Journal of Media Psychology, 20*(3), 97–105. doi:10.1027/1864-1105.20.3.87.

Banks, M., Read, J., Allison, R., & Watt, S. (2012). Stereoscopy and the human visual system. *SMPTE Motion Imaging Journal, 121*(4), 24–43. doi:10.5594/j18173.

Barker, M. (2008). The functions of fantasy: A comparison of audiences for *The Lord of the Rings* in twelve countries. In M. Barker & E. Mathijs (Eds.),

Watching The Lord of the Rings: Tolkien's world audiences (pp. 149–180). New York: Peter Lang.

Barker, M. (2009). Changing lives, challenging concepts: Some findings and lessons from the *Lord of the Rings* project. *International Journal of Cultural Studies, 12*(4), 375–393. doi:10.1177/1367877909104244.

Barwise, P., & Ehrenberg, A. (1988). *Television and its audience.* London: Sage.

Bielby, D. D., & Harrington, C. L. (2008). *Global TV: Exporting television and culture in the world market.* New York: New York University Press.

Biltereyst, D. (1991). Resisting American hegemony: A comparative analysis of the reception of domestic and US fiction. *European Journal of Communication, 6*(4), 469–497.

Biltereyst, D. (1995). Qualitative audience research and transnational media effects: A new paradigm? *European Journal of Communication, 10*(2), 245–270.

Bore, I. L. K. (2011). Transnational TV comedy audiences. *Television & New Media, 12*(4), 347–369. doi:10.1177/1527476410374965.

Bourdieu, P. (1984). *Distinction: A social critique of the judgement of taste.* Cambridge, MA: Harvard University Press.

Boyd-Barrett, O. (2015). *Media imperialism.* London; Thousand Oaks; New Delhi; Singapore: Sage.

Brown, J., Childers, K., Bauman, K., & Koch, G. (1990). The influence of new media and family structure on young adolescents' television and radio use. *Communication Research, 17*(1), 65–82. doi:10.1177/009365090017001004.

Chamorro-Premuzic, T., Kallias, A., & Hsu, A. (2013). What type of movie person are you? Understanding preferences and uses: A psychographic approach. In J. C. Kaufman & D. K. Simonton (Eds.), *The social science of cinema* (pp. 87–122). Oxford: Oxford University Press.

Chan, B. (2005). Imagining the homeland: The internet and diasporic discourse of nationalism. *Journal of Communication Inquiry, 29*(4), 336–368. doi:10.1177/0196859905278499.

Chin, B., & Gray, J. (2001). 'One ring to rule them all': Previewers and pretexts of the *Lord of the Rings* films. *Intensities: The Journal of Cult Media, 2.*

Dahlgren, P. (1988). What's the meaning of this? Viewers' plural sense-making of TV news. *Media, Culture and Society, 10*(3), 285–301.

Davis, C. H., Michelle, C., Hardy, A. L., & Hight, C. (2014). Framing audience prefigurations of *The Hobbit: An Unexpected Journey*: The roles of fandom, politics and idealised intertexts. *Participations: Journal of Audience & Reception Studies, 11*(1), 50–87.

De Kloet, J., & Kuipers, G. (2007). Spirituality and fan culture around the *Lord of the Rings* film trilogy. *Fabula: Journal of Folktale Research, 48*(3/4), 300–319. doi:10.1515/FABL.2007.023.

Dekie, A., Meers, P., Vande Winkel, R., Van Bauwel, S., & Smets, K. (2015). Nollywood online: Between the individual consumption and communal reception of Nigerian films among African diaspora. *Journal of African Media Studies, 7*(3), 301–314. doi:10.1386/jams.7.3.301_1.

Desilla, L. (2014). Reading between the lines, seeing beyond the images: An empirical study on the comprehension of implicit film dialogue meaning across cultures. *The Translator, 20*(2), 194–214. doi:10.1080/13556509.20 14.967476.

Dill, K. E. (2009). *How fantasy becomes reality: Seeing through media influence.* Oxford: Oxford University Press.

Elasmar, M. G., & Bennett, K. (2003). The cultural imperialism paradigm revisited: Origin and evolution. In M. G. Elasmar (Ed.), *The impact of international television: A paradigm shift* (pp. 1–16). Abingdon, UK: Routledge.

Fiske, J. (1989). Moments of television: Neither the text nor the reader. In E. Seiter, H. Borchers, G. Kreutzner, & E. Warth (Eds.), *Remote control: Television, audiences, and cultural power* (pp. 56–78). London: Routledge.

Fu, W. W. (2012). National audience tastes in Hollywood film genres: Cultural distance and linguistic affinity. *Communication Research, 40*(6), 789–817. doi:10.1177/0093650212442085.

Giles, D. (2003). *Media psychology.* Oxford: Routledge.

Gillespie, M. (1995). *Television, ethnicity and cultural change.* London: Routledge.

Gould, R. K., Ardoin, N. M., & Kamakanipakolonahe'okekai, Hashimoto, J. (2010). 'Mālama the āina, Mālama the people on the'āina': The reaction to Avatar in Hawai'i. *Journal for the Study of Religion, Nature & Culture, 4*(4), 425–456.

Gray, A. (1992). *Video playtime: The gendering of a leisure technology.* London: Routledge.

Gray, A. (1999). Audience and reception research in retrospect: The trouble with audiences. In P. Alasuutari (Ed.), *Rethinking the media audience* (pp. 22–37). London: Sage.

Gray, J. (2007). Imagining America: *The Simpsons* go global. *Popular Communication, 5*(2), 129–148. doi:10.1080/15405700701294111.

Gudehus, C., Anderson, S., & Keller, D. (2010). Understanding *Hotel Rwanda*: A reception study. *Memory Studies, 3*(4), 344–363. doi:10.1177/1750698010374 923.

Haag, O. (2014). Racializing the social problem: Reception of *Samson and Delilah* in Germany. *Continuum, 28*(5), 666–677. doi:10.1080/10304312. 2014.942025.

Häkkinen, J., Kawai, T., Takatalo, J., Leisti, T., Radun, J., Hirsaho, A. & Nyman, G. (2008). Measuring stereoscopic image quality experience with interpretation based quality methodology. In S. P. Farnard & F. Gaykema

(Eds.), *Image Quality and System Performance V: Proceedings of SPIE-IS&T Electronic Imaging, 68081B* (pp. 1–12). doi:10.1117/12.760935.

Hall, A. E., & Bracken, C. C. (2011). 'I really liked that movie'. Testing the relationship between trait empathy, transportation, perceived realism, and movie enjoyment. *Journal of Media Psychology, 23*(2), 90–99.

Haluza-DeLay, R. B., Ferber, M. B., & Wiebe-Neufeld, T. (2013). Watching *Avatar* from 'AvaTar Sands' land. In B. Taylor (Ed.), *Avatar and nature spirituality* (pp. 123–140). Waterloo, Canada: Wilfred Laurier University Press.

Hamelink, C. J. (1983). *Cultural autonomy in global communications.* New York: Longman.

Harindranath, R. (2005). Ethnicity and cultural difference: Some thematic and political issues on global audience research. *Participations, 2*(2).

Hasebrink, U. (2012). Comparing media use and reception. In F. Esser & T. Hanitzsch (Eds.), *The handbook of comparative communication research* (pp. 382–399). London: Routledge.

Hoffner, C., & Cantor, J. (1991). Perceiving and responding to mass media characters. In J. Bryant & D. Zillmann (Eds.), *Responding to the screen: Reception and reaction processes* (pp. 63–101). Hillsdale, NJ: Lawrence Erlbaum.

Hoskins, C., & Mirus, R. (1988). Reasons for the US dominance of the international trade in television programmes. *Media, Culture and Society, 10*(4), 499–515.

Jensen, K. (1995). *The social semiotics of mass communication.* London: Sage.

Ji, Q. & Lee, Y. S. (2014). Genre matters: A comparative study on the entertainment effects of 3D in cinematic contexts. *3D Research, 5*(15). doi:10.1007/s13319-014-0015-6.

Jordin, M., & Brunt, R. (1988). Constituting the television audience: A problem of method. In R. Paterson & P. Drummond (Eds.), *Television and its audience: International research perspectives: A selection of papers from the Second International Television Studies Conference, London, 1986.* London: BFI Publishing.

Katz, E., & Liebes, T. (1985). Mutual aid in the decoding of *Dallas*: Preliminary notes from a cross-cultural study. In P. Drummond & R. Paterson (Eds.), *Television in transition* (pp. 187–198). London: BFI Publishing.

Katz, E., & Liebes, T. (1990). Interacting with 'Dallas': Cross cultural readings of American TV. *Canadian Journal of Communication, 15*(1), 45–66.

Kersten, A. (2014). National cultural repertoires of evaluation in a global age: Film discourse in France, the Netherlands, the United Kingdom, and the United States. *European Sociological Review, 30*(6), 717–727. doi:10.1093/esr/jcu069.

Kim, S. (2004). Rereading David Morley's *The 'Nationwide' Audience. Cultural Studies, 18*(1), 84–108. doi:10.1080/0950238042000181629.

King, G. (2003). Spectacle, narrative, and the spectacular Hollywood block-buster. In J. Stringer (Ed.), *Movie blockbusters* (pp. 114–127). London and New York: Routledge.

Klinger, B. (2008). What do female fans want? Blockbusters, *The Return of the King* and US audiences. In M. Barker & E. Mathijs (Eds.), *Watching The Lord of the Rings: Tolkien's world audiences* (pp. 69–82). New York: Peter Lang.

Kuipers, G., & de Kloet, J. (2008). Global flows and local identifications? *The Lord of the Rings* and the cross-national reception of characters and genres. In M. Barker & E. Mathijs (Eds.), *Watching The Lord of the Rings: Tolkien's world audiences* (pp. 131–148). New York: Peter Lang.

Kuipers, G., & de Kloet, J. (2009). Banal cosmopolitanism and *The Lord of the Rings*: The limited role of national differences in global media consumption. *Poetics, 37*, 99–118. doi:10.1016/j.poetic.2009.01.002.

La Pastina, A. C. (2004). Telenovela reception in rural Brazil: Gendered readings and sexual mores. *Critical Studies in Media Communication, 21*(2), 162–181. doi:10.1080/07393180410001688056.

Lacalle, C. (2015). Young people and television fiction: Reception analysis. *Communications: The European Journal of Communication Research, 40*(2), 237–255. doi:10.1515/commun-2015-0006.

Lamont, M. (1992). *Money, morals, and manners: The culture of the French and the American upper-middle class*. Chicago: University of Chicago Press.

Lamont, M., & Thevenot, L. (Eds.). (2000). *Rethinking comparative cultural sociology: Repertoires of evaluation in France and the United States*. Cambridge: Cambridge University Press.

Lee, F. L. F. (2006). Cultural discount and cross-culture predictability: Examining the box office performance of American movies in Hong Kong. *Journal of Media Economics, 19*(4), 259–278. doi:10.1207/s15327736me1904_3.

Lee, F. L. F. (2008). Hollywood movies in East Asia: Examining cultural discount and performance predictability at the box office. *Asian Journal of Communication, 18*(2), 117–136. doi:10.1080/01292980802021855.

Leurs, K., & Ponzanesi, S. (2014). Intersectionality, digital identities and migrant youths: Moroccan Dutch youths as digital space invaders. In C. Carter, L. Steiner, & L. McLaughlin (Eds.), *The Routledge companion to media and gender* (pp. 632–642). London: Routledge.

Liebes, T., & Katz, E. (1990). *The export of meaning: Cross-cultural readings of Dallas*. Oxford: Oxford University Press.

Livingstone, S. (1994). Watching talk: Gender and engagement in the viewing of audience discussion programmes. *Media, Culture and Society, 16*(3), 429–447.

López-Sintas, J., & García-Álvarez, E. (2006). Patterns of audio-visual consumption: The reflection of objective divisions in class structure. *European Sociological Review, 22*(4), 397–411. doi:10.1093/esr/jcl004.

Mankekar, P. (1999). *Screening culture, viewing politics: An ethnography of television, womanhood, and nation in postcolonial India*. Durham, NC: Duke University Press.

McKeown, B., Thomas, D. B., Rhoads, J. C., & Sundblad, D. (2015). Falling hard for *Breaking Bad*: An investigation of audience response to a popular television series. *Participations: Journal of Audience and Reception Studies, 12*(2), 147–167.

Michelle, C. (2007). Modes of reception: A consolidated analytical framework. *The Communication Review, 10*(3), 181–222. doi:10.1080/10714420701528057.

Michelle, C., Davis, C. H., & Vladica, F. (2012). Understanding variation in audience engagement and response: An application of the composite model to receptions of *Avatar* (2009). *The Communication Review, 15*(2), 106–143. doi:10.1080/10714421.2012.674467.

Michelle, C., Hardy, A. L., Davis, C. H., & Hight, C. (2015). An unexpected controversy in Middle-earth: Audience encounters with the 'dark side' of transnational film production. *Transnational Cinemas, 6*(1), 49–66. doi:10.1080/20403526.2014.941185.

Mikos, L., Eichner, S., Prommer, E., & Wedel, M. (2008). Involvement in *The Lord of the Rings*: Audience strategies and orientations. In M. Barker & E. Mathijs (Eds.), *Watching The Lord of the Rings: Tolkien's world audiences* (Vol. 3, pp. 111–128). New York: Peter Lang.

Miller, T., Govil, N., McMurria, J., Maxwell, R., & Wang, T. (2005). *Global Hollywood 2*. London: BFI Publishing.

Moon, S., Bayus, B. L., Yi, Y., & Kim, J. (2015). Local consumers' reception of imported and domestic movies in the Korean movie market. *Journal of Cultural Economics, 39*, 99–121. doi:10.1007/s10824-013-9214-x.

Morley, D. (1980). *The nationwide audience: Structure and decoding* (BFI Television Monograph No. 11). British Film Institute.

Morley, D. (1986). *Family television: Cultural power and domestic consumption*. London: Comedia.

Morley, D. (1992). *Television audiences and cultural studies*. London and New York: Routledge.

Oliver, M. B., Sargent, S. L., & Weaver, J. B. (1998). The impact of sex and gender role self-perception on affective reactions to different types of film. *Sex Roles, 38*(1–2), 45–62.

Oliver, M. B., Weaver, J. B., & Sargent, S. L. (2000). An examination of factors related to sex differences in enjoyment of sad films. *Journal of Broadcasting & Electronic Media, 44*(2), 282–300. doi:10.1207/s15506878jobem4402_8.

Olson, S. R. (1999). *Hollywood planet: Global media and the competitive advantage of narrative transparency*. London and New York: Routledge.

Pölönen, M., & Aaltonen, V. (2012). '3D looks more real and is funny': Comparing the children's and adults' 3D-related experiences. *SID Symposium Digest of Technical Papers, 43*(1), 958–960.

Potter, W. J. (2012). *Media effects*. Los Angeles; London; New Delhi; Singapore; Washington DC: Sage.

Press, A. (1989). Class, gender and the female viewer: Women's responses to *Dynasty*. In M. E. Brown (Ed.), *Television and women's culture: the politics of the popular* (pp. 158–181). London: Sage Publications.

Press, A. (1991a). Working-class women in a middle-class world: The impact of television on modes of reasoning about abortion. *Critical Studies in Mass Communication, 8*, 421–441.

Press, A. (1991b). *Women watching television*. Pennsylvania: University of Pennsylvania Press.

Press, A. L., & Rosenman, E. (2016). Consumerism and the languages of class. In T. Shary & F. Smith (Eds.), *ReFocus: The film of Amy Heckerling* (pp. 77–96). Edinburgh: Edinburgh University Press.

Ratnasingam, M., & Ellis, L. (2011). Sex differences in mass media preferences across four Asian countries. *Journal of Media Psychology, 23*(4), 186–191. doi:10.1027/1864-1105/a000054.

Rentfrow, P. J., Goldberg, L. R., & Zilca, R. (2011). Listening, watching, and reading: The structure and correlates of entertainment preferences. *Journal of Personality, 79*(2), 223–258. doi:10.1111/j.1467-6494.2010.00662.x.

Richards, J., & Sheridan, D. (1987). *Mass observation at the movies*. London: Routledge & Kegan.

Riggs, K. (1996). Television use in a retirement community. *Journal of Communication, 46*(1), 144–156.

Schrøder, K. C. (1994). Audience semiotics, interpretive communities and the 'ethnographic turn' in media research. *Media, Culture and Society, 16*(2), 337–347.

Scodari, C. (2012). 'Nyota Uhura is not a white girl': Gender, intersectionality, and *Star Trek* 2009's alternate romantic universes. *Feminist Media Studies, 12*(3), 335–351. doi:10.1080/14680777.2011.615605.

Scodari, C. (2014). Breaking dusk: Fandom, gender/age intersectionality, and the 'Twilight Moms'. In C. L. Harrington, D. D. Bielby, & A. R. Bardo (Eds.), *Aging, media, and culture* (pp. 143–154). Lanham, MD: Lexington Books.

Seiter, E. (1999). *Television and new media audiences*. Oxford: Clarendon Press.

Seiter, E., Borchers, H., Kreutzner, G., & Warth, E. (1989). 'Don't treat us like we're so stupid and naïve': Towards an ethnography of soap opera viewers. In E. Seiter, H. Borchers, G. Kreutzner, & E. Warth (Eds.), *Remote control: Television, audiences and cultural power* (pp. 223–247). London and New York: Routledge.

Sigismondi, P. (2011). *The digital glocalization of entertainment*. New York: Springer.

Skeggs, B., Thumim, N., & Wood, H. (2008). 'Oh goodness, I am watching reality TV': How methods make class in audience research. *European Journal of Cultural Studies, 11*(1), 5–24. doi:10.1177/1367549407084961.

Smets, K. (2012). Connecting Islam and film culture: The reception of *The Message (Ar Risalah)* among the Moroccan diaspora. *Participations: Journal of Audience and Reception Studies, 9*(1), 68–94.

Smets, K. (2014). 'Turkish Rambo' going transnational: The polarized reception of mainstream political cinema among the Turkish diaspora in Belgium. *Turkish Studies, 15*(1), 12–28. doi:10.1080/14683849.2014.897409.

Smets, K., Bauwel, S. V., Meers, P., & Winkel, R. V. (2016). Film-viewing in Turkish and Moroccan diasporic families: A gender and place perspective. *Gender, Place & Culture, 23*(4), 556–571. doi:10.1080/0966369X.2015.1034243.

Straubhaar, J. D. (2003). Choosing national TV: Cultural capital, language, and cultural proximity in Brazil. In M. G. Elasmar (Ed.), *The impact of international television: A paradigm shift* (pp. 77–110). London and New York: Routledge.

Tan, S. K. (2011). Global Hollywood, narrative transparency, and Chinese media poachers: Narrating cross-cultural negotiations of *Friends* in South China. *Television & New Media, 12*(3), 207–227. doi:10.1177/1527476410372094.

Thussu, D. K. (Ed.). (1998). *Electronic empires: Global media and local resistance.* London: Arnold.

Turnbull, S. (2008). Beyond words? *The Return of the King* and the pleasures of the text. In M. Barker & E. Mathijs (Eds.), *Watching The Lord of the Rings: Tolkien's world audiences* (pp. 181–190). New York: Peter Lang.

Van Ommen, M., Daalmans, S., Weijers, A., de Leeuw, R. N., & Buijzen, M. (2016). Analyzing prisoners', law enforcement agents', and civilians' moral evaluations of *The Sopranos. Poetics, 58*, 52–65. doi:10.1016/j.poetic.2016.07.003.

Volz, Y., Lee, F. L. F., Xiao, G., & Liu, X. (2010). Critical events and reception of foreign culture: An examination of cultural discount of foreign-language films in the US before and after 9/11. *International Communication Gazette, 72*(2), 131–149. doi:10.1177/1748048509353865.

Weaver, J. B., Brosius, H. B., & Mundorf, N. (1993). Personality and movie preferences: A comparison of American and German audiences. *Personality and Individual Differences, 14*(2), 307–315.

Willis, J. (1995). Staying in touch: Television and the over-seventies. In D. Petrie & J. Willis (Eds.), *Television and the household: Reports from the BFI's audience tracking study* (pp. 32–48). London: British Film Institute.

Wilson, T. (2001). On playfully becoming the 'Other': Watching Oprah Winfrey on Malaysian television. *International Journal of Cultural Studies, 4*, 89–110. doi:10.1177/136787790100400105.

Wühr, P., & Schwarz, S. (2016). *Die Hard* in *Notting Hill*: Gender differences in recalling contents from action and romantic movies. *Applied Cognitive Psychology, 30*(4), 491–503. doi:10.1002/acp.3238.

Wyatt, J. (2010). *High concept: Movies and marketing in Hollywood.* Austin: University of Texas Press.

Zalipour, A., Michelle, C., & Hardy, A. (2014). Modes of engagement among diasporic audiences of Asian New Zealand film. *The Communication Review, 17*(4), 311–335.

Zenor, J. (2014). Reading the President: Audience reception of The West Wing. In J. Zenor (Ed.), *Parasocial politics: Audiences, pop culture, and politics* (pp. 9–18). Lanham, MD: Lexington Books.

CHAPTER 10

Conclusion and Methodological Reflections on a Unique Project

INTRODUCTION

In the previous chapters we have used an innovative methodological approach to trace the evolution of audience responses to the *Hobbit* film trilogy from the immediate pre-viewing period until after the final film screened in movie theatres. Our findings suggest that while *An Unexpected Journey* (*AUJ*) delighted and enchanted a clear majority of respondents, key creative decisions progressively alienated a growing number of Tolkien and *Lord of the Rings* (*LotR*) enthusiasts as the trilogy unfolded, while also frustrating even some former *Hobbit* fans. Using a combination of qualitative and quantitative methods, our research has pinpointed the underlying reasons for the clearly more polarised responses to Jackson's second Middle-earth trilogy—most notably, the use of stereotypical Hollywood blockbuster formulae, an unusual digital aesthetic and too obvious use of CGI, excessive focus on extended action scenes showcasing special effects at the expense of narrative and characterisation, and considerable artistic licence taken with respect to Tolkien's original novel and vision. Our research thus offers a detailed insight into why *The Hobbit* has not become a popular cultural phenomenon in its own right, having fallen short of replicating the extraordinary critical, financial and popular success of Jackson's *LotR* film trilogy.

But beyond identifying the primary sources of viewers' pleasure and discontent, we have argued that the underlying theme unifying an eclectic array of criticisms of the *Hobbit* trilogy is an intensifying audience

© The Author(s) 2017
C. Michelle et al., *Fans, Blockbusterisation, and the Transformation of Cinematic Desire*, DOI 10.1057/978-1-137-59616-1_10

resistance to the processes, practices, conventions and imperatives that collectively constituted the blockbusterisation of Tolkien's original novel and its transformation into a tentpole event-film franchise. In concluding our discussion, we revisit this growing ambivalence toward blockbusterisation, before reflecting on the theoretical insights that can be gleaned from this study of *The Hobbit*'s transnational reception. Then, we address a few remaining issues arising from our unique methodology, highlighting its strengths as well as limitations, both in the interests of transparency about our methodological choices and for the benefit of audience researchers who may be contemplating similar projects.

BLOCKBUSTERISATION AND THE TRANSFORMATION OF CINEMATIC DESIRE

While the analysis offered in this book is consciously audience-centred rather than being a study of *The Hobbit*'s production per se, it is clear that the trilogy itself constituted a contested ground over which various stakeholders sought to assert creative control (Johnson 2013). Among these stakeholders were Warner Bros and New Line Cinemas, Jackson and his large production team, Weta Digital, fans of Tolkien and the wider Middle-earth franchise (many of whom claimed a personal stake in the outcome) and even the New Zealand government. Various sets of interests thus came into play in *The Hobbit*'s production and reception; at some moments competing and at others, aligned. In keeping with Warner Bros' now firmly established investment strategy, rather than offering a faithful cinematic interpretation of the unexpected adventure of a small but courageous homebody hobbit, the Jackson-Warner adaptation applied a broad range of blockbuster conventions intended to create a spectacular immersive experience, one loosely based on Bilbo's journey as a reluctant hero, but not focused exclusively on it. Echoing the three-part structure from *LotR*, a third episode was added to the *Hobbit* film series, purportedly to allow Jackson and company to 'tell more of the story' of Middle-earth, a decision that also yielded millions of dollars in additional profits and was seen by some commentators early on as a blatant 'cash grab'—a reading that became more widely shared among our respondents as a disappointing trilogy unfolded. The introduction of elf-guard Tauriel was clearly intended to appeal to women and others accustomed to seeing 'kick-ass' women in action films, but the (evidently) studio-requested placement of her within an unlikely and uncanonical love triangle angered many knowledgeable Tolkien readers, as well as some female *LotR* fans and casual viewers who had initially appreciated her presence within an overwhelmingly masculine universe. Incorporation of advanced visual effects and the experimental use of HFR 3D was consistent with Warner Bros' fundamental business imperative to offer a screen experience so compelling that only theatres could provide it (as well as Jackson's own creative interest in enhancing narrative transportation), but the particular combination of technologies and heavy reliance on CGI produced an unusual visual aesthetic that looked very different to that of the *LotR* trilogy, and more like small-screen genres that are culturally devalued. This displeased both those more committed to a traditional cinematic aesthetic and those who had been enchanted by the look and feel of the original *LotR* trilogy, and impeded or disrupted their immersion in the storyworld. And while the studio's need for a product that would appeal to a broad global audience of non-English-speakers no doubt influenced the *Hobbit* trilogy's emphasis on highly visual storytelling and narrative transparency, this was seen by many as undermining the rich themes and characterisation in Tolkien's written work.

In important respects, our case study of *The Hobbit*'s reception demonstrates that the processes of collaborative creativity that produced this prominent exemplar of the industrial processes of Hollywood blockbusterisation were deeply contested. Many of our respondents strongly proclaimed their own interests as stakeholders in *The Hobbit*'s production and the cinematic re-presentation of Tolkien's work, and increasingly expressed opposition to the way in which these interests were marginalised and denied by other, more powerful stakeholders in the process of translating the book to screen. Thus, while we initially set out to chart the evolution of audience responses to the *Hobbit* trilogy, we have simultaneously traced the emergence of growing audience resistance to blockbusterisation and the franchise model of film production among fans of a well-established collective cultural property and resource.

While it might be tempting to dismiss many of the criticisms of Jackson's re-visioning of *The Hobbit* as merely reflecting purist objections to any cinematic sullying of Tolkien's original vision, many of those who considered the *Hobbit* trilogy a failed adaptation greatly enjoyed the *LotR* films, and were not, in fact, averse to Jackson's previous interpretations of Tolkien's written works. Such dismissal would also fail to recognise the more fundamental changes in the nature of Hollywood blockbuster film production that have occurred in the decade since those earlier films were produced—changes that meant *The Hobbit* was specifically designed to be not simply an adaptation, but also a *blockbuster prequel event-film franchise* with international playability. These revised imperatives shifted the orientation of these films in ways that meant the outcome diverged quite considerably from Tolkien's brief novel, and also from Jackson's previous Middle-earth trilogy, in a manner that was all too evident for some. Such divergences were not merely displeasing; they radically undermined the nature and intensity of many viewers' previously enthusiastic cinematic desire for the *Hobbit* sequels. Our research suggests that before the trilogy began, and even after the first instalment screened in cinemas, audiences for *The Hobbit* had formulated certain desires and expectations about the pleasures and experiences these films might offer. When these were unforthcoming or differed substantially from those hoped for, cinematic desire for more of the same began to wane, replaced by deepening discontent in some quarters.

In an important sense, then, the growing disaffection for *The Hobbit* among existing fans of the wider franchise, and among Tolkien enthusiasts in particular, might be better understood as simultaneously a *protest* against growing corporate ownership and control over collective cultural and creative resources by individuals who claim a stake in the re-presentation and expansion of those shared properties. Following Johnson (2013, p. 11), our research thus illustrates how 'the multiplied cultural reproduction of media franchising, as a materially structured industrial practice' was 'tied into more subjective struggles over identity, meaning, and affect' among those with personal and psychological investments in the wider Middle-earth universe. Many of our respondents were intimately familiar with Tolkien's written works, Jackson's earlier trilogy, or both; many used these widely shared and enjoyed public properties as sources of insight, sociability and creativity. They, too, had a stake in any extension of this well-established and much-loved franchise.

The evolution and extension of collective resistance among a significant number of pre-existing fans of the wider franchise can be traced over the course of our project. An explicit critique of *The Hobbit*'s blockbusterisation was nascent in the views of *Jackson Critics* even before *AUJ* hit cinemas, and Jackson's own problematic role in a New Zealand labour dispute fuelled many of their criticisms of this transnational blockbuster film production. Concern about the adverse impact of commercial imperatives became progressively more central to the critiques offered by Tolkien-oriented respondents following each instalment. *AUJ* convinced *Bored and Disillusioned Hobbit Critics* as well as many *Disappointed*

Tolkien Readers and *Mildly Entertained Casual Viewers* of the detrimental impact of financial interests on the design of the film, but these were minority views at this stage. Following *DoS*, *Disenchanted Hobbit Critics* and *Aggrieved Tolkien Aficionados* strongly agreed with a statement condemning the film for its Hollywood blockbuster characteristics, while the (now significantly depleted) core group of *Happy Hobbit Defenders* strongly disagreed. After viewing *BotFA*, all groups except *Fulfilled Hobbit Fans* and *Frustrated Middle-earth Fans* agreed that the trilogy seemed like a blatant cash grab. While remaining fans greatly valued Jackson's adaptation as a compelling, visually impressive, action-packed expansion of the wider Middle-earth franchise that mostly delivered on its promise, our many disaffected respondents made their antipathy explicit. Respondents' objections to the trilogy, well documented in the preceding chapters, appear to collectively reflect and indeed crystallise an underlying opposition to and reaction against the transformation of a beloved cultural property into a widely consumed cultural commodity and its reduction to 'just another Hollywood blockbuster, nothing more!'

However, it is important to note that others defended the processes and practices of blockbusterisation as inevitable given the practical 'realities' of contemporary filmmaking within a capitalist film industry, and furthermore as *necessary* to bring *The Hobbit* to life, given the technological requirements of realising the more fantastical elements of Tolkien's Middle-earth on screen. Successfully doing so required a significant capital investment from which film studios could reasonably expect a return, some argued—which meant the trilogy needed to have broad international audience appeal:

> I think people judge too harshly, especially the purists, and most of them do not understand the difference between printed text and visual media, or the difference between catering to fans vs. the wider general public (who are the ones mostly contributing to the box office and filling cinema halls). The fans, passionate as we are, only make up a small percentage. Unfortunately many book purists I've met seem to lack the understanding of the 'business' part of the movie business. (Sri Lankan man, 32; *Happy Hobbit Defender*)

Clearly, many of our participants perceived an alignment or accordance between their own interests as fan stakeholders in enjoying a long-awaited (and, we would suggest, fetishised) cultural commodity, and those of *The Hobbit*'s creators. Consequently, they found grounds to downplay or rationalise the trilogy's more excessive elements, or to mini-mise claims of labour exploitation or studio interference in the course of its production lest such concerns spoil a deeply desired entertainment experience. Others attributed problematic characteristics of the films to the forgivable missteps of a well-intentioned (if overly zealous) direc-tor; one who has subsequently claimed he 'didn't know what the hell' he was doing while making *The Hobbit* (Child 2015; see also Ahsan 2015) and likely faced extraordinary pressure to meet predetermined windows for the release of the three *Hobbit* films. Notably, this intense pressure itself stemmed from the financial interests associated with blockbuster film production in terms of maximising box-office takings and revenues from sales of ancillary merchandise during the lucrative Christmas holi-day season. Some defenders also argued that while the *Hobbit* films bore the clear imprint of Hollywood, they were still much better than its typi-cal blockbuster fare, and expressed a genuine effort by the filmmakers to honour Tolkien's legacy, suggesting an alignment between the corporate and creative interests of Jackson and Warner Bros and their own interests as fans:

> While the studio may reap the benefits of an extended franchise, this is the last time to visit Middle-earth for the fans. The breadth of Tolkien's writ-ings are only touched on in the *Hobbit* book, and incorporating the back story from the Appendices and Silmarillion is a delight. The mere men-tions in the script of Istari and Ungoliant give the viewer the satisfaction that the writers really GOT IT—and were committed to fully realizing Tolkien's works. (American woman, 59; *Enchanted Hobbit Fan*)

Ultimately, then, the *Hobbit* case suggests that the capital-intensive com-modification of established cultural properties in the form of block-buster adaptation film franchises has moved beyond earlier antagonisms between high and low culture and is fuelling new tensions between dif-ferently empowered stakeholders with different sets of interests, most notably through the alteration and extension of canonical storyworlds, through the displacement of print stories by screen stories, through the conversion of familiar narratives into immersive visual spectacles, but perhaps more fundamentally, through the radical transformation of cin-ematic desire among loyal and enthusiastic pre-assembled audiences. That some of the strategies adopted by Jackson and team appear to have backfired, in some minds at least, was variously attributed to studio interference, directorial hubris, corporate greed, taking too many liberties with a beloved cultural property, and underestimating audience commitments to the *LotR*'s more conventional cinematic aesthetics. But more fundamentally, the perceived failures of *The Hobbit* reveal that the blockbusterisation of cultural properties in which individuals have deep psychological and imaginative investments potentially entails a profound sense of *loss*.

This loss relates to the threat that an unsatisfactory adaptation, sequel or prequel presents to the aura of specialness or exceptionality attributed to the 'original' object, whether a physical book or film or an imaginatively projected version of it. While fan audiences often greatly enjoy the opportunity to re-immerse themselves in familiar narrative worlds, the commercial and critical failure of a succession of recent instalments to established franchises suggests they are rather less tolerant of an adaptation, sequel/prequel or reboot that undermines or degrades a previous heightened personal and collective experience. As Pallotta (2016) observes and our research also bears out, poor quality prequels/ sequels potentially taint the legacy of a successful franchise, while much has been written about the risks of adaptations straying too far from an original work (see for instance Joshi and Mao 2012; Leitch 2009). Evidently, *The Hobbit* trod dangerous ground on both counts. While most of our respondents made a clear separation between the book and its adaptation, and while many *Hobbit* defenders saw the films as actually improving the novel or extending their enjoyment of the *LotR* trilogy, more than a few critics expressed profound loss and regret as they contemplated an unsatisfactory outcome that simultaneously tainted and degraded something *else* which had great personal value:

> The films did not honour the book in the way the *LotR* films did for Tolkien's other work. I was insulted by the work and felt like a strong part of my childhood had been taken away. It depressed me. I honestly feel like the writers should apologise for what they have done to the fans of the book and the Tolkien estate. (Welsh man, 42; *Unhappy Tolkien Adherent*)

> I want to get Jackson's version out of my head so that I can rediscover my superior memory of this story. (American man, 49; *Unhappy Tolkien Adherent*)

> The Royal Family of Mirkwood is everything to me. I won't go into why, as it's deeply personal. Watching them get destroyed in front of my eyes

literally made me feel like a part of my heart died. I was in legitimate pain for days. (American woman, 22; *Unhappy Tolkien Adherent*)

Blockbusterisation can thus be seen as potentially effecting a deeper transformation of cinematic desire among fan audiences in particular, through its conversion of familiar collective cultural properties beloved by distinct communities of interest into extravagant, visually impressive, action-heavy cultural commodities that bear the clear hallmarks of corporate ownership and control.

In this important respect, then, receptions of the *Hobbit* trilogy's form as a blockbuster franchise adaptation-prequel clearly possessed ideological dimensions, which can be usefully evaluated in line with the final set of categories proposed in Michelle's (2007) Composite Model (See Chap. 2, Fig. 2.1). While many of our passionate and often very knowledgeable respondents celebrated the *Hobbit* trilogy as the product of an alignment of their interests with those of the trilogy's creators and thus expressed preferred or *hegemonic* readings (as is clearly the case with *Enchanted Hobbit Fans*, *Happy Hobbit Defenders* and *Fulfilled Hobbit Fans*), others evidently perceived these films as tarnishing or destroying the 'special aura' of previously cherished exceptional works, and in some cases radically transforming their experience of them. These respondents can be seen to have adopted readings that were either *contesting*, in the sense that they rejected certain aspects of the capitalist form of the *Hobbit* trilogy while accepting others, or *counter-hegemonic* in the sense that they rejected that form in full. The latter is generally true of those viewpoints that critiqued the professional or industrial intentions and imperatives shaping *The Hobbit*'s creative realisation, which we have argued were intimately connected to its blockbusterisation—as was the case with *Bored and Disillusioned*, *Disenchanted* and *Angry Hobbit Critics*. By the trilogy's conclusion, *Unhappy Tolkien Adherents* were similarly articulating a counter-hegemonic reading, or very close to it.

THEORETICAL IMPLICATIONS FOR UNDERSTANDING MODES OF RECEPTION OF BLOCKBUSTER FILM ADAPTATIONS

Flowing from these insights into audience resistance to *The Hobbit*'s blockbusterisation, our research has clear implications for theoretical understandings of audience reception per se. Our purpose in writing this book was not merely to survey global responses to *The Hobbit* as an exemplar of the contemporary blockbuster fantasy film franchise; we also sought to contribute to understanding the nature of audience reception itself, in a more general sense. For analytical purposes, and to allow the findings of this study to be compared with those of other studies, we have interpreted the viewpoints identified in each post-viewing survey as reflecting the underlying modes of reception charted in the Composite Model. More specifically, we have explained *The Hobbit*'s radically divergent receptions in terms of the success or failure of each film to induce and sustain the preferred *transparent* mode of response, characterised by pleasurable feelings of being transported back to Middle-earth and becoming completely immersed in the narrative storyworld. As Fowkes (2010) notes, the capacity to escape into an alternative fantastical imaginary world is one of the pleasures afforded by fantasy film as a genre (see also Saler 2012). It is also clear that the filmmakers consciously sought to elicit this fully transported viewing mode among fans and mainstream audiences, most notably through the use of HFR 3D projection; the inclusion of characters and themes associated with the *LotR* trilogy and the use of a musical score with familiar elements; the introduction of new characters and tropes designed to capture the attention of contemporary audiences and introduce novelty; and the creation of numerous visually impressive set pieces.

Paradoxically, however, our research suggests that several of these strategies were experienced as disruptive and even objectionable by certain subgroups among the wider viewing audience, who instead adopted variations of a mediated mode of reception focused on textual aesthetics, generic form, professional or industry-based intentionality or some combination of these. For these respondents, the *Hobbit* films failed in full or part to secure and maintain the preferred, and often deeply desired, transparent mode of reception, and was thus reconstituted as a 'bad object', one perhaps *unworthy* of their devoted attention. This core distinction between a larger central audience group who adopted a transparent mode of reception and various smaller groups who assumed distinct variations of the mediated mode persisted across the cinematic life of the *Hobbit* trilogy.

The recent publication of key findings from our larger 'sister' project, the *Hobbit* World Audiences study, confirms that very similar lines of division were evident among their participant sample, offering a source of external cross-validation of our previously published findings and those presented here. Most notably, Barker (2016) identifies a very broad separation between 'Enthusiasts' and 'Critics', while Jerslev et al. (2016) describe the qualitative responses of their most enthusiastic Danish respondents in terms essentially very similar to our own descriptions of *Hobbit* fans, who adopted a transparent mode of reception. Conversely, Hipfl and Kulterer (2016, p. 253) observe that *The Hobbit* left 'a bad taste of greed and commercialization for many' who attributed the excessive action scenes, decision to make a trilogy and overuse of CGI to commercial interests and the profit motive—consistent with our own analysis of growing resistance to blockbusterisation. Ilan and Kama's (2016) thematic analysis of Israeli responses highlights very similar distinctions between those who were immersed in the storyworld and saw the *Hobbit* films as perfect reflections of the novel, or even an improved version of it that unified the wider Middle-earth series, and those concerned (and angry) about the adaptation's deviation from the original story and the spirit of Tolkien's work. Just as we have observed, others expressed criticism of the films' commercial orientation (which these authors term Hollywoodisation, as personified by Jackson and reflected in the expansion of the story into a trilogy designed to make more money), or *The Hobbit*'s 'cinematographic methods'. All of these are familiar themes in the responses of our own participants.

While we believe our analysis offers a rather more refined and methodologically robust picture of the main lines of division among fans as well as critics of the *Hobbit* trilogy, the same core distinctions are clearly echoed in the findings of the larger and more global World Audiences study, which used a different methodological approach in the form of surveying audiences at the trilogy's conclusion only. The consistency between the two very different sets of findings suggests that this fundamental division between transparent and mediated modes of reception is not the artificial by-product of a particular research process or participant sample, but most likely existed within the wider *Hobbit* viewing audience globally. The fact that this basic division appeared regardless of cultural, geographical or linguist context also suggests that these subjective modes of engagement and response are likely universal, and reflect the particular interpretive capacities and predilections of different individuals—ones that they presumably take with them to *other* media encounters.

Assuming this is the case, we can perhaps go one step further and tentatively suggest that the particular modes of reception we have identified here are likely to be most prevalent among viewers of other adaptations, particularly highly anticipated blockbuster fantasy film franchises that are simultaneously sequels, prequels or adaptations of popular novels (such as the *Harry Potter, Hunger Games* or *Divergent* series). That is, transparent and mediated modes of reception—and more specifically, that variation of the mediated mode focused on generic form (in this case, as an adaptation, prequel or sequel)—might be reasonably anticipated as the predominant modes shaping audience responses to films of this particular *kind*. So, we might anticipate a core distinction between those who are very transported and fully engaged in the narrative world, evaluating it on its own terms as though it were real life, versus those who express explicit awareness of the text as a constructed media product and critically evaluate it in relation to relevant intertexts (most obviously, the original novel on which the film is based, and/or other films in the same franchise), and perhaps secondarily in terms of the quality of its textual aesthetics or the processes, imperatives and intentions governing its production. The latter sub-variants of the mediated mode are, we suggest, probably more likely to be evident in cases where the adaptation, sequel or prequel is judged and found wanting as failing to enchant or transport—something that requires explanation.

More tentatively still, we postulate that unless the narrative content has overt personal or real-world relevance that lends itself to *referential* readings, or contains explicit messages that are controversial or subject to debate, thereby prompting the adoption of a *discursive* mode among certain viewers, fantasy film adaptations seem likely to elicit a relatively narrow range of responses. While we have not identified a significant viewpoint that could be considered primarily referential or discursive, there were a (very) small number of respondents who expressed concerns about the trilogy's excessive violence, while many others highlighted the importance of *The Hobbit*'s deeper themes—but not in a sustained way that might be said to constitute a predominant mode of response in its own right. And as Michelle (2007) notes, there is a discursive dimension to *all* receptions, with acceptance of textual messages being an inherent feature of the transparent mode.

Interestingly, Hipfl and Kulterer (2016) analysed German-speaking respondents' answers to a question in the *Hobbit* World Audiences questionnaire that specifically invited respondents to reflect on whether the *Hobbit* films 'raise any broader issues or themes'. When asked to do so, some noted connections with real-world conflicts and wars, and the plight of growing numbers of refugees. Hasebrink and Paus-Hasebrink (2016) similarly point to examples of German and Austrian viewers making connections between *The Hobbit*'s 'symbolic material' and their everyday lives, and suggest 'quite a few' explicitly related the homeless dwarves to the ongoing refugee crisis in Europe. However, it is unclear from their analysis whether such reflections emerged independently or as the by-product of the researcher effect in that the respondents were explicitly invited to think about the trilogy's relevance to broader social and political issues. We subsequently examined whether themes relating to (real-world) wars, refugees and homelessness featured in the open-ended responses of our respondents (including their responses to Q statements specifically noting the 'real-world' relevance of the story or its message content), conducting a systematic search for these terms within our data. Only three such instances were found in the English language *AUJ* survey data, while one respondent in the *BotFA* survey mentioned relating to the dwarves as refugees, since she was herself a political refugee. Surprisingly, we found no such references in the German data, but this sample was considerably smaller. The relative absence of unsolicited references to real-world issues and events appears to confirm that the referential and discursive modes were not primary interpretive frames adopted by very many of our respondents, if at all.

In making a claim for the universal nature of modes of response and the likelihood that the transparent and mediated modes will predominate within audience receptions of blockbuster fantasy film adaptation/sequels, we do not seek to deny the unique aspects of this particular film trilogy. Obviously, the content of *Hobbit* viewers' responses is highly specific to these three films, their (deeply) contested relationship to Tolkien's written works, their narrative, characterisation, visual effects and so on. While this is undoubtedly true, we believe the underlying form of those responses is not unique to any one film or set of films, because interpretation (or textual decoding, in Stuart Hall's formulation) is a process that emanates from embodied and socially situated actors as they adopt and move between distinct modes of reception that frame their relationship to the text, shape their approach to sense-making and utilise specific knowledges and capacities. Those knowledges and capacities may be more or less accessible depending on a given individual's particular social location; hence we were also interested in exploring the possible relationship between reception and the social locations of viewers.

THE COMPLEX RELATIONSHIP BETWEEN RECEPTION AND SOCIAL LOCATION

As detailed in Chap. 9, we found a substantial number of significant effects relating to location, gender, age, education, occupation, political beliefs and fandoms. On that basis, we can confidently say that those who expressed the most favourable responses to the *Hobbit* trilogy were more often female, with males being more likely to adopt non-preferred modes of reception. While *AUJ* appealed to relatively young viewers, relatively old viewers were more likely to adopt the preferred reading in the case of *DoS* and *BotFA*. The more highly educated the viewer, the less likely she or he was to assume the preferred reading. In the final analysis, however, many of these effects were small and cumulative, and the individuals who loaded significantly on a particular factor were quite diverse, even if there were some statistically significant trends in their shared characteristics. In most cases, what ultimately united the various audience clusters we have identified was not so much their nationality, gender, age or any combination of socio-demographic attributes, but rather their *shared perspective*. That is to say, the viewpoints we identified, and the modes of reception underlying them, were themselves the unifying elements.

This finding is important for the wider field of audience studies, because it shows that Q methodology can reveal the most important and salient distinctions within a broader population, based on their actual rather than assumed subjective responses to a given text. Doing so makes it possible to objectively categorise respondents in ways that are more reliable, replicable and also more meaningful than is possible in other commonly used approaches to studying audience reception. Q methodology, we believe, offers a new way to think about and research the relationship between social location, interpretation and response to a wide range of media texts, and potentially also to explore whether and why different subgroups within a wider audience might consistently adopt particular modes of reception for specific mediums and genres.

One additional point bears further comment. While we have postulated that the modes of reception charted in the Composite Model are universal, this does not mean they are equally accessible to all. Some draw on knowledges and competencies that are not evenly distributed within social networks, but rather depend on the intersection of multiple identities (nationality, gender, age, ethnicity etc.) and experiences relating to occupation, education, life stage, and so on. The level of media literacy that characterises highly detailed articulations of the mediated mode, in particular, is not an innate characteristic; it has to be acquired or learned. It is no coincidence, then, that we found that advanced media production education and industry experience were significantly associated with particular critical viewpoints on *The Hobbit*'s technologies and visual realisation; other studies have similarly noted an association between media education and mediated modes of reception (see Michelle 2009, for an overview). As one respondent noted, such training produces a particular *way of seeing* films, a distinct mode of reception that sits at odds with unreserved narrative immersion:

> More than 30 years ago I worked in Film and TV. For five years after that, I never could enjoy a film because I was thinking about the lighting, audio, staging and such. Eventually, I forgot all that and learned to enjoy films again. I know now that people who work in film do not see precisely the same film that I am currently seeing. (American man, 65; *Happy Hobbit Defender*)

Interestingly, Skeggs et al. (2008) reveal that the research process itself can encourage the mobilisation of particular forms of cultural capital, including self-reflexive and mediated modes of media engagement (particularly in relation to historically derided genres—of which fantasy is one), as part of a performative production of class identity. This tendency is important to acknowledge in relation to our own explorations of the roles that education, occupation and class may have played in shaping responses to the *Hobbit* trilogy. To some unknown extent, the adoption by certain respondents of a mediated mode of reception may actually reflect a self-reflexive performance of how they felt they should properly talk about these films in the context of academic research, or in light of considerable (and often critical) public discussion and debate about their quality—from a position of objective distance, cool evaluation, using the language of a film critic or Tolkien buff, for example, rather than the more effusive language of a besotted fan. (Although the anonymity afforded by online research offers considerable protection in this regard; knowing their identities remained concealed, respondents may have felt little need to engage in what is, in effect, a form of impression management.)

Nonetheless, there were moments where it was possible to observe the conscious, self-reflexive mobilisation of specific subject positions and related forms of economic, symbolic, social and cultural capital by respondents to explain and provide support for their evaluations, as in cases where they prefaced their remarks with statements asserting particular expertise, such as 'I am a literary scholar, particularly of English literature', or 'As a Screen and Media student', or 'I'm a classically trained musician'. As sociologist Pierre Bourdieu's (1986) work implies, mobilising such forms of capital can help constitute a subject's symbolic value and sense of self. Such responses can thus be understood, in part, as a self-reflexive production of the Self as a certain *kind* of subject; one with specialist knowledge perhaps, or specific motivations for viewing that separate oneself from culturally derided identities such as the fan, historically at least.

METHODOLOGICAL MATTERS

While we hope our research contributes to theoretical understandings within the wider field of reception studies, any potential contributions depend on the veracity of our findings, and hence the validity of our methodological choices and analytical processes. For readers more familiar with ethnographic audience research, our use of Q methodology will likely raise eyebrows, as it may for those based within media psychology, despite Q now having made inroads within the wider social sciences. With time, Q is likely to become better understood by other media scholars. So, rather than recite a well-worn defence of Q methodology (interested readers should see McKeown and Thomas 2013; Watts and Stenner 2012), we confine our discussion to a few key issues regarding our research approach.

First, some readers may perceive the viewpoints we have identified as reductive and overly simplified, and as compartmentalising our respondents into neat little boxes when their individual perspective may have been rather more nuanced. However, we take the view that analytic generalisation (and thus theory-building and testing) requires the creation of meaningful categories using a clear, reliable and replicable process. Reduction and simplification are inevitably part of that process. It is true that these categories alone cannot capture the full complexity of each individual respondent's perspective, nor their final views on the topic, both because the views expressed are in response to a specific condition of instruction and rely on the 'tools' provided, and because processes of reception may be ongoing with repeated re-engagement with a text and may also shift and change following discussion and debate with others. This is why Q is typically used in conjunction with interviews, or in our case, a questionnaire inviting open-ended qualitative responses. Nonetheless, we emphasise that the factors *do* reflect statistically significant distinctions in the expressed viewpoints of our respondents, as operationalised through their own independent actions in preferentially sorting the Q statements. To provide external confirmation of their relevance, we included the following question in our three post-viewing surveys: *To what extent did the statements in the previous ranking exercise allow you to convey your own responses?* On a 4-point scale from 1 = 'not at all' to 4 = 'almost completely', the average score was slightly over 3 for each survey. This indicates that most respondents were satisfied that the provided Q statements allowed them to broadly represent their viewpoint. We thus believe that the identified positions can be considered naturally occurring, and reflect the most salient distinctions among different subsections of our participant sample.

Of course, what those viewpoints mean and the underlying modes of reception they might reflect is subject to interpretation (see Watts and Stenner 2012). Our analyses were informed both by the extensive open-ended comments of our participants and our chosen analytical framework—the Composite Model. Ultimately, however, the viewpoints don't have to be interpreted with reference to this particular model. Indeed, the primary reason for drawing on this analytical framework was to make it possible to make meaningful connections with the findings of other studies across the wider field of audience research (somewhat difficult to do without a common conceptual schema), and to avoid creating the (false and misleading) impression that global receptions of *The Hobbit* are entirely unique in their underlying form and in the subjective orientations to sense-making they express—a point to which we return below.

Questions will also likely be asked about the composition of our participant sample, which was slightly gender-skewed from the outset. This gender bias became even more pronounced as the project continued, likely a flow-on effect from the more positive reception of the first film among women respondents. It possibly also reflects our use of Theonering.net and Facebook as recruitment tools (among various others, but these were clearly the most successful in generating responses). A significant majority of Theonering.net users are women (58%) (Klear n.d.), while 77% of women Internet users use Facebook versus 66% of men (Duggan 2015). Part of the challenge of online research is accessing potential respondents in a rapidly transforming, relatively fluid environment. At the time we commenced this project back in 2012, MySpace was still in operation, while the more male-dominated site Reddit was nowhere near as popular as it is today—neither were Tumblr and Instagram. While Facebook continues to consolidate its impressive market dominance, future online research would benefit from a more diversified approach to recruitment.

Our vast number of respondents will also raise eyebrows within Q methodology circles for reasons that may surprise audience researchers, given the current drive for large-scale, cross-national audience research. Bigger isn't necessarily better in the world of Q methodology; it is considered redundant to include a large number of respondents merely to identify the typology of viewpoints within a population. However, we hoped to do rather more than simply chart the different perspectives among *Hobbit* viewers: we wanted to be able to explore *patterns* of response and to investigate whether there were significant associations between viewing positions and aspects of social location or fan affiliation. To do this, we needed to recruit larger numbers of respondents than is typical for Q studies. Our aim was 1000 per survey, which we achieved or exceeded in all but one case, although only for English-speaking respondents. Having comparatively large P sets has enabled us to identify some significant associations between viewpoints and the socio-demographic and other characteristics of our respondents, and these findings should be of considerable interest to fellow audience researchers.

Of course, while we are satisfied that our research has produced a wealth of valuable insights that contribute in meaningful ways to our understanding of audience engagements with blockbuster film adaptations and of audience reception more generally, we are keenly aware of its limitations. Among these include the project's limited global reach, the lack of representativeness of online research, and factors relating to our survey's usability and the lack of familiarity with Q sorting among most respondents.

GLOBAL AMBITIONS ONLY PARTIALLY REALISED

One of the things we were less successful in achieving was to make this a truly global longitudinal study of *The Hobbit*'s reception. Ideally, that would have meant conducting each reception survey in a wider range of languages and having a larger international research team to assist with recruitment and interpretation in each context. In the end, our global ambitions were stifled by a combination of insufficient funding and the lack of familiarity with Q methodology among audience researchers internationally. Nonetheless, we were able to attract a handful of scholars at Roskilde University in Denmark, Ghent University in Belgium, Erasmus University in the Netherlands and the University of Navarra in Spain to contribute in various capacities. With their involvement and the help of a diverse team of research assistants comprised of Spanish, German and French speakers along with professional translators, we were able to construct versions of our *AUJ* reception survey in seven languages and to recruit a reasonable number of respondents to complete most of these. While the findings from these multilingual surveys are certainly suggestive, the numbers of respondents were not sufficient to perform some of the analyses we had hoped to undertake. And unfortunately, while the other three surveys were open to respondents living anywhere in the world, they were available in English only, meaning we can make only limited claims regarding the global reach of our research.

QUESTIONS OF 'REPRESENTATIVENESS'

While our sample is substantial and diverse, it is not representative of the wider *Hobbit* audience for several reasons. Firstly, our use of exclusively online surveys means we have primarily reached people who are active on the Internet, access to which is not evenly distributed. At the time we commenced our project, estimates suggested that 70–90% of people in Western developed nations had Internet access, but in the developing world, only 25% were online (International Telecommunication Union 2012). Also, within Western countries, there are often significant differences in access to ICT based on socio-economic class, age and ethnicity. Hence, our research is likely to overrepresent the views of Internet-savvy '"cosmopolitans": people whose life orientation revolves around global interconnectedness rather than their local communities' (Hannerz 1990, as cited in Kuipers and Kloet 2009, p. 104). These are likely to be relatively economically empowered individuals both in the developing *and* developed worlds. This bias appears to be a significant shortcoming of online research generally and was evident to some extent in our *Hobbit* participant sample.

Furthermore, our reliance on convenience sampling means the generalisability of our study is limited by a self-selecting sample bias. We had no control over who participated and did not know if those who completed surveys were representative of the demographic make-up of the wider population of *Hobbit* viewers globally or nationally (see also Trobia 2016). It is rather more likely that our research overrepresents the views of highly motivated *LotR* fans and committed Tolkien enthusiasts with a strong prior interest in the subject matter. While fans are not a singular monolithic group and often have diverse views about their object of interest (Jenkins 1992; Hills 2002), they are also not representative of the general population of cinemagoers. Fans typically exhibit deeper, more intense forms of psychological and emotional engagement, and often possess specialist knowledge of relevant intertexts. Not surprisingly then, Jerslev et al. (2016) found significant differences between the responses of a systematically selected quota sample representative of Danish *Hobbit* viewers and those who self-selected to participate in response to its online/networked recruitment strategies.

Seeking to mitigate this potential sample bias, we attempted to maximise variation among our respondents by posting our invitation in a wide range of *non*-fan forums and making it clear we hoped to capture diverse viewpoints. We also targeted certain special interest groups that were likely to have unique perspectives on the topic at hand. This approach to recruitment is standard within Q methodology, the specific aim of which is to identify the range of viewpoints on a topic and characterise them so that they may be interpreted, as opposed to constructing a representative sample of the wider population to measure the distribution of particular beliefs or values. As noted by Stenner et al. (2008, p. 221),

> Participants in Q studies are ... treated as strategic 'sites' from which a limited independent variety of subjective viewpoints can be heard. The aim is to gain access to that range of viewpoints, and not to make claims about the frequency of their occurrence amongst the general population.

For these and other reasons, we make no claims about the distribution of the subjective orientations we have discovered within the wider population of *Hobbit* viewers, although these viewpoints are sure to be present among them. And, while we have found several striking patterns in our data along socio-demographic and other grounds, we want to stress that these trends are particular to *this* research project, and should not be assumed to reflect tendencies among the wider viewing audience. They may well do, but we have not investigated this and make no claims of that nature.

Usability Issues and Lack of Familiarity with Q Sorting

Some more significant limitations of our study relate to the survey itself and Q sorting as a still unfamiliar approach within social science research. Some respondents found the survey instrument rather cumbersome and time-consuming, possibly compounding the high dropout rate that tends to blight online research. Some experienced usability issues with the 'drag and drop' function in the second stage of Q sorting, while others found it difficult to scroll through the statements to review them due to the survey layout and size of the font, especially on smaller screens. The forced distribution grid was perplexing to some since it meant statements sometimes had to be placed into columns that did not accurately reflect their sentiments. In the respondent information blurb that preceded the survey we noted it would take around 30–40 minutes to complete, but in more than a few cases, it took much longer, judging by the very detailed comments some respondents offered (and several noted as much).

Nonetheless, we believe the depth and quality of the data generated through longer surveys adequately compensated for the potentially higher dropout rate. And, while some experienced technical problems with the survey instrument, we received very positive feedback from others who enjoyed the process of sorting the statements on screen, one describing it as a pleasant kinaesthetic experience. Several praised the depth and comprehensiveness of the survey and its unusual design, while many thanked us for the opportunity to share their views in what some described as a cathartic process, or as one suggested, 'A therapeutic way for me to vent my "anger"'.

Ultimately, we believe any potential costs of using Q methodology were adequately counterbalanced by the analytical power of the method. As is always the case with human research there is a trade-off between the numbers of respondents, the quality of the data generated, the manageability of the resulting data set, and the researcher's capacity to systematically identify objectively meaningful patterns and trends within that data. We believe our data is of exceptional quality for an online survey where respondents received no recompense for participating, other than the opportunity to share their views and contribute to knowledge production. Many offered detailed and insightful comments on a broad range of topics, and while our use of an unfamiliar and quite time-consuming survey method may have biased our results even further toward those most highly motivated to share their views, there is no reason to suppose that high motivation to participate correlates with one uniform perspective on the *Hobbit* films. Our respondents include those who were deeply critical of the films on various grounds as well as those effusive in their praise, and many in between. In the end, we managed to obtain just under 5800 responses to our core surveys. Including the additional survey and interviews focusing on reactions to *The Hobbit*'s use of HFR 3D, the final tally for the whole project is 6450, making this one of the largest audience research projects ever conducted, almost certainly the biggest Q methodology study to date, and (to our knowledge) the first published reception study to systematically adopt a longitudinal approach to data collection over the life of a serialised screen product.

METHODOLOGICAL CONTRIBUTIONS

On balance, we believe this project has made some significant methodological contributions to the wider field of audience research, most particularly in illustrating how Q methodology can be used for large-scale, cross-cultural online reception research, and in exemplifying a workable longitudinal approach to studying audience engagements with serialised screen media content. With a high degree of confidence, we have been able to identify and track over time the specific textual elements, issues and concerns that became particularly controversial and indeed polarising among a large and widely dispersed participant sample. Q allowed us to reliably identify similarities and differences in how respondents interpreted the same stimuli, and to perceive how and why distinct groups of respondents attributed significance to particular issues and concerns over others. In sorting the same set of statements, respondents conveyed different emphases and nuances within the context of expressing their holistic perspective, or point of view. These important distinctions and their contribution to a shared subjective orientation toward these texts would have been lost had we merely asked our respondents to rate a series of statements in turn (using Likert scales, for instance) because such an approach assumes viewers' reactions to different issues can be understood in isolation from each other. Q methodology, conversely, seeks to discern how particular concepts, ideas and issues are *related to* each other from the vantage point of those individuals who share a perspective, while also highlighting the specific aspects that are the most salient. The key concerns and distinctions identified using factor analysis were cross-validated by independent inductive analysis of participants' open-ended responses. Through the triangulation of different methods of data collection and analysis, we believe our project has achieved a high degree of internal validity.

Furthermore, in light of the growing reliance in both film and television production on serialisation, there is an urgent need for audience researchers to develop alternative approaches to the static and singular sampling strategy typically used to date. Serialisation is a dynamic process of narrative and character evolution as texts unfold over weeks, months and years, in ways that sometimes diverge quite radically from source materials and may even outpace their creation, as witnessed with HBO's hugely successful *Game of Thrones* fantasy series. To imagine that we can fully understand the reception of such texts among the wider viewing audience by surveying loyal followers at one moment in an extended and very complex narrative is, at best, wishful thinking. Conversely, the kind of longitudinal approach we have attempted makes it possible to capture the evolution of audience viewpoints over time by taking a series of snapshots at different moments, while the use of Q methodology allows the analyst to characterise and hold steady shared positions for the purposes of comparison with the views of others at the same moment, or at *different* times. Such an approach even makes it possible to isolate and compare a single respondent's views at various points in the life of a complex narrative text—as we have done in juxtaposing the opinions of the same individuals at different moments over the course of the *Hobbit* trilogy. This kind of approach makes it possible to capture the complex set of expectations and evaluations that characterise an audiences' dynamic and evolving relationship to media productions over time. Our findings reveal some significant transformations in respondents' views over the course of the trilogy, clearly illustrating the value of a longitudinal approach.

QUESTIONS FOR FUTURE RESEARCH

But of course a great deal remains unanswered, and there are various issues we have not been able to address here fully. For one, we have not systematically analysed the marketing and promotion of these films and the presence of other prefigurative materials in different national contexts, which some suggest play a major role in establishing viewers' interpretive frameworks (Biltereyst et al. 2008; Gray 2010; Luthar 2008). While potentially interesting, systematically collecting and analysing these materials across different national contexts was beyond our resources. We also took the view that it was not so much the materials themselves but the shared meanings they informed that was important to track. Hence, we included an array of such materials in the cultural trawl conducted for the first stage of the project, which helped ensure that major prefigurative frameworks for interpretation became embedded in our research process. We also asked our respondents directly about their engagement with a range of prefigurative materials and activities, in the belief that this would gather more useful information about the possible impact of ancillary paratextual materials in shaping receptions of the *Hobbit* films. The diverse responses we have charted suggest that while marketing and other prefigurative materials may be effective in stimulating general awareness within a wider potential audience (i.e. marketability) and in providing possible interpretive frames for viewers in the pre-viewing period, the level and nature of engagement with those materials is individually idiosyncratic and sits alongside a large number of other potential influences on how viewers will subsequently make sense of a fully realised, complexly layered and polysemic text, the nature of which can never be fully anticipated, as Chap. 5 illustrates. The outcome of encounters between texts and audiences is thus not determined by prefigurative discussions or marketing materials, and cannot be predicted from studies of pre-viewer expectations or their preoccupations with particular intertexts.

Another issue we have not addressed is the ways in which the extended editions and special features released on DVD and Blu-ray may have shaped the interpretations of viewers, as it is clear that these can be keenly anticipated as well as influential in reshaping receptions among some fans (Egan and Barker 2008; Hight 2005). Some of our respondents considered the extended editions to be the definitive versions, with several expressing hopes for what they might see developed there in greater depth. A few were reluctant to offer their final evaluations of a given film or the series as a whole without having yet watched the 'author's cut' edition, since this represented the version of the film Peter Jackson wanted to bring to the screen. It is also clear that many respondents experienced the films 'as part of, or in relation to, a broader storyworld' (Koistinen et al. 2016, p. 356)—the *Hobbit* or wider Middle-earth universe—which they accessed through various mediums, including the books, the films, games, visiting locations, cosplay, writing fanfiction and so on, all of which potentially impacted on their viewing experience. While we addressed this in relation to prefigurative activities, we have yet to systematically analyse the 'participatory and transmedial' (p. 356) nature of the subsequent *Hobbit* viewing experience. Likewise, we have largely neglected the evident importance for some respondents of film soundtracks and the emotional impact of Howard Shore's *LotR* and *Hobbit* scores.[1]

It is evident too that further research is needed on viewers' complex engagements with new and emerging cinematic technologies, and in particular, the new ways of seeing demanded by the combination of ultra-high-resolution stereoscopic 3D and HFR projection. While specifically intended to break down the cinematic 'fourth wall' and draw viewers further into the fantastic world of Middle-earth, our research suggests that the combination of live action, green screen, computer-generated imagery and high-resolution 3D HFR was not experienced as seamless by many viewers but rather appeared to create a hyperreality paradox in which the juxtaposition of real, simulated and CGI elements was rendered more apparent, effectively exposing the artificial means through which cinematic 'magic' had been created. These perceptual anomalies disrupted engagement for some viewers, including some positively predisposed fans of the *LotR* franchise. While professional film critics have subsequently suggested HFR 3D may simply be better suited to genres other than fantasy, the harshly critical reviews of Ang Lee's *Billy Lynn's Long Halftime Walk* (2016) indicate that at least some of the problems we have documented relate more specifically to the use of ultra-high-resolution HFR 3D (in this case 120 fps) projection itself. *The Guardian*'s Jordan Hoffman (2016, n.p.) went so far as to proclaim that after two 'very costly, public humiliations', HFR 3D should now be buried as 'another bold-but-bad idea in theatrical cinematic presentation'. It remains to be seen whether James Cameron can successfully resolve these kinds of perceptual anomalies in his forthcoming *Avatar* sequels, or risk alienating influential critics and viewers habituated to a more traditional cinematic aesthetic.

Some Final Thoughts

In many respects this project has itself been an unexpected journey; one that evolved in directions we had not anticipated at the outset. We have faced numerous challenges along the way, and we have achieved most but not all of our ambitions. Nonetheless, it was a journey well worth taking, and there is much we have learned in the process. We hope we have succeeded in providing sufficient detail here to offer meaningful insight into the underlying reasons for *The Hobbit*'s highly ambivalent reception and its failure to replicate the success of *LotR* as a cultural phenomenon, to clarify to our very generous participants why we asked the questions we did and how we have made sense of their often detailed responses, and to provide a roadmap of sorts for audience researchers interested in adopting a similar approach in their own studies. We hope our methodological choices, as well as our many significant findings and their potential contribution to theory-building, stimulate further discussion and debate around what is possible, and desirable, in this rapidly expanding field.

Note

1. Interested readers may wish to consult White (2016).

References

Ahsan, S. (2015, November 20). Peter Jackson admits to 'making it up as I went along' while shooting the Hobbit trilogy. *National Post*. Retrieved January 15, 2017, from http://news.nationalpost.com/arts/peter-jackson-admits-to-making-it-up-as-i-went-along-while-shooting-the-hobbit-trilogy.

Barker, M. (2016). An investigation of the role of affiliations to 'authors' on audience responses to *The Hobbit* films. *Participations: Journal of Audience and Reception Studies, 13*(2), 198–222.

Biltereyst, D., Mathijs, E., & Meers, P. (2008). An avalanche of attention: The prefiguration and reception of *The Lord of the Rings*. In M. Barker & E. Mathijs (Eds.), *Watching The Lord of the Rings: Tolkien's world audiences* (pp. 37–58). New York: Peter Lang.

Bourdieu, P. (1986). The forms of capital. In J. Richardson (Ed.), *Handbook of theory and research for the sociology of education* (pp. 241–258). New York: Greenwood Press.

Child, B. (2015, November 19). Peter Jackson: 'I didn't know what the hell I was doing' when I made *The Hobbit*. *The Guardian*. Retrieved January 15,

2017, from https://www.theguardian.com/film/2015/nov/19/peter-jackson-battle-of-the-five-armies-i-didnt-know-what-the-hell-i-was-doing-when-i-made-the-hobbit.

Duggan, M. (2015). The demographics of social media users. Pew Research Center. Retrieved August 2, 2016, from http://www.pewinternet.org/2015/08/19/the-demographics-of-social-media-users/.

Egan, K., & Barker, M. (2008). The books, the DVDs, the extras, and their lovers. In M. Barker & E. Mathijs (Eds.), *Watching The Lord of the Rings: Tolkien's world audiences* (pp. 83–102). New York: Peter Lang.

Fowkes, K. A. (2010). *The fantasy film*. Hoboken, NJ: John Wiley & Sons.

Gray, J. (2010). *Show sold separately: Promos, spoilers, and other media paratexts.* New York: New York University Press.

Hasebrink, U., & Paus-Hasebrink, I. (2016). Linking fantasy to everyday life: Patterns of orientation and connections to reality in the case of *The Hobbit. Participations: Journal of Audience & Reception Studies, 13*(2), 223–245.

Hight, C. (2005). Making-of documentaries on DVD: *The Lord of the Rings* trilogy and special editions. *The Velvet Light Trap, 56,* 4–17. doi:10.1353/vlt.2006.0006.

Hills, M. (2002). *Fan cultures*. London: Routledge.

Hipfl, B., & Kulterer, J. (2016). Greed, war, hope, love and friendship: Contemporary structures of feeling and the audience's readings of broader themes in *The Hobbit. Participations: Journal of Audience & Reception Studies, 13*(2), 246–262.

Hoffman, J. (2016, November 11). Too big? Too loud? Too real? *Billy Lynn* and other failed cinematic innovations. *The Guardian.* Retrieved January 11, 2017, from https://www.theguardian.com/film/2016/nov/11/billy-lynn-long-halftime-walk-3d-cinema-innovation-movies.

Ilan, J., & Kama, A. (2016). Where has all the magic gone?: Audience interpretive strategies of *The Hobbit*'s film-novel rivalry. *Participations: Journal of Audience & Reception Studies, 13*(2), 289–307.

International Telecommunication Union. (2012). *Measuring the information society: Executive summary.* Geneva, Switzerland. Retrieved August 10, 2013, from https://www.itu.int/dms_pub/itu-d/opb/ind/D-IND-ICTOI-2012-SUM-PDF-E.pdf.

Jenkins, H. (1992). *Textual poachers: Television fans and participatory culture.* New York: Routledge.

Jerslev, A., Kobbernagel, C., & Schrøder, K. C. (2016). The importance of sampling: Building complementary insights about reception experiences of *The Hobbit* film trilogy with different survey sampling strategies. *Participations: Journal of Audience and Reception Studies, 13*(2), 328–355.

Johnson, D. (2013). *Media franchising: Creative license and collaboration in the culture industries.* New York: New York University Press.

Joshi, A., & Mao, H. (2012). Adapting to succeed? Leveraging the brand equity of best sellers to succeed at the box office. *Journal of the Academy of Marketing Science, 40*(4), 558–571. doi:10.1007/s11747-010-0241-2.

Klear. (n.d.). Theonering.net. Retrieved August 12, 2016, from http://klear.com/profile/theoneringnet.

Koistinen, A. K., Ruotsalainen, M., & Välisalo, T. (2016). The world *Hobbit* project in Finland: Audience responses and transmedial user practices. *Participations: Journal of Audience and Reception Studies, 13*(2), 356–379.

Kuipers, G., & de Kloet, J. (2009). Banal cosmopolitanism and *The Lord of the Rings*: The limited role of national differences in global media consumption. *Poetics, 37,* 99–118. doi:10.1016/j.poetic.2009.01.002.

Leitch, T. (2009). *Film adaptation and its discontents: From Gone with the Wind to The Passion of the Christ.* Maryland: Johns Hopkins University.

Luthar, B. (2008). Promotional frame makers and the meaning of the text: The case of *The Lord of the Rings*. In M. Barker & E. Mathijs (Eds.), *Watching The Lord of the Rings: Tolkien's world audiences* (pp. 59–68). New York: Peter Lang.

McKeown, B., & Thomas, D. (2013). *Q methodology.* Newbury Park, CA: Sage.

Michelle, C. (2007). Modes of reception: A consolidated analytical framework. *The Communication Review, 10*(3), 181–222. doi:10.1080/10714420701528057.

Michelle, C. (2009). (Re) contextualising audience receptions of reality TV. *Participations: Journal of Audience & Reception Studies, 6*(1), 137–170.

Pallotta, F. (2016, 23 June). Is Hollywood's sequel bubble about to burst? *CNN.* Retrieved January 7, 2017, from http://money.cnn.com/2016/06/23/media/hollywood-sequel-bubble-independence-day-resurgence/.

Saler, M. (2012). *As if: Modern enchantment and the literary prehistory of virtual reality.* Oxford, UK: Oxford University Press.

Skeggs, B., Thumim, N., & Wood, H. (2008). 'Oh goodness, I am watching reality TV': How methods make class in audience research. *European Journal of Cultural Studies, 11*(1), 5–24. doi:10.1177/1367549407084961.

Stenner, P., Watts, S., & Worrell, M. (2008). Q methodology. In C. Willig & W. Stainton-Rogers (Eds.), *The Sage handbook of qualitative research in sociology* (pp. 215–239). London: Sage.

Trobia, A. (2016). Selecting significant respondents from large audience datasets: The case of the world *Hobbit* project. *Participations: Journal of Audience and Reception Studies, 13*(2), 440–468.

Watts, S., & Stenner, P. (2012). *Doing Q methodological research: Theory, method and interpretation.* London: Sage.

White, D. (2016). Middle-earth music: The sonic inhabitation of a fantasy world. *Participations: Journal of Audience and Reception Studies, 13*(1), 488–511.

Appendix A: Summary of Audience Segments

	Number	Proportion of Survey Sample
Pre-Viewing Survey: N = 1000		
LotR Film Fans	516	51.6%
Jackson Critics	27	2.7%
Tolkien Aficionados	182	18.2%
Anxious Investors	36	3.6%
Celebrity Followers	17	1.7%
An Unexpected Journey Post-Viewing Survey: N = 2870		
Enchanted *Hobbit* Fans	2125	74.0%
Bored and Disillusioned *Hobbit* Critics	91	3.2%
Disappointed Tolkien Readers	199	6.9%
Critics of Technological 'Enhancements'	119	4.1%
Mildly Entertained Casual Viewers	43	1.5%
The Desolation of Smaug Post-Viewing Survey: N = 1051		
Happy *Hobbit* Defenders	606	57.7%
Disenchanted *Hobbit* Critics	15	1.4%
Aggrieved Tolkien Aficionados	307	29.2%
Hobbit Sceptics	30	2.9%
Middle-earth Appreciators	7	0.7%
The Battle of the Five Armies Post-Viewing Survey: N = 840		
Fulfilled *Hobbit* Fans	405	48.2%
Angry *Hobbit* Critics	14	1.7%
Unhappy Tolkien Adherents	229	27.3%
Ambivalent Middle-earth Enthusiasts	41	4.9%
Appreciative Film Critics	25	3.0%
Frustrated Middle-earth Fans	17	2.0%

Note Only classifiable responses are reported here

© The Editor(s) (if applicable) and The Author(s) 2017   287
C. Michelle et al., *Fans, Blockbusterisation, and the Transformation
of Cinematic Desire*, DOI 10.1057/978-1-137-59616-1

Appendix B: Questionnaire, *An Unexpected Journey* Post-Viewing Survey

Translated into French, German, Spanish [European and South American variants], Danish, Dutch and Flemish

About the Statements you just Sorted

1. To what extent did the statements provided in the previous ranking exercise allow you to express your own responses to *The Hobbit? Not at all. None of the statements really reflected my reactions to the film; To a limited extent. Other important aspects of my response weren't covered, though; Generally. I could express most of my reactions using the statements provided, but not fully; Almost completely. I was able to communicate my response very effectively through the ranking process.*

2. If you don't feel you have fully expressed your own responses to this film in the previous ranking exercise, please describe them here [OPEN RESPONSE].

About The Hobbit

3. How important was it for you to see *The Hobbit? Extremely important; Quite important; Somewhat important; Hardly important; Not at all important.*

4. What does *The Hobbit* mean to you? [OPEN RESPONSE]

© The Editor(s) (if applicable) and The Author(s) 2017   289
C. Michelle et al., *Fans, Blockbusterisation, and the Transformation of Cinematic Desire*, DOI 10.1057/978-1-137-59616-1

5. With which character in *The Hobbit* do you most identify? Why? [OPEN RESPONSE]
6. To what extent were your prior expectations about *The Hobbit* met? [OPEN RESPONSE]
7. How many times have you watched *The Hobbit*? (for example, 3) [OPEN NUMBER RESPONSE]
8. In which of the following formats have you seen *The Hobbit*? *Yes; No; Don't know*
   a. In 3D?
   b. At the higher frame rate of 48 fps?
   c. In 2D?
   d. Online?
   e. As a download?
   f. On DVD?
9. Was the film version you most recently viewed: *Yes; No; Don't know*
   a. Dubbed from English into your own language?
   b. Subtitled?
10. With whom did you watch *The Hobbit* the first time you saw it? *Family members; A spouse or partner; A romantic date; Friends; Other fans; I watched alone*
11. Did you attend a special screening of *The Hobbit*? *Yes; No;* If yes, did you wear a 'Middle-earth' costume for the event? *Yes; No*
12. Have you purchased, or do you intend to purchase, a copy of *The Hobbit* on DVD or Blu-ray? *Yes; No; Maybe*
13. Which of the following MOST motivated you to see *The Hobbit*? *I'm a fan of The Hobbit book or of J. R. R. Tolkien; I'm a fan of Peter Jackson; The Lord of the Rings films; One of the actors starring in the film; The film trailer(s); Other marketing materials such as posters; News coverage of the film; A magazine article; A social invitation from friends; A romantic date; A film review; The LotR video game; Word of mouth from friends or acquaintances; Comments on Twitter, Facebook, or other social media; Peter Jackson's production videos or blogs; Other*
14. How many times have you read Tolkien's original novel, *The Hobbit* (for example, 3)? [OPEN NUMBER RESPONSE]
15. If you have not read *The Hobbit* before, how likely are you to read it now that you've seen the film? *Not likely; Somewhat likely; Very likely; Definitely; Not applicable—I've already read the book*

About you

16. Please enter your age: (for example, 24) [OPEN NUMBER RESPONSE]
17. Please select your gender: *Female; Male*
18. Which of the following best describes the nature of your present or former employment? *Student; Homemaker/caregiver; Manual worker; Tradesperson; Clerical or administrative worker/service and sales worker/office worker/call-centre worker, etc.; Salaried or self-employed creative worker: artist/musician/media producer/graphic designer; Self-employed technical or professional worker; Small business owner-operator; Manager or executive in public or private sector; Salaried professional: e.g. school teacher, nurse, accountant, public servant; Higher level professional: e.g. doctor, lawyer, lecturer/professor, scientist, engineer; Military; Other*
19. Relative to the average income in your country of residence, which of the following best describes your income level? *Lower income/unpaid; Lower-middle income; Middle income; Higher-middle income; High income; Decline to answer*
20. What is your nationality? [OPEN RESPONSE]
21. What is your present country of residence? [OPEN RESPONSE]
22. Do you belong to an ethnic minority? *Yes; No*; If yes, which ethnic minority/minorities do you see yourself as belonging to? [OPEN RESPONSE]
23. What is your highest level of education? *Masters or Doctoral degree; Bachelors degree; Professional qualification; Baccalaureate or A-levels; University entrance; High school diploma or leaving certificate; I did not complete secondary/high school*
24. Have you ever worked in the film or television industries, or studied media production at an advanced level? *Yes; No*
25. What is your religion? *No religion; Buddhist; Protestant; Catholic; Orthodox (Russian, Greek); other Christian; Confucian; Hindu; Jewish; Muslim; Spiritual; New Age; Pagan; Pantheist; Other; decline to answer*
26. How would you describe your political beliefs? *Progressive/ Liberal/Social Democrat; Conservative/Republican; Centrist; Libertarian; Communist/Socialist; Anarchist; Nationalist; Monarchist; Communal—e.g. ethnic, tribal; Faith-based; Neutral, No strong beliefs; Other; Decline to answer*

27. Were you aware of any controversy surrounding the production of the film? *Yes; No*

28. If you were aware of any controversy surrounding the production of the film, did that knowledge change how you felt about *The Hobbit* at all? [OPEN RESPONSE]

29. With which countries do you most closely associate *The Hobbit*? Why? [OPEN RESPONSE]

30. Have you ever participated in political activism in support of environmental protection? *Yes; No*

31. Have you ever participated in political activism in support of human rights or the pro-democracy movement? *Yes; No*

32. Have you ever engaged in union activism in support of workers' rights? *Yes; No*

33. Is there anything else you would like to say about your response to this film that hasn't been addressed in the survey? [OPEN RESPONSE]

Appendix C: Q-Sample Statements and Scores by Viewpoints—Pre-viewing Survey

	Statement	Viewpoint				
		LotR Film Fans	Jackson Critics	Tolkien Aficionados	Celebrity Followers	Anxious Investors
1	I remember reading the book when I was younger. I hope the film reflects, in every way possible, the spirit of the book	0	0	+4	−1	+1
2	I don't care that much about *The Hobbit*, but will probably watch it just to see what all the fuss is about	−1	+1	−4	0	+1
3	I hope that the feel of the movie is fantastical and fun and mystical and like a children's movie. Because that's how the novel was	0	0	+1	0	+2
4	Using 48 fps will destroy the film experience for me; it detracts from the warmth and artistry of film	−1	+1	−1	0	−1
5	*The Hobbit* is one of my favourite books, so I really want this film to be perfect	0	0	+4	−4	−1

(continued)

© The Editor(s) (if applicable) and The Author(s) 2017
C. Michelle et al., *Fans, Blockbusterisation, and the Transformation of Cinematic Desire*, DOI 10.1057/978-1-137-59616-1

Statement	Viewpoint				
	LotR Film Fans	Jackson Critics	Tolkien Aficionados	Celebrity Followers	Anxious Investors
6	I have waited so many years for this movie and now am scared that it will only be a disappointment	−1	+1	+2	−1	−3
7	My disinterest grows with each passing bit of media and publicity released. I am underwhelmed by what I've seen and heard so far	−3	+3	−2	−4	+1
8	Peter Jackson has just used these films as a testing ground for his new technology and it sounds like it has backfired big time, because he has sacrificed the story and the look of the films	−3	+3	−1	−2	−2
9	I have complete trust in WETA workshops. This film will be groundbreaking in its use of digital effects	+2	−2	0	+1	+2
10	Peter Jackson is a genius and I have complete faith that he knows what he's doing	+4	−4	−2	0	+1
11	I was very concerned to hear about Warner Bros' exploitation of workers on *The Hobbit* set	−1	+1	0	0	+3
12	I'm looking forward to seeing the beautiful New Zealand landscape on the big screen again	+1	-1	+2	+3	+2
13	*The Hobbit* is definitely on my 'must go see' list for this year. It will be a major cinematic event	+2	−2	+3	+4	−1
14	The switch to 48 fps will greatly improve the viewing experience with no strobing or flickering, more depth of detail and smoother motion	+1	−1	−1	0	0

(continued)

Statement	Viewpoint				
	LotR Film Fans	Jackson Critics	Tolkien Aficionados	Celebrity Followers	Anxious Investors
15 Based on the trailer, this film seems like some producer's attempt to appeal to the lowest common denominator	−2	+2	−1	−3	−1
16 I really wish I could have been part of this film production, creating movie magic	+2	−2	+1	+1	0
17 What a great cast! Perfect choices in most cases	+1	−1	0	+3	0
18 I worry that there will be a lot of cheap slapstick and family-friendly script gimmicks and cheesy one-liners in the film	−1	+1	+1	−2	−2
19 The more I hear about what they are doing with this movie, the more I don't want to see it	−2	+2	−3	−3	−2
20 I am especially looking forward to going to see the film with my friends/family	+1	−1	+3	+2	0
21 All the non-book additions and story and character changes are starting to concern me. Tolkien would turn in his grave if he saw how far Jackson has diverged from his original work	−3	+3	0	−1	0
22 I seriously doubt this film will do justice to J. R. R. Tolkien. It doesn't feel like an adaptation of his work, more like an adventure-comedy. It has lost its epic scope	−2	+2	−1	0	0
23 I'm very happy that one of my favourite actors will appear in *The Hobbit*	0	0	0	+4	−1

(continued)

	Statement	Viewpoint				
		LotR Film Fans	Jackson Critics	Tolkien Aficionados	Celebrity Followers	Anxious Investors
24	Making *The Hobbit* into a trilogy is just Jackson and the studio stretching out a short book to make more money at the box office. They're milking it for all it's worth	−4	+4	+1	+2	+3
25	I've heard negative comments about *The Hobbit*, but I will reserve judgement until I see the film for myself	0	0	+1	+1	+4
26	Peter Jackson is an immature, sloppy, artistically tone-deaf director with no ability to edit, and I enjoy few of his films	−4	+4	−3	−3	−4
27	No one but Peter Jackson could tell this story and do it justice	+4	−4	−2	−2	−2
28	I refuse to pay full price to see the films and give Warner Bros any more of my hard earned money	−1	+1	−3	−1	−1
29	This film seems to have only one significant female role and it doesn't have as many 'heart-throbs' as *LotR*. It will be interesting to see how many women will go to watch the movie	0	0	−2	−2	+1
30	What I've seen so far looks breathtaking and the colours are fantastically vivid; I feel like I'm really there	+1	−1	0	+2	0
31	I don't like the *LotR* films or fantasy films in general, and probably won't watch *The Hobbit*	−2	+2	−4	−1	−3
32	I really hope that the fantastic once-in-a-lifetime movie experience that was *LotR* can happen again	+2	−2	+2	+1	+1

(continued)

Statement	Viewpoint				
	LotR Film Fans	Jackson Critics	Tolkien Aficionados	Celebrity Followers	Anxious Investors
33 Middle-earth is a massive world with a rich history and Jackson is doing the best he can to bring as much of that history into these movies as possible	+3	−3	0	+2	+2
34 I am enjoying discussing, speculating and debating about *The Hobbit* before seeing it	+1	−1	+2	+1	−3
35 This film can't get here soon enough. I've been waiting for this my whole life, and I can't wait to see this adventure up on the big screen	+3	−3	+1	−1	−4
36 I feel excited and proud when I think about my country's contribution to this major international film production	0	0	−1	+1	+3
37 This film will really help to spur tourism in New Zealand, which is great for the economy. I understand why the government would provide some public support	0	0	0	+3	+4
38 I am really looking forward to returning to the wonderful world of Middle-earth	+3	−3	+3	0	0

Appendix D: Q-Sample Statements and Scores by Viewpoints—*An Unexpected Journey*

	Statement	Viewpoint				
		Enchanted Hobbit Fans	Bored and Disillusioned Hobbit Critics	Disappointed Tolkien Readers	Critics of Technological 'Enhancements'	Mildly Entertained Casual Viewers
1	More editing was needed. Not only was the fat not trimmed, but it was stretched out and expanded to fill the time. The film's extraordinary length wasn't justified	−2	+2	+3	0	+4
2	The soundtrack, especially the Misty Mountain song, was very beautiful and powerful	+2	−2	+2	+2	+1

(continued)

© The Editor(s) (if applicable) and The Author(s) 2017
C. Michelle et al., *Fans, Blockbusterisation, and the Transformation of Cinematic Desire*, DOI 10.1057/978-1-137-59616-1

	Statement	Viewpoint				
		Enchanted Hobbit Fans	Bored and Disillusioned Hobbit Critics	Disappointed Tolkien Readers	Critics of Technological 'Enhancements'	Mildly Entertained Casual Viewers
3	The scenic New Zealand landscapes were gorgeous—it seems like a beautiful fantasy land	+1	−1	+3	+3	+4
4	Overall, it lacked much of the energy, passion and epic scale of the *LotR* films, and wasn't particularly successful as a prequel to the earlier trilogy	−2	+2	0	+1	−1
5	The story related in *The Hobbit* teaches people about the real values in life: honesty, loyalty, friendship, sacrifice, courage, faith and hope. Such stories are very uplifting, and can help us become better people	+1	−1	0	0	+1

(continued)

Statement	Viewpoint				
	Enchanted Hobbit Fans	Bored and Disillusioned Hobbit Critics	Disappointed Tolkien Readers	Critics of Technological 'Enhancements'	Mildly Entertained Casual Viewers
6 The magic of the novel was missing, and the sense of charm and childlike delight was greatly diminished. The film doesn't quite reflect the spirit of J. R. R. Tolkien's original novel	−2	+2	+3	−2	0
7 The clarity and detail were incredible; everything looked so real and lifelike, it was breath-taking! I felt as though I'd stepped into Middle-earth and was going along for the adventure	+3	−3	+1	−3	+1
8 The sheer amount of graphic violence in the movie is far beyond what is in the book. The level of violence is unsuitable for young children	0	0	0	−3	−4

(continued)

	Statement	Viewpoint				
		Enchanted Hobbit Fans	Bored and Disillusioned Hobbit Critics	Disappointed Tolkien Readers	Critics of Technological 'Enhancements'	Mildly Entertained Casual Viewers
9	Watching *The Hobbit* was like seeing old friends again, after missing them for ten years	+2	−2	−1	+2	0
10	I thought the film was a great balance between fun targeted at children, and linking it to the more adult content of LotR	+1	−1	−4	0	+2
11	Time flew by so quickly, I barely noticed. I wished the film didn't have to end so soon; I could easily have kept watching for another hour or two	+4	−4	−4	−1	−4
12	The casting and acting were real strengths of this film. Particular performances were especially strong	+4	−4	0	+3	+2

(continued)

Statement	Viewpoint				
	Enchanted Hobbit Fans	Bored and Disillusioned Hobbit Critics	Disappointed Tolkien Readers	Critics of Technological 'Enhancements'	Mildly Entertained Casual Viewers
13 It took me back to the place I love the most—Middle-earth. You really get the sense that this is an old world rich in history, places, people, kingdoms, magic and wonders	+2	−2	0	+2	0
14 All the controversy prior to this film's release made me feel a bit conflicted about seeing *The Hobbit,* and I think I enjoyed it less as a result	−1	+1	−2	-3	+2
15 The film is not about a reluctant hero drawing courage from some deep personal well. It is just a showcase for Jackson's visual effects and has lost much of its deeper meaning	-3	+3	+1	−2	-2

(continued)

Statement	Viewpoint				
	Enchanted Hobbit Fans	Bored and Disillusioned Hobbit Critics	Disappointed Tolkien Readers	Critics of Technological 'Enhancements'	Mildly Entertained Casual Viewers
16 The Hobbit fails to balance the demands of good cinema against catering to its hordes of fans; the film falls a long way short of cinematic excellence	−3	+3	+2	−1	0
17 There was too much deviation from the book and too much emphasis on adding action scenes. I wish it had stuck more closely to J. R. R. Tolkien's original story in tone and emphasis	−1	+1	+4	−1	−2
18 Within seconds I was transported back to Middle-earth, completely immersed, and upon leaving the theatre felt like I was having culture shock, back in the modern world. I just wanted to go back	+3	−3	−3	+1	−1

(continued)

Statement	Viewpoint				
	Enchanted Hobbit Fans	Bored and Disillusioned Hobbit Critics	Disappointed Tolkien Readers	Critics of Technological 'Enhancements'	Mildly Entertained Casual Viewers
19 I felt proud of my country's association with this film production	0	0	−2	−2	0
20 The character scenes were too few and too brief in between the rushing plot points. They spent more time on battle scenes than making us actually care about the characters	0	0	+2	+1	−1
21 Watching this film I felt enchanted and had an overwhelming sense of joy. I laughed and smiled much of the time, and almost cried in some parts	+3	−3	−3	0	−2

(continued)

Statement	Viewpoint				
	Enchanted Hobbit Fans	Bored and Disillusioned Hobbit Critics	Disappointed Tolkien Readers	Critics of Technological 'Enhancements'	Mildly Entertained Casual Viewers
22 The film was too whimsical and too silly at times. While the book relied on Bilbo's quirky nature and wit, the film took a more slapstick approach, with some rather immature humour	−1	+1	+1	+1	−3
23 Changes have to be made when a book is adapted for the big screen. Jackson did a great job of following the story line for the most part, and adding events from Middle-earth's history in great spots for cinematic effect	+2	−2	−3	+1	+3
24 I really enjoyed seeing this film with others who are important to me	+1	−1	−1	+2	+1

(continued)

Statement	Viewpoint				
	Enchanted Hobbit Fans	Bored and Disil-lusioned Hobbit Critics	Disappointed Tolkien Readers	Critics of Technological 'Enhancements'	Mildly Enter-tained Casual Viewers
25 The film was badly let down by one or two over-the-top and un-subtle characterisations	−1	+1	−1	0	−3
26 I appreciate the message of *The Hobbit*, which is that no matter how small or insignificant you are, with courage and determination you have the power to influence the world	+1	−1	+1	+1	+1
27 The computer generated imagery was too obvious. I wanted to be able to immerse myself in the film and not be constantly reminded that actually this is a movie and all this stuff is just computer generated	−2	+2	−1	+4	−3

(continued)

Statement	Viewpoint				
	Enchanted Hobbit Fans	Bored and Disillusioned Hobbit Critics	Disappointed Tolkien Readers	Critics of Technological 'Enhancements'	Mildly Entertained Casual Viewers
28 The Hobbit is a coming of age tale for me, of finding who you really are and breaking from social norms if need be to get there. It transcends gender, age or time, because there is a little bit of Bilbo in all of us	0	0	0	−1	0
29 The film was too similar to the LotR series. Greater originality would have allowed it to stand on its own merits. It felt like a cynical attempt to recreate the epic greatness and success of the earlier trilogy	−1	+1	+1	−2	−1
30 This movie really brought back old memories and invoked a strong sense of nostalgia in me	0	0	−1	+3	−1

(continued)

Statement	Viewpoint				
	Enchanted Hobbit Fans	Bored and Disil- lusioned Hobbit Critics	Disappointed Tolkien Readers	Critics of Technological 'Enhancements'	Mildly Enter- tained Casual Viewers
31 The grain of film was replaced by the gloss of high definition video, giving everything and everyone a fake, artificial sheen. I could see the sets and makeup for what they were, which spoiled the romantic illusion of film	−1	+1	−2	+4	−1
32 I felt bored and uninterested at times. It was very long and drawn out, and lacked momentum	−4	+4	+1	−1	+3
33 This first film just didn't give me enough to make me care. I probably won't watch the next two films in theatres	−4	+4	−2	−4	−2

(continued)

Statement	Viewpoint				
	Enchanted Hobbit Fans	Bored and Disillusioned Hobbit Critics	Disappointed Tolkien Readers	Critics of Technological 'Enhancements'	Mildly Entertained Casual Viewers
34 The commercial motivation is clear when such a short and well-crafted book is split into three films. The story was diluted to turn a single book into three billion dollar movies. It was a cash grab, aimed at making even bigger profits	−3	+3	+4	−1	+3
35 This film is a technological milestone, and a game-changer for the industry. I was amazed by how the spectacular visual effects blended almost seamlessly into the action on screen	+1	−1	−1	−4	+2

(continued)

Statement	Viewpoint				
	Enchanted Hobbit Fans	Bored and Disillusioned Hobbit Critics	Disappointed Tolkien Readers	Critics of Technological 'Enhancements'	Mildly Entertained Casual Viewers
36 The themes in *The Hobbit* are very relevant to the real world today. Greed, war, betrayal, and alienation from one's homeland are not unique to Middle-earth alone	0	0	+2	0	+1

Appendix E: Q-Sample Statements and Scores by Viewpoints—*The Desolation of Smaug*

Statement	Viewpoint				
	Happy Hobbit Defenders	*Disenchanted Hobbit Critics*	*Aggrieved Tolkien Aficionados*	*Hobbit Sceptics*	*Middle-earth Appreciators*
1 *The Hobbit* is one of the greatest fantasy novels ever written, a near perfect execution of comedy, drama, and tragedy. This is a story that doesn't need to be rewritten, yet that's what was done with this second film. It's a travesty, and it infuriates me	−2	+2	+3	−2	−4
2 Throughout the film, Bilbo and the company's journey to reclaim the Lonely Mountain is not forgotten as the driving force of this tale	+1	−1	−1	0	+1

(continued)

© The Editor(s) (if applicable) and The Author(s) 2017
C. Michelle et al., *Fans, Blockbusterisation, and the Transformation of Cinematic Desire*, DOI 10.1057/978-1-137-59616-1

313

	Statement	Viewpoint				
		Happy Hobbit Defenders	Disenchanted Hobbit Critics	Aggrieved Tolkien Aficionados	Hobbit Sceptics	Middle-earth Appreciators
3	I'm happy that Jackson doesn't change the core story so much as treat it like an outline. Less than 50% of what's on screen comes from *The Hobbit*. The rest is culled from Tolkien's notes, the Appendices, and Jackson's imagination	+1	−1	−3	+1	+1
4	This film was never going to be equivalent to the *LotR*, yet unfortunately that is why I have found fault in it. The epic scale of the *LotR* films could never be matched in the *Hobbit* movies	−1	+1	−1	+2	+3
5	Even though I'm a fan of the book, the films are allowing for more depth and more character development, and I appreciate that	+2	−2	−2	+1	0
6	Tauriel, even though an entirely new character, is frankly a welcome female face in a fictional universe that revolves around its men	0	0	-4	+2	+1

(continued)

	Statement	Viewpoint				
		Happy Hobbit Defenders	Disenchanted Hobbit Critics	Aggrieved Tolkien Aficionados	Hobbit Sceptics	Middle-earth Appreciators
7	The film is paced more swiftly than the previous *Hobbit* film, and offers some exciting set pieces	+1	−1	0	+1	−1
8	I came out feeling that, despite the care and love that has gone into the making of the 'look' of the film, it just doesn't have the spirit, or the 'feel', of Tolkien anymore	−1	+1	+4	+1	0
9	Another instalment of *The Hobbit* means reuniting with what has come to be an extended part of my family	+2	-2	0	-1	+4
10	I am pleased that Jackson is taking the longer view. The *Hobbit* and *LotR* trilogies will make a remarkably consistent six-film arc. What you get isn't exactly Tolkien, but it's faithful to Tolkien's world	+2	−2	−2	0	−1

(continued)

	Statement	Viewpoint				
		Happy Hobbit Defenders	Disenchanted Hobbit Critics	Aggrieved Tolkien Aficionados	Hobbit Sceptics	Middle-earth Appreciators
11	They needed more money and had to make three films, so they invented some crowd-pleasing rubbish and put a bunch of kung-fu fighting elves in it, after testing it on an audience of high school kids	−4	+4	+2	−4	0
12	Many scenes looked incredibly fake. One of the greatest things of the original *LotR* trilogy was that it looked so realistic. *The Desolation of Smaug* often looks and feels more like a video game than a motion picture	−1	+1	+1	+3	+4
13	There isn't a single poor performance to report here, as Jackson had the fortune of working with a wonderful cast filled with talent	+3	−3	0	+2	+3
14	*The Hobbit* is a gentle story. Bilbo, with some help from Gandalf and the Dwarfs, is able to accomplish amazing things, despite his small size, because of his luck, wits, and strength of character	+1	−1	+2	+1	+1

(continued)

Statement	Viewpoint				
	Happy Hobbit Defenders	Disenchanted Hobbit Critics	Aggrieved Tolkien Aficionados	Hobbit Sceptics	Middle-earth Appreciators
15 For me, these films have lost their feeling of wonder and anticipation. This latest movie didn't get me emotionally invested in it in a positive way at all	−4	+4	+2	+2	−2
16 I mainly watched this film to see my favorite actor in a leading role, and I was very happy with their performance	0	0	−2	−2	−3
17 This is such a classic tale that it will be retold over and over in new ways and in new mediums for generations. We may not always agree with each adaptation, but the story lives on	+3	−3	0	+1	+2
18 The movie was fast paced; I never once looked at my watch, and I felt sad when it ended. I could have kept watching for longer	+2	−2	−2	−3	+3

(continued)

	Statement	Viewpoint				
		Happy Hobbit Defenders	Disenchanted Hobbit Critics	Aggrieved Tolkien Aficionados	Hobbit Sceptics	Middle-earth Appreciators
19	I don't really like the new movies, there are too many battles. I really loved the scenes of Hobbiton and hobbit parties in the earlier films; there was more fun, more colour, more creativity and interesting details	−2	+2	+1	−1	−2
20	It was hard to be concerned about all the changes to the book when the movie not only just drew you in but wouldn't let you go	+1	−1	−3	−4	−1
21	Jackson's *The Hobbit* could have been a grand, stirring adventure, a story of how even the small, reluctant and unimposing have the ability to become heroes. Instead this movie is just another bloated cookie-cutter action adventure fantasy	−3	+3	+3	0	−2

(continued)

Statement	Viewpoint				
	Happy Hobbit Defenders	Disenchanted Hobbit Critics	Aggrieved Tolkien Aficionados	Hobbit Sceptics	Middle-earth Appreciators
22 Tolkien spent his whole life developing and refining his vision of Middle-earth, not just in order to entertain us, but to leave us a vision of truth, goodness, and beauty that would change our lives for the better. This vision is lost in translation	−2	+2	+3	−1	−3
23 I absolutely LOVED it. To be submerged into the movie as if it were real life was breathtaking. I felt closer to the story than I ever thought possible	+1	−1	−3	−3	−1
24 The CGI team deserves a standing ovation for conceiving this abomination that is Smaug; the emotions, scales, movements, wings, and fire effects have been exhaustively and meticulously shown in great detail	+4	−4	+2	+3	+2

(continued)

	Statement	Viewpoint				
		Happy Hobbit Defenders	Disenchanted Hobbit Critics	Aggrieved Tolkien Aficionados	Hobbit Sceptics	Middle-earth Appreciators
25	The visual virtuosity is wasted, because the scenes have no emotional impact. The characters are undeveloped, and barely interact with each other. There is no tension, no texture, no warmth	−3	+3	0	+4	−1
26	The visual texture was akin to a high-definition home video, while the richness and depth of field associated with cinema was lost. It looked and felt like a movie set	−2	+2	−1	−1	+2
27	The trouble is, as Jackson shovels on the visual awesomeness, the characters can feel like cutout figures bobbing about against a gorgeous diorama	−2	+2	+1	+2	+1
28	The Desolation of Smaug was made to a high level of quality and with much respect for Tolkien's work, while necessarily updating and adapting the story to fit a modern audience's expectations	+2	−2	−4	−1	0

(continued)

	Statement	Viewpoint				
		Happy Hobbit Defenders	Disenchanted Hobbit Critics	Aggrieved Tolkien Aficionados	Hobbit Sceptics	Middle-earth Appreciators
29	While Howard Shore's score is good, it doesn't have the same heart-lifting epic-ness as the *LotR* soundtracks. I was hoping for something more memorable	−1	+1	+1	+3	+1
30	New Zealand is a stunning spectacle in its own right, and makes an ideal setting for Middle-earth	+4	−4	+4	+4	+4
31	*The Desolation of Smaug* completely transported me to another world that is wholly fantasti-cal, wonderful, and exciting	+4	−4	−1	−2	+2
32	The special effects were absolutely superb. The days of being able to tell what is CGI and what is not are long gone, by the looks of it	0	0	−1	−3	−4

(continued)

	Statement	Viewpoint				
		Happy Hobbit Defenders	Disenchanted Hobbit Critics	Aggrieved Tolkien Aficionados	Hobbit Sceptics	Middle-earth Appreciators
33	An adaptation does not extend to creating new characters and storylines, rewriting canon, and changing the themes/tone/plot of the book. That's called fan fiction, a much more accurate description of Jackson's screenplays	−1	+1	+4	−4	−3
34	The continued survival of all the protagonists despite their endless brushes with death doesn't just strain credibility — it utterly eliminates it. We are left with fantasy action in the truest sense, to be enjoyed for choreography, not plausibility	−1	+1	+1	+4	−2
35	The book is the book, and a masterpiece. The artistic, interpretive movie adaptation of Peter Jackson and crew is in a separate category, and it is also a masterpiece	+3	−3	−2	−1	+3

(continued)

Statement	Viewpoint				
	Happy Hobbit Defenders	Disenchanted Hobbit Critics	Aggrieved Tolkien Aficionados	Hobbit Sceptics	Middle-earth Appreciators
36 The barrel scene down the river was breathtaking. It felt like something real instead of a typical movie action scene filled with blur that just loses you. Everything was there, crystal clear, to enjoy and appreciate	0	0	−3	−2	−4
37 New film technologies should aim to enhance the immersive experience of cinema, not detract from it. I was so distracted by the visual effects I couldn't follow the story	−3	+3	0	0	0
38 Laketown, Mirkwood Forest, and Smaug's subterranean kingdom under Lonely Mountain are exceptionally well crafted	+3	−3	+2	+3	+2
39 The film runs over 2.5 hours, and is filled to the brim with padding, narrative strands, and pointless invented characters that exist purely to fill up the time and/or attempt to raise the stakes in a journey that has few to speak of	−3	+3	+1	0	−3

(continued)

	Statement	Viewpoint				
		Happy Hobbit Defenders	Disenchanted Hobbit Critics	Aggrieved Tolkien Aficionados	Hobbit Sceptics	Middle-earth Appreciators
40	The fight scenes and chases are shot and staged with genuine creativity, while edited in long fluid takes for maximum clarity	0	0	−1	−2	−1
41	Jackson's risky move of inventing his own Tolkien character—the elf guard Tauriel—as a love interest for Legolas pays off. These two bring some badly needed heat to the woodlands	0	0	−4	−3	−2
42	The film, to an even greater extent than its predecessor, embraces three things I despise about Hollywood: catering to the lowest common denominator, showcasing special effects at the expense of storytelling, and blatantly treating filmmaking as a business	−4	+4	+3	0	0

Appendix F: Q-Sample Statements and Scores by Viewpoints—The Battle of the Five Armies

Statement	Viewpoint					
	Fulfilled Hobbit Fans	Angry Hobbit Critics	Unhappy Tolkien Adherents	Ambivalent Middle-earth Enthusiasts	Appreciative Film Critics	Frustrated Middle-earth Fans
1 I was genuinely on the edge of my seat, and felt a great deal of tension at times	+1	−1	−2	−1	−3	−3
2 This film gets bogged down with additional material that takes us away from the main plotline, disrupting the story's momentum	−1	+1	+3	0	0	0

(continued)

© The Editor(s) (if applicable) and The Author(s) 2017
C. Michelle et al., *Fans, Blockbusterisation, and the Transformation of Cinematic Desire*, DOI 10.1057/978-1-137-59616-1

	Statement	Viewpoint					
		Fulfilled Hobbit Fans	Angry Hobbit Critics	Unhappy Tolkien Adherents	Ambivalent Middle-earth Enthusiasts	Appreciative Film Critics	Frustrated Middle-earth Fans
3	The film was funny, romantic, sad, and action-packed. I felt thrilled watching it	+2	−2	−2	0	−2	−2
4	*Five Armies* is a circus of freaks, marvels, and high-flying pageantry. Like any circus, we're there to gasp and to laugh, but not to feel	−3	+3	0	−3	−1	0
5	Jackson's team made the necessary technical adjustments to smooth out the visuals, creating a robust and seamless CGI-dominant film	+1	−1	−2	0	+3	−3

(continued)

Statement	Viewpoint					
	Fulfilled Hobbit Fans	Angry Hobbit Critics	Unhappy Tolkien Adherents	Ambivalent Middle-earth Enthusiasts	Appreciative Film Critics	Frustrated Middle-earth Fans
6	The script took a bit of a dive, with some laughable clichés and a rather cheesy love scene	−1	+1	+3	+3	−1	+2
7	Tauriel has been a fine addition to the series. I'm happy they added her	0	0	−4	−4	+4	+2
8	The filmmakers invented battles, minor storylines, and a love triangle simply to attract the widest possible audience	0	0	+3	+3	0	+1
9	The images were very sharp and clear, and when the camera moved you could actually see what was going on	+1	−1	0	+2	+2	+1

(continued)

	Statement	Viewpoint					
		Fulfilled Hobbit Fans	Angry Hobbit Critics	Unhappy Tolkien Adherents	Ambivalent Middle-earth Enthusiasts	Appreciative Film Critics	Frustrated Middle-earth Fans
10	Jackson seems confused about who his main character is: taciturn, gold-obsessed dwarf Thorin, or the surprisingly cunning, homebody hobbit Bilbo	−2	+2	0	+1	−2	−1
11	Few directors can mount such a massive war and keep us interested throughout	+1	−1	−1	+1	+3	−1
12	We've seen it all before in the far superior *LotR* trilogy. *Five Armies* is just an action flick in the *LotR* world	−3	+3	0	+2	+1	−1
13	I felt completely engrossed in the story and barely noticed time passing	+3	−3	−3	−1	−3	−2

(continued)

Statement	Viewpoint					
	Fulfilled Hobbit Fans	Angry Hobbit Critics	Unhappy Tolkien Adherents	Ambivalent Middle-earth Enthusiasts	Appreciative Film Critics	Frustrated Middle-earth Fans
14 Jackson has gutted the quieter, character-driven moments in the story and filled them with non-stop bad action and battle scenes	−2	+2	+4	−2	+2	+1
15 I liked the movie and thought it was a good way to introduce the world of Middle-earth to new people	0	0	−4	0	0	−2
16 I felt bored by this film, and wanted to leave before it ended	−4	+4	0	−4	−3	−4

(continued)

	Statement	Viewpoint					
		Fulfilled Hobbit Fans	Angry Hobbit Critics	Unhappy Tolkien Adherents	Ambivalent Middle-earth Enthusiasts	Appreciative Film Critics	Frustrated Middle-earth Fans
17	This was the film I had been hoping for. It was an emotionally powerful, spectacle-filled ending to one of the greatest fantasy series of all time	+3	−3	−4	−3	−4	−4
18	This film is predict-able, poorly plotted and directed, and the editing cre-ates holes where there needn't have been	−3	+3	+1	−3	−2	−2
19	Despite my reserva-tions, I still appreciate this huge achievement by Peter Jackson and his talented cohorts	0	0	−1	+4	+4	+3

(continued)

	Statement	Viewpoint					
		Fulfilled Hobbit Fans	Angry Hobbit Critics	Unhappy Tolkien Adherents	Ambivalent Middle-earth Enthusiasts	Appreciative Film Critics	Frustrated Middle-earth Fans
20	Peter Jackson has destroyed a piece of my childhood soul with his poor adaptation of an epic book	−4	+4	0	−4	−4	−4
21	It's no classic but it's still worth seeing, if just to get a sense of closure with Tolkien's universe	−1	+1	−2	+3	+4	+3
22	This film is inflated with superfluous, self-indulgent stuff, losing the concentrated brilliance and wonder of Tolkien's novel	−3	+3	+4	−1	+1	+1

(continued)

	Statement	Viewpoint					
		Fulfilled Hobbit Fans	Angry Hobbit Critics	Unhappy Tolkien Adherents	Ambivalent Middle-earth Enthusiasts	Appreciative Film Critics	Frustrated Middle-earth Fans
23	Jackson plays to his strengths, creating dynamic action sequences that excite in their level of detail, but also dazzle in their aesthetic design	+2	−2	−3	+1	0	−3
24	The film often ignores the laws of physics (e.g. Legolas's acrobatics). This made it hard to suspend disbelief and took me out of the movie	−1	+1	+2	−1	−1	+4
25	Thorin's struggle to overcome gold-fever suggests that the desire for wealth is complex and layered with meanings	+2	−2	0	+1	+1	−1

(continued)

	Statement	Viewpoint					
		Fulfilled Hobbit Fans	Angry Hobbit Critics	Unhappy Tolkien Adherents	Ambivalent Middle-earth Enthusiasts	Appreciative Film Critics	Frustrated Middle-earth Fans
26	Alfrid's character seemed pointless, and out of kilter with the rest of the film. He was inserted for comic relief, and that decision fell flat	0	0	+3	+1	+1	+3
27	With this film, *The Hobbit* trilogy truly becomes part of the Middle-earth saga. It provides a conclusion and a beginning to what follows	+3	−3	−3	0	0	0
28	The characters are given no real depth and I found it hard to connect with any of them, so when major characters were brought to an end I felt no remorse	−4	+4	+2	−3	0	−1

(continued)

	Statement	Viewpoint					
		Fulfilled Hobbit Fans	Angry Hobbit Critics	Unhappy Tolkien Adherents	Ambivalent Middle-earth Enthusiasts	Appreciative Film Critics	Frustrated Middle-earth Fans
29	This film is about finding home, fighting for it, and learning the value of the journey. It reflects timeless themes of honour, love and self-sacrifice	+4	−4	−1	+2	+2	+1
30	I felt a certain sadness when the film ended and the credits rolled	+4	−4	−1	0	−1	+4
31	The love story between Kili and Tauriel detracts from the movie, rather than adding any value to it	0	0	+4	+4	−3	0
32	The acting was top notch from nearly everyone	+4	−4	+1	0	+3	0

(continued)

	Statement	Viewpoint					
		Fulfilled Hobbit Fans	Angry Hobbit Critics	Unhappy Tolkien Adherents	Ambivalent Middle-earth Enthusiasts	Appreciative Film Critics	Frustrated Middle-earth Fans
33	The ideal screen adaptation of *The Hobbit* would have been a two-part venture. Turning it into a 3 part 9-hour long movie seems like a cash grab	−1	+1	+2	+3	+3	0
34	The soundtrack is moving and elegant, and among Howard Shore's best Middle-earth work	+3	−3	+1	−2	+2	0
35	The over-reliance on poorly executed CGI left the action feeling weightless and disjointed, and so the bad guys felt unconvincing as a serious threat	−2	+2	+2	−2	−2	+3

(continued)

	Statement	Viewpoint					
		Fulfilled Hobbit Fans	Angry Hobbit Critics	Unhappy Tolkien Adherents	Ambivalent Middle-earth Enthusiasts	Appreciative Film Critics	Frustrated Middle-earth Fans
36	An emotional rollercoaster from start to finish, *Five Armies* left me an emotional wreck by the end	+1	−1	−3	−2	−4	−3
37	While *Five Armies* was an entertaining action fantasy, it strayed too far away from Tolkien's strong spirituality, which helped make the *LotR* films so exceptional	−2	+2	+1	+4	+1	+2
38	It was a joy to share the experience of watching this film with others who are important to me	+2	−2	−1	+2	0	+2

(continued)

	Statement	Viewpoint					
		Fulfilled Hobbit Fans	Angry Hobbit Critics	Unhappy Tolkien Adherents	Ambivalent Middle-earth Enthusiasts	Appreciative Film Critics	Frustrated Middle-earth Fans
39	I would have preferred a more comprehensive ending that tied up all the loose plot points. I was left wanting more	0	0	+1	−1	−1	+4

INDEX

© The Editor(s) (if applicable) and The Author(s) 2017
C. Michelle et al., *Fans, Blockbusterisation, and the Transformation
of Cinematic Desire*, DOI 10.1057/978-1-137-59616-1

Printed by Books on Demand, Germany